Sustainable Property Developm

A guide to real estate and the environment

Sustainable Property Development

A guide to real estate and the environment

Miles Keeping
David E. Shiers

Department of Real Estate and Construction
Oxford Brookes University

Blackwell
Science

© 2004 by Blackwell Science Ltd
a Blackwell Publishing company

Editorial offices:
Blackwell Science Ltd, 9600 Garsington Road, Oxford OX4 2DQ, UK
    Tel: +44 (0) 1865 776868
Blackwell Publishing Inc., 350 Main Street, Malden, MA 02148-5020, USA
    Tel: +1 781 388 8250
Blackwell Science Asia Pty Ltd, 550 Swanston Street, Carlton, Victoria 3053, Australia
    Tel: +61 (0)3 8359 1011

First published 2004

Library of Congress Cataloging-in-Publication Data
is available

ISBN 0-632-05804-8

A catalogue record for this title is available from the British Library

Set in 10 on 12.5 pt Palatino
by Kolam Information Services Pvt. Ltd, Pondicherry, India
Printed and bound in Great Britain using acid-free paper by Ashford Colour Press, Gosport

For further information visit our website:
www.thatconstructionsite.com

Contents

Foreword

Sustainability is a broad church. It covers the creation of living and working environments which are culturally and economically diverse and are capable of surviving in the long term with minimum intervention. It is about reducing consumption – property development as part of the energy supply chain – providing the most energy efficient buildings possible. It means having respect for the natural environment and being kinder to the planet.

Sustainable Property Development is about the location, design and development of property which is economically viable, environmentally responsible and which has a positive, material effect on quality of life. This book explores the ways in which the built environment can be made more sustainable. It will help students and practitioners to be better prepared for these challenging new approaches to property development in order to set new standards for best practice.

Jonathan Falkingham RIBA FRSA
Co-founder and CEO, Urban Splash

Preface

This book has been written in response to a perceived need among built environment students, lecturers and practitioners for a single, introductory text examining the relationship between environmental issues and the design and development of property.

Whilst there are now a great many excellent sources of information focusing on specific aspects of property-related environmental issues, for those coming to the subject for the first time such material can be hard to follow, often appearing to require considerable prior knowledge. This basic 'primer' makes no such demands upon the reader – all that is required is an interest in learning more about this increasingly important field of study. It should be noted, however, that the study of environmental impacts is still relatively new and, as such, our understanding of the issues is still very much evolving. Consequently, the requirement to remain up-to-date is even more critical than in other, more established fields.

In this book, four key property-related environmental issues are discussed: the environmental implications of the location of property development, the development of previously used land, the nature and design of low environmental impact 'green' buildings and sustainability within the UK construction industry. Each are dealt with in terms of key concepts, 'headline' issues and, finally, practical problems and solutions. In dealing with these issues, we have sought to provide an overview of current thinking and to help the student or practitioner identify what they *need to know* rather than to attempt to explain all there *is to know*.

The issue of sustainability is undoubtedly an international one, but this book is concerned primarily with the situation in the UK and other developed countries. The situation in many developing countries is obviously very different to that in more developed nations, and they may have different priorities, for example health and sanitation being more important than, say, green architecture. However, the reasons for sustainable development are similar wherever the context (such as the over-consumption of natural resources) and so we have also endeavoured to provide some understanding of the background to the often complex issues under discussion – the global nature of this topic means that international political, social and economic dimensions must be considered. Ultimately though, it is hoped that this book will help the reader to better understand the relationship between property and the environment and provide

a useful reference when seeking further practical guidance on a range of property-related environmental issues.

Because this book was written at the Department of Real Estate located within
the faculty of the Built Environment of our university, the text often moves freely
between several disciplines. We believe this approach not only widens and
informs the discussion but also more accurately reflects the professional world
in which we work; one which increasingly promotes the idea of the 'integrated
team'.

There are seemingly innumerable definitions of *sustainable development*, each
with their own subtleties and emphases. From the relatively recent past, the
definition provided by the *Brundtland Report* encourages us to think about the
concept of *futurity* – how future generations will be left to cope following our
custodianship of the planet (World Commission, 1987):

> 'Development that meets the needs of the present without compromising the ability of
> future generations to meet their own needs.'

The theme of futurity is common to most definitions of sustainable development, as is the concept of *equity*. Equity is variously explained as a need for far
more environmental protection or greater fairness within and among societies or
more appropriate levels of economic development. Many people disagree about
the emphasis placed on the three key issues of the environment, society and the
economy but we prefer not to get too bogged down in what might be called a
semantic minefield. As Cox *et al.* (2002) point out:

> 'Sustainability will continue to be a term that defies precise definition. Those who wait
> for an "answer" will be left behind. Sustainability is, at least, described, and practition-
> ers should work within the boundaries of the description.'

As this comment rightly suggests, we also believe that there is an urgent need
for all to come to terms with sustainable development and to assist
in its achievement. Practitioners working within the field of the built environment have very important parts to play in this. Since the issue of sustainable
development has risen to towards the top of the political agenda, the
need for a sustainable means of developing the urban environment has
become increasingly urgent. The Earth Summit on Environment and
Development held in Rio de Janeiro in 1992 resulted in the Agenda 21 Declar-
ation, which provided 27 principles setting out the ways that countries
should contribute to global sustainability. Many of these principles are of
direct relevance to the use and management of urban environments and
property generally. Following the Rio Earth Summit, governments around
the world have promoted sustainable development both internally and internationally.

In the UK, successive governments have promoted Local Agenda 21
policies and, in 1999, the Labour Government produced a strategy for sustainable development called *A Better Quality of Life*. This promotes the idea of
using indicators of sustainability so that we can measure progress towards
sustainable development. The indicators comprise the three sustainable

development themes of environment, society and the economy. There are also seven sub-themes, some being particularly relevant to the property development context, such as:

- Prudent use of resources
- Environmental protection
- Better access to local amenities, services and transport networks
- Design of the environment and public realm.

More particularly aimed at property development, the Government has also produced a further seven key indicators for evaluating the success of urban regeneration schemes. Three of these are:

- Minimisation of resource consumption
- Protection and enhancement of local *environmental capital*
- High quality design

All these indicators are themes that run through this book.

It is therefore important for property developers and their advisers to understand the relevance of sustainability indicators to assess, record and manage the move towards sustainable development. While such indicators may cover international, national and regional issues, developers need to be aware of the indicators at local, neighbourhood and site-specific level. They may feel that some (e.g. those indicators pertaining to participation in local governance) are not relevant to their activities. They may point out that empowerment of local people should include their involvement in making decisions about their immediate environment, such as the determination of planning applications and/or consultation about development proposals. These sorts of issues are undoubtedly important for sustainable development but it is the environmental aspects of sustainable development that are the focus of this book.

Many communities have developed sustainability or *quality of life* indicators that may affect the work of developers. For example, residents, businesses and the local authority in Bristol have produced 60 such indicators divided into 12 themes for their City. These themes include the following seven that have direct relevance to property development:

- Community safety
- Energy
- Environmental protection
- Housing and shelter
- Land use and development
- Transport
- Waste management

Often, locations considered by developers may be in an area where such indicators are in place. These may masquerade under different names (for example, not only under the headings *quality of life* or *sustainability*, but also *triple bottom line* or other terms). Whatever they are called, developers should be aware of them and consider the implications of the development proposals within their context. Thus a good understanding of development plan policy and sustainable development policy is required, but developers should also be aware of how to make their developments more environmentally sustainable *per se*. Those who do not consider these issues will be left behind, and increasingly so.

Miles Keeping and David Shiers

Cox, J., Fell, D. & Goodwin, M. (2002) *Red Man, Green Man*. RICS Foundation, London.
World Commission on Environment and Development (1987) *Our Common Inheritance*, OUP, Oxford.

ACKNOWLEDGEMENTS

Thanks are due to the following individuals and organisations:

Professor Martin Avis
Bennetts Associates, Architects
Feilden Clegg, Architects
Professor Anthony Heath, University of Oxford
James Honour, BRE
Ray Kearney, Architect
Dr Karen Kearley
Ilona Keeping
Professor Charles Kibert, University of Florida
Madeleine Metcalfe, Blackwell Publishing
Dr Paul Oliver MBE, Oxford Brookes University
Professor Paul Macnamara MBE, Prudential Property Investment Managers Ltd
Dr Nicholas Walliman, Architect

The location of property: greenfield and brownfield development

1

Suggested learning outcomes

After studying this chapter and discussing its contents you should be able to:

- Describe the factors which identify suitable locations for property development.
- Appraise the sustainability of such locations.
- Set out government policy relating to location-finding for sites.
- Provide a framework for the historical development of urban regeneration policy.
- Discuss current policy relating to urban regeneration in terms of its sustainability.

This chapter discusses the traditional concepts pertinent to location issues for property development, as well as considering approaches to locating developments which are more appropriate to the recent and continuing transition towards more sustainable land use patterns. This is because the issue of sustainable development as it relates to the location of property has recently come to mean an emphasis on urban regeneration which should be brought about by an 'urban renaissance' (Urban Task Force, 1999).

HEADLINES: BIG ISSUES AND IMPORTANT QUESTIONS

If you ask people in the property world what is the most important factor in determining value, the overwhelmingly common reply is 'location'. The reasons for this are principally:

- Economic advantage: the 'best' locations are those to where business customers and suppliers can most easily get.
- Proximity to goods, services and amenities.
- Transport: proximity to public transport nodes and road networks.

- Environment: preferences for urban convenience or rural tranquility or a suburban combination of these.

It is important to remember that the nature and character of locations can change over time, sometimes quickly and dramatically. This underlines the need for developers and their advisers to remain abreast of marketplace changes by thorough and up-to-date market research. For example, the supply of developments can affect the demand for buildings, while changes in town planning policy, either at national or local levels, can affect this supply.

When attempting to find a suitable site for a new development developers and their advisers must therefore follow systematic site finding and site investigation procedures. These include consideration of site-specific matters as well as more 'strategic', policy-based issues. In recent years, government policy relating to property development has changed course quite significantly. Whereas in the past there was a laissez faire attitude towards property development, policy now positively promotes development of brownfield land whilst discouraging greenfield development. Furthermore, it is also encouraging developers and town planners to ensure that urban regeneration is achieved via an 'urban renaissance'. The importance of urban regeneration cannot be overstated, given that over 90% of the UK population lives in urban areas (DTLR, 2001). The essence of this policy means that there should be a greater move towards sustainable property development, which will be effected by:

- Reliance upon mixed use development becoming the norm for development proposals.
- Greater reliance on public transport rather than the road network.
- A mixture of tenure types in new developments (e.g. freehold and leasehold, private and social housing).
- High quality urban design, both in the sense of the public realm and of individual buildings.
- Promotion of 'green buildings' and remediation of polluted land.
- Economic regeneration of urban areas, combined with greater encouragement of urban living.

These will only be achieved if developers and town planners work in a public–private partnership. This might mean that developers have to alter their modus operandi, for example, by finding and developing sites which are reliant on public transport rather than car use. Town planners might find that they must increasingly adopt flexible attitudes to what constitutes appropriate development in order to approve financially viable development proposals.

The important questions that must be addressed are:

- How do developers determine where 'good locations' are for different property types?
  The traditional means of determining good locations for property development have stemmed from an understanding of theories such as 'central place theory'. There has been a gradual evolution of such early theories that has mirrored the changes that have taken place in society, including those

engendered by the market economy. Examples of this include the transition towards out-of-town retail developments that are largely reliant upon private car transport, the use of which stems from significant expansion of the 'car economy' in many countries.

- What is government policy concerning location issues and how has government policy evolved to encourage a move away from the traditional model towards ones which are more sustainable?
  Town planning policy has been particularly influential in the context of the location of property developments since the middle of the twentieth century. This initially reflected the need for environmental control of development in order to ensure, *inter alia*, a check upon unfettered development activity and 'betterment' of the public realm. Since the early 1990s, UK town planning policy has continued to influence property development in this respect, but it has turned its focus towards a more sustainable approach by seeking to ensure that development is concentrated upon formerly developed land and the regeneration of urban environments. This means that developers have had to change the ways in which they appraise sites for development, largely by placing greater emphasis upon brownfield development and the use of existing infrastructures, such as transport networks.

- How has urban policy with regard to regeneration evolved, and what is the current policy context for this?
  Urban policy measures used to tackle the decline of town and city centres have gone through a series of metamorphoses, involving shifts in focus on economic and fiscal measures, tactics to improve the health of populations, both enhancement and reduction of town planning powers, and improvement of the physical environment in strategic and *ad hoc* ways. Since the late 1990s, a new and consistent approach has been favoured which encourages the public and private sectors to agree and adopt a vision for the urban environment.

- What constitutes sustainable urban regeneration? How should developers respond to urban regeneration policy in terms of site finding?
  The main thrust of urban regeneration policy is based upon the principles of sustainable development, and attempts to encourage people to live in cities and halt migration from them. This means that policy measures and instruments are aimed at restoring the economies of urban areas (for example, by providing employment that is relevant for people living there), reviving communities in towns and cities (for example, by encouraging mixed communities in terms of age, ethnicity and wealth) and rejuvenating the physical environment (such as by demanding high quality urban design and respect for the public realm).

  In response to this policy initiative, developers will need to produce high quality, mixed use brownfield development which is less reliant upon transportation and demonstrates a greater respect for the needs of the community. For many developers, this means a change in their site finding and subsequent development activities, allowing them to grasp the opportunities that current urban regeneration policy could present, rather than to perceive it as a threat.

BACKGROUND

The historical reasons for the constant change in the built environment are perhaps obvious. Since settlements were first established, means of communication have changed and populations have become increasingly mobile. Urban theorists once explained locational influences upon places to live and to produce and sell goods and services with 'central place theory' and the development of complementary land uses (Christaller, 1933; Losch, 1938). More recently, it has been suggested that 'centrifugal forces for certain functions are replacing centripetal ones' (Ratcliffe & Stubbs, 1996, p. 10). This argument suggests that real estate developers respond to consumer demand by producing buildings in which to carry out the functions of day-to-day living, working and provision of goods and services.

In recent years, however, it is clear that this consumer-driven supply of property has been fettered to some extent by systems of land use planning and development control, more so in industrialised countries than elsewhere. In the UK, for example, a system of town and country planning has been in force at both national and local levels since the middle of the twentieth century. The planning system in the UK has more recently been reorganised to better achieve the principles of sustainable development. Unfortunately there are still only a few examples of property development which attempt to adhere to such principles. Traditional discussions about location issues pertinent to property development have espoused the need for proximity to, and reliance upon, private transportation networks and the benefits of development upon greenfield sites due to the difficulties of developing brownfield sites. It is now evident, however, that governmental policy directions in many industrialised countries are moving the discussion away from this sort of traditional standpoint towards a sustainable model.

PRACTICAL PROBLEMS AND SOLUTIONS, CURRENT APPROACHES, TECHNIQUES AND MODELS

The remainder of this chapter is divided into three parts. The first part takes in the traditional view of locations for development and considers how to undertake site finding investigations for different property types. The second part examines government policy relevant to this discussion and how this has evolved. The final part considers recent trends in seeking to place development within urban areas as part of a process of urban regeneration.

PART 1: LOCATIONS AND SITE-FINDING FOR DEVELOPMENTS

It is important to remember that developers are continually engaged in a balancing act between risk and return. Risks occur throughout the real estate development process and particularly at the outset, because this is when major strategic decisions are made about the development scheme and when there are still many uncertainties. Returns, on the other hand, usually occur at the end of the development process in the form of profit. In order for developers to ensure that the outcome of this balancing act is a satisfactory financial reward, they must always be aware of the factors that influence the value of the completed scheme. Finding the best site for a development is arguably the most important factor; it is probably worth remembering the old adage that the three most important determinants of real estate value are location, location and location.

Part of the process of assessing the risk associated with a development scheme therefore occurs when locating a suitable site. This is more than merely finding a piece of land which is physically capable of having a building placed upon it. It involves knowledge of geographical, town planning, engineering, construction, environmental, social, political and economic issues. As Ratcliffe & Stubbs (1996) stress, in addition to knowledge of these issues and the risks associated with them, developers who understand the range of complexities involved in finding sites will possess good research, presentation and negotiation skills.

When considering the site-finding process in relation to property development, we must consider site-specific and strategic issues. We must also accept that having sound information is the key to success. This information will include financial indicators such as rents and yields, as well as many others, like a firm grasp of national and local planning policies. Throughout the site finding and investigation processes, developers will harness all of the knowledge they gain to determine the most financially attractive outcome.

Developers often confine themselves to undertaking projects of a certain type or within a certain geographical area. All development companies will, to a greater or lesser extent, have mission statements and business plans that set out the limits of their activities. Within this context, the location of their development projects will probably depend on a number of issues (Cadman & Topping, 1995, p. 29). These include

- The location of their headquarters. If these are far away from the project, the developer will need to establish a network of contacts within the local authority there, with local estate agents, and even consider a partnership with a local developer.
- The need to diversify their portfolio of projects. Risks may be spread and thereby reduced through diversification.
- The availability of development funding and finance. Lenders prefer what they consider to be 'prime' property (well constructed buildings with a high specification), good locations (the most popular) and tenants 'of good

covenant' (i.e. those least likely to default on lease terms and rental payments). It is important to note that 'within and among funding institutions a preferential treatment exists towards certain situations in, around and between selected sites and facilities' and, therefore, that 'it is helpful to know the attitude and commitment of individual fund managers to particular towns, areas and regions' (Ratcliffe & Stubbs, 1996, p. 319).

- The results of market research. This is the most crucial element, upon which the money to finance a development largely depends. Developers need to display economic and property market growth potential in the given location with evidence of factors such as current and future supply and demand.

Market information and market research

To maximise the profit achieved from a development it is essential that the developer considers market research data when undertaking site-finding exercises. Indicators of market supply and demand exist as rents, yields and capital values. Some of the factors that can influence these include the following:

- Larger buildings or sites, such as business parks, can be difficult to sell or let as a single unit because only large organisations can afford them. If there is little demand, that is, when few organisations are competing for a property, this will tend to depress the property's marketability and thus its value.
- Accessibility is an important factor in determining a building's value. Rents and capital values may be higher if it is more accessible.
- The specification of a building will obviously have an influence on its value. Investors might prefer newly constructed buildings as they pose less risk than an older building, in terms of obsolescence. Similarly, tenants might prefer a building that is likely to have more modern facilities, lower maintenance charges or be more energy efficient. Both of these factors will assist in enhancing the building's value. Other issues such as natural light, the building's grounds or parking facilities might also have an effect.

Analysing supply and demand is not necessarily easy or even possible with any great degree of certainty. It is true to say that some property advisers, such as estate agents, can over-inflate the state of the market (this is known as 'talking up the market'). Apart from assessing demand, analysing the future supply of property can be even more problematic, as planning policies (which heavily influence the future supply of property) change direction, both at national and local levels.

Usually, the literature available considers different types of development (e.g. commercial, retail, industrial and residential) separately. This part of the chapter emulates this approach. We then contrast this with a discussion of whether considering types of property development as separate entities is in fact a truly sustainable approach.

Investigating sites for different uses

Office properties

'Office properties' consist of those premises which are classified under the Use Classes Order[1] in classes A2 and B1. The former class contains uses such as 'professional services' that one would typically find in town centres and which members of the public might be expected to visit off the street, like firms of solicitors and accountants, estate agencies and post offices. The B1 class consists of offices and light industry, although the latter use could not be one which would affect the amenity of neighbouring occupiers.

In considering locations for office uses, we would traditionally have divided the sorts of locations as being either on business parks (usually out-of-town or edge of town) or in urban areas, i.e. within a town or city (see, for example, Cadman & Topping, 1995; Havard, 2002; Ratcliffe & Stubbs, 1996). As you will be able to determine from the discussion in this book relating to urban regeneration, the development of greenfield land for single-use schemes such as business parks is not encouraged by policy because it is not sustainable. The reasons for this are excellently portrayed in the following description of their characteristics:

> The basic concept of the business park is low-density development of relatively low-rise buildings in landscaped, pleasant environments. These locations are on the edge of major urban areas and need to have both good car access to the motorway network and extensive car parking. (Havard, 2002, p. 56)

In terms of issues over and above those common to all property development site investigations, developers of business parks need to ensure that the site is large enough to accommodate extensive areas of car parking and landscaping (in addition to providing for possible future expansion of the site). Given the car-reliant nature of this form of out-of-town development, site investigations also need to ensure that access to the site is adequate. It should be the case that this would also include access by public transport – for social and environmental reasons – but few commentators appear to place much emphasis on this. Lastly, the provision of amenities, such as shops and leisure facilities, should be checked, as potential occupiers of these often isolated properties consider them to be an added attraction when comparing out-of-town with in-town properties.

Of course, the developer of in-town office properties does not have to look as far from potential development sites for amenities, particularly if the proposed development follows the more sustainable vogue for incorporating a mixture of uses. It is increasingly common for office developments to include some retail and/or leisure type of development at ground floor level. Not only does this mean in-built amenity for the office space occupiers, but it also serves well as a means of diversifying away risks and is more than likely to make the scheme attractive to local planning authorities. Even if the new office development is not mixed use, it is often within or very near to the central business district (CBD) and its associated mixture of retail, leisure and, increasingly, residential properties. Wise office developers, in undertaking site investigations, will consider the needs of the occupiers of the completed property in terms of their certain desire to work near retail and leisure facilities and even be within walking distance or a short journey of their homes.

Again, the traditional view (Cadman & Topping, 1995, p. 31) is that such properties' location must be influenced by the 'vital consideration' of road, rail and air communications. However, whilst it is acknowledged that 'proximity to good public transport is important for office locations in central areas', it has also been put forward that in the UK, 'in relation to office development in provincial towns and 'out-of-town' business or office parks, proximity to the national motorway network and airports is important. This has been demonstrated in the South East with the growth of towns along the motorways (M3, M4 and M25) and near London's airports (Heathrow and Gatwick)'.

The same authors contend that the locational choice of an office occupier is determined by such diverse factors as:

- Tradition
- Proximity to markets
- Staff availability
- Quality of housing
- Complementary businesses
- Provision of car parking
- Individual directors' preferences

Within this sector of users, we have seen in recent years a change in the working patterns of the workforce to a limited extent. In the early 1990s, the concepts of 'hot-desking' (i.e. where employees share desk space within offices, particularly if they may be out of their office for certain, long or frequent periods) and 'tele-working' (i.e. where employees work away from their employer's facilities, often at home and communicate with colleagues via web-based or telephone systems) were vaunted in certain circles as representing the future for many office-based employees. It is evident, however, that the demand for such working practices has reached a plateau. It is possible that technology will advance sufficiently in the coming years for such practices to become more feasible than they currently are. Given the parlous and over-crowded state of our transport networks, the popularity of out-of-town office working may increase, but whether or not it will become more popular with workers and employers is perhaps a moot point. If they do, it is probable that the result will be a continuing downsizing of office space requirements and, it has been suggested, a continuing decentralisation of them (Cadman & Topping, 1995).

Retail properties

Retail uses are those buildings that are designed to be used as shops under class A1 of the UCO 1987.[1] Again, we can divide the locations for A1 uses into two: out-of-town and city/town centre/village locations (which will collectively be referred to here as 'town centre' locations).

It would be true to say that the retail sector is the most analysed and monitored sector of all property sectors; the revenue generated by retailers is most heavily influenced by the location of their premises. This fact is not one which has only recently been recognised. Urban economists have studied the effects of retailing locations on urban form and socio-economic issues for some time and these historic analysis tools are still used today. In the early 1930s, Christaller proposed that there was a vertical hierarchical relationship from villages to towns to cities due to economic reliance. Inhabitants of the smallest settlement, i.e. a village, were reliant upon towns to provide some goods and services and then cities for other goods and services. What Christaller (1933) was postulating was the concept of the catchment area. Other economists have considered the location of retail premises and produced theories which still hold true today. We can see many examples of a hierarchical relationship between shopping uses where the most popular (and profitable) shops locate in the centre of towns and less used shops locate towards the periphery of the centre. The relationship between location and rents, which tend to be higher in the centre of the town, can be seen as being of vital relevance to the developer.

The nature of retailing has changed considerably in the UK since the 1960s. Havard (2002) highlights the principal changes, which he notes are fuelled by an increase in disposable incomes:

- The rise of the 'national multiple', i.e. the consolidation of the number of retailers into fewer retail groups. This has led to such groups becoming very influential in determining the commercial success of retail locations.
- The massive increase in influence of supermarkets. These stores have increased in size largely because of the increased range of products they offer. In the early 2000s, we are seeing further consolidation of this group of retailers, with international companies seeking to enter the UK market and domestic retailers seeking to buy out the competition.
- Because of the above factors, smaller retail companies are diminishing in number and influence.
- Shopping is becoming increasingly 'decentralised'. Although 'the traditional town centre is still important to retailers ... there has been a considerable gravitation to the edge of town. This has been caused by the development of out-of-town shopping centres and retail warehousing' (Havard, 2002, p. 58).
- The increase in demand and supply for covered shopping centres and for leisure to be associated with retailing. An example of this is the Trafford Centre (Figure 1.1), near Manchester, a Regional Shopping Centre which attracts 465 000 visitors per year, most of whom make use of the 10 000 free car parking spaces (Peel Holdings, 2001).

Evidently, in recent years, town centre shopping provision has suffered due to the competition provided by out-of-town retail developments. Whereas in years gone by shoppers were content to have their needs met by a range of speciality and small retailing establishments, lifestyles have changed to the extent that, certainly for day-to-day requirements at least, consumers prefer to have such needs met by single retailers like supermarkets. Often, these new providers have chosen to locate outside of city or town centres at stand-alone

Figure 1.1 The Trafford Centre, Manchester (Paul Roach, Oxford Brookes University).

locations on arterial roads, with access provided by 'comfortable driving' conditions (i.e. at a controlled junction and with a petrol filling station at the exit) (Hawking, 1992). The reasons for this are many. It has been noted that:

> A major debate rages around the future of town centres and the impact upon them of out-of-town developments. Many town centres have experienced a decline in fortune over recent years, principally as a result of competition from out-of-town shopping facilities, but also as a result of such factors as an increase in car ownership. (Ratcliffe & Stubbs, 1996, p. 22)

The issue of out-of-town retailing is one that is hotly debated, particularly in the UK, but also in many other jurisdictions. Recent UK Government town planning policy has been drawn up to curtail its development and Planning Policy Guidance Note 6 (DoE, 1996) specifically states that developers need to apply a 'sequential test' in the site-finding process for retail developments. This means that in applying for planning permission, developers must demonstrate that they have considered the possibility of town centre locations before deciding upon out-of-town sites for their application schemes. Whatever the policy situation, developers will need to consider certain generic issues when attempting to find a site for retail use and these are discussed below.

It is evident from a review of the literature, as well as looking at the situation at first hand, that the impact of increased car use has had a most significant effect on retail development location. Cadman & Topping (1995) tell us that retail developments take place in a hierarchy of shopping locations from regional, to district to local centres and then superstores and retail warehouses. A development's position in the hierarchy depends upon its catchment population, which they define as the size of the population within 10 to 20 minutes' drive time of the centre/store. Ringer (1989) includes within a list of the seven most important factors dictating the success of a shopping centre that access by private transport is vital. Furthermore, it has been suggested that for retail warehouses, location is the 'single most important factor' dictating success in terms of specification and design, as a 'catchment population of 70 000 within a minimum drive time of 20 minutes is seen as a minimum' (Ratcliffe & Stubbs, 1996, p. 375). The area within which the catchment population lives is analysed, therefore, in terms of the size and economic status of population within given drive times. On the other hand, it is suggested that within town centres, the most important factor regarding the location of retail premises is the pedestrian flow past the site. However, it should be noted that the most important generators of pedestrian flow have been regarded as car parks first and then public transport nodes, pedestrian crossings and magnet stores (Cadman & Topping, 1995).

In considering catchment areas and possible locations for a retail development, the developer will need first to consider four key issues:

- *Accessibility*: does the topography allow for new development; are adequate public transport links available to the shopper; is 'pedestrian flow' past the intended shop sufficient to generate trade; what is the relationship between the intended location, other centres and the shopping public?
- *Competition*: which are the direct competitors to the potential shop(s) and what share of trade might they take from it (them)?
- *Prosperity*: what is the current level of provision of retail use generally; what are the levels of income and retail expenditure in the area; is there a good proportion of multiple shops; how many refurbished shops are there locally?
- *Potential*: what are the population and employment trends locally; what is the attitude of the town planners to future retail development; are there any schemes in the development pipeline?

Armed with this sort of information, developers will be able to assess with a degree of certainty the quality and appropriateness of the catchment area in order to assess the suitability of a potential development site.

Industrial properties

Industrial uses are taken to be those which would be classified under either class B2 (General Industrial) or B8 (Storage and Distribution) of the UCO 1987. Whatever the type of industrial property, the traditional view is that they need to locate close to raw materials and markets and must have good access to major roads.

In this sector, sources of information are often confined to the public sector, although market information might best be gleaned from local property consultants. Local and regional authorities are very often seeking industrial employers in their localities and they can thus help the developer in providing a wealth of relevant information. What the industrial occupier will most often be concerned about, after the expense of the scheme itself perhaps, is whether or not there is a readily available supply of labour. This information is available to local and regional authorities, but whether or not there are recently moved companies in the area will also give an indication of this. Other sources of information include central government departments, such as the Department of Trade and Industry. Other more local organisations which are usually willing to assist in the provision of information include Chambers of Commerce and, of increasing importance in the UK at least, Regional Development Agencies (Cadman & Topping, 1995; Ratcliffe & Stubbs, 1996).

As with other types of property development, the location of industrial space has, over recent years, moved away from city and town centre locations to out-of-town ones. This has been for a number of reasons. In the main, industrialists have chosen to locate in places where access to communication networks has been favourable. With the decline of rail freight systems coupled with the increased expense involved in their use, location in proximity to motorway networks has become of prime importance. Ratcliffe & Stubbs (1996, p. 444) suggest that quick and ready access to clients, markets, suppliers, labour and services is an 'absolute prerequisite to modern industry. Thus motorway linkage and high carparking standards are crucial'. They go further to explain that the 'push' away from town centres has been due to the levels of traffic congestion, increasing transportation and land costs and longer commutes for workforces. Furthermore, the 'pull' factors to out-of-town locations have included cost savings (in lower land prices), more pleasant environments, and adequacy of parking facilities and accessibility. However, it is noted that amenities, facilities for workforces, public transport links and shopping and recreation facilities are absent from such locations. It could be suggested that herein lies a problem for industrialists and their workforces when it comes to choosing locations for their installations. According to Adams *et al.* (1993), rational behaviourists suggest that the optimal industrial location is driven by profit maximisation. More recently, however, it has been seen that the pretence of optimal location has been abandoned in favour of personal preferences and uncertainties (e.g. owners' expectations and behaviour, costs of redevelopment and upheaval and planning controls). Thus, it is put forward that there is only ever a partial equilibrium in the market, where supply (which is controlled by the planning system) and demand (from the private sector) do not equate. It is, therefore, very difficult to apply competitive market analysis to the industrial land market.

Despite this view, we can see from other published research that there has been a shift away from town and city locations and why this is so. Debenham Tewson Research (1990) noted the willingness of users of industrial space in the mid 1980s to move to 'off-centre' locations. It was held that this was because of the related shift in populations and economic activity from major urban locations to smaller and rural ones. Furthermore, at that time, it was suggested that the ranking of economic prosperity of local labour market areas indicated that performance was strongest in smaller, recently industrialised districts. Most interestingly, however, the most important influences for the move to off-centre locations were given as motorway proximity **and** environmental quality, followed by access to markets, airports, the rest of the organisation, and staff availability, attraction and skills all coming well ahead of the suitability of arrangements for public transport, leisure and housing for the workforce.

This view of trunk road proximity being at the forefront of requirements of users of various types of industrial space is again supported by earlier commentators. Williams (1982) and Taylor (1985) note that for high technology developments, motorway access is vital. More recently, Cadman & Topping (1995) suggest that warehousing must also have good motorway access. Clearly this is true in the UK (and probably most other industrialised countries), given that there is a lack of adequate public sector transport infrastructure.

In finding a site upon which to erect a building for industrial use, there are several more issues which will have to be considered, such as the necessary working area within the building (particularly its height), how many doors will be needed and whether internal offices will be necessary. Access to the site by large vehicles (whether they be rail or road) must also be considered.

Ratcliffe & Stubbs (1996) note that the following four factors are influential in determining good locations for industrial properties:

- *Communications*: motorway linkages and car parking being predominant.
- *Flexibility*: space to expand and reorganise working practices.
- *Environment*: pleasing external and internal appearances.
- *Design*: identifiable character and quality and low running costs.

Residential properties

Although there are a large number of small property development companies involved in residential development, by far the largest market share of development of new property is undertaken by the so-called 'volume house builders' who benefit from economies of scale. These organisations have come to realise that, in terms of a marketing strategy, their best chances of success lie in the concept of selling a 'lifestyle' rather than selling houses. This has important implications when they are attempting to find sites for their products and perhaps the key issue they will consider at this stage is whether or not the character of the neighbourhood is appropriate for the lifestyles of the people who are likely to buy their houses. For example, the developer will want to know about the levels of reported crime in the area, whether there are schools to which house purchasers would wish to send their children, whether there is an appropriate 'shopping offer' nearby and what sort of provision there is for leisure activities.

Site-finding activities are undertaken partly in-house by land buyers. These people spend a great deal of their time travelling within cities and towns and in the countryside looking for suitable sites on which to develop houses. Often, developers will be given details of potentially suitable land by estate agents or may find them in press advertising. Because large pieces of developable land rarely come onto the market, developers need to spend time in building up 'land banks' – i.e. land which may be developed at a later date. In building up a land bank, developers will usually take out 'options' to purchase land at a later date. These are contracts which bind the land owner, usually for a limited period of time (say 5 to 10 years), to selling the land to the option holding developer at a given price (usually open market value) unless the developer decides not to buy the land. Taking out an option to buy land does not mean that developers are necessarily buying land at reduced prices but they are guaranteeing that they will have the first right to buy the land by edging out any competing purchasers. Land banks may consist of very large parcels of land and sites capable of taking only a handful of houses.

In determining where they will focus their attention when land banking, developers will consider current and future planning policies. Their knowledge of the development plan for an area should be detailed and they will certainly benefit from being involved in the forward planning process (i.e. by making representations about changes to development plan policy). Furthermore, good developers will maintain close links with the personnel in planning authorities and will discuss policy directions with them.

Despite a stable population in the UK, the nature of demand for household type has changed in recent years, with a significant growth (both actual and predicted) in the number of small or single person households and a drop in the amount of married couple housing, as depicted in Figure 1.2.

The recent history concerning the development of significant amounts of housing to satisfy the demand of an increasing population and number of households has been influenced by three main types of provision, infill development, new settlements and urban villages. Within their development planning activities, local planning authorities are required to maintain an adequate supply of land for housing development. The Government issues housing target figures, following consultation with local and county councils and regional planning bodies. These are hotly debated, particularly in the South East of England where pressures for housing are very high, but where councils often do not wish to see too much land taken for development.

Government policy in this area is set out principally in PPG3. An early version (DoE, 1992) of this policy statement stated that:

> The planning system must provide an adequate and continuous supply of land for housing, taking account of market demand and of government policies for the encouragement of home ownership and the provision of rented housing. It must also ensure that established environmental policies are maintained and enhanced. These policies, to which the Government is firmly committed, include the continuing protection of the green belts, National Parks and Areas of Outstanding Natural Beauty, the conservation of natural habitats and the protection of the countryside and the best and most versatile agricultural land, and the conservation and enhancement of the urban environment and built heritage.

More recently, an updated version of PPG3 (DETR, 2000a – see Part 2 below, p. 25) suggests that a 'sequential test' will be applied to planning applications, which will favour redevelopment of brownfield sites above that of greenfield sites. Furthermore, policy statements have suggested that in future, 60% of new housing development will have to occur on brownfield sites. Given the intention of PPG3 to see urban land reused for housing development, it could be held that

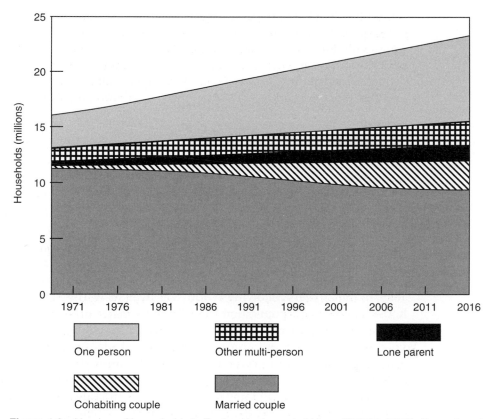

Figure 1.2 Number of households in England by household type (ODPM, 2003). Reproduced with kind permission of the publisher.

it is likely that we shall see more by way of infill and urban villages development than the continuance of large-scale new settlement type development.

Infilling consists of building new houses within the gaps between existing buildings and usually facing them onto the same road as the existing properties. There are principally three forms of infill development:

- 'Backland' development, where new properties are built in the back gardens of existing houses.
- 'Tandem' development, where a new house is constructed immediately behind another, sharing the existing access to the original property. The main difference between 'backland' and 'tandem' development is the proximity of the original and new houses and the sharing of the access.
- 'Houses to flats' development, where the original house(s) are demolished and rebuilt as flats or are converted at a higher density.

Such development clearly meets the current objectives of PPG3 of seeing densities being increased and urban land being reused. But, is it really sustainable, from the sense of residential amenity? Between the late 1960s and late 1980s, it has been noted that land values increased sevenfold (Cheshire, 1993), causing much infilling as developers sought to cash in on increasing sale prices of new housing development. Similar sorts of price rises were experienced between 1998 and 2002, with similar effect. As Ratcliffe and Stubbs (1996) note, the character of many suburban areas changed significantly over a long period by way of greatly increased densities. A further benefit was the increase in supply of small-sized, low cost units.

New settlements v. urban villages

In the recent past, the main debate concerning the provision of large-scale residential development (i.e. the most significant 'land take' form of development) has centred upon whether this should be provided in new settlements or urban villages.

According to Ratcliffe & Stubbs (1996), debate has existed about whether to develop new settlements or to increase the density and/or size of existing residential areas for many years. Early planners, such as Ebenezer Howard, suggested large-scale, planned new settlements (or Garden Cities) as early as 1898. In the 25 years following World War II, 29 New Towns were designated to house the overspill population from Britain's major urban areas. In 1985, Consortium Developments Limited (CDL) was formed by an amalgamation of volume house builders to promote and present planning applications for new settlements. There were certain similarities between the rationales of Howard and those for the more recent proposals for new settlements, such as to generate settlements away from cramped conditions in existing towns. Many planners (Hall, 1989) endorsed the idea of CDL's approach, suggesting that new, balanced developments (i.e. having a mixture of uses, property sizes and types of tenure) away from high grade agricultural land and integrated with existing transport infrastructures would remove pressure from existing towns and villages and protect the countryside. However, CDL's applications never received the official approval needed, often having issues of environmental harm, traffic generation and visual impact being cited as the reasons for rejection. It could be suggested that greater co-operation between CDL and regional and local planners might have caused greater success. However, in these cases, there was often confusion between 'planning' and 'political' issues. The proposed developments were speculative and sponsored outside the development plan process. That they were opposed by vociferous NIMBY objections only furthered the cause to see them being rejected. Proponents of the new settlement concept are still encouraged by Government support for 'model' settlements to be developed. Although the issues are never absolutely clear cut, proponents of sustainable development fear that such settlements will become 'a new generation of commuter dormitory towns' (Blackman & Lipman, 2003). Campaigners who are keen to see the preservation of greenfield sites are right to continue to be concerned about this matter. In February 2003, the Government announced the launch of its 'Sustainable Communities Plan' (ODPM, 2003), which set out funding arrangements for urban regeneration, as well as plans for what one campaigning group termed 'massive greenfield sprawl' (CPRE, 2003, para. 2), but the Government preferred to call the provision of hundreds of thousands of new houses a desire 'To accommodate the economic success of London and the wider South East and ensure that the international competitiveness of the region is sustained, for the benefit of the region and the whole country' (ODPM, 2003). In preparing its Sustainable Communities Plan, the Government undertook studies to assess the capacity for development activity and growth in Ashford in Kent, the region around Milton Keynes, Luton and Northampton and the 'M11 corridor' stretching from inner London to Cambridge. The CPRE states that:

> The studies assume new housing will be built at the higher densities which national planning guidance calls for (30–50 dwellings per hectare) rather than the lower densities currently prevailing (the current average is 25).... This gives a total, for all four growth areas, of between 482 000 to 556 000 homes on greenfields, covering between 12 530 and 14 730 hectares of countryside – equivalent to around 113 square kilometres or 44 square miles. This is in addition to all the other greenfield building continuing elsewhere in the South East and around England. And all this in the most crowded, congested, and highly pressured region in the country. (CPRE, 2003, para. 8)

Alternatives to new settlements are occasionally accused of being likely to result in 'town cramming'. Proponents of other forms of development aimed at meeting housing need, such as urban villages, on the other hand, present an argument which suggests that new settlements are more likely to result in a 'monoculture' of housing than a planned mixed use, mixed tenure and more sustainable development. The Urban Villages Forum was formed in 1989 as a reaction against typical post-war planning which was seen as promoting the zoning of land for separate uses that resulted in a wasteful use of resources, particularly in terms of transportation. Ratcliffe & Stubbs (1996, p. 491) suggest that 'what was needed was a revitalized form of housing and employment land use to bring life back to cities, and new large-scale housing proposals'. The key features of such urban villages are:

- Mixed-use buildings and areas comprising housing, small businesses, shops and social amenities (a sense of 'community' being an important element).
- Mixed ownership with rented and owner-occupied housing.
- High standards of urban design, particularly incorporating public open spaces.
- Populations of 3000 to 5000 people.
- Development suitable for the redevelopment of existing urban areas, but also possible for greenfield sites.

Proponents of the concept of urban villages (and any form of large-scale mixed-use development) are not without their detractors. As with most forms of large-scale development in a market economy, the momentum behind schemes rests principally with the financiers. Institutional investors have historically been blamed for a lack of support of mixed-use developments, it being argued that they are not in favour of risking investment in multi-use buildings which are considered to be expensive to manage and may have lower future values than single-use ones. However, it is clear that planning policy runs contrary to such views and it is suggested that developers and financiers of housing development – and commercial property development – who adhere to the traditional view will lag behind and lose out to more adventurous ones. This is discussed further below, in Part 3 of this chapter, p. 30–33.

Investigating site-specific characteristics of potential development sites

Having considered the strategic issues pertaining to a potential development scheme, such as the economic suitability of the general location and the town planning policies relevant to the locality, developers need to consider site-specific issues. What should be at the top of the developer's mind at this stage is whether or not the selected site is physically and functionally capable of taking the proposed development.

Developers will commonly use a form of checklist when visiting a site in the first instance. Box 1.1 below is an edited extract of a site investigation checklist used by a developer. This shows the sort of level of detail that is required at an early stage in site investigation. Much of the information will be gleaned from a physical inspection of a potential development site and the remainder, such as legal information, can be gathered during a 'desktop' study following the physical inspection. The sort of information being gathered with the checklist in Box 1.1 is appropriate to most forms of development. This would be supplemented with additional information which would be required in order to assess site suitability for particular types of development (e.g. retail or residential).

Consideration of the contents of Box 1.1 would serve most developers well when undertaking a site-finding exercise. If developers were to approach their task from a sustainable property development perspective, they might wish to add supplementary headings and questions. As examples, the following issues could be investigated:

- *Highways*: can the local public transport infrastructure support the proposed development?
- *Parking*: how little parking can we provide on the site?
- *Drainage*: could a sustainable urban drainage system be provided? Could reed-bed drainage be viable?
- *Water*: is there a watercourse on or adjacent to the site and how could this be retained/enhanced?
- *Design*: what is the local vernacular and how could we complement this?
- *Habitats*: are there important or valuable habitats or flora on the site and how could these be retained/enhanced?

Many of these ideas would not need to mean significant additional expenditure or reduced profit. Indeed, some aspects of sustainable property development can either add to the value of completed schemes and/or assist planning authorities to see the benefits of a scheme. Furthermore, some of these ideas can add to the marketability of the scheme.

Environmental impact assessment

Some property developments, by virtue of their potential effects upon the wider environment, are required to be assessed in terms of their environmental impact before they are given permission to proceed. The formal process of environmental impact assessment (EIA) has been described as:

> a process by which information about the environmental effects of a project is collected, both by the developer and from other sources, and taken into account by the relevant decision-making body before a decision is given on whether the development should go ahead. (DoE, 1995)

EIAs were first systematically used in the USA in the early 1970s. The European Union established the legal framework for EIAs in 1985 (EU Directive 85/337/EEC) and the UK complied with the requirement to establish a national regulatory system for EIA in 1988 (Town and Country Planning (Assessment of Environmental Effects) Regulations 1988). These Regulations have been updated, the current ones being the Town and Country Planning (Environmental Impact Assessment) (England and Wales) Regulations 1999 (there are comparative Regulations in Scotland).

A schedule of the projects which are required to be subject to an EIA are set out in Schedules 1 and 2 of the 1999 Regulations. Schedule 1 projects are those which automatically require an EIA to be undertaken (e.g. power stations, waste disposal facilities, motorways and steel works) and are relatively few and far between. More common are projects listed in Schedule 2 of the 1999 Regulations (e.g. industrial estates and urban development of more than half a hectare in size), which will often require an EIA to be undertaken, but only if they meet certain criteria and thresholds, which are set out in Schedules 2 and 3. Further advice concerning the criteria, thresholds and implementation of EIA can be found in Circular 02/99: Environmental Impact Assessment (ODPM, 1999).

In essence, an EIA is an investigation to assess the environmental and socio-economic effects of a proposed development on the wider environment. These effects could be upon natural resources (e.g. soil, water, air quality, flora and fauna and landscape) or upon 'man made' resources (e.g. transport systems, cultural heritage, the economy and housing).

The process of EIA   In undertaking an EIA, developers are required first to understand whether an EIA is required. The process for determining this is known as screening and local planning authorities will screen development proposals upon request. Thereafter, there is a seven-stage process, which is set out in the 1999 Regulations. Glasson *et al.* (1999) and Morris & Therivel (2001) provide an excellent summary of the process (Figure 1.3).

The first two stages of the EIA process, scoping and baseline studies, provide the basis upon which the remainder of the EIA will be undertaken. Scoping should involve site visits and the use of checklists to identify the probable key impacts, potential mitigation measures and the likely assessment methods to be

Box 1.1   Extract from a site investigation checklist (Crawford, 2002).

Highways

- Who is the Highway Authority?
- Access – is this adequate or will alterations be necessary?
- Road widths – are on-site and access roads of adequate width or will alterations be necessary?
- Other highway considerations:
  —Specification – are road surfaces of appropriate quality?
  —*Ransom strip(s)* – does access to the site cross land in another ownership?

Drainage

- Who is the Drainage Authority?
- Are sewers to which the site connects public ones or will private authorisation be required?
- Existing pipe specifications – are these adequate for the proposed development?
- Spare capacity – is the drainage system adequate for the proposed development?
- Does the site drain by gravity or will pumping be required?
- Is there a storage facility for drainage (if so, what are the area and positions and will such area be allowed for open space purposes)?

Off-site requirements

- Is the sewer to be requisitioned?
- Is there a major sewer works or pumping station nearby and are they adequate for the proposed development?
- What is the condition of watercourses or existing ponds (and what is the depth)?
- Is any remedial treatment required to sewer system?

Soil investigation

- Does the vendor have a soil survey?
- Has an independent soil survey been carried out?
- What are the ground conditions (soil type, filled land)? What are the subsequent foundation recommendations?
- Is the site on a flood plain?
- Where is the water table in relation to the site?
- What are the existing or adjacent tree types and positions?
- Have contaminated land enquiries been carried out?
- Is any report available?

Services

- Is there existing availability of services or will diversions be necessary?
  —Gas
  —Telecoms/fibre-optic cables
  —Electricity
  —Water
  —Other infrastructure
- What are the likely costs of all of the above?

Planning

- Who is the Planning Authority?

- What is the status of the development plan?
- What is the planning history of the site?
- Is there existing planning permission (ref. and date)?
  —What for?
  —Are there any Section 106 planning agreements (existing/proposed)? What are their requirements?
  —Is a development brief available?
  —What were the requirements for phasing the development?
  —Is all the land on offer included within the planning permission?
  —Are there any special considerations attached to the planning permission (for example, special materials, conservation area, listed buildings, tree preservation orders)?
  —Is there any landscaping requirement?
  —Are there other land use requirements (for example, tree belt, noise barrier)?
- Has a meeting with the planning authority been arranged?
- Are any other planning reports available?

Legal

- Is the land registered or unregistered at the Land Registry?
- Does the contract for the purchase of the site have an attached plan?
- Do any other titles abut the site?
- Do the site's dimensions reconcile with Land Registry and planning permission site measurements?
- Does the site abut the public highway?
- Are there rights over drainage or services?
- Have rights of light been checked?
- Is there a party wall?
- Are there any restrictive covenants and does the proposed scheme comply with these?
- Will vacant possession be transferred upon completion of the purchase?
- Do the vendors approve of the proposed plan?
- Are there any tenancies or third party uses of the site?
- Can the site connect to existing public highways (including visibility splays) without crossing the land of a third party?

Site visit

- Do you have an Ordnance Survey plan?
- Has a full land survey and/or boundary survey been undertaken?
- Have the site boundaries been physically checked as being clearly defined?
- Are there any overhead lines, cables or pipe markers or inspection covers visible?
- Are there any encroachments, gates from the site into rear gardens, retaining walls, overlooking windows or private accesses affecting the site?
- Is the site occupied in any way (for example, garages, allotments)?
- Will the slope of the site warrant retaining walls between plots?
- What is the condition of existing trees and hedges?

employed. Conducting baseline studies involves both desktop and on-site studies and is crucial to undertaking an effective EIA. The third stage of the process, describing and evaluating the baseline conditions, sets out the value of key receptors of any potential impact and, importantly, whether there are any 'limitations in data accuracy and completeness' (Morris & Therivel, 2001, p. 6).

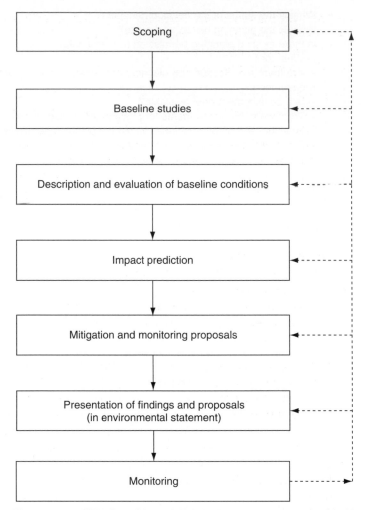

Figure 1.3 The process of EIA (from Morris & Therivel, 2001, p. 4, reproduced with permission).

Predicting impacts is, of course, the most fundamental aspect of the EIA process. It is important that the direct and indirect consequences of the proposed development are predicted, as are the cumulative impacts that are likely from the proposed and other developments. It is also important to note that impacts may be positive as well as negative and that they may be felt in the short, medium or long term. That any impact may be reversible is relevant to the next stage in the process – impact mitigation and monitoring proposals. Morris & Therivel (2001, p. 8) note, 'Mitigation measures aim to avoid, minimise, remedy or compensate for the predicted adverse impacts of the project' and then set out the sorts of measures that exist:

- Selecting alternative techniques and/or locations for the development.
- Modifying the methods and timing of development.
- Redesigning aspects of the development.

- Minimising operational aspects, e.g. polluting activities.
- Specific measures to minimise impacts, including off-site measures, e.g. alterations to highways.
- Compensating for losses, e.g. provision of new habitats.

The visible output of the EIA process is the 'Environmental Statement', as discussed below, which is produced in order to support a planning application and contains information about all of the previously set out steps in the EIA process. It need not include information on monitoring, the final phase of the process. This is partly due to the fact that monitoring is not strictly a requirement of the statutory EIA process. However, as Morris & Therivel (2002, p. 10) point out, 'lack of monitoring is a serious deficiency in current EIA practice'. Effective monitoring, which is necessary in order to attempt to achieve sustainable property development, should include:

- Baseline monitoring, e.g. a survey programme over time, usually relying on existing data, on the state of the environment prior to the development.
- Compliance monitoring.
- Impact and mitigation monitoring to assess the accuracy of impact prediction and the effectiveness of mitigation measures.

Methods of assessing environmental impact   It is interesting to note that the burden of undertaking the EIA falls upon the developer. Developers will therefore engage consultants to undertake the assessment, who will report to the developer rather than to the planning authority. This is not the case in some other countries, for example Canada, where the EIA is undertaken by independent environmental consultants selected from a panel of approved organisations and reporting is to the planning authority.

In the UK, the developers' consultants, who may be a firm of environmental consultants or a collection of specialists from different organisations, will possibly need to have specialisms in areas as diverse as ecology, soil science, geology, economics, transport, noise, archaeology, historic buildings and air quality. The project management skills needed to co-ordinate the personnel involved in a large scale EIA are tremendous, particularly given that the process's outcome, in the form of the Environmental Statement, must constitute a cogent assessment of the potential impact of a development, rather than a collection of studies by individual experts.

Environmental Statements

The required content of Environmental Statements (ESs), i.e. the information that needs to be presented, is set out in Schedule 4 of the 1999 Regulations and Annex C of Circular 02/99. The ES needs to be an integrated document and must be transparent in terms of setting out limitations caused by a lack of data. All ESs must include a non-technical summary which is comprehensible to non-experts.

Contaminated land

Any site being considered for development should be regarded as potentially contaminated. The importance of this cannot be overstated and every site investigation should reflect this. The issue of contaminated land is considered in some detail in Chapter 2 of this book and will thus not be discussed again here.

PART 2:   GOVERNMENT POLICY REGARDING LOCATION OF DEVELOPMENT

Box 1.2   Outline of key recent brownfield and greenfield policy developments

1987

- *Our Common Inheritance* (a.k.a. 'Brundtland Report' (World Commission on Environment and Development, 1987))
  —Suggests need to preserve the environment, reduce resource consumption, reduce world poverty – all within a neo-classical economic paradigm;
  —Defines 'sustainable development' as: Development that meets the needs of the present without affecting the ability of future generations to meet their own needs.

1990

- *This Common Inheritance*: UK Government response to *Our Common Inheritance*
  —Suggests need to protect environment and see economic growth.
- Town and Country Planning Act:
  —Development plans mandatory for the whole of the country;
  —Section 54A suggests that planning decisions should be made in accordance with development plan provisions and any other material considerations (e.g. PPGs).
- Environmental Protection Act:
  —Presents a framework for pollution control. Much debate and wrangling over s. 143 (never actually enacted) which proposed a register of sites subject to previous contaminative uses.

1992

- Rio Earth Summit: UK (plus 140 or so other governments) signs up to 'sustainable development', including that of land resources. Government suggests planning system is the way to see sustainable development implemented.

1995

- Environment Act enshrines contaminated land policy in law, by inserting Part IIA into Environmental Protection Act 1990. This:
  —Defines 'contaminated land';
  —Enforces local authorities to inspect their areas for contamination;
  —Establishes a 'liability hierarchy' – polluters responsible first (in accordance with EU law), owners of land thereafter;
  —However, legal and financial wrangling means that the Contaminated Land Regulations only become effective in 2000/2001.

1999

- The 'Urban Task Force' reports (see below).
- Government produces a strategy for sustainable development: *A Better Quality of Life* (DETR, 1999). This:
  —Provides indicators for measuring sustainable development;
  —Encourages local initiative for sustainable development by promoting Local Agenda 21.

2000

- Contaminated Land (England) Regulations 2000.
- DETR Circular 02/2000 'Contaminated Land'.
Both of these documents set out how the legislation should be enforced and responded to by local authorities.
- Urban White Paper: *Our Towns and Cities: The Future – Delivering an Urban Renaissance* (see below, p. 28).

PPG1: general principles of the planning system

PPG1 (DETR, 2001) sets out the basic tenets of planning policy in England and Wales and as such guides both development plan policy-making and development control decision-making. Amongst the overriding concerns that the planning system needs to address, according to PPG1, is sustainable development. Principal amongst the ways in which planners and developers can assist the move towards sustainability is the encouragement and provision of mixed use development. Whilst PPG1 does not define this term, it does stress that 'mixed use can help create vitality and diversity and reduce the need to travel. It can be more sustainable than development consisting of single use.' The major motivation for this emphasis on mixed use is therefore that locating such developments in central locations with good access to public transport is likely to reduce dependency on the use of private transport. PPG1 charges local planning authorities with promoting mixed use development in specifically designated areas: 'Development plans should identify individual sites where development should incorporate a mixture of uses'.

PPG3: housing

PPG3 (DETR, 2000a) provides guidance for planners and developers on the provision of housing in England and Wales. PPG3 stresses the need for planners to promote the redevelopment of brownfield sites above that of greenfield sites and has instituted a 'sequential test' approach which needs to be followed when submitting and approving development applications (similar to that in PPG6 concerning retailing). It states that development plans should 'focus new housing development in areas where previously-developed land is available in preference to developing greenfield sites.' Furthermore, following the principle laid down in PPG1, PPG3 also makes significant reference to the role of mixed use development in future housing provision. It is interesting to note that the authors of this most recent version of PPG3 have extended the scope and meaning of sustainable development to include social matters rather than just environmental ones. Whilst there is reference to the environmental objective of conserving greenfield sites through brownfield development, PPG3 also promotes the development of 'inclusive communities which offer a choice of housing and lifestyle'. In this sense, PPG3 attempts to underpin what much of the current government's policy making has sought to achieve – i.e. 'social inclusion'. PPG3 comments that the principle of good mixed use development 'does not accept that different types of housing and tenures make bad neighbours.'

PPG6: retailing and town centres

PPG6 (DoE, 1996) supports town centre initiatives, including active town centre management (TCM) and transport strategies. Local authorities need to judge retailing proposals on grounds of potential impact upon town centre 'vitality and viability'. The 'index of vitality' is based on the comparative study of various factors, such as (Ratcliffe & Stubbs, 1996, p. 381):

- Relative rental levels
- Vacancy and occupation levels
- Relative branch performance of major retailers
- Retail mix and level of retailer representation
- Presence of covered malls and speciality centres
- Presence of pedestrianisation schemes
- Relative access by public and private transport
- Ratio of carparking to retail floorspace
- 'Health' of secondary shopping areas
- Presence of TCM schemes
- Presence of other unique attractions (e.g. tourism and leisure)
- Size of local town and town centre employment base

Out-of-town developments are now only considered as acceptable if in-town congestion cannot be tackled in any other way. PPG6 requires the 'sequential test' approach to be adopted (as per PPG3 above), in that when submitting and approving development applications, it must be clear that town centre locations have been considered before edge-of-centre ones, which in turn must be considered before edge-of-town locations and so on until out-of-town locations are considered as a last resort. Regional Shopping Centres (RSCs – i.e. stand-alone shopping centres offering in excess of 100 000 square metres of retail provision) are only considered to be suitable if they are supported by development plan policy, if there is a sufficiently large population to be served by them and if adequate expenditure growth is likely. Furthermore, there now also needs to be proof that an adequate public transport infrastructure exists to support them (Ratcliffe & Stubbs, 1996).

PPG13: transport

PPG13 (DETR, 2000b) attempts to ensure that planners and developers square the circle between development and transport decision-making. Echoing the promotion of mixed use development in PPG1 and elsewhere, PPG13 calls upon decision-makers to consider the sustainability benefits that can be brought about through such a form of development. The focus of PPG13 is upon environmental benefits, principally through reduced atmospheric pollution, that should follow a reduction in developments which cause greater reliance upon private transport. As per PPG1 and 3, PPG13 recommends that highly accessible sites could be well utilised by having mixed use developments built upon them. The reason for this is that the office and retail elements of them are classed as travel intensive. PPG13 comments that: 'Mixed-use development can provide very significant benefits in terms of promoting vitality and diversity and as promoting walking as a primary mode of travel'.

In focusing upon the environmental aspects of transport, it is perhaps unfortunate that PPG13 misses a chance to set out the social and economic benefits which can result from better public transport and less reliance upon private transport.

PPG23: planning and pollution control

PPG23 (DoE, 1997) states that contamination is a 'material consideration' when planning applications are being determined. Given that this PPG ensures that the remediation of contaminated land is a benefit that can be derived from granting permissions, developers should be able to use this to their advantage in securing planning permissions on brownfield sites. PPG23 notes that local authorities may demand from developers the results of site investigation surveys, as well as guarantees that remediation has been undertaken which is consistent with the 'suitable for use' approach for reusing contaminated land (see Chapter 2 for more on this approach).

The Urban Task Force

The Urban Task Force report was published in 1999 (UTF, 1999), just over a year after the Task Force, which was chaired by the architect Lord Rogers of Riverside, was appointed by the Government. The report, *Towards an Urban Renaissance*, made several recommendations that were highly important in terms of their influence on subsequent Government policy. In essence, these were:

- *Recycling land and buildings*: it is important to limit the release of greenfield land, to reuse contaminated land and empty properties.
- *Improving the urban environment*: it is necessary to improve the quality of urban design, in part by increasing densities, improving public transport systems and creating 'Home Zones' (i.e. where there is a 'pedestrians first' policy).

- *Achieving excellence in leadership, participation and management*: 'positive planning' is needed which encourages the redevelopment of neglected areas. This can be facilitated by devolving detailed planning processes to the neighbourhood level, by ensuring a mix of tenures and incomes within neighbourhoods and by strengthening strategic management in local authorities.
- *Delivering regeneration*: Urban Priority Areas should be designated where decision-makers can streamline planning procedures, enable easier land acquisition and provide fiscal incentives for certain redevelopment initiatives. In order to achieve this, it will be necessary to place resources at the local level and make public expenditure at all levels of government focus on the urban renaissance.
- *Designing the urban environment*: a national urban design framework should be established, as well as demonstration projects which will assist designers, developers and the public to experience high quality urban design. At the local level, local authorities should produce a single 'public realm strategy', which establishes a framework for increased density of development and sets the context for area regeneration schemes, which should have 'integrated spatial masterplans'. At the site level, new housing should be rated in terms of its environmental characteristics and performance and its running costs.
- *Making the connections*: 'Home Zones' (see above) should include lower speed limits and traffic calming measures. These should be within the context of Local Transport Plans, which should have a statutory status and should include car-use reduction targets. At the national and local levels, there should be more effective regulation of bus service franchises and policy should be for a maximum of one car parking space per dwelling in urban areas.

Urban White Paper: Our Towns and Cities: The Future – Delivering an Urban Renaissance

The response by Government to the Urban Task Force report (UTF, 1999) and other influential research findings (DETR, 2000c) was an almost complete adoption of their recommendations. The Government produced a White Paper (ODPM, 2000) which set out the 'key steps' needed to make urban areas 'places for people':

- The design and quality of urban fabric must be good and 'right' for the place.
- All towns and cities should be able to create and share economic prosperity.
- Quality services that are needed should be available to all.
- People should be able to participate in developing their communities.

The Government has committed resources to assist the implementation of the Urban Renaissance. Furthermore, the Government has begun the process of facilitating the necessary changes in the planning system in a Green Paper (DTLR, 2001). It will be interesting to see how the policy initiatives for urban regeneration are played out. Their potential implications as far as determining good locations for property developments are discussed in Part 3.

PART 3: RECENT TRENDS IN DEVELOPMENT WITHIN CITY/TOWN CENTRES (AS ELEMENTS OF URBAN REGENERATION)

Urban regeneration: an introduction

Government policy concerning urban regeneration has gone through several metamorphoses. In the UK in the 1960s, policy was formulated which followed, to some extent, experiences in attempting to seek regeneration in the USA. At that time, the problem was seen as relating to the ghettos, inner city areas which had succumbed to significant economic and physical decay. Characteristically, such areas and their populations demonstrated high levels of unemployment, low levels of educational attainment, poor health and continually rising levels of crime. The 'Urban Programme', both in the USA and the UK, has, over the years, adopted different instruments and approaches in order to revitalise inner city areas. Initially, it was thought that the economic situation needed reversing in order to bring about the hoped-for benefits to the physical environment often associated with economic growth. To this end, the focus was initially on employment generation. Fiscal incentives were given to encourage employers to move to, or remain in, inner cities. With varying degrees of success, the policy focus later shifted towards improving the health of the inner city population. It was believed, rightly so, that a healthier population was likely to perform better both educationally and as a workforce and that targeted investment in healthcare provision in such areas would later reap dividends.

Effective fiscal and healthcare provisions for inner city dwellers were (and still are) essential to stop the long-term spiral of decline evidenced by the vicious cycle of economic, societal and environmental deterioration. But, in the 1980s, such an interfering approach by a government was not politically fashionable. Whilst it is certainly not the case that the Conservative Government of the UK in the 1980s absolutely stopped such intrusive involvement in improving inner cities, it is true to say that it favoured an altogether different approach. Rather than using the controlling hand of government to organise inner cities, the proponents of Thatcherism preferred to trust the free market. Given that a quick bureaucratic solution to inner city decay had not been found, it was felt that the market, unfettered by the restrictive practices of the planning system, would have to be relied upon to solve the problems. To this end, the property market was let loose, in certain places, by being given what are known as 'planning freedoms'. Simplified Planning Zones (SPZs) and Development Corporations were examples of these. The theory was that improvement of the physical environment would cause investment in the area, jobs would follow and general prosperity thereafter. To supplement the freedom of property developers to disregard what were considered to be 'limiting' planning policies, fiscal freedoms (such as 'tax holidays') were granted to business occupiers of the newly developed environment.

There is still debate, much of it politically motivated, about the relative merits of the bureaucratic/democratic model versus the market model. It is certainly the case that market-led urban regeneration has caused hugely significant change in the fabric of many urban areas, such as in London's Docklands. It is also true that many of the original residents of areas such as Docklands have not benefited directly from the changes, whereas developers and others have. Nor is it at all clear that the environmental changes have all been for the better. In terms of an assessment of the sustainability of the Thatcherite model of property-led urban regeneration, we would certainly have to weigh up the pros and cons of environmental enhancement and democratic deterioration. It is clear that property-led regeneration initiatives are not at the heart of the Urban Task Force's proposals for an urban renaissance and it is unclear, therefore, why the UK government should propose, in the Urban White Paper, the resurrection of the idea of zoning areas of deregulated planning control (in the form of Business Planning Zones (BPZs)) in 'deprived' areas. Critics of this proposal, which include the Commission for Architecture and the Built Environment (CABE), Campaign for the Protection of Rural England (CPRE) and the Royal Institution of Chartered Surveyors (RICS), suggest that BPZs would probably result in increased greenfield development, increased reliance on car use and a reduced likelihood of mixed use development. Such a policy could best be described as anti-sustainable.

Since the early 1990s, UK government policy on urban regeneration began to focus upon reusing derelict land and/or brownfield sites, which can be defined as 'any areas of land which have previously been the subject of a man-made or non-agricultural use type' (Syms, 1994, p. 63) or 'that which is or was occupied by a permanent structure (excluding agricultural or forestry buildings)' (DETR, 2000a, Annex C). More recently, the emphasis has been upon sustainable development of urban areas. To this end, government policy statements, such as PPGs and White Papers, have stressed the need to see mixed use development promoted and undertaken (see Part 2 above). Given that most urban land, certainly in inner city areas, is by definition brownfield land, policy has sought to promote mixed use development on brownfield sites within the planning system.

Mixed use developments

Mixed use development involves, as its name suggests, the development of a mixture of uses of buildings and land. This can mean that a number of single-use buildings are built on a site or that a building or buildings are occupied by different types of users. There has been much discussion on this type of development in the recent past and it has been heralded as an obvious contributor to sustainable urban development for a number of reasons. In particular, it is suggested that mixed use developments can encourage:

- Reduced reliance upon private transport
- Mixed tenure developments
- A 'dynamic' community
- Good aesthetics
- High quality urban design

Perceived problems with mixed use development

Traditionally, however, mixed use development has been resisted by a large number of developers and investors for a variety of reasons. Principal amongst these are that (RICS, 1992):

- Costs associated with this form of development are higher per square metre than single use developments. The reasons for this include expenditure required for health and safety reasons (e.g. to comply with fire regulations and means of escape from buildings which will need to be different for different users).
- Developers have traditionally been specialists in a type of construction. Whilst entering into joint ventures with developers of other types might solve this problem, this might well also bring with it procedural problems and greater uncertainty.
- The costs of managing a mixture of uses within a completed development scheme can be prohibitive, often as a result of differing lengths of leases and subsequent problems associated with the cost and timing of maintenance and refurbishment and multiple rent reviews.
- There has been a perception that certain occupiers of certain uses do not wish to be associated with other types of occupiers, such as office occupiers being co-located with what might be termed 'downmarket' shops.

As has been noted elsewhere, the involvement of the public sector in developing brownfield sites in order to regenerate an area is nearly always necessary. An example of this is the Gloucester Green development in Oxford. The local authority owned the site and was the driving force behind the initial stages of the scheme. It is argued that the key to the success of this scheme was that the site assembly from different interests and ownerships was reduced significantly and that public ownership of the development site meant that profit maximisation was not necessarily given primacy over social objectives associated with urban regeneration.

This example is not necessarily typical of the attempts to undertake the regeneration of an area with the development of a mixed use scheme, however. A number of problems associated with mixed use regeneration development have been identified (Rowley, 1996), in addition to those discussed above:

- Regeneration sites are very often outside what might be considered the 'prime pitch' for office and retail developments, thereby reducing their desirability to developers and investors.
- Often, sites proposed to be elements of regeneration schemes are small and do not offer economies of scale in their redevelopment.
- Sites which have previously consisted of housing use are often limited with regard to the ways in which they can be altered due to construction techniques employed.

- Mixed use schemes often rely upon small businesses to occupy space. Small businesses are often perceived to be financially vulnerable and therefore more risky than large businesses as occupiers.

Funding mixed use developments

Evidently, a problem exists with encouraging investors to consider involvement in many mixed use schemes. This is because 'The investing institutions include pension funds and life insurance companies, whose objective is to invest their contributors' premiums in safe, reliable investments' (Coupland *et al.*, 1997, p. 118). Such institutional investors are known to be 'risk averse' and are certainly very much 'risk aware'. Overexposure to property investments in the early 1990s saw many of their portfolio returns suffering during the economic downturn and the associated and spectacular property crash of that time (the expression 'once burnt, twice shy' comes to mind when considering their caution in becoming involved in apparently risky ventures in more recent times). This is why single use and, ideally, single tenanted, buildings in prime positions are attractive to them. An outcome of this situation is that in order to undertake these sorts of developments, developers need to find funding and finance from elsewhere. They tend to be loathe to expose much of their own money to a risky venture and banks tend to prefer to lend money against the development of existing or proven income streams, for which there are seemingly no limitations in terms of applications. Failing the opportunity to borrow from institutions or banks, developers would have to attempt to convince other lenders and/or commence a scheme in order to demonstrate its viability.

Planning issues and mixed use developments

Even if developers were able to source development funding and finance from a willing source to permit them to undertake mixed use development, there are significant systemic obstacles facing its achievement. An example is the lack of flexibility presented by development plans, which are often based upon historic land use patterns being continued in future land use suggestions. There is often, for example, a presumption in favour of 'employment generating' land uses within development plans in certain areas where there has been a history of manufacturing industry. The sub-text for such a policy is that, despite manufacturing uses no longer being economically viable in a given location, local authorities perceive a need to see the land returned to use which is labour intensive, rather than, say, combining a mixture of uses which may include housing or retail. Syms (1994) criticises such a lack of flexibility in decision-making and calls for each case to be treated upon its own merits.

Given the continuous updating of development plans and that this area of policy is developing rapidly, however, it could be the case that the flexibility that has been called for will become the norm. Recent government proposals for changes to the way in which forward development planning functions are undertaken, and its outputs are presented, represent a new departure for the planning system. It is proposed in the Planning Green Paper (DTLR, 2001) that development planning should be undertaken at a national level (in a spatial planning strategy), at the regional level (by unelected regional assemblies) and at a local level (by District authorities). What would be effected by such change is a removal of the Structure Plan level of town planning, often undertaken by County Councils, and a greater emphasis on the production of Local Development Frameworks (LDFs) in place of Local Plans. It is proposed that the LDFs would be more flexible and locally relevant than the current provisions and would be required to be updated every five years rather than every ten as at present.

The requirement to see greater flexibility in the planning system is one which occurs often in the literature on sustainable urban development and regeneration. As noted above, recent thought in this area has recommended that trends in centralising economic and development planning be replaced with regional, more localised policy-making and implementation. The Urban Task Force (1999) argues that such decentralising of decision-making will facilitate more appropriate development. The Urban Task Force (UTF) recommendation that local authorities are given considerably more scope than they currently possess to make merit-based decisions for development proposals will assist that process more easily than at present. It should, the UTF argues, allow for more efficient land assembly and financial aid for necessary redevelopment. Each of these issues is considered in turn below.

Land assembly and partnerships between developers and local authorities

In addition to their important function as a planning authority, local authorities have another key facilitating role to play in successful urban regeneration – as partners with developers. Prior to the 1980s, local authorities were often actively involved in the regeneration of urban areas. As noted previously, the 1980s and 1990s saw an increasing role being taken by the private sector in regeneration and there was a decrease in influence of the public sector in development activity generally. Partnerships between developers and the local level public sector can take a variety of forms and the roles that local authorities can take can also vary. Ratcliffe and Stubbs (1996) set out the key areas where local authority involvement in the development process can mean the difference between the success and failure of development projects generally. The following are particularly pertinent in urban regeneration:

Planning allocation: development plan land allocation greatly influences development potential and value. A partnership approach can be adopted at this very early stage of the planning and development process through consultation and negotiation for the mutual benefit of developers (in seeing their sites become allocated for development) and local authorities (whose regeneration objectives can be met) alike.

Land assembly: compulsory purchase powers can be used, when necessary, to 'assemble' land from different ownerships into one parcel of developable land.

The need for this occurs because developers need to be able to dispose of a finished scheme without constraints affecting legal title, services, planning and access. An authority's use of compulsory purchase powers depends on the perceived need and political will for regeneration and creating, often, employment-generating land use. Land assembly also can be assisted by land reclamation, provision of buildings, infrastructure and services, relocation of tenants and the promotion of the locality as suitable for businesses to locate to. The amount of money authorities can spend on economic development by way of capital expenditure is restricted by their credit approval limit and assisted by additional funding from central government. Assistance by negotiation with private landowners in achieving a realistic price for elements of a site can be significant. However, the system of compulsory purchase takes much time, which is largely why Compulsory Purchase Orders (CPOs) have been little used since their heyday of the 1960s and 1970s. It is argued (Fulford, 1999) that the CPO system is 'antiquated, bureaucratic and costly' and this is probably why the use of CPOs 'has long been a last resort for many councils' (Gummer, 2002).

Compulsory Purchase, under the Local Government Planning and Land Act 1980, can be effected if:

- Land is suitable for and required to secure development, redevelopment and improvement;
- Land is necessary to be acquired for proper planning of an area.

The time-consuming aspect of the current compulsory purchase system stems from the fact that all interests in land (which may be hundreds in city centre regeneration schemes) need compensating. Public Inquiries are held, followed by potentially lengthy negotiations between the affected parties' valuers and the District Valuer or other independent valuer. 'Disturbance compensation' may be payable to occupiers who suffer loss due to relocation and loss of profit. Furthermore, criticism exists due to inadequate compensation usually being paid, particularly as it is based on existing, not new premises' value and the system for payment can be very drawn out.

The Government, in response to such criticisms, has introduced legislation to liberalise the compulsory purchase and compensation regimes. The Planning and Compulsory Purchase Bill 2002 aims:

> 'to speed up the planning system. The provisions introduce powers which allow for the reform and speeding up of the plans system and an increase in the predictability of planning decisions, the speeding up of the handling of major infrastructure projects and the need for simplified planning zones to be identified in the strategic plan for a region or in relation to Wales. The Bill also provides for a number of urgent reforms to make the handling of planning applications both by central government and local authorities quicker and more efficient.' (House of Commons, 2002)

Infrastructure provision: often, regeneration sites have suffered from a lack of recent renewal of suitable roads, sewers, open space, schools and other public services. A lack of infrastructure will result in lower demand for developable sites. Whereas planning obligations (see below) may be used to provide for these on an ad hoc basis, there is an obvious need to prepare land for suitable redevelopment. Furthermore, by ensuring that adequate infrastructure is in place, local authorities are likely to see land values increased and, potentially, revenues also rising. Local authorities often approach retailers and other businesses for payment to enhance local infrastructure.

Business partnerships with developers: local authorities sometimes grant a long lease to developers, rather than selling the freehold of a development site, receiving a ground rent (sometimes linked to a scheme's performance) rather than a capital sum. Negotiations for the legal agreement between the two (or more) parties are often lengthy and are usually dependent upon finance being available for the developer. The social and financial objectives of authorities sometimes conflict and the internal resolution of these can take a very long time, which may frustrate the redevelopment scheme. To avoid delays, some authorities enter into limited partnerships with developers, which are regulated by law to ensure public accountability. These allow for quicker decision-making and risk-sharing.

Financial aid for necessary redevelopment

It is clear that the public and private sectors need to operate efficiently together in order to ensure effective regeneration. It is a commonly held view that public sector organisations, such as local authorities and regeneration agencies, need to 'pump prime' regeneration schemes with investment funding. Adair *et al.* (1998, p. 16) rightly point out that their responsibilities in bringing in private sector finance should go further and require 'the use of facilitating mechanisms such as pump priming, flexible administrative procedures, land assembly and disposal of sites on performance'. Without these and possibly other assistance from the public sector, private sector developers and investors are unlikely to bear the risks, which they perceive as significant, associated with regeneration schemes. The principal way in which developers and investors traditionally account for such risks is by requiring a financial premium on top of their usual returns. If a regeneration scheme is unlikely to deliver usual returns plus the premium, as is often the case, the gap between actual and required returns needs to be bridged – that is, gap funding is usually required to secure private sector finance. However, gap funding from European Union sources is unlikely to provide such a bridge in future:

> The ways in which public sector monies can be invested in regeneration have been heavily affected by the EC's state aid rules. In December 1999, the EC declared gap funding (which filled the gap between end-value and development costs in order to make development commercially viable) under the Partnership Investment Programme (PIP) constituted illegal state aid, and breached its Competition Directorate's rules on fair competition within the single market.

In summer 2001, the EC approved a suite of replacement schemes, providing new mechanisms for gap funding. The Regional Development Agencies (RDAs) are generally reluctant to use the new gap funding regime within their Single Pot allocations, favouring greater use of direct development and joint venturing. This requires greater initial funding, and involves longer delivery times – one factor being the need for additional skilled personnel, and hence a greater emphasis on training. (Anon, 2002b)

Arguably, it could be suggested that those considering investing in a regeneration scheme might accept a lower premium if they were to be guaranteed a given return on their investment, the risk of uncertainty being eliminated to some extent. Other means of reducing risks associated with regeneration must be found for the private sector to participate in it. From the developer/investor perspective, suggestions to do so include (KPMG, 1999):

- The removal of stamp duty on purchases of brownfield sites and schemes completed upon them. Interestingly, the Town and Country Planning Association (TCPA) suggests that stamp duty should go up (by 4%) at sites near transport hubs in order to fund future regeneration (Anon, 2002a).
- Delaying or deferring corporation tax payments for those developers involved in regeneration projects.
- Insurance cover to account for potential delays in completing and/or disposing of development schemes often associated with regeneration and brownfield redevelopment schemes.

Solutions to reduce the risk associated with suitable land not being used for regeneration schemes – i.e. what might be termed the risk to the 'public good' – include the imposition of a tax on 'vacant land'. This would have obvious implications for developers and others who undertake 'land banking' in the hope that land values will increase prior to its disposal or development. However, it should be pointed out that there are various potential problems associated with such a scheme. For example, the definition of 'vacant land' may, in certain circumstances, be unclear. Also, the suitability of certain sites for regeneration schemes might be an arguable point.

At a more site-specific level, fiscal measures can be used as incentives for the use of sites located in areas which may be part of regeneration schemes. Syms (1994) suggested that tax credits in respect of remediation costs would encourage and enable developers to become involved to a greater extent with brownfield site redevelopment. Since then, tax relief for this activity has been granted. Further than this, Syms also suggested that a tax upon greenfield development would act as another inducement to develop brownfield sites. The benefits associated with this proposal can at times seem obvious, but again, those who argue against this form of inhibition of greenfield development could suggest that circumstances pertinent to individual sites and situations might indicate that it is inappropriate. However, the proposition that brownfield redevelopment must be promoted and the importance of greenfield development demoted is if course endorsed by all supporters of urban renaissance and regeneration.

Taxation of inappropriate development might, therefore, be one of the best ways of securing this, as well as a means of local authorities raising revenue which might be ring-fenced for supporting regeneration efforts.

Regional Development Agencies

Regional Development Agencies (RDAs) are the latest in a line of organisations that have been established to promote regeneration in the UK. Although their main focus is on economic regeneration, they also undertaken many different activities that directly or indirectly assist in physical urban regeneration. The first RDA, the Welsh Development Agency, was established in 1976. Scottish Enterprise, another RDA, was set up in 1991. Their counterpart in Northern Ireland, Invest Northern Ireland, was established following the amalgamation of a number of different economic development organisations in 2002. In England, there are nine RDAs, all established in 1999 (except the London RDA, which was set up in 2000). The English RDAs are:

- Advantage West Midlands
- East Midlands Development Agency
- East of England Development Agency
- London Development Agency
- North West Development Agency
- One North East
- South East England Development Agency
- South West England Regional Development Agency
- Yorkshire Forward

The roles of RDAs have been set out succinctly (Anon, 2002b) as:

- 'Acquiring and assembling sites.
- Preparing sites for development by the private sector, such as through the remediation of brownfield sites and the provision of infrastructure.
- Entering into partnerships/joint ventures with the private sector, local authorities etc.
- Attracting relocating companies to their regions.
- Securing inward investment.
- Providing finance, loans, guarantees.
- Working with the local planning authority on a masterplan for the area.
- Assisting with the formulation of long-term strategic planning.
- Undertaking direct development.
- Carrying out the usual property management functions.

Regional development agencies are able to compulsorily acquire land but, unlike their predecessor urban development corporations, do not have any statutory planning powers. Instead, they operate within the usual planning system.

Whereas previous regeneration initiatives were predominantly property specific, the RDAs' roles extend to bringing about the long-term overall economic growth of an area. This is achieved by the provision of support to new and existing businesses and the promotion of training and development initiatives for local communities and businesses.

RDAs also seek to build a strong brand to assist in dealings with businesses and the general public.'

Sources of public finance for regeneration

The most significant amounts of public money for regeneration schemes come essentially from or through two sources: RDAs and the European Union. RDAs have what is known as a 'Single Pot' of funding from government, in addition to the Single Regeneration Budget (SRB), which is being phased out. The European Union provides a European Regional Development Fund (ERDF), but this has only been guaranteed until 2006. The importance of the RDAs is therefore increasing in terms of their financial weight. Other sources of funding for regeneration include local authorities, non-governmental organisations (e.g. the Prince's Trust and the Peabody Foundation) and the National Lottery. The use of European Union money, which was for a long time a lifeline for many regeneration projects, is definitely on the wane, as discussed above.

Planning obligations

In terms of financial aid for redevelopment necessary to promote regeneration, local authorities are restricted in the manner in which they can use finance for the benefit of developments, particularly if those benefiting from the profits generated include private organisations. In order to derive public advantage from private developments, local authorities may, in certain circumstances, oblige developers to provide, for example, infrastructural benefits necessitated by the development itself. The system of planning obligations (or 'planning gain' as it has been dubbed by some) represents an occasionally significant means of funding the aims of regeneration and, for some authorities, the most significant means of raising funds to meet regeneration objectives. This system has been criticised by the UTF (Punter, 1999) for a number of reasons, as set out below.

Although developers face risks when taking on regeneration schemes it is also clear that local authorities, as promoters of them, face a certain amount of risk and uncertainty when seeking their implementation. Many developers, partly because of their desire to reduce risks and their attempts to increase returns from any development scheme, will seek to offer relatively little to a community by way of 'betterment'. Local authorities often seek to secure positive impacts resulting from developments by way of planning obligations, often through s.106 agreements. However, it is evident that this method of ensuring that the objectives of a local authority to regenerate an area is not ideal. The UTF report suggests that these are the principal obstructions within the planning obligations system:

- The use of s. 106 legal agreements takes too long, thereby slowing down the regeneration process.

- No matter how carefully local authorities' development plans are drafted, in meeting the stated primary objectives of a plan, developers are not required to meet secondary objectives which may have become of primary importance since the plan was written.
- The lack of a standardised way in which to secure developer contributions towards meeting local authority objectives means that authorities have to deal with each case as if from a new standpoint. This lack of consistency hinders both the decision-makers and developers.
- Planning obligations do not need to consider the viability of the scheme as a whole. This means that some authorities might seek to impose obligations which will prevent a scheme that might benefit an area from going ahead.

If the use of these obligations can act as an obstacle to regeneration, then what sort of alternatives can we consider? In the USA, the common form of securing 'betterment' from development activity is via means of impact fees, where these are standardised methods of calculating a financial gain which should be granted to local authorities. This is, in effect, a form of development tax of the sort which has been used in the UK in the past. There are critics of this method, however. Their principal objections relate to the fact that standardised methods of securing public benefits from private developments do not allow local authorities to reflect local needs in their requests for 'betterment'.

Another objection is that the use of negotiated s. 106 agreements on a case-by-case basis does not result in a transparent method of assessing needs against possible gains. This adds to the uncertainty borne by developers in any development activity, thereby increasing the risks associated with it.

POSSIBLE FUTURE DIRECTIONS

This chapter set out to describe traditional approaches to the consideration of locational issues pertinent to property development and then to explain why recent policy changes have come about and what the impact of these has been on the property development process. Whereas, traditionally, property developments have tended to be of the single use variety, produced by specialists in developing buildings of that use, we hope that you will have seen that mixed use developments offer a practical and sustainable alternative to these.

Of course, understanding the traditional view is still helpful in some contexts – we still need to know, for example, what sort of population is needed to support the provision of retail facilities and what sorts of obstacles lie in the path of engendering mixed use developments on a wider scale than is presently seen. However, we also need to appreciate that a more sustainable approach to property development must progress, for example by appreciating that a viable retail facility should not rely upon its catchment population using private transport, nor that funding institutions will always be sceptical of investing in mixed use schemes.

The change in focus of the planning system and development activity towards trying to engender an 'urban renaissance' has been fundamental. Since the early 1990s, when the aims of sustainable development became politically pertinent to town planning (and thus property development) in the UK, we have seen a significant move away from practices such as promotion of out-of-town greenfield development towards the regeneration of brownfield urban locations. The Government has used a range of policy instruments, such as PPGs and fiscal and legislative tools, to enforce concepts such as 'sequential testing', brownfield development land allocation, remediation of contaminated land, land assembly and mixed use development. All of these, as discussed in this chapter, have a profound influence upon the ways in which developers and others consider the appropriate location of new property developments.

Notwithstanding this point, the UK Government is still attracted to the concept of large-scale greenfield development, particularly of residential properties. The announcement in February 2003 of the Sustainable Communities Plan (ODPM, 2003) is likely to mean a lot more greenfield development than in recent years and that 'The Government appears to be returning to the discredited "predict-and-provide" approach to planning for housing which Mr Prescott abandoned less than five years ago' (CPRE, 2003, para. 3). We shall need to see how this policy statement is delivered in practice. The CPRE (2003, para. 9) has urged the Government to ensure that the Sustainable Communities Plan meets quality of life objectives by:

- 'Taking full account of an area's environmental capacity to absorb new development when determining the scale and location of growth.
- Providing genuinely affordable housing to meet identified needs, not simply feeding speculative development of large, detached houses for sale.
- Making much better use of land – raising average housing densities well into the 30 to 50 dwellings per hectare range, and above – including by applying the new Density Direction across the country.
- Raising the Government's 60% brownfield housing target – which it has already exceeded eight years early – to at least 75%.
- Minimising the use of primary aggregates, water, energy and other natural resources in construction – in line with the objective of making better use of minerals and other natural resources ('getting more out of less') in the Government's Sustainable Development Strategy.
- Ensuring that new development mixes housing, jobs, shops and services together to reduce the need to travel, especially by car.
- Preventing new development from creating more dismal dormitory sprawl which just adds to congestion and pressure for new road building, severs communities and contributes to noise, air pollution and climate change.'

Good developers, i.e. ones which respond to the challenge of contributing towards an urban renaissance, will take up the opportunities which this fundamental shift in development policy presents. They will, through investment in the resources and intellectual capital needed to respond to this new challenge, have to consider the following issues:

Changing perceptions about the quality of different locations: given the emphasis on using brownfield, urban sites for development, it is clear that the way in which land is valued will be different from the past. Land values will change as policy reduces the supply of greenfield sites and enhances the demand for urban sites. Many sites that are labelled as derelict need not be, particularly if local authorities designate and promote them as developable land. This would encourage owners of contaminated brownfield sites to instigate remedial and/or development activity.

In the short term, policies aimed at altering perceptions about locations in this way might mean developers beginning to change the ways in which they 'bank' land. Over the medium and longer terms, divestment of greenfield site holdings will be appropriate as the balance of land holdings shifts towards more of an emphasis upon a greater compactness of town centres and urban extensions (Jenks *et al.*, 1996).

Changing perceptions about the nature of the properties demanded: the UTF is clear about the nature of change required in order to meet future demand for property. Properties will have to comprise a far greater mixed use component, be more flexible (in terms of their layout and use) and be developed to greater densities. Within the residential context, properties will have to be smaller and allow people to use them as live–work units. The issue of car parking also needs to be carefully addressed, as PPG 3 has begun to do (DETR, 2000a). This may seem a tall order and too significant a change of culture for developers to bear. However, it should be borne in mind, for example, that mixed use development should comprise flexible space, which is able to adapt to market place changes and therefore be of a long term higher value.

Currently, most private sector (and increasingly public sector) housing is provided by volume house builders. They need to change the style of house they provide from suburban family houses to that which is appropriate for the massive majority of housing need that the UTF estimates will be taken up by single people in future.

All of these changes to the types of properties that will be increasingly demanded have an obvious connection to site-finding and appraisal – developers need to understand what it is they intend to build when they identify sites for their products.

Changing the way development sites and schemes are appraised: given the above, it is evident that the costs associated with development will be different in future. There will probably be more cost 'up-front' to be spent on market research, the design process (often due to public participation) and on construction itself (as the quality of buildings improves and developers increasingly contribute to a higher quality public realm). All of this may be used, indeed it is used, by detractors of recent urban regeneration policy to suggest that it will not work. This view is short sighted. Although costs will probably rise, at least in the short and medium terms, developers must also appreciate that many of the policy changes represent positive opportunities. There will, for example, be less risk in securing planning permissions if extensive design consultation is undertaken. Furthermore, there is likely to be more revenue received by developers from increased densities and thoughtful designs.

In terms of policy implementation, we are beginning to see UTF proposals becoming accepted. For example, the concept of spatial masterplans (see Part 2 above) has been taken up in the Urban White Paper (ODPM, 2000). Furthermore, Local Planning Frameworks (LPFs), which have been proposed as a replacement for Local Plans, are intended to be relevant at the neighbourhood level (rather than district-wide), quicker to produce and derived from public involvement in decision-making. Other UTF proposals (e.g. for reforming planning obligations, increasing densities, mixed use development and appropriate car parking standards) also need a policy context in order to make them enforceable and comprehensible.

Changing the nature of the work of property professionals: traditionally, property professionals working in private practices have foregone the opportunity to work on regeneration projects unless on behalf of private or public sector clients who are prepared to pay for their services at normal rates of pay. An organisation based in Liverpool, Kensington New Deal for Communities (NDC), suggests that there is another way in which their help might be useful in 'kick-starting' regeneration projects (Box 1.3). The Chairman of Kensington NDC, Bishop James Jones, suggests that: 'While NDC is community-led, there is still a need for property professionals to get involved. They should try to find the time or money to make a difference.'

Box 1.3 How property professionals can help kick-start regeneration.

'Agents and surveyors can help with the large volume of valuation and acquisition work needed to demolish abandoned, poor-quality housing stock and transfer ownership to approved registered social landlords.

Developers and investors can match-fund NDC money to build homes, a school or an adult training centre. Kensington NDC alone needs to match its £62 m of NDC money with £180 m of other public- and private-sector funds to meet its targets.

Volunteer mentors from agencies and surveyors can help to start up businesses and find premises in untapped edge-of-city markets.

Property professionals can help to uncover profitable markets in deprived communities. How can the level of homeownership be improved, cheaply and efficiently? How can surplus, derelict shopfronts best be brought back into use on busy arterial roads?

Research assistance is needed by four pilot City Growth Strategies (CGSs) in Nottingham, Plymouth, St Helens and London to map inner-city business bases. Rather than focusing on social disadvantage, CGSs emphasise the economic advantages of locations, workforce availability and underserved retail markets. The aim is to encourage private-sector investment and help to develop plans for business growth.

Venture capital investors can back the government's forthcoming Community Development Venture Fund, which will provide finance for firms operating in disadvantaged areas.'
(Unger, 2002, reproduced with permission)

It is clear that many potential regeneration schemes will not succeed until such a time as they are able, *inter alia*, to demonstrate their commercial viability in order to attract long-term funding and until they prioritise revamping of their environment. In order to achieve these, communities will need expert advice for which they are unlikely to be able to pay in the short term. Some people may think Bishop Jones' comment that professionals should 'find the time or money to make a difference' as being commercially unrealistic. However, it could be suggested that such professionals could 'speculate to accumulate', in that work as a loss-leader could later result in profitable consultancy once the regeneration project is up and running. Unger (2002) stresses that much of the £2 billion of Government funding set aside for NDC use (there are, at the time of writing, 39 NDCs) has not been spent because NDCs have not been able to demonstrate the financial sustainability of their proposals. Surely property professionals could enable the release of such funds, to their own and the communities' benefit as well as that of regeneration generally.

In terms of development practice, all of the above changes mean that:

- Accuracy and currency of market research information will be of paramount importance if competitive advantage is to be maintained.
- Different skills will have to be employed, by designers, market researchers and developers in the private sector, as will new approaches in some public sector agencies where a 'can do' attitude which fosters innovation will be required.
- Financial institutions will still have to be involved in funding development schemes but conservatism amongst financial institutions currently has a tendency to stifle innovation in development. If, for example, regeneration through mixed use development and the development of live–work units is to be possible, financiers will need to be convinced of the benefits of the way policy is changing before it can be put into practice on a wider scale than at present. Some financial institutions are making some progress in this respect. Prudential Property Investment Managers, for example, have a commitment to 'Socially Responsible Investment' (SRI). Apart from addressing a range of issues concerning their own performance in this respect, they also mention in their Environmental and Social Report 2002 that they will, *inter alia*:

'promote increased awareness and debate in the wider property investment community about SRI and how it might be conceptualised for property investors. This will be done through the support of relevant research and by conference papers and publications'. (PruPIM, 2002, p. 36)

- Furthermore, PruPIM stress that as a major property owner, they have an obligation to 'help in the upgrading of UK [property] stock'. Apart from the benefit to the community, they stress that whilst investing about £100 million each year in refurbishing properties, the beneficiaries include themselves and their tenants.

There now exists a real opportunity for positive, beneficial change to our environment through sustainable property development. We shall have to see whether it works or goes the way of previous regeneration policies, which we suggest have failed largely because the policies suffered from a lack of consideration of their full implications. The current policy regime has advantages over previous ones because it is based upon the concepts of sustainable development and the need to consider development projects and plans in terms of their environmental, social and economic implications. Fundamental to this is that sustainable property development requires support from private and public sectors, in the form of funding from both sectors and from effective partnerships rather than paying lip service to this sort of approach. The proposals set out by the Urban Task Force and in the Urban White Paper have the support of the public and private sectors, which should encourage us to believe in their probable effectiveness.

One of the potential obstacles to issues like urban regeneration, promotion of the redevelopment of brownfield sites and mixed use development is objection from those who fear that it might lead to 'town cramming'. What needs to be ensured is that 'town cramming' objectors are convinced of the benefits of such development over, say, new town developments. High density development does not necessarily mean town cramming and if local authorities engage with their populations, this message should be capable of being put across. Better still, demonstration projects should exemplify the issue.

We need to remember that the issue of location of property developments, including urban regeneration, is only a part of a wider picture. We must also consider site-specific issues relating to the redevelopment of land, particularly the beneficial reuse of contaminated land, as well as the design and procurement of environmentally sensitive buildings. These issues are considered in the following chapters.

LEARNING MATERIALS

Some questions and issues for discussion

(1) **Consider the reasons for selecting sites with a large amount of car parking when site finding for different property types**

- There has traditionally been a reliance on private transport when determining suitable locations for most property, though only since car ownership has been commonplace.
- The state of public transport provision is poor and apparently increasingly so.
- Working practices seem to dictate that car use at work is important, but we need to consider how necessary this is. Many occupiers are beginning to devise transport strategies to determine such need, partly because car parking space is not cheap.
- Government policy (e.g. in PPGs 3, 6 and 13) suggests that developers and planners should limit the provision of car parking spaces.

(2) **What are the possible means of financing the 'urban renaissance'?**

- There is a clear need for partnerships between the public and private sectors. In recent years, the Government has announced it will supply billions of pounds of investment in regeneration which it expects will attract far more private investment.
- Other ways that the public sector can assist with reducing costs of regeneration include site assembly.
- Taxation of greenfield development and Impact Fees (a form of development tax) have been suggested as means of revenue raising.
- The use of planning obligations continues and suggestions have been made by the UTF to change this system.

(3) **What is the 'sequential test' and how should developers consider this when making planning applications?**

- In making planning applications, developers must be aware of 'material considerations', including the provisions of the development plans and government guidance. Many development plans and PPGs (e.g. PPGs 3 and 6) indicate that the sequential test must be followed.
- In essence, the test involves developers proving that they have considered brownfield sites before greenfield ones. Furthermore, they should demonstrate that they have considered central locations, before moving away to edge of centre, then the edge of built-up areas, with out-of-town locations as a last resort.
- If this policy is relevant to an application, there is little point in submitting an application for greenfield development if a lack of brownfield availability cannot be demonstrated.

(4) **How will the UTF proposals and those in the Urban White Paper promote environmental sustainability?**

- In essence, the more compact an environment is, the fewer resources are required to build it and live and work in it.
- The issue of transport is vital, as high density towns and cities require less transport movement than low density ones. Proposals for Home Zones and mixed use developments are important here.
- The White Paper and UTF proposals stress the need for a high quality public realm, which includes the appropriate use and design of public spaces, as well as high quality design of buildings in terms of their aesthetics and functionality.
- Energy efficiency within the built environment is important and the White Paper and UTF state a need for more efficient buildings.

(5) **What are the key environmental differences between urban villages and new settlements?**

- Essentially, the key difference is that of brownfield versus greenfield development.

- Urban villages are likely to be more efficient in terms of transportation requirements, given that they usually rely on far higher density of development and mixed use buildings and sites.
- Other sustainable development issues (i.e. social and economic) are important too.

(6)   **What are the advantages and disadvantages of mixed use development proposals over other forms?**

- Apart from allowing for the possibility of mixed tenure and balanced communities (which are important for socially sustainable reasons), environmental reasons are relevant here. Compactness and density of development and consequentially less need for transportation are key issues.
- It is important to understand the attitudes of investors towards mixed use development. Institutions tend not to favour these (largely due to alleged high running costs), whereas other investors, such as property companies, might.
- On the other hand, many planning authorities' attitudes are very favourable and planning permission might be easier to secure than for single use proposals.

Examples of media coverage of the issue of regeneration

(1)   **In the following article from the *Estates Gazette*, John Gummer, a former Secretary of State for the Environment, berates an organisation that promotes the concept of new towns (which were discussed above).**

SAY NO TO GREENFIELD HOMES

The Joseph Rowntree Trust has a fine record of intervening to raise the quality of life for the poor and the disadvantaged. It therefore grieves me to have to belabour it regarding the latest report that calls for further extensive building in the countryside.

Rightly concerned at the decline in house building and the increasing number of people for whom decent housing seems beyond their grasp, Rowntree has come up with the outdated prescription of massive new greenfield developments designed to increase the supply in order to cut the price of homes. This contention plays well with many developers, the Town and Country Planning Association, and even some local authorities. It is nonetheless wholly wrong.

Our failure to get the building we need is not because we have refused permission on greenfield sites. It is because we have failed to facilitate building on already-used land. We are so institutionally hidebound and administratively inept that we are beginning to convince ourselves that only by indulging ourselves with the easy and environmentally destructive option of splurging on greenfield can we deliver the goods.

In fact, the opposite is the case. Yet more suburban estates, executive closes, and new designer settlements will betray the cities and besmirch the countryside.

From Gummer (2002b). Reproduced with kind permission of the publisher.

---

(2)   **Consider all sides of the above debate, as suggested by the Council for the Protection of Rural England (CPRE: www.cpre.org.uk), Town and**

Country Planning Association (TCPA: www.tcpa.org.uk) and the Urban Task Force (www.urban.odpm.gov.uk/whitepaper/taskforce/). What are the key issues put forward by each party? What are the benefits of each party's proposals? Consider the extent to which the arguments are 'clear cut' or more complex.

(3)   The following article (Allen, 2002) sets out a number of interesting issues that relate to sustainable property development generally and to urban regeneration in particular.

FIRMS WITH A HEART GO AHEAD

Giving things back to the community and being aware of environmental and social issues can often pay dividends for firms. Lucy Allen looks at the trend towards corporate social responsibility.

You're a young, urban Londoner. Pounding your way around the capital's streets and its shops, you get tired of the same old scene. Street after street duplicates itself, with the same coffee shops, bars, and retail. So when Sunday rolls around, your favourite place to hang out is the old market.

Here you find some respite from the bustle of corporations vying for your attention. You meet friends, eat from an independent stall, buy some fresh organic vegetables and choose a shirt that has been handmade somewhere in Hackney. You go home feeling you have given something back, rather than boosted the coffers of corporations that you really don't trust.

So imagine how you feel when you hear that developers are planning to raze your market to the ground, and build more of the same big shiny city offer in its place.

These situations fuel the public perception that developers are only really interested in money. And such negative public perceptions are dangerous.

Public expectations are changing. The consumer is more sophisticated and people are becoming keener to scrutinise companies. It is no longer enough to donate to charities, as this is seen as paternalistic. The public want brands to give back.

People demand social responsibility

Paul Cornes, director of community investment at Prudential Property Investment Managers, explains: 'People are demanding that companies be socially responsible. It's the way of the world nowadays.'

So what used to be termed 'good business practice' has been re-branded. The new catch-phrase in global corporate public relations is 'corporate social responsibility', or CSR. It's a North American idea, spawned by global brands like Starbucks, which applies ethical ideals on environmental and social issues and incorporates them into business under the CSR umbrella.

Cornes believes he is the first director of CSR to be appointed within the property industry in this country. 'Having a CSR strategy has shone a headlight across all parts of our business, making us consider whether they are all socially responsible and whether our shareholders would find them acceptable,' he says.

CSR requires corporations to stop treating philanthropy as a separate issue from business by incorporating it into their business plans. Companies with CSR policies aim to analyse the impact of their business activities on their stakeholders and on the local and global environment. This might encompass human rights, workplace issues, the environment, marketplace issues or the community.

Continued

Emma Denne, corporate communications manager at Land Securities, explains what CSR means to her company. 'CSR is a framework within which we engage with the community and communicate our environmental and ethical policies as a corporate citizen,' she says. 'We see it as good business sense.'

The FTSE4Good index

Land Securities is 43rd in the FTSE4Good UK 50 index series for socially responsible investment (SRI). Prudential is 17th. Launched in July 2001, the FTSE4Good criteria covers environmental sustainability, the development of positive relationships with stakeholders, and universal human rights. Mark Makepeace, chief executive of the FTSE group, describes FTSE4Good as 'an investible financial tool that also sets attainable CSR standards for companies worldwide'. British Land is also involved in CSR, and has been listed in the FTSE4Good index since its inception.

Advocates of CSR believe that corporate codes of conduct should be an integral part of business planning, and that the vision of corporations should not be wholly defined by profit. For them, it is the public that gives a company the licence to prosper and, increasingly, this licence depends upon the contribution a company is making to society.

'Many think CSR is just about giving money to charity,' says Cornes. 'But most companies now try to link their corporate giving with their business objectives.'

The idea that businesses need to make money to prosper, but can also prosper by doing good, is not rocket science. Large corporations have often had elements of philanthropy. In the 19th century, the Lever factory at Port Sunlight provided quality housing for its workforce.

But what is new is the concept that shouting about the social good you are doing can improve your public image.

Starbucks now employs a senior vice-president of CSR to market its good works. Through emphasising its Fair Trade brand of coffee, Starbucks has always promoted an image of social responsibility.

So how can firms in the property industry give back to their communities? The social and environmental debates that immediately affect the property industry are well reported: concern over CO_2 emissions, urban regeneration, location – brownfield or greenfield – raw materials and use.

Publicly scrutinised policies

Yet with emphasis increasingly being placed on CSR, property companies could soon be required to develop policies or corporate codes of conduct on these issues that will have to be released into the public domain. There are many examples of property companies throughout the UK that are keen to sponsor charity events for good causes, local or global. The difference is that these good works are not yet part of many companies' business plans.

Few signs have emerged of any commercial property agents having completely come to terms with the concept of CSR. Both Jones Lang LaSalle and Knight Frank admit that they have all the elements of CSR in place in terms of values, but that they are not yet incorporated under the CSR banner. Quentin Langley, head of public relations at Knight Frank, says: 'Our values permeate every aspect of what the firm does. We don't go shouting about them, because they are what clients expect and what we deliver.'

A spokesperson for GVA Grimley says: 'It's something we can't comment on at the moment, because we haven't got anything in place. But we are looking seriously at it.' DTZ has the same message: 'We take CSR seriously, and it is something we are moving towards. We are not there yet, but we are committed to doing it,' says a spokesperson.

HSBC holdings, number two in the FTSE4good UK 50 index, obviously sees CSR as an integral part of its business. It recently announced that it is donating £35 million over five years to three environmental charities, including the World Wide Fund for Nature.

But is this really a publicity coup? Is CSR just a way of measuring social and environmental impact to create more transparency, or is it just more PR 'spin'?

Important part of branding

PruPIM's Cornes describes CSR as 'an increasingly important part of branding, which differentiates you from your competitor and enhances your reputation'. His colleague, Paul McNamara, adds: 'CSR is expected to be an essential way of doing business soon. If it is a form of branding, then everyone is going to be adopting it.'

But cynics believe that, because there is no legislation or auditing method yet that verifies that businesses are actually making a contribution to society, what companies are actually doing is exploiting ethical concerns for profit and good PR.

Others believe that CSR is another form of damage limitation, driven by concern over the negative consequences of avoiding the issue of reputation.

A CSR policy may protect against negative publicity for property companies. Those companies that focus on brownfield sites and encourage energy efficiency may be seen more positively and have a competitive advantage over those that do not.

But CSR could actually create a negative image for a company: in the same way that public relations disasters can drive away customers, shareholders and sometimes even employees, companies that act in an ill-judged manner in terms of CSR can find themselves in trouble (see below).

The bottom line is, just as your young urban Londoner trusts independent retailers at his local market more than those on the high street, customers may increasingly trust pressure groups more than corporations. Businesses who refuse to acknowledge this are not doing their shareholders any favours.

The CSR route: not risk free

By engaging with CSR, Starbucks opened itself up as a target for environmental and social pressure groups and anti-globalisation protesters, who have claimed that the company gives little to its farmers while generating huge profits. This arguably had a negative impact on the public perception of the company. Protesters damage the brand when they attack the firm, and adverse publicity can rapidly affect share values.

But ignoring the implications of CSR may turn out to be risky. The impact of campaigning groups on the reputation of corporations has been well documented. When the Monsanto genetically modified foods scandal erupted, consumers in the UK heard about it from Greenpeace, rather than from the food industry. This damaged the public view on GM foods to such an extent that it will be years – if ever – before UK consumers accept such food, despite the fact that GM foods are the norm in the US.

In the property sector, a bad reputation may have an impact on the price of buildings. CSR issues can also affect investment returns. Clients may begin to question property managers over whether their investments are being dealt with in a socially responsible manner, and whether this responsibility or lack of it will enhance their business.

From Allen (2002). Reproduced with kind permission of the publisher.

Continued

Exercises

- Obtain CSR reports and identify the key environmental and other sustainability issues within them (these are increasingly available on the internet).
- How do environmental issues fit within the CSR reports – do you think that they are given more or less emphasis than social or economic issues?
- Do CSR reports commit the organisations to specific environmental objectives? If so, do the objectives relate to existing buildings or development projects?
- What are the strengths and weaknesses of the CSR reports and what opportunities and threats do they present for the organisations that published them?

Resources

www.mallenbaker.net/csr/: a website containing many CSR related resources, including basic information concerning the advantages and disadvantages of CSR, news items, internet resources and publications.
www.csrcampaign.org/: a website produced by campaigners for CSR.
www.prudential.co.uk/prudentialplc/csr_home/: the CSR site for the financial institution, 'Prudential'.
www.pggm.nl/: the website for the Dutch financial institution, 'PGGM'.
www.boots-plc.com/: the website of the retailer, including its on-line CSR. Examines the influence of property, particularly the issues of location and transport.

NOTE

1   The Town and Country Planning (Use Classes) Order 1987. Note that this is due to be revised in 2003 (see: www.planning.odpm.gov.uk/consult/ucotup/01.htm).

REFERENCES

Adair, A., Berry, J., Deddis, W., McGreal, S. & Hirst, S. (1998) *Accessing Private Finance: The Availability and Effectiveness of Private Finance in Urban Regeneration*, London, RICS.

Adams, C.D., Russell, L. & Taylor-Russell, C. (1993) 'Development constraints: market processes and the supply of industrial land', *Journal of Property Research* **10**(1), 49–61.

Allen, L. (2002) 'Firms with a heart go ahead', *Estates Gazette*, 23 March.

Anon (2002a) 'Stamp Duty hike urged to fund transport revamps', *Estates Gazette*, 2 November.

Anon (2002b) 'Pump-priming for prosperity', *Estates Gazette*, 7 September.

Blackman, D. & Lipman, C. (2003) 'New settlements will turn into dormitories, MPs told', *New Start*, www.newstartmag.co.uk/news440.html, visited 28/1/03.

Cadman, D. & Topping, R. (1995) *Property development*, London, E&FN Spon.

Cheshire, P. (1993) 'Why NIMBYISM has gone BANANAS', *Estates Gazette* 9321, 104–5.

Christaller, W. (1933) Die zentralen Orte in Süddeutschland. Jena, Gustav Fischer

Coupland, A. (ed) (1997) *Reclaiming the City: Mixed-use Development*, E&FN Spon, London.

CPRE (Council for the Protection of Rural England) (2003) 'Half a million homes on greenfields in South East England?', press release, 31 January, www.cpre.org.uk/press/rel2003/press-brief-communities-plan.htm

Debenham Tewson Research (1990) *Development trends*, Debenham, Tewson & Chinnocks, London.

Department of the Environment (DoE) (1992) *Planning Policy Guidance Note 3: Housing*, DoE, London.

DoE (1995) *Preparation of Environmental Statements for Planning Projects That Require an Environmental Assessment: A Good Practice Guide*, HMSO, London.

DoE (1996) *Planning Policy Guidance Note 6: Retailing and Town Centres*, DoE, London.

DoE (1997) *Planning Policy Guidance Note 23: Planning and Pollution Control*, DoE, London.

Department of the Environment, Transport and Regions (DETR) (1999) *A Better Quality of Life: A Strategy for Sustainable Development in the UK*, DETR, London.

DETR (2000a) *Planning Policy Guidance Note 3: Housing*, DETR, London.

DETR (2000b) *Planning Policy Guidance Note 13: Transport*, DETR, London.

DETR (2000c) *The State of English Cities*, DETR, London.

DETR (2001) *Planning Policy Guidance Note 1: General Policy and Principles*, DETR, London.

DTLR (2001) *Planning: Delivering a Fundamental Change* (a Green Paper), DTLR, London.

Fulford, C. (1999) 'Righting the land assembly process', *EGi Archive*, 9 January.

Glasson, J., Therivel, R. & Chadwick, A. (1999) *Introduction to Environmental Impact Assessment*, 2nd Edition, UCL Press, London.

Gummer, J. (2002a) 'Grease the wheels to lift city centres', *Estates Gazette*, 16 March.

Gummer, J. (2002b) 'Say no to greenfield homes', *Estates Gazette*, 30 March.

Hall, D. (1989) 'The case for new settlements', *Town and Country Planning* **58**(4), 111–14.

Havard, T. (2002) Contemporary Property Development. London, RIBA Enterprises.

Hawking, H. (1992) 'Checkout superstores', *Estates Gazette* **9205**, 146.

House of Commons (2002) *Planning and Compulsory Purchase Bill: Explanatory Notes*, House of Commons, London.

Jenks, M., Burton, E. & Williams, K. (1996) *The Compact City: A Sustainable Urban Form?*, E&FN Spon, London.

KPMG (1999) *Fiscal Incentives for Urban Housing: Exploring the Options*, Urban Task Force, London.

Losch, A. (1938) 'The nature of economic regions', *Southern Economic Journal* **5**, 71–8.

Morris, P. & Therivel, R. (eds) (2001) *'Methods of Environmental Impact Assessment,'* 2nd Edition, Spon Press, London.

ODPM (1999) *Circular 02/99: Environmental Impact Assessment*, ODPM, London.

ODPM (2000) *Urban White Paper: 'Our Towns and Cities: The Future – Delivering an Urban Renaissance'*, ODPM, London.

ODPM (2003) *Sustainable Communities: Building for the Future*, ODPM, London.

Peel Holdings (2001) *The Trafford Centre Information Pack*, Peel Holdings, Manchester.

PruPIM (2002) *Environmental and Social Report 2002*, Prudential, London.

Punter, L. (1999) *The Future Role of Planning Agreements in Facilitating Urban Regeneration*, Urban Task Force, London.

Ratcliffe, J. & Stubbs, M. (1996) *Urban Planning and Real Estate Development*, UCL Press, London.

RICS (1992) *Living Cities: An Initiative by the RICS*, RICS, London.

Ringer, M. (1989) 'Is the shopper really king?', *Estates Gazette* **8945**, 109–12.

Rowley, A. (1996) *Mixed-Use Development: Concept and Realities*, RICS, London.

Syms, P. (1994) 'The funding of developments on derelict land and contaminated sites', in R. Ball & A. Pratt, *Industrial Property: Policy and Economic Development*, Routledge, London, pp. 63–82.

Syms, P. (2001) *Releasing Brownfields*, Joseph Rowntree Foundation, York.

Taylor, R. (1985) 'New high-technology survey', *Estates Gazette* **275**, 20.

Unger, P. (2002) 'Residents of a deprived area of Liverpool are looking for help from above – but not all their prayers have been answered', *Estates Gazette*, 14 December.

Urban Task Force (1999) *Towards an Urban Renaissance*, DETR, London.

Williams, J. (1982) *A Review of Science Parks and High-technology Developments*, Drivers Jonas, London.

World Commission on Environment and Development (1987) *Our Common Inheritance*, OUP, Oxford.

FURTHER RESOURCES: WEBSITES

www.urban.odpm.gov.uk/atoz/index.htm#uv   The website for the Office of the Deputy Prime Minister which indexes many useful policy-related websites, including Urban Task Force publications.

www.tcpa.org.uk/   The website for the Town and Country Planning Association, a campaigning group which seeks to promote sustainability in the built environment and promotes new settlements.

www.princes-foundation.org/   The website for the Princes Foundation: a campaigning group which seeks to promote sustainability in the built environment, including through the development of Urban Villages. It has a number of demonstration projects which are well worth examination.

www.cpre.org.uk/   The website for the Council for the Protection of Rural England: a campaigning group which seeks to promote sustainability in the built environment and promotes protection of greenfield land.

www.cabe.org.uk   The website for the Commission for Architecture and the Built Environment, which promotes high quality that prioritises the quality of the built environment through both public and private investment.

www.bura.org.uk/main/content.htm   The website for The British Urban Regeneration Association, which seeks to encourage and disseminate best practice in the regeneration sector.

www.hbf.co.uk/   The website for the House Builders Federation, the trade federation for private house builders in England and Wales that promotes the cause of developers.

www.rics-foundation.org/   The website for the RICS Foundation, which provides and sponsors research into land, property, construction and development. A significant focus is upon sustainable development.

www.regen.net/   The website for Regen.net – an information network for regeneration partnerships and a good source of information on regeneration good practice.

Contamination: dealing with polluted land

2

Suggested learning outcomes

After studying this chapter and discussing its contents, you should be able to:

- Define contaminated land under the law and explain changes in the definition of land contamination over time.
- Discuss possible causes of contamination and the reasons why it must be addressed.
- Explain what could be involved in the remediation process and describe how contaminated land can be investigated and cleaned up.
- Appraise the nature of Government policy in this area in terms of its sustainability.
- Provide sustainable solutions to given problems pertaining to contaminated land.

HEADLINES: BIG ISSUES AND IMPORTANT QUESTIONS

In the property world at least, 'contaminated land' has come to represent one of the most significant environmental issues faced by owners and developers of land and their professional advisers. The reasons for this are that contaminated land:

- Represents a continuing state of environmental damage that possibly originated hundreds of years ago and is, as yet, unchecked.
- Can and does irreversibly harm living organisms, people, animals and plant life.
- Can cause building materials and components to fail, such that buildings may become unfit for their intended purpose.
- Often reduces the value of sites through a poor public image and reduced marketability.
- Usually means that redevelopment costs of certain sites are higher than otherwise, partly because it is less safe for contractors to handle the soil, and that alternative uses have to be considered for some sites.
- Can result in some highly and widely polluted urban areas becoming stigmatised with a 'dirty' image, leading to no-go development areas (often where urban regeneration is most needed).

53

- May result in legal liability of polluters and owners or occupiers of land for the costs of cleaning up pollution.

The important questions that need to be addressed are as follows. They are given some context here and then are discussed in more detail further below.

What is 'contaminated land'?

The precise definition of contaminated land has changed over the last few years. Although this might appear to be an issue merely of semantics, it is important to understand the differences between 'contaminated land' and other types of polluted land if we are to be able to advise owners about their legal liabilities. The legal definition of contaminated land is contained within the Environmental Protection Act 1990 (EPA 1990), as discussed below.

How and why does it occur?

It stems from unchecked pollution of the soil from by-products of industrial processes. Often, these processes were carried out some time ago (e.g. during the Industrial Revolution) but their effects, in the form of contaminated land, are only now being felt. Again, we should not get bogged down in semantics, but in applying the law, environmental regulators will need to determine whether someone *'caused'* or *'knowingly permitted'* contamination to occur (in accordance with s. 78F of the EPA 1990). Defining these terms is not as straightforward as it might initially seem.

What problems does it pose and to whom?

Contaminated land can harm people, animals and plants and the wider environment. It can, for example, be ingested by people, pollute water supplies and cause vegetation to die, thereby harming ecosystems.

How can it be cleaned up and avoided in the future?

There are many different clean-up ('remediation') techniques available, all with different cost implications and effects upon the environment. For example, it might be relatively cheap to excavate the affected soil and place it in a landfill site, but this does not really address the problem of the existence of the pollution, except for the site from which it was removed. In order to prevent future contamination, those who operate potentially polluting installations should implement pollution prevention and control strategies. It might be helpful to operate an Environmental Management System (e.g. under the ISO14001 standard). The European Union Directive on Integrated Pollution Prevention and Control (Directive 96/61/EC (OJ L182 16.7.99)) stated specific requirements for the inclusion of conditions to prevent soil pollution in permits for industrial installations. These were translated into UK regulations (Pollution Prevention and Control (England and Wales) Regulations 2000 (SI 2000/1973)).

How can other problems associated with it be avoided?

In order to understand this, we need to be able to appreciate the wider, non-physical effects that contaminated land can create. These include various financial problems (e.g. for regulators, developers, landowners and their advisers) and legal liabilities.

Who is responsible for cleaning it up and how much can this cost?

Responsibility for remediation should be determined by reference to current legislation and supplementary government guidance. A hierarchy of liability exists which is, arguably perhaps, in accordance with the 'polluter pays principle'. However, responsibility rests with someone known as 'the appropriate person' and this might be the owner or occupier of the land. The cost of remediation varies from site to site and 'ballpark' figures are rarely given. The principle of using the best available technique not entailing excessive cost (BATNEEC) is enshrined in legislation (EPA 1990, s. 7) and best *practicable* techniques in the statutory guidance (DETR, 2000a, Annex A, paras. 6.23–6.24), although this has to be balanced with effectiveness.

BACKGROUND

Definitions of 'contaminated land' have changed, even in the recent past, as policy makers have shifted the emphasis within the definitions from the presence of pollutants to the possibility of damaging the environment. Previously, the following definitions have been given:

- Land that contains substances which, when present in sufficient quantities or concentrations, are likely to cause harm, directly or indirectly, to man, to the environment, or on occasion to other targets. (NATO/CCMS, 1985)
- Land which is being or has been put to a contaminative use (EPA, 1990, s.143)

Essentially, contamination of land occurs when soil contains chemical pollutants and/or physical obstructions that can either harm the wider environment, people, animals and plants or inhibit future uses in, on, over or under the land. Furthermore, it usually occurs when a polluting occupier has used the land.

Historical causes of contamination

As mentioned above, pollutants and obstacles in sites are very often there as a result of the activities of former occupiers, perhaps those who were in occupation many years ago. Prior to recent regulation on waste management, occupiers of sites frequently saw land as a resource to be used, in part, as a refuse dump. Unwanted by-products of many industrial activities were simply disposed of or 'stored' in unrecorded landfill tips that were covered over with topsoil and, very often, built upon at a later date. Fortunately, many of these sorts of activities are now illegal (even though we still manage to landfill approximately two thirds of our industrial, commercial and household waste (DETR, 2000b)) but in the past, it was considered to be an acceptable part of industrial processes. Because much of this sort of activity went unrecorded, many current-day occupiers and developers of land often have to deal with the environmental legacy of pollutants and obstacles in soil in a reactive manner. The sorts of industrial processes and land uses which often created this sort of pollution are set out in Box 2.1.

Box 2.1　Examples of former industrial activities which often resulted in land contamination

---

Manufacturing industry sites

- Asbestos works and buildings containing asbestos
- Brickworks and potteries
- Chemical works, including pharmaceutical, acid and alkali works
- Dry cleaners
- Food processing plants
- Glass and ceramic works
- Metal mines, smelters, foundries, steel works, metal-finishing and plating works
- Munitions production and testing sites
- Paint-manufacturing works
- Paper, pulp and printing works
- Rubber industry sites
- Tanneries
- Textile mills

Infrastructure sites

- Cemeteries, crypts and other burial areas
- Docks, canals and ship-breaking yards
- Mineral extraction sites (quarries, china clay mines, etc.)
- Railway land (including sidings and depots)
- Sewage works and farms, sludge disposal sites and sites where sewage sludge has been applied to land

Industrial storage sites

- Landfills and waste disposal sites
- Military airfields
- Oil refineries, petroleum distribution and storage sites
- Scrap yards

Power generation sites

- Gasworks, coal-carbonisation plants and associated by-product works
- Nuclear power stations, radioactive storage/disposal works

There are numerous sources of possible contaminants. The Rosehaugh Guide (RIBA, 1990) lists the following possible sources:

- Accidental leakage and spillage from pipes and tanks during plant operation.
- The storage and disposal of raw materials, by-products and waste materials.

- The disposal of unwanted wastes and residues on or adjacent to a site by disposal to properly designated landfills, dumps or tips.
- The deposition of airborne particles from stack or volatile exhaust emissions.
- The uncontrolled demolition of industrial plant, which may contain contaminating materials such as asbestos lagging, chemically impregnated brickwork, tars in pipes and underground tanks, etc.
- Further dispersion of contaminants as a result of soil disturbance, or leaching and drainage of the more soluble and mobile contaminants into surface water and groundwater.

Government action to address contaminated land

Governmental policies on addressing the issue of land contamination have been in existence for some decades. It was in the USA where the first comprehensive set of policies was established. The issue of pollution of land and water was raised notably in the 1960s by the American author Rachel Carson, in her seminal work *Silent Spring* (Carson, 1962). In that and the following decade, environmentalism grew in popularity. Sixteen years after Carson's work was published, the environmental pollution disaster at Love Canal, in the City of Niagara Falls, caused President Carter to declare a state of emergency for the area. The Love Canal incident served as a reminder of Carson's warnings of damage that was likely to haunt future generations due to our industrial legacy. In 1980, when another state of emergency was declared at Love Canal, the American Government enacted legislation known as the Comprehensive Environmental Reclamation and Contaminated Land Act (CERCLA). This attempted to deal with the issue of liability for past pollution of the soil and was thus the first attempt by a national government to address this issue comprehensively.

Within the European Union, certain governments have acted more quickly and comprehensively than others. For example, the Dutch government introduced very high standards for the clean-up of contaminated land fairly soon after CERCLA was introduced in the 1980s (Ministry of Housing, Physical Planning and the Environment, 1983), whereas the UK government only introduced them, and to lower standards (ICRCL, 1987), following European Union policy (Wilkinson, 1992). Even then, powerful lobbying by vested interests (such as the property industry and manufacturers) prevented the introduction of the first attempt at comprehensive legislative powers (i.e. elements of the Environmental Protection Act 1990, such as the proposed s. 143 Registers). In hindsight, it can probably be said that objection to these ill-considered laws was appropriate, given the poorly constructed early regulations. In July 1995, the Environment Act amended the 1990 Environmental Protection Act and inserted the all-important (in this respect at least) Part IIA into it. This, now, is the principal legislation concerning contaminated land in the UK and it is supported by supplementary regulations (Contaminated Land (England) Regulations 2000 (S.I. 2000, No. 227)) and guidance from the Government (DETR, 2000a). It is important to note that the issuing of this guidance came five years after the legislation was enacted (that is, 10 years after the initial legislation). The guidance went through numerous draft forms and several consultation periods existed for the draft guidance and policy statements between 1990 and 1999. This caused considerable confusion within the property industry and is certainly symptomatic of the complexity of the issues that are involved.

Defining contaminated land today

Currently, it is vitally important to know of and understand the legal definition of contaminated land in order to appreciate the nature of the liabilities for remediating it or to ensure that it is cleaned up at all.

Part IIA of the Environmental Protection Act 1990 contains the definition of contaminated land and some vitally important qualifications to the definition. Understanding of the definition and these qualifications is not straightforward, but, as stressed previously, is absolutely essential for anyone with an interest in this topic. The definition of contaminated land (EPA 1990, s. 78A (2)) is:

> 'any land which appears to the local authority in whose area it is situated to be in such a condition, by reason of substances in, on or under the land, that:
>
> (a)   significant harm is being caused or there is a significant possibility of such harm being caused; or
> (b)   pollution of controlled waters is being, or is likely to be, caused'.

This definition implies that, in fact, land has to be in such a condition that 'significant harm' is resulting (or is likely to result) from the existence of pollutants rather than it merely being capable of causing any harm. In other words, the definition of contaminated land has changed since 1990. Then, there was an emphasis upon the current and former uses of the land. (The EPA 1990, s. 143 proposed the use of public registers of land subject to 40 contaminative uses (DoE, 1991), but the list of uses was later reduced to the eight most contaminating ones (DoE, 1992).) By 2000, the emphasis was upon the **actual condition of land** and whether this would cause significant harm. This is obviously an important change in policy and it is discussed below.

The 'suitable for use' standard

In a qualification to a draft definition of contaminated land, the term 'significant' was combined with the word 'harm' at the report stage of the Environment Bill (Act) 1995 in the House of Lords. The consequence of this qualification was very far reaching. This was for two reasons: first, it was an attempt to bring the definition into line with the Government's intention to maintain the 'suitable for use' approach to remediation of contaminated land, which means that any cleaning up or remediation of land should be done to a standard which is suitable for the current or proposed use of the site. Second, the related concept of assessing the risk of harm resulting from contamination was introduced, i.e. there is now a new test relating to the possibility of contamination resulting in actual harm rather than just being in existence, or even only possibly in existence. Indeed, the statutory guidance states 'the definition of contaminated land is based upon the principles of risk assessment' (DETR, 2000a, para. A9). The guidance follows the source–pathway–target (also referred to as contaminant–pathway–receptor) model of risk assessment. This is discussed further below when we consider the concept of 'remediation', or cleanup, of contamination.

Who is liable for contamination?

The use of the risk assessment model makes it possible for authorities to undertake inspections of their jurisdictions, and landowners of their own sites, for contaminated land. It also allows regulators to identify the person or persons responsible for the contamination and thus financially liable for its remediation. Under the law (EPA 1990, s. 78E(1)), such a person is known as the 'appropriate person', upon whom a 'remediation notice' will be served by the enforcing authority (either the local authority or the Environment Agency if the site is, unusually, so severely contaminated that it is deemed to be a 'special site' (EPA 1990, s. 78C)). The appropriate person bears all or part of the remediation expenses, except in cases of hardship. The 'polluter pays principle' persists (EPA 1990, s. 78F(2)) unless the polluter cannot be found, as may be the case with historically polluted sites. If this is the case, the appropriate person is deemed to be the current landowner (that is, under the law, the person entitled to receive a 'rack rent' for the land (EPA 1990, s. 78F(4))). If there is more than one appropriate person, the regulator is obliged to apportion costs for remediation, having first applied six exclusion tests (EPA 1990, s. 78F(7) and DETR, 2000a).

Amount of land that is contaminated

One of the important effects of the change in the definition of contaminated land over time has been upon the amount of land thought possibly to be suffering from it. In 1993 (i.e. under the 1990 definition), for example, it had been estimated that there were 200 000 ha (CBI, 1993), whereas after the change to the EPA 1990 s. 78A(2) definition, it was estimated that there were 2800 ha (Syms, 1999). Prior to the change in definition, some very broad estimates of the potential identification (£400 million) and remediation costs (£20–£40 billion) for the national UK contamination burden were made (Timothy, 1992; CBI, 1993). However, these cannot be relied upon as accurate measures of the problem, due to both the change in definition and the 'ball park' nature of the figures themselves. What they do perhaps indicate is the view at the time that contamination was a very significant problem but that it was difficult to estimate the scale of the problem. This latter point has not changed significantly. Even the 2800 ha estimate carries the caveat that the total amount of polluted land in the UK might be up to 20 times greater than the amount of land which falls within the relatively narrow statutory definition of 'contaminated land' (Syms, 1999).

Controlled waters

The statutory definition contains reference to pollution of 'controlled waters', which are:

- Territorial waters
- Coastal waters
- Inland waters
- Groundwater

The statutory guidance does not provide very comprehensive advice to help with the determination of whether pollution of controlled waters has occurred or will happen. Furthermore, the guidance suggests, perhaps alarmingly from a perspective of desiring certainty in this area of the law, that 'the Government is proposing to review the wording of the legislation on this aspect and to seek amendments to the primary legislation' (DETR, 2000a, Annex 2, para. 6.30). The reason for this is that pollution of controlled waters simply means the entry into such water of *any* polluting matter.[1] This could easily result in minute amounts of relatively harmless polluting matter triggering the definition of contaminated land under the law. Despite assurances in the guidance that a clear entry into the relevant register stating the nature and amount of a contaminant would be made by the enforcing authority, were a remediation notice to be served upon a landowner under such circumstances, then problems may arise later with blight and/or stigma. It is to be hoped that the legislation and guidance in this area becomes more robust in future, offering certainty to landowners and regulators alike.

PRACTICAL PROBLEMS AND SOLUTIONS, CURRENT APPROACHES, TECHNIQUES AND MODELS

Why does it matter whether a site is contaminated?

If a contaminated site is developed without sufficient recognition of the potential dangers or their appropriate remediation, there is a high probability that the contamination may give rise to a number of hazards. The effects of each hazard vary with each individual development. For example, the development of a car park on contaminated land will not usually pose the same risk as the development of residential houses. The degree of remediation required in this example will thus be correspondingly lower.

Phytotoxicity

Phytotoxicity is the prevention or inhibition of plant growth. The effect varies between species and can be caused by a number of factors including soil contamination, absence of soil nutrients and waterlogging. Principal phytotoxic elements include boron (water-soluble), copper, nickel and zinc. These elements are essential for plant growth at low concentrations, but are toxic at higher concentrations. Gases such as methane may give rise to phytotoxic effects by reducing the oxygen content of the soil in the root zone. A number of substances such as oils and phenols give rise to phytotoxic effects at concentrations which are not directly hazardous to human health.

Phytotoxic contaminants can cause the death of vegetation which can affect health (loss of food crops), financial wellbeing and be unsightly. If the vegetation has been planted to provide landscaping around offices or industrial developments or forms residential gardens, the marketability of these developments could be impaired.

Chemical attack on building materials and services

A number of contaminants are known to attack building materials and services either in or on the ground. Sulphates attack concrete, which may lead to the weakening of structures such as foundations. Sulphate attack may be heightened in acid soils and solutions. Other known contaminants detrimental to materials are acids, oily and tarry substances, and other organic compounds. These contaminants can accelerate the corrosion of metals in soils and damage plastics, rubber and other similar materials, which are often used in pipework and service conduits or as jointing seals and protective coatings for concrete and metals.

Combustion

Contaminants such as coal and coke particles, oil, tar, rubber, domestic waste and plastic are all combustible. They can ignite if heated by buried power cables, hot ashes or surface bonfires. Some organic materials such as carbon, hides, milk products and fertilisers are prone to self-heating under certain conditions. This can lead to ignition. Underground fires can burn out of control for many years with little evidence on the surface. These fires leave voids that may cause settlement and affect the structural integrity of buildings. Toxic gases may be liberated during combustion.

Explosion

Flammable gases such as methane may be produced on former waste disposal sites. Gases can migrate laterally or vertically for long distances. If these gases accumulate in a confined space, such as under or within buildings, there is an increased risk of explosion (see also 'landfill gas', below).

Leachate and groundwater contamination

Contaminated sites can give rise to leachate production, which may lead to contamination of aquifers surface water and groundwater. These hazards may pose a threat either on or off the site. They may also be subject to statutory obligations regarding protection of water sources.

Common contaminants that produce hazardous leachate include acid run-off from colliery spoils and sulphur-rich slag. Industrial sites can also produce hazardous leachate. Although leachate production and movement is frequently slow, it can give rise to considerable pollution over a long period of time.

Obstructions

As a result of their past use, many contaminated sites have had buildings and underground services placed on the site. When factories, for example, are decommissioned, structures such as the underground pipework and tanks are commonly left behind. If not identified at an early stage, these can cause obstructions to future development. Problems that can arise include:

- Interference with site investigations.
- Concentrations of contaminants (due to structures such as tar wells).
- Release of contaminants (from leaking pipes, etc.).

Stability

The presence of certain contaminated fill materials in a site can significantly affect its load-bearing capacity and thus threaten the stability of any structure erected on the site. A Construction Industry Research and Information Association (CIRIA) report (Leach & Goodger, 1991) states: On a fill site, settlement potential may impose severe constraints on building development, and extensive ground improvement and careful foundation design may be required before building works can be realised.

Landfill gas (LFG)

Gas generation from former waste tips and landfill sites has increasingly given great cause for concern. Flammable gases, which often form explosive mixtures (see above), are generated by the degradation of organic materials. Gas generation can continue for at least 15 years and stabilisation may take over 50 years. LFG is predominantly a mixture of methane and carbon dioxide. Methane is explosive at concentrations of 5%–15% in air. In high concentrations it is flammable. Mixtures of LFG and air should, therefore, always be regarded as potentially explosive. LFG is normally odorous, which helps identify its presence, although occasionally the odorous compounds are removed by passage through rock and soils. In the latter case, although then non-odorous, the gas remains volatile and can be explosive.

LFG is potentially a highly mobile gas and can slowly accumulate in buildings and structures above or adjacent to landfills. LFG can also affect structures situated some distance from the landfill site. If a site has been covered with low-permeability materials such as car parks and concrete foundations, lateral diffusion of LFG may be heightened.

Health and environmental hazards

Contaminants can pose a threat to the health and safety of plant, human and animal life. In humans, i.e. those involved in site reclamation and redevelopment as well as those working or living on or close to the developed site, the effects may be short or long term. Effects can range from simple irritation to extreme toxicity and injury or death through poisoning or impact.

Commercial hazards

Land contamination can dramatically affect the viability of redevelopment of a site. Not only can remediation activities add to the costs of a development scheme, but also the existence of contamination (or even the suggestion of it) can lead to a 'stigma' effect occurring. 'Stigma' has been defined in this context as the valuation implications of uncertainty created by environmental issues (Wilson, 1994) and, more simply, a 'negative intangible' (Patchin, 1991) caused by:

- Fear of hidden clean-up costs.
- Hassle associated with clean-up.
- Fear of public liability.
- Difficulty in obtaining mortgages.

Registration of contaminated land

Previously, many people and organisations first became aware of the existence of contamination when attempting either to purchase or to occupy land or when applying for planning permission for development of it. As stated above, more recently (i.e. since April 2000 (DETR, 2000a)), owners or polluters of a site may have been served a Remediation Notice by the local authority under the provisions of the amended Environmental Protection Act 1990, s. 78E. Few local authorities' strategies for doing this were prepared before July 2001 (by which time they are required to have prepared their plans for inspecting their areas and establishing registers), given financial and human resources constraints, but progress has been made since then.

The problems that this posed for owners of sites, for example, were many and various:

- Owners found it very difficult to obtain planning permission from a local planning authority for a certain use of the land.
- Redevelopment of sites became difficult for a number of reasons.
- Lenders became wary of being associated with a scheme blighted by contamination.
- Building contractors insisted upon various necessary but expensive health and safety measures being established before they entered sites.
- Professional valuers might present further unwelcome news in the form of deeply discounted valuations of sites as in the model (Figure 2.1), which

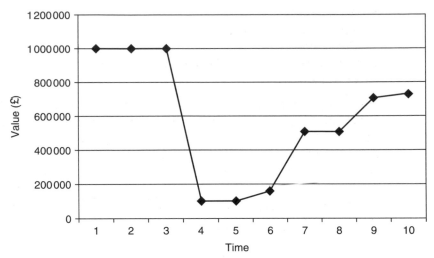

Figure 2.1 Potential effect of stigma on a contaminated site's value over time (adapted from Mundy, 1992).

demonstrates how values can be affected by the notification of the presence of contamination.

In Figure 2.1, we see how an evidently unimpaired site (that is, one which is not known to be suffering from contamination) has an open market value of £1 million. Assuming a stable market, at time period 3 the value suddenly drops due to the stigma attached to contamination being discovered (and, importantly, publicised). Thereafter, the site's value maintains a low value until time period five, when remediation actions are planned and are then undertaken in periods six and seven. During periods seven and eight, the value plateaus; only 'good P.R.', supported by accurate information pertaining to the remediation, will help the value to increase towards its former level. Whether or not, from period nine onwards, the value will reach its former unimpaired value will depend on a number of factors, such as results of pollutant monitoring, market conditions of supply and demand and ongoing public relations initiatives. The stigma effect on value may thus continue to be felt indefinitely.

Using a team of advisers

Many professional organisations (e.g. RICS, 2000) suggest that their members' clients' interests can best be served if the advisers adopt a teamwork approach to solving problems presented by contaminated land. An RICS model (RICS, 2000), for example, suggests that the team of necessary advisers could include the following:

- Asset managers
- Lawyers
- Geotechnical engineers
- Planners

- Accountants
- Regulatory authorities
- Developers
- Surveyors (of various disciplines)
- Insurers

It should be noted that others must be involved in the operation to find and adopt solutions to a problem posed by contamination. It would be unthinkable not to include the landowner and/or the 'appropriate person' as defined by statute in the decision-making process. Similarly, the inclusion of the expertise and knowledge from within the enforcing authority would usually be deemed as necessary for the successful solution of a contamination problem. Lastly, but by no means marginally, the attitudes and interests of local people must also be considered and involved in any decision-making, particularly if on-site works and future development of the site are proposed.

Professional advice

Governmental advice for local planning authority officers (DoE, 1995) suggests a system of risk assessment for identifying sites prone to contamination and this methodology (and other advice contained in this series[2]) can be well used by other professional advisers, although many have been slow to adopt it. Because of the nature of contaminated land and the relative ignorance of how it should be dealt with by many site owners (and, regrettably, their professional advisers (Keeping, 2001a and 2001b)), many of the surmountable problems associated with it are either not overcome at all or done so badly. For example, research evidence indicates that valuers often display ignorance as to how they should reflect the presence of contamination in a valuation report. It is axiomatic that all valuers should define the extent of their instructions with clarity before reporting to a client. The 'Red Book' guidance is quite clear on this and valuers should address the issue of contamination at this stage. It states (RICS, 1995, PS6) that unless otherwise agreed in advance, it is mandatory that all relevant issues (like contamination) should be reflected in a valuation. It also states that possible contamination is a relevant issue: 'unless instructed by or agreed with the client to the contrary, it is necessary to establish the existence and the extent of any contamination' (RICS, 1995, GN2). It lists the following important factors that should be taken into consideration by valuers when attempting to assess how important a factor contamination is likely to be in their provision of advice to clients:

'(a) the nature and extent of their instructions;
(b) the state of knowledge at any time of the existence and effect of the particular form of contamination;
(c) the current interpretation of the law;
(d) the extent to which the market is reflecting possible changes in legislation and technology;
(e) the previous use of the subject land/buildings and property nearby;

(f)   the existing use of the subject land/buildings and property nearby;

(g)   the proposed use of the subject land/buildings and property nearby as may be established from reasonable local enquiries and inspection of planning registers; and

(h)   the financial effect of the above.'

The most recent RICS guidance sets out the responsibilities of valuers on reporting and reflecting the possible presence of contamination in valuation reports. It aims *inter alia* to 'define [chartered surveyors'] professional responsibilities' (RICS, 2000, 1.3(a)) and notes that service provided by these professionals 'will be incomplete or inappropriate if it were to ignore any contamination implications for the property or the users of it' (RICS, 2000, v).[3]

RICS guidance on this matter is helpful up to a point (e.g. RICS, 1995) but it does not address the thorny issue of valuation methodology, which is discussed below.

Valuation advice

In attempting to value a contaminated site, valuers are somewhat hindered by three frequently occurring factors. First, they seldom possess sufficient knowledge about environmental matters to translate technical contaminated land investigation and remediation reports provided to them by other professionals. Second, their lack of expertise nearly always inhibits them from securing adequate professional indemnity insurance, without which professional valuers are disallowed from advising clients. Third, the paucity of information relating to comparable evidence means that typical comparison-based valuation methods are rendered somewhat difficult to rely upon. The first two matters urgently need to be addressed by the profession and its insurers. It is for the third reason that valuers are increasingly likely to turn to 'explicit' valuation models when advising clients about their contaminated sites (a trend which is likely to continue in all areas of valuation advice).

Research into the area of valuation advice for contaminated sites began, in the UK at least, in the mid 1990s. Richards' work (Richards, 1995 and 1996) drew upon North American literature and reported results from an empirical study of UK practitioners. Lizieri *et al.* (1996) similarly reported from American literature and went on to consider practitioners' approaches to valuation of environmental factors. Related work by other researchers, such as Syms (1997a), has concluded that valuation methodology amongst practitioners varies. Most researchers and many practitioners suggest that the advantages of explicit methods of valuation, such as the Discounted Cash Flow (DCF) model, tend to outweigh their disadvantages. Careful personal consideration of this topic should confirm this and that other, 'traditional' methods of valuation are less suitable for the valuation of a contaminated site. Admitting that the DCF approach is not without its problems, Gronow (1998, p. 31) has nonetheless summed up this particular issue succinctly: 'As in other areas of appraisal, as clients question the "what", and the "how", of what was taken into account, it will be inevitable that an explicit DCF model will be essential for appraising contaminated land.'

Legal advice during land transactions

Another example of inadequate professional advice concerns that of some solicitors involved in the conveyancing of contaminated sites. Purchasers of real property rely heavily upon the advice and services of legal advisers during the process of the transaction of freehold and leasehold land. This is due to the complex nature of the conveyancing process which grapples with the hindrance of the *caveat emptor* principle. In this research, the key method employed by legal advisers to protect their clients from entering into a contract to purchase potentially contaminated land, that is, enquiries before contract, have been seen to be inadequate in effect if not in purpose. Furthermore, research (Keeping, 2001b) has also shown that many conveyancers, while achieving the minimum that the Law Society might expect the reasonable and competent practitioner to achieve, are not acting much in excess of this, if at all. A significant proportion of firms are failing to raise even the most obvious and pertinent enquiries, such as details about a site's previous uses. Some firms of solicitors issue extensive and highly commendable lists of preliminary enquiries and it is only these firms who are approaching or meeting the suggestions submitted in guidance commissioned and approved by the Law Society. A number of 'core' environmental questions should always be asked in order to help protect the purchaser from acquiring contaminated land and any associated liabilities and additional expenditure. These are:

- Whether the owner is aware of any actual or potential pollution.
- The site's (and neighbouring sites') previous uses.
- The presence of hazardous wastes stored on the site.
- Whether any environmental audits have been carried out regarding the site.
- Whether there have been any actions against site owners in respect of polluting incidents.

Similarly the purchaser's solicitor needs to ascertain whether hazards are present on the site, as, after acquiring the site, clients would have to ensure the avoidance of:

- Causing a statutory nuisance (Part III of the EPA 1990).
- Allowing the escape of polluting substances from the land in a manner which affects neighbouring landowners (a potential common law liability).
- Breaching the duty of care in respect of waste (EPA 1990, s. 34).
- Treating, keeping or disposing of controlled waste in a manner likely to cause pollution of the environment or harm to human health (EPA 1990, s. 33(1)(c)).

It is during the pre-contract phase that conveyancers can assist potential purchasers both in not acquiring such liabilities and in reducing their likelihood of having to go to considerable expense with ground investigations. Government guidance (DETR, 2000a, Annex 3, para. E43) states that:

'The enforcing authority should bear in mind that the safeguards which might reasonably be expected to be taken will be different in different types of transaction (for example, acquisition of recreational land as compared with commercial land transactions) and between buyers of different types (for example, private individuals as compared with major commercial undertakings)'.

This indication that purchasers of sites and their professional advisers must reflect absolute thoroughness in their investigations is very clear. That it has not yet become as clear to some practising conveyancers as might be expected of a reasonably competent practitioner may prove worrisome to such professionals in the near future, let alone their clients.

Inspection methods

Syms (1997b, p. 68) succinctly reports that site investigations 'must be sufficiently comprehensive, so as to present a reasonably accurate picture of the site condition, and not a misleading impression'. In order to achieve this, it is recommended that a strategy with nine objectives is assumed (CIRIA, 1995), as set out in Box 2.2.

Box 2.2   Suggested objectives for a site investigation strategy (adapted from CIRIA, 1995)

(1)   Determine the nature and extent of any contamination of soils and groundwater on the site;
(2)   Determine the nature and extent of any contamination of soils migrating off the site;
(3)   Determine the nature and extent of any contamination migrating into the site;
(4)   Determine the nature and engineering implications of other hazards and features on the site, e.g. storage tanks, deep foundations;
(5)   Identify, characterise and assess potential targets and likely pathways;
(6)   Provide sufficient information to identify and evaluate a range of remedial strategies;
(7)   Determine the need for, and scope of, short and long term monitoring and maintenance (on and off site, as necessary);
(8)   Formulate safe site working practices and ensure effective protection of the environment during remedial works; and
(9)   Identify and plan for immediate human and environmental protection and emergency response.

Various commentators suggest staging the components of site investigations into two, three or four phases. However many phases are deemed appropriate, similar information should be sought such that a representation of the site's condition is arrived at. A model developed by a development agency in the early 1990s (WDA, 1993) demonstrates which information is required, as set out in Box 2.3.

As each contaminated site is unique from another, there is no singularly 'best method' for the investigation of a contaminated site. An often-favoured approach for site investigations is that of a phased or staged approach. The four typical phases can be seen in Box 2.4 (page 70).

Box 2.3   Information required from site investigations (adapted from WDA, 1993)

An historical study

Many sources of information, such as ordnance survey and geological maps, newspaper records, town planning records, historical photographs and utilities' records. Checking for previously undertaken environmental surveys can save considerable time at this stage, although its current relevance must obviously be checked.

Site characterisation

Pulling together initial evidence as to the hazards posed to the natural and built environments and human health. The source–pathway–receptor model should be employed.

Site reconnaissance

A visual survey of the site is necessary to check the veracity of documentary sources and to supplement them with apparent but unrecorded data.

Inspection and testing

This should only be necessary if the previous stages have been undertaken thoroughly and suggest this should be done. More detailed inspection of the site than previously undertaken and some initial soil testing will assist in determining the objectives of future investigation and designing an appropriate and cost-effective ground investigation. Consideration of any on-going activities on the site will be necessary.

Ground investigation

The purpose of this is to determine the presence, nature, distribution and amount of any contaminants. It will involve determination of systematic sampling patterns (before actual sampling is undertaken) and of the requirement for machinery and personnel to undertake the sampling.

Sampling and analysis

Various techniques might be employed, such as the digging of pits and trenches to expose and remove soil or the use of gas surveying equipment. On-site and off-site analysis of soil is recommended, the former to protect site workers and the latter for more thorough laboratory testing.

Supplementary investigation

This becomes necessary when, for example, unexpected contaminants are discovered, when a more detailed investigation of a certain area is required or when other on-site activities inhibit previous investigation.

Phase 3 in Box 2.4 indicates that a risk assessment should be included within site investigation methodology. It should be noted that risk assessment should be used with the aim of reducing the risks identified – that is, to ensure that the full range of risk management techniques is employed. Risk management in the context of contaminated land has been defined as follows:

'Risk assessment and risk reduction together comprise the overall process of risk management. There is an overlap between risk assessment (comprising hazard identification and assessment, risk estimation and risk evaluation) and risk reduction (comprising risk evaluation and risk control). In the context of contaminated land, the need to assess the risks associated with contaminants

Box 2.4   Typical phases of investigating a (potentially) contaminated site

---

Phase 1

- Review of site history
- Site reconnaissance
- Review of regulatory methods

Phase 2

- Site investigation to identify the nature and extent of contamination

Phase 3

- Risk assessment
- Assessment of remedial options
- Feasibility studies

Phase 4

- Remediation
- Final design
- Monitoring

---

and to decide appropriate levels of control is the primary consideration in the development of the investigation strategy. In developing the remediation strategy, the aim is to explicitly remove or control risks in a transparent and justifiable way.' (Smith & Harris, 1994)

In this respect, the RICS have issued guidance on the objectives of risk assessment (RICS, 2000). This advice promoted the following of a system or 'framework' which unsurprisingly commences with data collection. Having identified and evaluated potential hazards and receptors likely to be on site, the next phases of assessment involve estimating the extent and likely costs of intrusive site investigation and necessary remediation, including accounting for unforeseen expenditure. The advice reminds us that all risk assessment activities need to be undertaken within the context of the intended use of the site.

A summary of the suggested risk assessment framework is as follows:

(1) Data collection
    —analysis of information gleaned from desk-top study and site visit
    —identification of potential pollutants
(2) Exposure and toxicity risks
    —identification and assessment of all aspects of 'pollutant linkages' (see below)
    —use of toxicity data appropriate to circumstances
(3) Assess risk
    —determination of potential harm to receptors
    —communication of advice appropriate to circumstances

Remediation

A number of risk assessment methodologies have been developed for use by designers of works upon contaminated land, including its remediation. In 1992,

CIRIA published advice (CIRIA, 1992) which suggested means of reducing the incompatibility of intended uses upon a site to 'acceptable dimensions'. Between 1995 and 1998, CIRIA published far more 'best practice' guidance (CIRIA, 1995–8) on the matter of remediating contamination and it continues to provide the industry with demonstration projects and reviews of 'state of the art' clean-up techniques (Evans *et al.*, 2001).

Dealing with contaminants in soil can be done in a number of ways, depending upon factors such as the type of pollutants, the use of the site, the sensitivity of the surrounding environment and the finance available. Methods of decontamination are discussed further below, but before we consider technical approaches to dealing with contaminated land, we must first consider what the legal definition of and requirements for remediation are.

Remediation is often taken to mean 'clean-up techniques' or 'treatment of the soil'. However, the statutory definition of remediation is:

'(a)   the doing of anything for the purpose of assessing the condition of:
    (i)   the contaminated land in question;
    (ii)   any controlled waters affected by that land; or
    (iii)   any land adjoining or adjacent to that land;
(b)   the doing of any works, the carrying out of any operations or the taking of any steps in relation to any such land or waters for the purpose:
    (i)   of preventing or minimising, or remedying or mitigating the effects of, any significant harm, or any pollution of controlled waters, by reason of which the contaminated land is such land; or
    (ii)   of restoring the land or waters to their former state; or
(c)   the making of subsequent inspections from time to time for the purpose of keeping under review the condition of the land or waters.' (EPA 1990, s. 78A(7))

This definition thus encompasses the range of activities from assessment of contamination through remedial works and on to monitoring works. At first glance, it might appear that remediation could mean simply doing something by way of 'assessing the condition of the contaminated land in question' alone. This would be an erroneous interpretation of the law, however, as enforcing authorities have a duty when serving remediation notices to specify particular remediation actions, which must be appropriate to the 'suitable for use' standard (DETR, 2000a, C10) of cleaning up a site. Thus, the inclusive statutory definition of remediation enables enforcing authorities to require any number of its elements to be provided by the appropriate person. Furthermore, requirements for remediation must ensure that the 'pollutant linkage' is broken.

Pollutant linkages

In essence, an enforcing authority will require of an appropriate person that contaminated land becomes no longer 'contaminated' in its current use and that any effects of the contamination are corrected. In this respect, we must return to the basis of the definition of 'contaminated land' in risk assessment (see above), which dictates that contaminated land is caused by the presence of a 'significant pollutant linkage', that is, something which causes contaminants to be linked via a pathway to a receptor. The law tells us that the breaking of such a linkage means that no contamination continues to exist. So, remediation might mean eliminating the source (i.e. the hazard or contaminant), obstructing the pathway and/or removing the receptor (i.e. the target). Figure 2.2 shows the possible hazards, pathways and receptors.

Treatments

Given the necessity to break the pollutant linkage that is causing land to be unsuitable for the use to which it is being put (i.e. making it 'contaminated'),

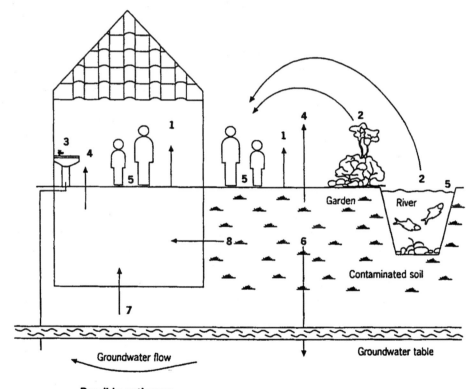

Possible pathways

Ingestion: of contaminated soil/dust (**1**)
                    of contaminated food (**2**)
                    of contaminated water (**3**)

Inhalation: of contaminated soil particles/dust/vapours (**4**)

Direct contact: with contaminated soil/dust or water (**5**)

Migration: to ground water (**6**)
                    into buildings (**8**)

Gaseous emission: into building structures (**7**)

Figure 2.2 Examples of hazards, pathways and receptors (Harris & Herbert, 1994). Reproduced with kind permission of the publisher.

common sense might suggest that there are several ways of achieving this. Nathanail (1999) sets out the broad approaches to remediation, which enable the pollutant linkage to be broken and the site to be determined as being suitable for its current (or intended) use. These approaches are:

- *Administrative*: this can include changing the use of the site (e.g. to a car park rather than residential), restricting the access to the site by human receptors and changing the layout of a proposed development (e.g. so that the pathway is blocked by a hard standing).
- *Civil engineering*: this might involve capping the site with an impermeable membrane, excavation of contaminated soil from the site or hydraulic movement of the contamination off the site.
- *Physical*: for example washing contaminants from the soil (on or off site), heating the soil to deactivate the contaminants, solidifying the contaminated soil such that it cannot move along the pathway and/or allowing the pollutants to attenuate naturally.
- *Chemical*: neutralisation of pollutants can be caused by addition of other chemicals (on or off site), for example to balance the pH of the soil.
- *Biological*: bioremediation of soil involves the neutralisation of the contaminant(s) by biological control rather than chemically or physically. Bacteria and other microbes can be added to the soil, for example, which will remove the contaminant from it.

Which technique is best?

Sustainability criteria dictate that a lasting, non-polluting solution is needed. The removal of the problem and placement of it elsewhere, for example in a landfill site, is hardly sustainable, nor is any technique which causes any off-site problems. Furthermore, it is increasingly likely that as energy costs increase, transportation costs will continue to rise along with the cost of disposing of waste to increasingly taxed and scarce landfill sites. Developers and their advisers should therefore consider the advantages that a more sustainable approach to remediation offers. Innovative, on-site treatment of contamination should present a more sustainable solution to remediation options, particularly as the results of research into this area become more widely available. A CIRIA report (Evans *et al.*, 2001) has attempted to demonstrate the costs and benefits associated with a number of different remediation process options, as summarised in Box 2.5.

The statutory guidance (DETR, 2000a) suggests that a balance needs to be drawn up between effectiveness of any treatment and the initial, on-going and disruption costs. Site owners and their advisers should also bear in mind value as well as cost. A discounted site value, following Mundy's (1992) model above, might be best countered with an expensive remediation programme, the cost of which may be seen as small in comparison to the enhancement in value that it offers the site. As with so many matters, the correct choice of method will depend upon the circumstances as they present themselves on a particular site and at a particular time, but there are a number of common criteria that should be considered in each case (Box 2.6).

Box 2.5 On-site remediation processes (adapted from Evans *et al.*, 2001)

Ex situ remediation

- *Bioremediation*: treatment of organic contaminants by degradation promoted by out-of-the-ground aeration or other treatment.
- *Soil washing*: separation of contaminants from uncontaminated soil by mechanical or aqueous means.

In situ remediation

- *Bioremediation*: treatment of organic contaminants by degradation by micro organisms in the soil.
- *Natural attenuation*: techniques include the degradation, dilution and stabilisation of contaminants such that their toxicity and/or mobility is within safe limits.
- *Vapour and liquid extraction*: venting of the soil to promote biodegradation.
- *Air sparging*: injection of compressed air or steam below the water table to promote biodegradation.
- *Bioventing*: treatment of biodegradable contaminants by aeration processes.
- *Fixation*: reduction of the mobility of contaminants by cement binding.

Box 2.6 Factors affecting the selection of remediation or treatment methods (adapted from Syms, 2002, pp. 119–20)

Legal

- Legislative and common law requirements for remediation standards (including town planning and waste disposal requirements)
- Contractual obligations (e.g. to land owners, neighbours and contractors)
- Criminal and/or civil liabilities

Political

- Current and future governmental policies
- Public and 'corporate' perceptions (e.g. timeliness and speed of remediation)

Commercial

- Valuation issues (e.g. land value to remediation cost ratio, especially risks associated with relatively untried remediation methods)
- Contractual guarantees
- Remediation timetable and cash flow requirements

Geographic

- Proximity to other, off-site contamination and neighbours
- Access to site for remediation plant

Environmental

- Proximity to sensitive environments and habitats (e.g. water extraction points)
- Hydrogeology of the site (e.g. presence of aquifers)

Engineering

- Groundwater levels
- Volume of contaminated soil (i.e. the cost-effectiveness of treatment)
- Availability of plant and machinery

Health and safety

- Toxicity of materials (e.g. necessity for special protective equipment)

> * Presence of obstacles in the ground and overhead
>
> **Managerial**
>
> * Project management (e.g. availability of sufficient expertise)
> * Quality control
> * Regulatory regimes
>
> **Technical**
>
> * Limitations of and confidence in remediation methods
> * Auditing requirements (e.g. monitoring and reporting needs)

POSSIBLE FUTURE DEVELOPMENTS

It is interesting to note that the UK's 'Suitable for Use' approach for dealing with contaminated land, which was condemned by many environmentalists when originally established as being too weak, is now being mimicked in other jurisdictions (such as the Netherlands which formerly had far more stringent clean-up requirements). Indeed, the European Commission's White Paper on Environmental Liability (CEC, 2000) states that contaminated soil clean up will be required to a standard with actual and plausible future uses of the site in mind. The White Paper also states that thresholds of pollution are to be determined, however, with regard to the protection of people and the environment. Quite how the Commission proposes to marry the concept of thresholds and 'suitable for use' remains to be seen, but it is unlikely that the systems that operate in the UK will change as a result of any future Directive coming after the Environmental Liability White Paper.

It is unlikely, in the foreseeable future at least, that regulation of liability for and remediation of contaminated land will become stricter. Specifically, the Environmental Liability White Paper states that, for example, any change to the regime will not include new provisions for retrospective liability nor lender liability. Notwithstanding this general point, however, current trends in domestic policy and that of the European Union indicate that in the future, remediation of historic pollution might have to comply with 'sustainable criteria'.

As can be seen in Chapter 1 on location of property developments and urban regeneration, recent Government policy concerning town planning and property development identifies contaminated land as one of the principal obstacles to efficient or successful regeneration. The Urban Task Force (UTF) suggests that the greatest risks associated with contamination, as far as seeing urban regeneration occur, include the fact that future uncertainties remain, either because of people's perceptions or because of physical and technical problems occurring after remediation. In order to reduce fears of this and, therefore, risks associated with it, the UTF suggests a 'blue flag' system of marking sites considered to be safe from contamination (UTF, 1999). Clearly it is the view of the UTF, therefore, that the current regulatory system for the identification and registration of contaminated land is insufficient to overcome the problem that contaminated land presents to what it perceives is sustainable property development, i.e. urban regeneration and use of brownfield sites.

If the regulatory regime is not yet adequate to oversee a sustainable way of dealing with contaminated land, we can only hope that it will become so as soon as possible. In order to effect this, it is doubtless that considerable investment will have to be made in our public services which undertake the identification and registration of contaminated land. Notwithstanding this, however, the private sector must also recognise that it has a very significant role to play in achieving a sustainable response to the problem of contaminated land. Many of the causes of the problems associated with seeing contaminated land brought back into beneficial reuse relate to the restrictions placed upon developers and others by the fear of becoming liable for the often prohibitive costs associated with remediating contamination. Given that some professional advisers have been found to be lacking in terms of their advice about contaminated land, it is suggested that comprehensive environmental due diligence investigations should be undertaken. In the case of a purchaser of real estate, an environmental due diligence investigation would possibly include the following processes as a minimum:

- A chain-of-title search.
- A property condition report (to assess repair and replacement costs of build-ings).
- A desk-top environmental assessment.
- Evaluating and monitoring any necessary new construction works.
- Phase II environmental audits (intrusive investigations).
- Approving and monitoring any necessary remediation works.
- Monitoring the site for any possible residual contamination.

The results of such an investigation, if properly executed, should indicate to a potential purchaser the extent to which the vendor has complied with their responsibility to ensure that all environmental liabilities have been met and that none will be transferred with the property.

Prima facie, it might seem that the above list of activities which ought to be included in an environmental due diligence investigation is little different from the activities that would ordinarily be undertaken by a purchaser's various professional advisers. The main benefit, perhaps, of a single environmental due diligence investigation over having a number of professionals undertaking these different tasks lies in the potential for minimising the number of indi-viduals involved in the process; a simplistic approach can be more easily adopted and monitored. Furthermore, it is suggested that this approach is more likely to enable a focus on sustainable solutions to problems that may be encountered.

LEARNING MATERIALS

Some questions and issues for discussion

(1) **What is the difference between 'contaminated land' and land which is polluted but not necessarily 'contaminated'?**

- Contaminated land is that which falls within the definition provided by the EPA 1990, s. 78A(2).
- Land which is polluted but does not fall within this relatively narrow definition may cause a statutory nuisance (EPA 1990, Part III). Local authorities' planning departments might require clean up of such land during the development process.

(2) **Why does pollution of soil represent a problem to people other than the land's owner and/or the actual polluter?**

- Harm to animal and human health, damage to ecosystems, damage to buildings and crops.
- Represents a continuing state of environmental degradation.

(3) **Why did the definition of 'contaminated land' change under provisions of Part IIA of the EPA 1990? Who objected to the previous definition and why?**

- Change from focus on previous land use to current condition of the land.
- Allowed 'suitable for use' criteria to be followed.
- Introduced a risk-based model of prioritising environmental protection.
- Objectors included the property industry (led by the RICS) due largely to the issue of potential 'blight' of land not contaminated.

(4) **How might a potential site purchaser discover if a site is contaminated without entering it?**

- Site investigations, a component of remediation, begin with desktop surveys of historical records. These should indicate the likelihood of land being polluted or contaminated.
- Examination of the local public register of remediation notices should provide site-specific information. It is intended that these will be comprehensive once authorities have completed the inspections of their areas.

(5) **Who might be involved in a site investigation on behalf of a site owner and what would their key responsibilities be?**

- An owner's property adviser, such as a chartered surveyor, might act as a co-ordinator of a team of advisers and the person who will report the findings of an investigation back to the client. A surveyor might undertake a desktop survey and rely upon the services of engineers, soil scientists or environmental consultants.

(6) **How can professional advisers attempt to reduce the possible implications of 'stigma' devaluing a potentially or actually contaminated site?**

- 'Stigma' derives, in part, from uncertainty. The provision of complete and accurate information about remediation (including monitoring) should help to diminish this uncertainty.
- Active marketing of the site, using reassuring information provided about the extent of any remediation would be necessary.
- Focusing upon stakeholders (e.g. neighbours, the press, potential purchasers, lenders and regulators) in the marketing process would be advisable.

Examples of media coverage of the issue of contaminated land

(1) **In a press release on the same date as the coming into force of the statutory guidance on contaminated land, the environmental campaigning group Friends of the Earth indicted the new regime for contaminated land for providing inadequate standards for cleaning up contamination.**

- Consider facts and opinions which support and counter Friends of the Earth's argument.
- How sustainable is the Government's policy of 'suitable for use' pertaining to contaminated land?

PRESS RELEASE

The new regime is based on the principle of 'suitable for use'. This implies different clean-up standards depending on the use of the land (e.g. buildings or playing fields). This ignores real-life risks from contact with contaminated soils, and could lead to remediation to low value uses rather than high value (e.g. car-parks rather than playing fields) and also leaves future generations with the problems of contaminated land. (FoE, 2000)

---

(2) **We have considered above that in attempting to develop a site, or to make it attractive to potential developer purchasers, site owners will have to balance matters of legal requirements, cost, environmental good practice and publicity.**

One site more than any other in the UK became infamous at the end of the twentieth century for the state of its soil. The former British Gas site at Greenwich in London was selected as the home of the Millennium Dome. Prior to its decommissioning after the year 2000 celebrations were due to finish, the site's owner (the Government) attempted to attract bidders for the site. The following *Financial Times* article (Cohen, 2000) highlights some of the problems it encountered when it was entertaining a bid for the future use of the site as a business park.

- What are the factors that would have been considered in determining the selection of clean-up techniques employed?
- If the decontamination efforts of British Gas complied with extant government guidance and best practices, why were bidders worried about future litigation? Why did experts believe that the clean up was not suitable for the preferred bidder's intended use of the site?
- Which other forms of clean up could have been undertaken to offer a more sustainable solution to the contamination problem?

CONTAMINATION THREAT TO DOME SITE

With Legacy now the government's preferred bidder for the Millennium Dome, the negotiations can begin in earnest. But while the opposition voices attack ministers' decision to overlook the advice of their own independent advisers, the site faces far greater difficulties.

Among the thorniest issues are those related to environmental considerations: those familiar with the area claim the site was once heavily contaminated. Indeed, other bidders for the site have said that environmental concerns and the possibility of litigation stemming from such issues proved one of the biggest stumbling blocks in trying to agree a price.

The ground beneath the Dome contains 'potentially harmful contaminants, the volatile hydrocarbon benzene, and the gases methane and carbon dioxide', according to an engineering report by Halcro, prepared to assist prospective bidders in June 1998. The report, made available on a confidential basis to bidders, describes in detail the efforts made by the site's former owners, British Gas, to clean up the land. It concludes that the decontamination efforts to date comply with government guidance and best practices.

The 24 acres directly underneath the Dome have been carefully decontaminated and isolated, bidders say. But it is the perimeter areas – which any prospective bidder would want to develop to make the site commercially viable – that are problematic. According to one Legacy adviser, the 15 acres to the south of the Dome are 'poison'. Simon Fullalove, editor of *Civil Engineering*, the professional journal of the Institution for Civil Engineers, says that is a harsh assessment. 'The big problem with the Dome was that it was over a huge tar pit,' he says. 'The rest of the area has a huge, thick clay cap – a geo-technically engineered process used to cap the contaminants.'

The decontamination involved the excavation of about 1.25 m cubic metres of material, of which 850 000 cubic metres was deemed suitable, after processing, for landfill across the site. Nevertheless, says Mr Fullalove, construction of large buildings, such as offices, is likely to penetrate the clay cap. Although what lies underneath has been cleaned, it would require further decontamination.

This is the bidders' concern. According to the report from Halcro, any developer will be required to take specific remediation, including 'such measures as the removal or isolation of residual contamination, specific to the actual after-use'. There is a layer of soil beneath the Dome. Under that is a 6 metre-thick concrete 'raft', and beneath that, a 20 mm layer of an impermeable plastic known as 'Sevidrain', says the report.

There is a gas membrane to divert dangerous gases, and the structure is supported by a series of concrete piles, each 350 mm in diameter and spaced at intervals of roughly 12 metres. Beyond this, the level of decontamination is less elaborate.

The issue for bidders is not just how to pay for the cost of decontamination. It is also whether there are any future liabilities that could arise from contamination. Privately, bidders have said that government ministers were offering guarantees to pick up the bill for any liabilities for a 15-year period following the sale. This, however, falls far short of the sort of guarantees that a financier is likely to want to see before providing construction finance. 'No

Continued

> banker will lend without an environmental liability guarantee of at least 50 years,' said one bidder. The bidder notes that one insurer offered to extend the guarantee to 25 years, provided he received a £1.2 m premium.
> 'To extend to 50 years would take millions more,' the bidder said.
>
> From Cohen (2000). Reproduced with kind permission of the publisher.

(3) **Despite the problems faced by the owners and developers of London's Millennium Dome site due to capping of contamination on site, the possible implications of advising a client to adopt an innovative bioremediation technique, rather than capping, are also not without potential problems. Consider the extract below from an article in *The Daily Telegraph* (Elsworth, 2000):**

- The use of an innovative technique might add to the levels of uncertainty surrounding a decontamination project. Consider what the uncertainties and risks might be.
- Why would such remediation schemes be considered to be more sustainable than, say, contamination capping?

> ### Biobugs give brownfield site a greener future
>
> Bugs that eat toxic chemicals are being used to clean a polluted industrial site in a pioneering project to turn a brownfield site green.
>
> In just 12 months, bacteria in the soil at a former tar works on Merseyside have eaten up most of the oil and heavy metals that have contaminated the land for more than 100 years. The derelict ground in Bootle, Liverpool, is now likely to become the site of a superstore, as part of the Litherland Initiative, a project to regenerate the area.
>
> Toxic land is usually excavated and the polluted soil carted away and buried in landfill sites at great expense. The new method, termed 'soft technology' or bioremediation, relies on tiny bugs that live in the soil. Given the right nutrients, air and light, the bacteria thrive on the dangerous compounds, breaking them down into harmless elements.
>
> From Elsworth (2000). Reproduced with kind permission of the publisher.

NOTES

1 'Pollution' need not involve harm being caused to water, but can, after *R. v. Dovermoss Ltd* [1995] Env. L. R. 258, mean simply 'to make physically impure, foul or dirty'.
2 See, for example, DoE (1994a); DoE (1994b); DoE (1997).
3 This guidance was first published in 1997 and updated in 2000.

REFERENCES

Carson, R. (1962) *Silent Spring*, Houghton Mifflin, Boston, MA.

CEC (Commission of the European Communities) (2000) *White Paper on Environmental Liability: COM(2000) 66 final*, Brussels, CEC.

CIRIA (Construction Industry Research and Information Association) (1992) 'Research project specification methane and associated hazards to construction – phase III stage 8, the assessment of degrees of risk', *CIRIA Project 475*, November, CIRIA, Oxford.

CIRIA (Construction Industry Research and Information Association) (1995) *Remedial Treatment for Contaminated Land, Vol. III (Special Publication 103)*, CIRIA, London.

CIRIA (Construction Industry Research and Information Association) (1995–8) *Remedial Treatment for Contaminated Land, Vols I–XII (Special Publications 101–12)*, CIRIA, London.

Cohen, N. (2000) 'Legacy must study the foundation for its plans', *Financial Times*, Financial Times Group, London, 23 November.

CBI (Confederation of British Industry) (1993) *Firm foundations: CBI proposals for environmental liability and contaminated land*, CBI, London.

DoE (Department of the Environment) (1991) *Public Registers of Land Which May Be Contaminated*, May, HMSO, London.

DoE (Department of the Environment) (1992) *Environmental Protection Act: Section 143 Registers*, July, HMSO, London.

DoE (Department of the Environment) (1994a) *Contaminated Land Research Report 2, Guidance on Preliminary Site Inspection of Contaminated Land*, DoE, London.

DoE (Department of the Environment) (1994b) *Contaminated Land Research Report 3, 'Documentary research on industrial sites'*, DoE, London.

DoE (Department of the Environment) (1995) *Contaminated Land Research Report 6, 'Prioritisation and Categorisation Procedure for Sites Which May Be Contaminated'*, DoE, London.

DoE (Department of the Environment) (1997) *Contaminated Land Research Report 12, A Quality Approach for Contaminated Land Consultancy*, DoE, London.

DETR (2000a) *Circular 02/2000: Contaminated Land*, DETR, London.

DETR (2000b) *Waste Strategy for England and Wales, Part 2*, DETR, London.

Elsworth, C. (2000) 'Biobugs give brownfield site a greener future', *The Daily Telegraph*, London, 26th March.

Evans, D., Jefferis, S., Thomas, A. & Cui, S. (2001) '*Remedial processes for contaminated land: principles and practice*', *CIRIA Report C549*, CIRIA, London.

FoE (Friends of the Earth) (2000) *Contaminated Land Threat. Minister told: set up independent clean-up body*, Press Release, FoE, London, 1st April.

Gronow, S. (1998) 'Contaminated land – the inevitability of an explicit appraisal model', *Property Management* **16**(1), 24–32.

Harris, S. & Herbert, M. (1994) *Contaminated Land: Investigation, Assessment and Remediation*, Thomas Telford, London.

ICRCL (Inter-departmental Committee on the Redevelopment of Contaminated Land) (1987) '*Guidance on the assessment and redevelopment of contaminated land, 59/ 83*', 2nd edition, July, HMSO, London.

Keeping, M. (2001a) 'The negligent valuation of contaminated land?', *Journal of Property Investment and Finance* **19**(4), 375–89.

Keeping, M. (2001b) 'The negligent conveyancing of polluted and contaminated land?', *Property Management* **19**(4), 249–64.

Leach, B. & Goodger, H. (1991) '*Building on derelict land*', CIRIA Report SP078, CIRIA, London.

Lizieri, C., Palmer, S., Charlton, M. & Finlay, L. (1996) *Valuation Methodology and Environmental Legislation: A Study of the UK Commercial Property Market*, RICS, London.

Ministry of Housing, Physical Planning and the Environment (1983) *Guidelines for Soil Sanitation*, State Printing Office, The Netherlands.

Mundy, W. (1992) 'The impact of hazardous material on property value', *The Appraisal Journal*, April, USA.

Nathanail, C. (1999) *Introduction to Contaminated Land Management*, Monitor Press, Sudbury.

NATO/CCMS (1985) *Contaminated Land: Reclamation and Treatment*, Vol. 8, Plenum Press, London.

Patchin, P. (1991) 'Valuation of contaminated property', *The Appraisal Journal*, January, USA.

RIBA (Royal Institute of British Architects) (1990) *Buildings and Health. The Rosehaugh Guide to the Design, Construction, Use and Management of Buildings*, edited by S. Curwell, C. March & R. Venables, RIBA, London.

Richards, T. (1995) *A Changing Landscape: The Valuation of Contaminated Land and Property*, College of Estate Management, Reading.

Richards, T. (1996) 'Valuing contaminated land and property: theory and practice', *Journal of Property Valuation and Investment*, **14**, (4–17).

RICS (1995) *The RICS Appraisal and Valuation Manual*, RICS, London.

RICS (2000) *Contamination and its Implications for Chartered Surveyors: A Guidance Note*, RICS, London.

Smith, M. & Harris, M. (1994) 'Available guidance on risk assessment and the use of guidelines and standards', paper presented to a *Clayton Environmental Consultancy* seminar, London, October (unpublished).

Syms, P. (1997a) 'Perceptions of risk in the valuation of contaminated land', *Journal of Property Valuation and Investment*, **14**, 38–47.

Syms, P. (1997b) *Contaminated Land: The Practice and Economics of Redevelopment*, Blackwell Science, Oxford.

Syms, P. (1999) 'Redeveloping brownfield land: the decision-making process', *Journal of Property Investment and Finance* **17**(5), 481–500.

Syms, P. (2002) *Land, Development and Design*, Blackwell Publishing, Oxford.

Timothy, S. (1992) *Contaminated Land: Market and Technology Issues, 'Industry and the Environment'*, Centre for Exploitation of Science and Technology, London.

UTF (Urban Task Force) (1999), *Towards an Urban Renaissance: Sharing the Vision*, DETR, London.

Welsh Development Agency (1993) *The WDA Manual on Remediation of Contaminated Land*, WDA, Cardiff.

Wilkinson, S. (1992) 'Maastricht and the environment: the implications for the EC's environmental policy of the Treaty on European Union', *Journal of Environmental Law* **4**(2), 221–39.

Wilson, A. (1994) 'The environmental opinion: basis for an impaired value opinion', *The Appraisal Journal*, LXII, 3.

FURTHER RESOURCES AND WEBSITES

CIRIA (2000) *Land Contamination: Management of Financial Risk (publication C545)*, CIRIA, London (very good look at the financial implications and considerations pertaining to this topic, e.g. insurance, investment and liabilities).

Tromans, S. & Turrall-Clarke, R. (2000) *Contaminated Land: The New Regime*, Sweet & Maxwell, London (contains full text of EPA 1990 Part IIA, the 2000 Regulations and Circular 02/2000 as well as excellent commentary on these).

www.defra.gov.uk   Follow the links to 'Land – soil and contamination' for advice and links concerning statutory guidance on issues relating to contamination of land under Part IIA of the Environmental Protection Act 1990.

www.environment-agency.gov.uk/subjects/landquality The site detailing Environment Agency information, such as statutory guidance and technical publications pertaining to contaminated land and waste management.

www.exsite.org   The website of an organisation committed to finding sustainable solutions to remediation and reuse of contaminated land.

www.ecoregen.com/   The website of an organisation committed to finding sustainable solutions to regenerating communities and polluted land.

Green property: the design of buildings that have lower environmental impact

---

Suggested learning outcomes

After studying this chapter and discussing its contents, you should be able to:

- Define what is meant by the term 'green building' and describe the key features of green property development projects.
- Analyse the principal historical, environmental and technological factors which have led to the evolution of a more environmentally responsible approach to the design and construction of buildings.
- Explain key technical principles and common practical solutions used in the design, construction and management of green property.
- Evaluate the ways in which building owners, occupiers and the community might benefit from green buildings.
- Discuss recent government policy and current attitudes within the property sector regarding sustainability and the built environment.

HEADLINES: BIG ISSUES AND IMPORTANT QUESTIONS

In the context of mainstream commercial and residential property in the UK, *sustainability* has, only relatively recently, become a significant factor in the design, construction and management of buildings. The principal driver in this process has been an evolving national and international political consensus that the use of the earth's resources, environmental pollution and climate change were matters which required urgent action, rather than mere expressions of concern.

As previously discussed, the UN conference of 1987, at which the Bruntland definition of sustainability was first put forward, the Earth Summit at Rio de Janeiro in 1992 and the Kyoto Protocol of 1997 resulted in the UK Government developing a set of environmental aims, objectives and targets, including a commitment to reduce CO_2 emissions resulting from energy use. The property sector in general and, more specifically, the design, construction and occupancy of buildings, have been identified as key areas in which more could be done to reduce energy consumption, provide healthier, safer working and living environments and minimise waste.

As a consequence, designers, engineers and other property professionals have sought to reduce the environmental impact of the built environment through a range of green building design and management features including:

- *Minimising energy consumption*: achieved by a range of techniques including the use of 'natural ventilation' (the utilisation of natural convection as a means of ventilating buildings) rather than air conditioning, more efficient heating and heat storage systems, control of solar heat-gain in order to reduce cooling requirements, and use of low-energy lighting.
- *Minimising site impact*: through sensitivity to site ecology, flora and fauna.
- *Minimising the use of resources*: for example, by the use of 'grey-water' recycling for landscape irrigation and low water consumption WCs.
- *Minimising the environmental impact of building materials*: through careful specification in both new building design and in maintenance and repair work on existing buildings.
- *Minimising the use of harmful chemicals*: in the construction process and in the management of the building, for example some timber preservation treatments, cleaning fluids, paints and solvents, landscaping, weed and pest control.
- *Minimising waste*: in the construction phase of the building through more careful ordering of materials thereby reducing the amount of new materials thrown away unused, by separating site waste materials for recycling and in the management of post-occupancy waste disposal.
- *Maximising the use of existing transport networks*: by careful location of proposed buildings close to existing public transport routes and by having greener transport policies within the occupier's organisation, for example car-sharing schemes for building users, facilities for staff using cycles.
- *Maximising the re-use of existing buildings*: by refurbishment, conversion and adaptation or extension wherever possible.
- *Maximising the quality of indoor environments*: healthier working and living environments, for example through greater use of natural daylight in offices, and by ensuring a high standard of air quality and individual environmental control.

In Feilden Clegg's design for the Building Research Establishment's Building 16 (Figure 3.1), green design features include five 3-m-high stainless steel 'chimneys' forming part of the natural ventilation system, external glass louvres reducing glare and solar gain, large areas of recycled facing brickwork and an area of photovoltaic panels generating sufficient power to light the building. Figure 3.2 shows a cross-section of Building 16, illustrating how air is drawn through the building for ventilation.

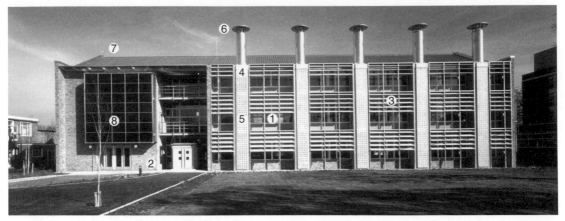

Figure 3.1   Building 16, Building Research Establishment (architects: Feilden Clegg; photograph and graphics: View Pictures Ltd/Gilbert & Callaghan).

1 Automatic opening windows linked to environmental control system; 2 recycled bricks; 3 external glass louvres; 4 ventilation stacks linked to natural ventilation system; 5 glass blocks reducing solar gain but allowing natural light in; 6 stainless steel chimneys; 7 high insulation value roof; 8 photovoltaic panels.

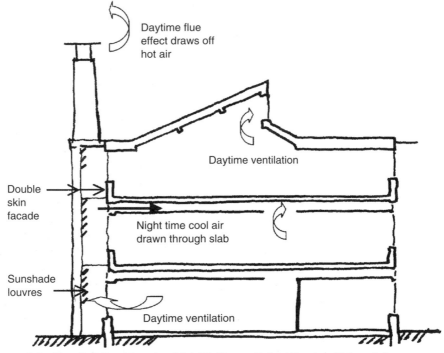

Figure 3.2   How Building 16 works (Nick Walliman, Oxford Brookes University).

Defining green buildings

It should be remembered that in the same way that the term *sustainable development* has many different definitions and interpretations, there is no single view of what constitutes a green building or a green development. However, most green buildings are characterised by an integrated approach to their design and management; they are projects which seek to reduce environmental impact through careful consideration of **all** aspects of the building's design and post-occupancy management, over the whole life-cycle of the building. So, we could say that a green building is one which seeks to minimise its environmental impact in an integrated and holistic way.

All green buildings should, therefore, seek to *minimise* environmental impact although the degree to which an individual building succeeds or fails in this objective can be difficult to measure.

Building owners and designers have been encouraged by the government to adopt a greener approach to their buildings whilst at the same time trying to help the property industry remain commercially competitive. They have sought to do this by using a 'carrot and stick' approach – voluntary schemes, green badging plus new legislation: thus far, the new legislation has been carefully designed to have minimal cost-impact.

The UK government, supported by the green lobby and many within the design, construction, research and academic communities, has sought to drive change through support of such initiatives as:

- *The Building Research Establishment Environmental Assessment Method (BREEAM)*: an environmental rating scheme which awards individual buildings green performance credits based on a range of building design and management criteria. Following an environmental appraisal carried out by a BREEAM accredited assessor, projects are rated on a four-point scale as Excellent, Very Good, Good or Pass (www.bre.co.uk/breeam).

  Originally devised as a marketing tool to demonstrate the green credentials of office buildings, this scheme has, perhaps, done more than any other initiative to raise the awareness of designers and building owners regarding property and its environmental impact.

- *Key Performance Indicators and Environmental Performance Indicators:* developed by the construction industry and government to give industry access to the main UK-based benchmarking organisations, including a search facility to retrieve performance graphs, charts and toolkits to measure and improve performance (www.sustainable-development.gov.uk and www.kpizo ne.com).

- The UK government has developed its own set of environmental objectives and targets for the 'greening' of the government estate, including such measures as the use of energy management systems, and more environmentally responsible supply chain policies (www.sustainable-development. gov.uk). In 2000, the Treasury set as an objective that all new government building projects should achieve an *Excellent* BREEAM rating and that refurbishments should be to a *Very Good* BREEAM standard (see Office of Government Commerce website www.ogc.gov.uk for information on Government Procurement).

- As discussed in Chapter 1, there was a shift in planning and development policy towards the development of 'brown land' (previously used) rather than 'green field' sites, in order to conserve and protect the natural environment and to ensure that towns and cities remain economically viable. The key changes were:

(1) Planning Policy Guidance Note 3 (PPG 3) – Housing: introduction of 'sequential test' for planning applications – brownfield/central urban before edge of town, before out of town, before greenfield (2000).
(2) PPG 6 – Retailing and Town Centres: determined that out-of-town shopping centres are not a good idea due to over-reliance on car transport and importance of existing town centres remaining *vital* and *viable* (1996).
(3) PPG 13 – Transport: developments to assist reduction in car use and increase in use of public transport (2000).

(www.planning.odpm.gov.uk)

- The 'One Million Sustainable Homes' initiative, sponsored by the World Wide Fund for Nature, is a campaign which has the backing of the UK Government and seeks to construct and refurbish 1 million low environmental impact homes by 2012. The question as to what exactly constitutes a 'sustainable home' is to be determined by using the BRE's Ecohomes standard (www.bre.co.uk/ecohomes); the use of this standard will, however, be reviewed during the evolution of the programme (www.wwf.org.uk).
- New legislation such as the Climate Change Levy also known as CCL – an energy tax on industry – designed to reduce energy consumption in both buildings and manufacturing processes (see www.hmce.gov.uk/business/othertaxes/ccl).
- Higher building insulation standards as in the recent amendments to Part L of the Building Regulations (www.safety.odpm.gov.uk/bregs/index.htm).

Some important questions that need to be addressed when considering green buildings

- *Are there degrees of 'greenness'?*
  When defining a green building, does one green feature, for example, the extensive use of recycled or low-impact materials in construction, mean that the entire project can be defined as green? Similarly, could a building in which all features but one are green, for example, a project where there is over-reliance on private car use, still be considered green?
- *Why should organisations or individuals wish to own or occupy a green building?*
  Are they cheaper to build, own or to rent? What financial benefits or incentives are there?
- *Are special skills needed to design and construct green buildings?*
  If green buildings differ from conventional buildings in terms of special techniques and materials, what level of new skills is needed to design and build them and how is this expertise being developed and taught?
- *What are the downsides to green buildings?*
  Is the learning curve too steep for many organisations to handle and are the risks, both financial and practical, too great? Does innovation inevitably

involve a degree of risk? Is greater input required of project managers and are there likely to be more individuals involved in the consultation process?

- *What is the level of government support for green projects?*
  Are there any grants, tax breaks and what are the likely penalties, now and in the future, for non-participation?

BACKGROUND

Review, evaluation and adaptation are necessary steps in developing faster, less wasteful, more economically viable human systems and technologies. Periodically though, an individual or a small, influential group goes further than simply questioning the efficiency of a specific process and will actually challenge the bottom-line objectives of the process itself. Such re-evaluations ask the question not only 'is there a better way of doing this' but also 'should we be doing this at all?'

In the context of the location and management of property development, prevailing attitudes regarding the nature of the built environment have been challenged in the past and this has, on occasions, lead to radical new ideas being put into practice. For example, driven by a vision of better living and working environments for all, the ideas of Ebenezer Howard and the Garden City movement caused a revolution in the way we thought about the design and planning of our towns and cities (see Howard, 1898). Plans for these landscaped, spacious environments provided a stark contrast to the polluted and overcrowded conditions in many nineteenth-century industrial cities and sought to address widely felt concerns about the social and environmental harm caused by over-industrialisation. The Garden Cities of Letchworth, Port Sunlight and others provided countrified housing, industry and cultural amenities in a single independent development and the influence of these designs can be seen in many of the post-1945 New Towns of Britain.

In 1947, the idea of a Green Belt policy, which formed part of the Town and Country Planning Act, was introduced to prevent what had been the unchecked sprawl of a number of major towns and cities. In this instance, property development became less a matter of building as much as possible at the greatest profit in the shortest time and more about containing the potentially harmful economic and environmental effects of such unrestricted development. A radical re-evaluation, led by the more far-sighted town planners and politicians, caused a major change in the way in which the built environment was planned and managed. In 1955, the details of the Green Belt policy were set out in Government Circular 42/55 (see www.cambridge.gov.uk and search for 'green belt' for more information and background).

Now, once again, driven by concerns about the use of resources, expanding human settlements and pollution, a radical reappraisal is taking place regarding man's relationship with the natural environment. Whether prompted by government-backed green initiatives, new environmental legislation or in response to their own sense of environmental responsibility, many architects, designers and property professionals have been re-evaluating the fundamental principles which determine the way we design, manage and locate buildings.

In the nineteenth century, the designers and scholars John Ruskin and William Morris challenged many Victorian attitudes toward economic growth through industrial progress by suggesting that much could still be learnt about the design of 'harmonious' buildings and towns from systems found in nature. Morris was one of the founders of the Arts and Crafts movement which sought to revive many traditional craft skills at a time when Victorian society was moving increasingly towards an industrialised, factory-based means of production (see Aho, 1987; Latham & Latham, 1991; www.speel.demon.co.uk/artists/morris.htm and www.morrissociety.org).

Pre-industrial revolution buildings can be seen to embody many of the principles of environmentally friendly design just as simpler, rural societies can, at their best, be seen as having a more harmonious relationship with the natural environment. The buildings were made of locally sourced, natural materials and relied on natural ventilation and very simple heating systems (Figure 3.3).

There can be no doubting the appeal of a simpler, less industrialised society with a closer relationship to the natural environment. Indeed, many of us choose to visit such places where they still exist and value their 'unspoilt' character. Internationally, however, some less-industrialised countries can suffer from over-dependence on tourism and locally produced, but vulnerable food sources. Local pollution and deforestation can also be common problems and weak national economies and low standards of rural living can mean that the major cities in some developing countries suffer the same uncontrolled cycle of over-development, pollution, overcrowding and health problems experienced in cities in nineteenth-century, industrial revolution England.

The attraction of simpler, low-tech, natural systems and materials, however, remains strong for many designers in more economically developed countries. This can be seen, at least in part, in a modern incarnation in such projects as straw bale housing, the use of basic recycled materials, and in the homes and settlements of more self-sufficient communities (Figure 3.4).

In the early part of the twentieth century, the American architect, Frank Lloyd Wright, urged designers not to forget the virtues of local, traditional materials and craft skills in their haste to use modern, industrialised products (Figure 3.5). It should be pointed out, however, that Wright did use modern, industrially produced materials in many of his buildings as well as employing traditional elements in often new and innovative ways. He was, first and foremost, an architect, albeit one with an interest in, and respect for, the natural environment; rather than an environmentalist with an interest in architecture (see Stower, 2002, www.franklloydwright.org and also www.GreatBuildings.com).

Another, alternative view of the relationship between the built and natural environments can be found in the work of Buckminster Fuller in the USA from the 1940s onwards and, in the UK, of Ron Heron, Peter Cook and the Archigram studio in the 1960s. These architects saw technology as something which would free mankind from want and would improve the environment;

Figure 3.3 Houses in Devon from the nineteenth and seventeenth centuries – local materials used in a simple, vernacular style (photograph: Oxford Brookes University Llibrary).

technology would enable us to both control the natural world and yet co-exist with nature in providing clean and healthy towns and cities (Figures 3.6–3.9).

The current generation of 'high-tech', green architects have developed an approach which has evolved from the work of Fuller and Archigram

Figure 3.4 Houses in Drop City, southern Colorado, USA. This is one of the original 1960s 'alternative lifestyle' communities which became a model for many of the subsequent eco-settlements. The houses were constructed from recycled materials, including car parts (photograph: Paul Oliver).

Figure 3.5 Taliesin West, by Frank Lloyd Wright, at Scottsdale, Arizona, 1937 onward. Exterior view of stonework and wood external roof beams (photograph: Oxford Brookes University Library).

Figure 3.6 The Wichita House (1946). An early example of a technological answer to the problems of poor housing which the architectural historian Charles Jenks describes as: 'A mass-produced house which can be flown in and placed anywhere because of its lightweight and pre-installed services … the result of intensive re-study of all the traditional requirements of living in a house' (photograph: Oxford Brookes University Library).

Figure 3.7 Photograph of the Union Tank Car Company factory dome, Louisiana, USA (1958). A lightweight geodesic dome envelope encloses a more conventional interior construction. Note the similarity to the Eden Project (see Figure 3.11) (photograph: Oxford Brookes University Library).

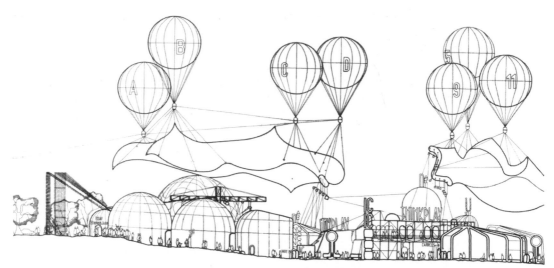

Figure 3.8 Instant City in a Field (1969, Peter Cook) (drawing: Architectural Association Library/ Archigram).

ELEVATION 1   COTE AVENUE PRINCESSE GRACE

Figure 3.9 Monte Carlo Entertainments Building (1969). Drawings produced by the Archigram design studio – a 'swinging sixties', pop-art influenced vision of the future where advanced building technology was seen as an opportunity, not a threat (drawing: Architectural Association Library).

known as 'Eco-tech'. The designs are typically lightweight, flexible buildings which sit *on* the landscape rather than *in* it. They claim to be without major environmental impact and suggest the capability of being removable at any time, leaving the natural world unharmed and unchanged (Figures 3.10, 3.11).

Prior to the early 1970s, the quantity of energy used in a building was not really considered to be of any great importance by the majority of either designers or building owners. Supplies of oil and coal were thought to be plentiful and were relatively inexpensive. Although a UN conference on the environment had taken place in 1972, resource depletion and the availability and cost of energy in buildings only really became an issue following the oil crisis of 1973. The UK Building Regulation requirements for the thermal performance of buildings pre- and post-oil crisis make interesting reading as they testify to a sea-change in attitudes towards energy use from virtual profligacy to conservation.

Thermal performance is usually measured in terms of 'U value' – this is the rate of heat loss through an element of building structure or a building material: the lower the U value, the lower the heat loss (Table 3.1). As we can see in Table 3.1, the issue of energy use and fuel conservation has resulted in insulation standards being continually reviewed and raised.

The Montreal Protocol of 1989 sought to eliminate the use of CFCs, used as a refrigerant in air-conditioning systems and in insulation products for buildings. It is suggested that the atoms of chlorine released from CFC molecules can help to destroy the ozone layer in the earth's stratosphere. It is the ozone layer which protects the planet from the more harmful part of the spectrum of solar radiation.

The phenomenon known as 'global warming' has been attributed to the production of greenhouse gases, which trap heat within the earth's atmosphere. Atmospheric gases allow the sun's radiation to heat the surface of the earth and then, under normal conditions, permit a percentage to escape again. One current theory is that this balance has been altered by the production of too much CO_2 through the burning of energy-producing fossil fuels – oil, gas and coal – and that the CO_2 is trapping heat within the atmosphere, which in turn leads to global warming.

The principal source of these greenhouse gases is the burning of fossil fuels for energy and the construction and occupancy of buildings is responsible for 60% of UK CO_2 emissions with a further 22% from energy used in travel between buildings (BRE, 1998).

In manufacture, the production of building materials alone accounts for over 10% of national UK energy use representing some 29% of national industrial energy use (CIRIA, 1994). The production of some materials results in VOC emissions (volatile organic compounds), which can be irritants or toxins. NO_x

Table 3.1 Change in 'U value' standards.

Building Regulations 'U value' minimum standard for external walls in dwellings (Watts/m^2/°C)	Year
1.7	1970
1.0	1976
0.45	1990
0.3	2002

Figure 3.10 Eagle Rock house, Sussex, UK, 1993. An eco-friendly, hi-tech design in the Sussex countryside (architect: Ian Ritchie; photograph: Architectural Association Library/Peter Cook). For other similar examples, see the work of the architect Jan Kaplicky and his Future Systems design studio.

Figure 3.11 Eden Project, Cornwall, UK, 2000. Eco-tech biospheres; lightweight domes in a disused quarry, now one of the most popular visitor destinations in the south-west of England (architect: Nicholas Grimshaw; photograph: Architectural Association Library/Gardner Halls).

(nitrous oxide), released in energy production and manufacturing combustion processes, is both a contributor to acid rain and reacts with VOCs in sunlight to produce photochemical smog which in turn is implicated in increased incidence of asthma and respiratory illness. SO_2, also released from the combustion of oil and coal products primarily, is the main contributor to acid rain (Anderson *et al.*, 2002).

As 50% of CO_2 is produced as a result of energy use in buildings – heating, lighting and cooling – the Kyoto Protocol of 1997 set targets for the reduction of energy use by an average of 5.2% for the period from 2008 to 2012. The UK Government made a manifesto pledge to cut CO_2 emissions to 20% less than 1990 levels by 2010 (www.sustainable-development.gov.uk).

The UK construction industry also accounts for around 30% of all controlled annual waste contributing significantly to an enormous national waste burden. At present, most of the industry's material is recycled as road sub-base or landfill engineering material. However, 30% of construction and demolition waste is disposed of in landfill sites or by incineration (BRE, 1998).

BREEAM: an environmental building design and management tool

As previously outlined, the introduction of the Building Research Establishment BREEAM programme (Building Research Establishment Environmental Assessment Method) in 1991 has proven to be one of the key property-related environmental initiatives of recent years in raising the awareness of, and providing guidance to, both building owners and designers. This voluntary scheme enables developers and building owners to submit designs for proposed projects or details of existing buildings for environmental assessment. Credits are awarded for good environmental design features; buildings are rated on a four-point scale: (excellent, very good, good and pass).

Commercial office buildings, for example, are assessed under a number of environmental issue categories (BRE, 1998):

- Management – policy and procedural issues
- Health and comfort
- Energy
- Transport – energy use and location issues
- Water – consumption and leakage issue
- Materials – environmental impact issues, for example use of energy, responsibly managed sources and recycling
- Land use
- Site ecology
- Pollution

The assessment process is carried out in three parts:

(1) *Core issues*: which assess the likely impact of the building when operative, for example energy consumption of heating, lighting and ventilation, site impact, etc.

(2) *Design and procurement*: for all new building and refurbishment projects, for example the specification of materials and how the project is constructed on site.

(3) *Management and operation*: for buildings which are already occupied. Assesses the building in terms of the way it is managed and offers the client guidance on environmental improvements which can produce financial, legal, health/wellbeing and image benefits (through reduced energy costs, reduced health and safety risks, improved indoor air quality and enhanced green credentials). Can include an action plan which can be carried forward by the client organisation.

Assessments are carried out by independent, BREEAM registered assessors. For more details see the BRE website (www.bre.co.uk/breeam). In the USA, the LEED system (Leadership in Energy and Environmental Design) offers a similar environmental rating system for buildings (see www.usgbc.org/Resources/leed_docs.asp).

Green buildings account for between 25% and 30% of all UK office space built since 1991 and an estimated 40% of all commercial schemes built during the period from 1996 to 1999. Based on the estimated number of BREEAM projects undertaken since 1991, there are now over 400 commercial buildings in the UK which could be considered to be 'green'.

One Million Sustainable Homes

Whilst the UK commercial property market has responded very positively to the idea of reducing property-related environmental impacts, the residential market has been less ready to embrace this new approach. Residential developers were unconvinced regarding the potential commercial advantages, particularly in terms of market demand. Larger residential development companies are, by nature, risk averse and are often wary of untried, new concepts.

It is possible, however, that as a result of a new, government-backed initiative, the residential developers will begin to match the commercial sector in the level of commitment to a greener approach to property development. In December 2001, with the involvement of a stakeholder group including the office of the Deputy Prime Minister, mainstream housebuilders, investors, the Housing Corporation and property researchers, the World Wide Fund for Nature launched a new programme 'One Million Sustainable Homes – Turning Words into Action' (see www.wwf.org.uk and www.odpm.gov.uk).

As previously stated, this programme aims to promote the construction and retrofitting of 1 million homes by 2012, which meet the Building Research Establishment's 'EcoHomes' standard. The programme is intended to address such issues as reducing energy use in homes through better insulation and more efficient heating systems, better transport links and access to improved local amenities (also see www.bre.co.uk/ecohomes).

As one of the parties involved in the project, Alan Knight, director of the property developer Kingfisher PLC, has stated, 'There is an urgent need to bring the concept of sustainability into the homes of all of the people in the UK that is both relevant and adds value to their lives. The One Million Sustainable Homes initiative provides a great vehicle for government and industry to do just this...Sustainable Homes will be good for government, good for business and good for customers' (World Wide Fund for Nature, 2001).

If successful, this programme could have a significant, widespread effect in terms of raising public awareness about sustainability in a way that has not really happened to date in the UK. Such programmes can, over time, lead not only to increased awareness and to more widespread interest but also, ultimately, to greater market demand – such demand can be the most powerful driver of all in the process of change.

PRACTICAL PROBLEMS AND SOLUTIONS, CURRENT APPROACHES, TECHNIQUES AND MODELS

Whole system solutions

Whatever definition of the term 'green building' is used, a key principle is that the design of a new green building is not simply a matter of 'bolting-on' a number of green features to an otherwise conventional design. In other words, buildings should be viewed as a series of inter-related systems, all which have the potential to adversely affect the environment and which therefore require inter-related, 'whole system' solutions.

For example, taking the decision to restrict car use within a residential development could impact across a wide range of inter-related building design issues. It may, as a consequence of fewer cars on site, be possible to reduce the widths and surface areas lost to car use allowing more trees and landscaping and even possibly additional properties. Minimising car use within residential developments can also reduce noise, result in less fuel consumption and consequent emissions, conserve land, increase the opportunities for social contact through pedestrian paths and make for a safer environment for children (RMI, 1998).

Whilst whole system solutions are preferable in new buildings, in the retrofit or refurbishment of existing buildings, even partial, small-scale green upgrades can be worthwhile, for example, by the replacement of older heating boilers by more efficient, low-emission modern equivalents or improved insulation within roofs and walls.

It can also be the case, however, that the more ambitious the retrofit, the greater the potential for both economic and environmental benefits. In the book *Green Development* (Rocky Mountain Institute, 1998) one project in the USA is cited in which an existing building of some 13 000 sq. m required the entire heating and ventilation system to be replaced.

Replacement of the system with new, high-efficiency equipment would have resulted in the building owners facing a 111-year payback period. However, by combining a new heating and ventilation system with a newly designed lighting system which incorporated low-energy, high efficiency fittings, the reduced heat gain and the simpler systems allowed significant reduction of the mechanical ventilation systems. By then adding an Energy Management System for the whole services package and by increasing rents to occupiers who would benefit from the energy cost reduction, the payback period was finally brought down to around two years. This project was successful because it addressed the 'whole system' rather than a single problem (RMI, 1998) (see also www.rmi.org).

The science of creating low-impact buildings is, however, still relatively new. As our understanding grows and lower-impact materials and technologies become more widely available, it will be possible to reduce further the impacts of buildings. At the present time, it could be argued that adopting a green approach is still primarily about raising awareness rather than achieving a really significant reduction in the environmental impact of property, due principally to vast numbers of existing, high-impact older buildings as yet unimproved.

For architects like Rab Bennetts, designer of the award-winning Wessex Water building, an honest attempt to reduce energy use, site impact, etc. of a project is almost enough, even if the final result is sometimes less than ideal:

> 'We're not saints and we're not religious about it – we're just normal architects trying to design good buildings. We don't have to be perfect but we all have to do something. You can probably reduce a building's CO_2 emissions by half if you design it thoughtfully. We renew our stock by 1% per annum, so for all new buildings, over 10 years, we only get a 5% improvement.' (Knutt, 2001)

Whilst Bennetts is proud of the 50% CO_2 emission reduction on some of his projects, he concedes that on others, where full air conditioning is required, there are only limited opportunities.

In this case, the architect is acknowledging that even with the best of intentions, compromise in the design of any building is almost always inevitable and the designer's or client's original vision is subject to a whole range of external interests and controls. This is not to devalue current efforts to reduce the environmental impact of property and many environmentalists would consider it extremely worthwhile to encourage building owners and building designers to, at the very least, 'move in the right direction'.

A green approach to the development of property can, on occasions, assist in negotiations with the Local Authority when applying for Planning Permission for a project. In an unusual case of bureaucratic constraints being compromised for 'the greater good', the BedZed project (Beddington Zero Emissions Development) in south London, built in 2001, achieved both higher than normal densities and reduced reliance on cars and space for car parking (Figure 3.12). This was due in part to the use of a green transport plan which aimed to reduce the need for cars by cutting the need for travel (e.g. through internet shopping links and on-site facilities) and by providing alternatives through a car pool. Other green features included:

- Building materials selected from natural, renewable or recycled sources and, wherever possible, brought from within a 35-mile radius of the site.

Figure 3.12 The BedZed project: a mixed-use development near London, in Beddington, Surrey, UK, 2002 (architects and photograph: Bill Dunster Associates/Arcblue).

- A combined heat and power unit able to produce all the development's heat and electricity from tree waste (which would otherwise go to landfill).
- Energy-efficient design with the houses facing south to make the most of the heat from the sun, excellent insulation and triple-glazed windows.
- A water strategy able to cut mains consumption by a third, including installing water saving appliances and making the most of rain and recycled water.
- Recycling bins in every home.

The BedZed project is a good example of how a green approach to design can not only minimise the environmental impact of property but also offer financial and social rewards, in the form of higher development densities, lower energy costs and enhanced quality of life for the occupiers. It is a 'whole-system' solution (see www.bedzed.org.uk and the BioRegional Development Group at www.info@bioregional.com).

There are also a number of one-off green homes which are, in effect, prototypes, designed to develop and test ideas for possible wider application. The Integer House at BRE in Hertfordshire (Figure 3.13) is one of the best known examples of this. It incorporated solar energy collecting photovoltaic panels for energy production, maintenance-free Western Red Cedar timber cladding and an earth roof for insulation and to act as an eco-friendly microenvironment.

The link between the introduction of the BREEAM green assessment programme in 1991 and the apparent dramatic rise in the numbers of green

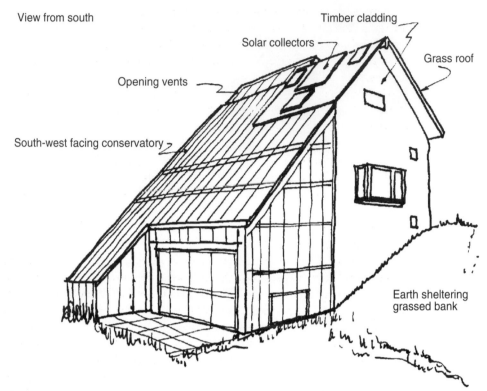

View from south

Timber cladding

Solar collectors

Grass roof

Opening vents

South-west facing conservatory

Earth sheltering
grassed bank

Figure 3.13   Diagram of The Integer House (Nick Walliman, Oxford Brookes University).

buildings (over 350 by 1998) is not coincidental. Building owners and designers could, for the first time, obtain clear guidance on how to design greener buildings and, having followed the guidelines, obtain an objective assessment of green performance.

Once a project has been assessed under BREEAM, its green rating can be used both for marketing purposes (publicising the green credentials of both building and building owner) and as a measure of performance. Building owners and Facilities Managers in particular like to be able to *measure* the performance of different characteristics of buildings: for example, value, capital costs, maintenance costs, energy consumption and downtime due to refurbishment or alterations. If something can be measured, it is then possible to record, audit and consequently improve its performance.

As previously discussed, the UK Government has a commitment to a range of environmental initiatives including reducing CO_2 emissions. The Government has determined that the property sector has a major role to play in achieving these objectives as part of the overall Sustainable Development Strategy (see www.defra.gov.uk).

When viewed in the wider context of the whole of UK industry, it is perhaps surprising that the design, construction and management of buildings has the potential to be responsible for very significant levels of environmental impact.

However, if, as now seems likely, there is a link between 'global warming' or the 'greenhouse effect' and increasing levels of gases such as carbon dioxide, chloro-fluorocarbons (CFCs) and nitrous oxide (NO_x), then the design and management of buildings is important in reducing the quantities of these climate-changing emissions.

Irrespective of the possible links between energy consumption and climate change, inefficient energy use is both wasteful of the earth's resources and expensive for the consumer. Greater use of renewable, less polluting sources of energy, more prudently expended are therefore in the interests of all organisations, on economic as well as environmental grounds.

There are implications too for the property investor as, according to one investment group 'the real cost of energy is set to increase above the rate of inflation. Energy inefficient buildings could see their costs of occupation rise and, in a competitive market, compensated for through lower (than otherwise) rents, rental growth may be hindered' (Prudential, 1998).

Property owners, managers and investors have also become more aware of the potential impact of the working environment on building occupants and of their increasing exposure to the risk of occupier health related litigation. Studies linking health, productivity, morale and absenteeism with the quality of the indoor environment provide compelling evidence that good environmental sense also makes good business sense and that organisations should constantly review investment in their most valuable asset, their staff.

In a study by the American Medical Association, it was shown that health problems resulting from poor indoor air quality cost 150 million workdays and about 15 billion US dollars in lost productivity every year (Rocky Mountain Institute, 1998). In the USA, there has been an increase in the number of lawsuits relating to Sick Building Syndrome (SBS) often involving all parties in the project including the manufacturers of the products used in the building. Recent cases include the award of some 26 million dollars to a client organisation for the costs of renovation of an eight-year-old public building suffering from SBS (ibid.).

As awareness of these issues has grown, a number of major public agencies and privately owned corporations have sought to benefit from the advantages and reduced exposure to risk offered by green property, by commissioning their own green buildings. In the USA these include AT&T, the US Post Office, Boeing Aircraft, Sony, United Parcel Services and Duracell. In the UK, British Airways, The Ministry of Defence, The DETR, Barclaycard, The University of East Anglia, Wessex Water, The Scottish Office, The British Council, The Inland Revenue and The Building Research Establishment and others have built and occupy green buildings. The UK Government has, as previously discussed, also introduced a policy which encourages all new central government buildings to achieve an *Excellent* rating using the BREEAM programme (see Office of Government Commerce website www.ogc.gov.uk for information on Government Procurement and www.sustainable-development.gov.uk).

It is also becoming apparent that these green buildings have different visual characteristics to their more conventional counterparts – they *look different*. It is possible that an entirely new aesthetic or architectural style is emerging as greener design methods and materials evolve.

The importance of taking the long-term view when designing green buildings cannot be over-emphasised. The location and site management of the building, the performance of the building fabric, its constituent materials, the internal environmental control systems and the future adaptability of the project should all be considered over the life-cycle of the building. The procurement and purchasing policy for the building's maintenance programmes, fixtures and fittings as well as the management of the operations or production processes within must also be considered at the initial design stage of the project.

Location and site issues

The 1998 edition of the BRE's Environmental Assessment Method for Offices (BREEAM) considers the priority issue to be the re-use of 'sites previously built on, or reclaimed from industrial processes particularly within existing urban areas'. The objective is the reduction of the rate at which land, previously not built upon, is being brought into urban use, not only for business accommodation and housing but also for leisure, shopping and transport. The rehabilitation of inner cities and town centres is also an important objective. In terms of development strategy, PPG3 (Housing), PPG6 (Town Centre and Retail Development) and PPG13 (Transport) set out current policy on the preferred locations of new development in terms of reduced car use and impacts on existing urban and rural infrastructures (see www.planning.odpm.gov.uk).

The importance of reducing energy use in transport has been discussed previously but it should be remembered that some 22% of UK national energy is used to transport people between buildings (BRE, 1998); a high proportion of which is commuter transport from home to work. The Government has made a commitment to reduce car use and to improve public transport; such commitments are likely to have major effects on the future location of new development as planners attempt to persuade developers to locate projects within existing conurbations or close to existing public transport networks.

When considering the impact of a proposed property development on the micro-environment of a site, the overall environmental objectives can perhaps be best summarised as being:

- The minimisation of ecological impacts.
- The protection and enhancement of ecological diversity.

These principles apply to both new and existing development sites. The techniques employed in the design and management of external works may include careful choice of landscape design features and plant species. This in turn may lead to such benefits as reduced cost or low-maintenance landscaping, the creation of wetland habitats from 'recycled' water, high-quality aesthetic impact value and enhancement of the image of the organisation as development sites are perceived as a community resource in the protection of local wildlife and flora.

The large areas involved in landscaping mean that the choice of materials for boundary protection or hard landscaping for car parking can be important in terms of environmental impact. Lowest impact materials for car parking tend to be either UK-produced Portland stone or precast concrete products; both using recycled aggregates as a sub-base. Of the other alternatives, granite and block are thicker and therefore have greater mass and consequently more environmental impact. Asphalt is possibly the least good option due to more intensive industrial processing and the fact it needs to be replaced more often (Anderson *et al.*, 2002).

Boundary protection (walls and fences) is best created using either natural materials such as hedging (the lowest environmental impact alternative even taking into account the energy used cutting and trimming) or lightweight options such as timber fencing or steel post and wire. The important environmental issues when assessing the impact of these materials relate to the mass of the minerals extracted and the waste generated at the end of the life of the materials (Anderson *et al.*, 2002).

It is important to be aware of the potential complexity of the ecological management of sites and of matters relating to land contamination. In both cases, it is prudent for client organisations to involve specialists, with a proven track record demonstrating appropriate expertise, at an early stage.

Energy systems

As stated previously, the principal concerns relating to energy use are the suggested link between the release of CO_2 and climate change and the breakdown of the ozone layer. Heat, light and power provision in buildings are major sources of energy consumption in the UK and hence any reductions in consumption can have significant environmental, as well as cost, benefits.

The oil crisis of 1973 reminded the industrialised countries that energy is a finite resource and, potentially, an extremely expensive one. Subsequent, incremental changes to the Building Regulations have meant that high levels of thermal insulation and energy efficiency in buildings are a legal requirement. As a response to Agenda 21, agreed at the Earth Summit in Rio in 1992, the Building Regulations underwent a further, radical upgrading of insulation and energy efficiency standards in Part L1: Conservation of Fuel and Power, in 1995 and a further raising of standards occurred in 2001. In the budget of March 1999, following Lord Marshall's report into possible ways of encouraging industry to be more sustainable, the Government announced a 'carbon tax' (the Climate Change Levy) which is intended to motivate businesses to further reduce energy consumption.

Other initiatives are voluntary, such as the DETR's Energy Efficiency Best Practice Programme, which since 1989 has promoted and advised business and industry on energy saving technology and good practice. The estimated energy cost savings derived from the programme have been estimated at some £370 million per year: equivalent to a reduction in CO_2 emissions of over four million tonnes per annum (DETR, 2000) (see www.energy-efficiency.gov.uk).

Advice for property owners on energy issues in the residential sector is available through the Building Research Establishment which has carried out extensive energy-modelling research and through NHER and SAP consultancies (page 116). BRECSU (The BRE's Energy Conservation Support Unit) provides advisory and consultancy services covering international energy issues, energy saving technology, statistics and energy management in residential and commercial property. For commercial property, additional guidance can be found in the DEFRA Energy Consumption Guide 19 and two guides specifically focused on energy efficiency in new and refurbished offices: GPG 34 and GPG 35 (see www.defra.gov.uk/and then follow environment/greening/land/offbuild).

In the design of a green building's energy systems:

- Every effort should be made to reduce heating, lighting and cooling loads to the lowest feasible levels whilst still maintaining correct comfort levels.
- All equipment should be of maximum efficiency in terms of energy consumption, running costs and maintenance requirements. Very often, specification, purchase and maintenance of reduced performance, cheaper heating and ventilation equipment can represent a false economy leading to inefficiency and additional technical and management costs.
- Full air-conditioning systems should be avoided wherever possible or, at the very least, kept to a minimum level. There will of course be some cases where air-conditioning systems are necessary such as industrial, 'high-tech' or other controlled environments.

In order to establish acceptable levels of energy use in green commercial buildings, a client's building services consultant can refer to energy consumption targets set out in the latest editions of the BREEAM programmes. The new Brighton Library (Figure 3.14) is an example of a more energy efficient building.

Energy-saving techniques, such as the use of heat recovery and heat exchange technologies, photovoltaic cells and so-called 'smart glass', are still at a relatively early stage of development. However, 'intelligent glazing' systems are now available which combine high light transmittance with low solar gain and the ability to reduce heat loss through the window. This is achieved by the use of sophisticated coating systems on the face of the glass panes and by the use of an argon gas-filled insulation gap within the double or even triple glazing panels to reduce heat loss.

Photovoltaic (PV) panels work by the conversion of light into direct electrical current through the reaction of silicon semi-conductor cells with solar energy. They can provide significant energy levels either for individual building use or, if used in great enough numbers, to an external network. Although still expensive, costs are being reduced as their use becomes more widespread and some government grants are available to offset the additional expense.

Other energy-saving design features which have been used in commercial buildings include:

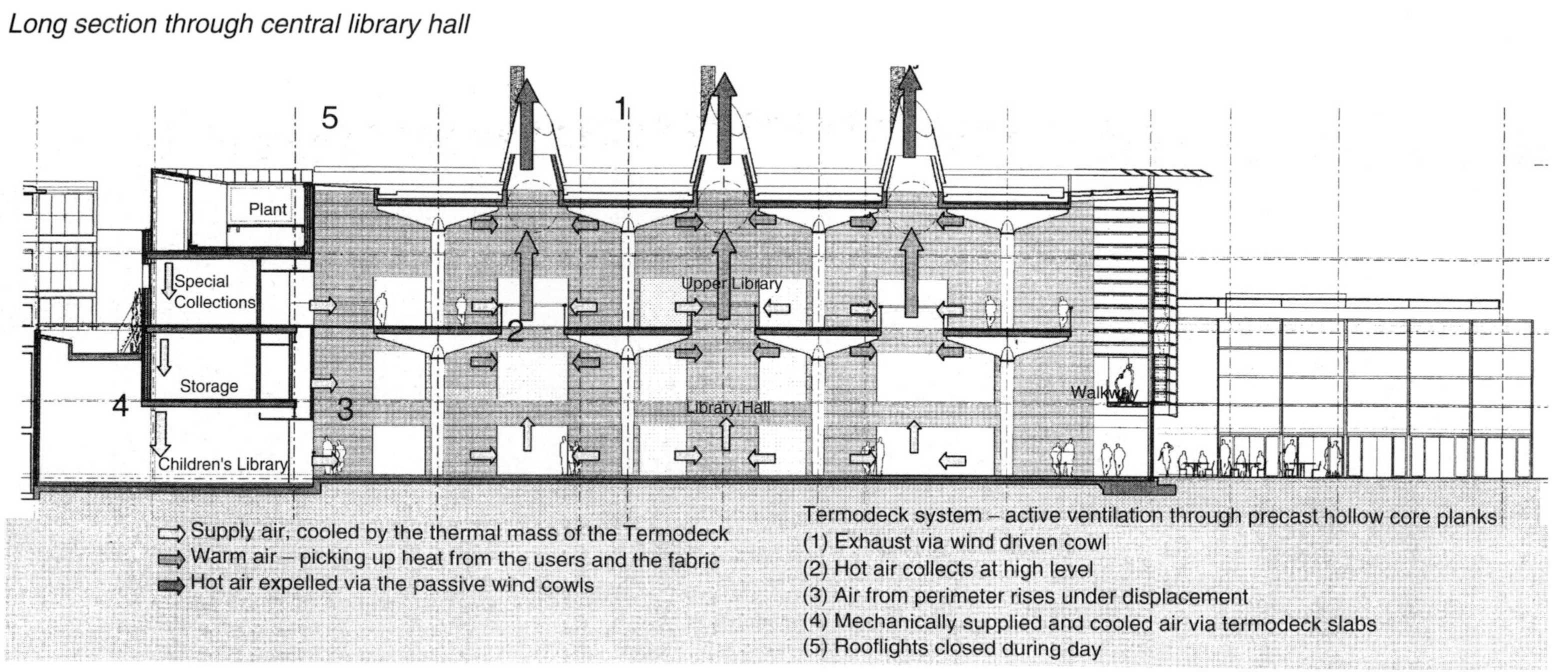

Long section through central library hall

Figure 3.14 Section through the new Brighton Library (architects: Bennetts Associates).

Termodeck system – active ventilation through precast hollow core planks:

(1) Exhaust via wind driven cowl
(2) Hot air collects at high level
(3) Air from perimeter rises under displacement
(4) Mechanically supplied and cooled air via termodeck slabs
(5) Rooflights closed during day

⇧ Supply air, cooled by the thermal mass of the Termodeck
⇧ Warm air – picking up heat from the users and the fabric
⬆ Hot air expelled via the passive wind cowls

Plant

Special Collections

Storage

Children's Library

Upper Library

Library Hall

Walkway

- The use of the building structure to store heat from internal heat gains (people, equipment and lights).
- Building heating provided by hot water radiators which use heat recovery systems linked to the lift motors and computer rooms.
- Air-to-air heat exchangers recovering heat from outgoing exhaust air.
- Simple, low-energy mechanical ventilation where required and natural ventilation via openable windows rather than large, complex air-handling systems.
- Daylight bounced from the top third of windows on to ceilings by the use of light shelves and thus into the centre of the floor plate.
- Window-lined atria combined with channelling of natural light providing a significant percentage of the building's lighting requirements.
- Artificial lighting by task light supplemented by low-level general lighting.

The Inland Revenue building in Nottingham and the Horniman Museum in London (Figures 3.15, 3.16) show some of these energy-saving features.

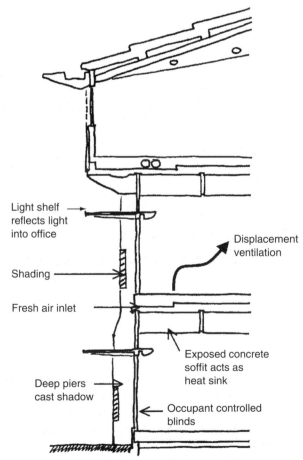

Figure 3.15 The Inland Revenue building, Nottingham (architects: Michael Hopkins and Partners).

In summer

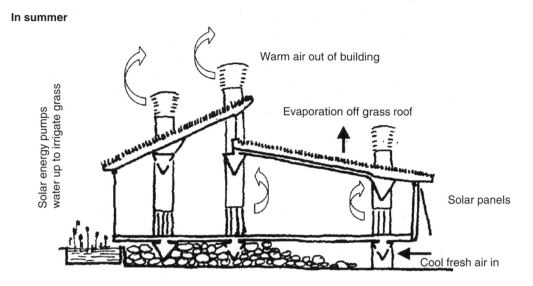

Warm air out of building

Evaporation off grass roof

Solar energy pumps water up to irrigate grass

Solar panels

Cool fresh air in

In winter

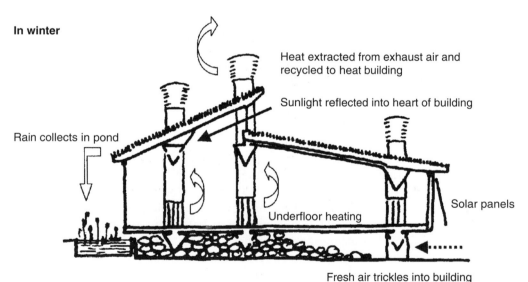

Heat extracted from exhaust air and recycled to heat building

Sunlight reflected into heart of building

Rain collects in pond

Solar panels

Underfloor heating

Fresh air trickles into building pre-warmed during passage

Figure 3.16 The Horniman Museum, London, showing typical green environmental control design features.

Energy savings can also be achieved in commercial buildings by the use of high-performance external walls. South-facing walls, often utilising a 'double skin' incorporating an air gap of up to 300 mm, can be used as solar collectors, where solar gain is controlled by blinds within the air gap and heat is collected and stored as it rises. Other walls can be designed to higher than minimum standards of insulation thus further reducing energy costs.

The utilisation of high-performance outside walls is significant: perceptions concerning the function of the external envelope appear to have changed from walls being regarded simply as *elevations*, designed for appearance and to satisfy Building Regulation minimum standards, to being seen as interactive, engineered component parts of an overall low-energy design strategy.

Each individual external wall is now more likely to be carefully designed to optimise thermal performance and to respond to specific microclimate and orientation considerations. Thus in many green buildings, south-facing and north-facing walls are no longer necessarily of the same design or even of the same materials.

Water use

The use of water in buildings is significant as the depletion and disruption of rivers and the associated ecosystems continues to generate concern. According to the Water Services Association, water consumption in the UK has risen by 70% in the last 30 years (WSA, 1997). Also, what was once regarded as a relatively cheap resource, provided by a non-profit-making state-run utility, has become an expensive and seemingly less plentiful commodity.

Savings in water bills can be made by innovations in leak detection, reduction in quantities being used in WC and urinal systems and in recycling water for a variety of purposes both inside and outside the building. According to BRE, in an average office, 43% of water is used in WC flushing, 20% for urinals, 27% for washing and 9% in staff restaurants (BRE, 1998). Specification of WC and urinal appliances and systems designed with water economy in mind, which are now available, can therefore make a significant impact on the quantity of water used in buildings.

Water consumption can also be reduced if drinking water is used only for personal hygiene, food and drink and rainwater used for all other purposes. By using carefully designed collection and filtration systems, rainwater from roofs can be held in cisterns and then used for irrigation, WCs and cleaning. Systems for wastewater management including the processing and reuse of water from sewage and grey water (e.g. water from baths and washbasins treated then reused for WC flushing and irrigation) are still under development. The key technical obstacles here concern health and economic viability.

In residential buildings, it has been estimated that a 40% reduction is possible in average family consumption by utilising such measures as dual-flush WCs, the fitting of flow limiters to taps, low-volume shower heads and more economical washing machines and dish washers. The increased costs in the appliances would have a payback period of between one and two years due to a typical family of four saving some 100 000 litres of water each year (Gauzin-Muller, 2002).

Construction materials

Awareness of the potential environmental impact of building materials and of the importance of making more environmentally responsible choices when selecting materials has grown steadily since the mid-1990s. Also, as more reliable methods of measuring the relative impacts of different materials have been developed, it has become possible for designers, developers and building managers to make more informed choices about the types of roofing materials, external claddings, floor structures and coverings, etc. chosen for a particular project.

As previously discussed, the production of building materials in the UK consumes approximately 30% of all industrial energy which is the equivalent of around 10% of total UK energy consumption. Given the Government's commitment to reducing CO_2 and other emissions arising from energy production and manufacturing processes, it is important for organisations to choose materials which require less energy generated by the burning of fossil fuels in manufacture.

For companies wishing to be seen as more socially and environmentally responsible, it is also important to select materials which have cleaner, less polluting manufacturing processes and require fewer resources and produce less waste. By specifying products which have a high percentage of recycled materials in them or can themselves be reused, as well as by more careful specification practices, it is possible to reduce the already enormous waste burden, currently around 25 million tonnes of construction and demolition waste per annum (BRE, 1998).

However, a recycled material may not necessarily be the best environmental option. In some cases, it may be better to choose a new, locally produced material rather than use a reclaimed material which may have been transported over long distances, using high-value polluting energy resources. Designers and property managers are probably best advised to consider each case on its own merits, weighing the potential benefits against the disadvantages for each material and location (Anderson *et al.*, 2002).

Prior to 1996, there was no reliable way of comparing the various environmental impacts of building materials and components. There had been a number of attempts to provide guidance for designers and building managers but these were mainly in the form of generalised notes, not based on quantitative data and therefore not actually measuring environmental impact. Other studies, usually of very small samples of materials, were complex, numerical analyses which were very difficult for designers and other property professionals to interpret and use.

The development of *The Green Guide to Specification – An Environmental Profiling System for Materials and Components* provided, for the first time, a reliable, easy-to-use rating system for materials. The system utilised quantitative measurements of amounts of energy used, emissions produced, wastes created, etc. for an extensive range of building products but then translated this complex information into a simple-to-use A, B, C system, where A equalled the best environmental option. The performance of each material or component was assessed against a range of environmental issues and then given an overall *summary rating* indicating general environmental impact (Table 3.2).

Green specifications

A *specification* is normally prepared by the design consultants and accompanies the project design drawings. It is a written description of the work to be carried

Table 3.2 An environmental rating system for materials and components (from Anderson *et al.*, *The Green Guide to Specification*, 2002). The *Green Guide* profiles some 250 commonly used materials and components, evaluating environmental impact. A=the best option.

	Summary rating	Climate change	Fossil fuel depletion	Ozone depletion	Human toxicity to air and water	Waste disposal	Water extraction	Acid deposition	Ecotoxicity	Eutrophication	Summer smog	Minerals extraction	Cost £/m²	Typical replacement interval	Recycled input	Recyclability	Recycled currently	Energy saved by recycling
Beam and blockwork floor with screed	A	A	A	A	A	A	A	A	A	A	A	A	47–73	60	A	C	C	A
Hollow precast reinforced slab and screed	A	A	A	A	A	A	A	A	A	A	A	A	47–73	60	C	A	C	A
Hollow precast reinforced slab with structural topping	B	B	B	A	B	B	B	B	A	B	A	B	50–80	60	C	A	C	A

out and contains information on the standards and types of materials to be used, site management requirements during the project, etc.

Many architects and designers maintain their own specification documents that contain standardised descriptions and clauses which can be adapted to suit individual projects. There are also industry standard specifications available, such as the National Building Specification (NBS), in which standardised clauses have been developed to reflect tried-and-tested specification practices. Specifications must provide clear and unambiguous descriptions of the work to be carried out and can therefore be very extensive, often running to many pages and can represent a great investment of time and expertise.

In writing green specifications, there are basically two approaches possible. The specification writer may wish to provide a special section on environmental considerations as an 'add-on' to the standard descriptions of the work to be carried out. Whilst such an addendum may be relatively easy to produce, it is also easier to miss; the importance of the environmental section may not be fully understood, it may become separated on site or not considered to be relevant to some sub-contractors.

As an alternative, it would seem preferable to weave green issues into the whole existing specification structure. In this way, it is made clear that environmental considerations are now part of the overall approach to design and construction rather than something peripheral, added-on to the main body of the specification. All aspects of the specification can then be subject to an appraisal of likely environmental impact and amended accordingly. Typically, a green specification would include clauses relating to:

- Low environmental impact requirements of materials (achieved by reference to, for example, *The Green Guide to Specification*), preferred sources of materials, recyclability issues, requirements for materials not specifically described in the specification, for example, a clause requiring that all timber used is to be supplied from responsibly managed sources.
- Content and types of adhesives or paints to be used.
- Waste disposal requirements relating to need to separate site waste for recycling, responsible disposal of potentially harmful solvents, etc.
- Client environmental objectives, for example, the percentage of construction materials to be from local sources.
- Energy and water use requirements during site operations.
- Environmental credentials of contractors, sub-contractors and suppliers.
- Requirements regarding 'considerate construction': that is, limitations on creation of noise, dust, effects on neighbours.
- Measures for briefing/monitoring of site personnel to ensure compliance with environmental objectives.

Life Cycle Assessments (LCAs)

The environmental impact of building materials should be analysed over the *whole life* of the product, not only in the manufacturing process but also in terms of the material's impact throughout its use within the building. This is known as Life Cycle Assessment or LCA and includes analysis of the impact of a material arising from:

- Winning of the raw materials, for example, the quarrying or extraction from the ground.
- Transportation of the raw materials to the factory.
- Production of the energy to be used in the manufacturing process.
- Manufacturing process in the factory.
- Production of the packaging materials for the product.
- Transportation to the building site.
- Assembly and construction of the product on site.
- Maintenance of the product or material throughout its lifetime.
- Demolition and removal of the materials.
- Processes and destination of the material as a waste product – recycling, incineration or landfill.

In a Life Cycle Assessment, the environmental impact of all materials is assessed over a typical 60-year building life and so, in some cases, the material or component will be replaced several times during that period. For example, in commercial offices, carpets may be replaced every five years and, given the large floor areas often involved, the overall environmental impact during the life of the building is potentially great. This may be somewhat surprising given the low mass and therefore relatively small quantities of raw materials and energy required for manufacture and processing. However, the 3rd edition of *The Green Guide* concluded that carpets had the potential to have the greatest environmental impact of all building elements (over 40% of all building impacts) if the carpet was the standard office specification; wool/nylon mix with a foam backing underlay. If the specification were to be changed to say a natural fibre underlay, this impact would be reduced to around 15% of all building impacts.

Otherwise, the general principle when selecting most building products is the lower the mass and the less industrial processing required, the lower the adverse environmental impact. Hence, products which utilise mainly natural materials tend to be the preferred environmental option.

The use and treatment of timber is potentially one of the most contentious and emotive building-related resource issues as deforestation and poorly managed plantations are a common cause of concern to environmentalists. The general rule is that preference should be given to timber from sustainable well-managed sources which have been independently certified under such schemes as Forests Forever or the Forest Stewardship Council (for more information see www.bre.co.uk/timber). The treatment of timber preservatives greatly extends the life of the wood with only minor additional environmental impact, as long as the treatments take place within the factory environment where the risk of environmental damage can be minimised.

Designers are also becoming aware of the need to design buildings in which it is easier to replace materials and, in the event of demolition, *de-construct* the building; waste materials can then be more easily separated for recycling. Also, replacement of a material which has reached the end of its life does not then involve the destruction and removal of other materials, potentially with many years of useful life left, simply to gain access to the material to be replaced.

Careful specification of low impact materials is now also a means of acquiring credits under the BREEAM programme by use of *The Green Guide to Specification*.

The benefits of green buildings

Supporters of green design claim that low environmental impact buildings offer a range of benefits including financial, improved public relations and reduced health and safety risks. Brian Edwards in the book *Green Buildings Pay* and the Rocky Mountain Institute, in *Green Development*, identify a number of potential advantages which are supported by specific examples and case studies. They include (RMI, 1998):

- Financial benefits:
    - —reduced running costs generally, in particular dramatically reduced energy costs.
    - —comparable or reduced capital costs of construction.
    - —buildings easier to let at higher rents because of market distinction and a more appealing product.
    - —reduced risk of financial loss arising from health and safety litigation.
- Benefits to building occupants:
    - —reduced health and safety risks to occupants from Sick Building Syndrome, legionnaire's disease – due to improved internal environments through better air quality – etc.
    - —lower absenteeism and improved productivity.
- Marketing and publicity benefits
    - —more positive, 'environmentally responsible' and therefore 'socially responsible' image for the organisations involved in projects.

(1)   Energy costs

When making a comparison between the energy costs of a conventional air-conditioned building and those of a green or naturally ventilated building (one relying on natural convection to draw fresh air into the building), we are not really comparing like with like. For example, the speed of response to changes in outside or inside temperatures or to humidity levels may be slower in the case of some naturally ventilated buildings when compared with their conventional air-conditioned counterparts. What is perhaps more important is to identify which buildings really require full air conditioning and which can function satisfactorily using lower tech systems. Research does seem to show that with simple heating and ventilation systems incorporating lower energy consuming equipment, naturally ventilated buildings will have, under optimum circumstances, lower running and capital costs but may not be suitable for all situations, for example, some city centre sites, or some computer environments.

It is possible to compare the likely energy costs of a proposed green building with those of a comparable, conventional building by making use of 'good practice' guides and energy cost predictors. As previously discussed, by using DEFRA's Energy Consumption Guide, the energy costs of an existing or proposed green building can be compared with the predicted expenditure for the equivalent conventional building, in terms of floor area and use, etc., using normal heating and ventilation systems.

For residential property, designers can use the National Home Energy Rating (NHER) scheme. This system calculates the energy use and energy costs of a property taking into account the building's location, design, construction, insulation, heating systems and ventilation. Buildings can be certified under the NHER scheme as having achieved the appropriate standard; the NHER scheme also incorporates the Government's Standard Assessment Procedure (SAP) which also gives an energy rating on a scale of 1–120. According to the energy consultants R&S, SAP ratings for newly built homes of below 80–85 are evidence that the properties will not have been designed with energy efficiency as a major concern (see www.energy-ratings.co.uk).

One indicator of the extent to which energy use in buildings has become of significance to property professionals can be seen by the award of the RICS Building of the Year prize for 2001 to the energy-efficient, green building, the Wessex Water Operations Centre near Bath, a building which achieved the highest ever rating under the BREEAM programme (Figure 3.17). This building operates at less than one-third of the energy consumption levels of a conventional building. The building's orientation is east–west and solar shading, natural ventilation and the use of photo voltaic panels for hot water all contribute to the minimisation of energy use (CSM, 2002).

The RICS Awards now include an Energy Efficiency category and, in 2001, the winners included the UCB Centre in Brussels, the Royal and Sun-Alliance Centre in Auckland, NZ, and the Central Square development in Newcastle, the UK, in addition to the Wessex Water building.

In 1997, the RICS Energy Efficiency prize was awarded to the Ministry of Defence complex at Abbey Wood, Bristol. The project's building economists undertook a very thorough Life Cycle Costing analysis as the design progressed because as a public agency, the MOD is accountable for its expenditure and was therefore required to justify the adoption of a green approach to the project. For this very large, new-build development of approximately $120\,000\,\text{m}^2$, net office space $97\,587\,\text{m}^2$, predicted energy savings were estimated at some £2 million per annum compared with the projected costs for a 'typical' comparable office (Table 3.3). The design utilises 'natural' or 'displacement' ventilation systems rather than traditional air-conditioning systems.

It should be noted that the report does not contain a fully itemised breakdown of these projected savings and so it is not possible to comment in detail on the figures shown below. However, it has been suggested that the energy needed specifically for the air conditioning operation would be no more than £5–£8 per m^2 net

Figure 3.17 Office building for Wessex Water, 1998 (architects and photograph: Bennetts Associates).

internal area and that therefore a saving of no more than a £500 000–£800 000 (1991 prices) would be found from this element (Williams, 1996). However, this would still be a significant cost saving for the client organisation concerned.

A further example of the design of green buildings reducing energy use and costs can be found in the much smaller, four-storey 3250 m², Elizabeth Fry Building at the University of East Anglia, completed in 1995.

The building's designers adopted a green approach to the design of the building's heating and ventilation systems involving the use of high levels of insulation and heat recovery systems. Following detailed monitoring of the building's energy and environmental performance between January 1996 and August 1997 under a joint BRE/BRECSU contract, it was found that the building's energy consumption was 61 kWh/m²/annum, 20% below the good practice figure for academic buildings and 50% below that normally found in a 'good' comparable office (PROBE, 1998).

Table 3.3   (a) Comparison of energy costs for Abbey Wood, a 'good' office and a 'typical' office (MOD, 1997).

	Abbey Wood (101 kWh/m² PA) cumulative PV	'Good' office (300 kWh/m² PA) cumulative PV	'Typical' office (600 kWh/m² PA) cumulative PV
Year 1	£411 000	£1 219 000	£2 437 000
Year 5	£1 728 000	£5 134 000	£10 268 000
Year 10	£3 020 000	£8 970 000	£17 940 000
Year 30	£5 648 000	£16 776 000	£33 552 000
Year 50	£6 647 000	£19 210 000	£38 420 000

(b) Where the cost savings can be attributed (MOD, 1997).

	Cost saving per annum*	Present value over 50 years
Low-energy lighting	£25 000	£400 000
Triple in lieu of double glazing	£28 000	£413 000
'Displacement' ventilation in lieu of air conditioning	£2 000 000	£32 000 000

Compared with a 'typical' comparable office. PV=present value. PA=per annum.

An occupant satisfaction survey carried out within the Elizabeth Fry building measuring comfort levels, building health, management and control strategies showed performance significantly higher than the National Benchmark Standard (Probe, 1998). This would indicate that good building performance can be achieved by the use of non-air conditioned, greener technology.

In a relatively early example of energy saving techniques applied to office design, the Dutch bank ING's headquarters in Amsterdam, completed in 1987, uses around one-fifth of the energy used in an adjacent, comparable bank building built at the same time but which used a more conventional approach to building design and management (Figure 3.18). The two buildings had roughly the same overall build cost, although ING's energy system cost around £470 000 more than a conventional system.

Energy savings are, however, estimated as being seven figure sums annually and the building is reputed to have the lowest energy costs in Dutch office building. Construction costs were £1050/m² which according to the project director were comparable or cheaper than other office buildings in The Netherlands (RMI, 1998).

(2)   Capital costs

As with the evaluation of running costs, it can be difficult to make meaningful comparisons between the capital construction costs of conventional and green buildings on a like-for-like basis. Some green buildings may indeed be less expensive than their conventional counterparts but may be different in terms of design concept and functional performance. However, in the case of the MOD

Figure 3.18   The ING building.

Abbey Wood project, both the project team and the client organisation make it clear in the project report that substantial cost savings were made as a result of the decision to 'go green'.

With a total shell-and-core cost of £100 million, the average construction cost of the project was £850/m^2, comparing favourably with such projects as Stanhope's 1992 Ludgate development which had a shell-and-core cost of £860/m^2 (Macneil, 1996). Savings arising from utilising a displacement system to assist natural ventilation rather than full air conditioning are reported as being £5 million. The adoption of a 'lower-tech', non-air-conditioned heating and ventilation installation involving much less air-handling equipment, including ducting, chillers, pumps, fans, cabling and control mechanisms, has, in this case, produced savings on the costs of services installations of around 40% (MOD, 1997).

Other capital cost reductions for the project include £1 500 000 arising from a low-impact approach to the use of the site involving the optimisation of existing site contours and the retention of existing features and planting.

In terms of other value-for-money advantages, the report also cites the optimisation of building layouts and the clear, simple and efficient planning of buildings due to requirements and constraints of natural ventilation systems, that is, the need for a 'stacking' effect. More careful specification practices, justifying decisions on the grounds of a range of life cycle considerations including maintenance, replacement, necessity and functionality, are also identified as an advantage.

The use of demountable partitions in offices is not a new idea but in the context of green building design their use enhances the green credentials of projects by minimising future waste and disposal costs, reducing management and 'down-time' costs due to lost productivity resulting from 'churn' and by providing flexible and responsive working environments. At Abbey Wood, the additional 40% capital cost of demountable 'monoblock' partitioning systems was offset by an estimated life-cycle cost saving of £135 000 per annum or £2 million over a 50-year period (Ministry of Defence, 1997).

Management of the landscape of the same project also produced savings of some £17 000 per annum by the planting of trees rather than large areas of 'manicured' grass, requiring high levels of irrigation and maintenance. As the landscape designers point out, this approach has produced a more 'natural' and mature landscape where 'staff would be made to feel more comfortable straight away by moving from the usual business park environment to something less "artificial" looking' (Findlay, 1998).

In one other project, the 28 885 m² Scottish Office Headquarters in Edinburgh, built in 1997, capital costs were reported as being approximately 20% lower, due in part to a 40% saving on services costs where a natural ventilation system replaced conventional air conditioning.

However, other studies have revealed that green projects do not always cost less than the conventional, equivalent building. In the Doxford International Solar Office, a scheme in northeast England which incorporates an entire elevation of photovoltaic panels to generate electricity for the building, construction costs were 30% higher than the normal, equivalent business park development. The approach adopted here was at the 'radical' end of green building design and the use of such unconventional and innovative technologies clearly incurred a cost premium.

(3)   *Letting green buildings*

Developers, investors and agents are traditionally wary of involvement in more 'radical' building solutions that are perceived to be unconventional and high-risk. In the case of one green building, it was felt that the unusual external appearance had 'put off' prospective tenants already nervous about lack of conventional air-conditioning. Moreover, some letting agents feel that tenants would not necessarily pay more for green property even if running costs were less, if a comparable property were available in the same location – particularly in areas such as business parks (Shiers, 2000).

It is also perhaps significant that at Leeds City Office Park, a green building by the architects Peter Foggo and Associates, a 'mixed-mode' ventilation system was introduced, comprising part low-energy or natural ventilation and part full air conditioning for special areas such as computer suites and high-use areas. It was felt that such a solution would have both practical and marketing advantages and reassure particular groups of prospective tenants that the buildings would in fact 'work'.

It may still be the case that in the eyes of many letting agents and tenants, prime office space which commands the highest rental values includes full air conditioning. It may also be that savings in running cost are still of relatively little interest to many tenants and that the importance of location, size and building quality remain paramount. It is, however, possible that with the introduction of an energy tax in April 2002 (the Climate Change Levy), the value of having lower energy costs may modify attitudes among tenants. Also, studies have shown that in locations where demand is high, good quality green accommodation can command an additional green premium on rent for 'value added', as long as other variables are strong (Goodman, 1994).

The developers Akeler have recently completed the first phase of a green business development at Leeds Valley Park. The scheme has achieved the highest BREEAM rating of *excellent* and Akeler have made much of the scheme's green credentials, as well as the more conventional selling points, in their marketing material (Akeler, 2002; see also www.leedsvalleypark.com):

'Leeds Valley Park is a landmark office park totalling 20.24 hectares (50 acres) which has planning consent for 67 818 sq. m gross (730 000 sq. ft) of high quality office accommodation and which benefits from generous on-site car-parking provision.

Akeler has committed to developing Phase One of the Park that will provide 11 148 sq. m net (120 000 sq. ft) in three separate buildings with future phases totalling 53 882 sq. m (580 000 sq. ft) available for bespoke development.

The masterplan provides for:

- Creation of a high quality business community capable of accommodating the sophisticated needs of modern business with the potential for an estimated 5500 people to be employed.
- A phased development process that takes into account infrastructure, topography and market issues.
- Plot sizes that can cater for buildings ranging from 30 000 sq. ft to 80 000 sq. ft, between two and four storeys high with generous car-parking provision.
- Creation of links to the Supertram with new bus stops, footways and cycleways.
- Development of nursery, café and retail facilities plus an on-site information and management centre, all within Phase One.
- Incorporate best practice in environmental and sustainable design, seeking to achieve the highest BREEAM (Building Research Establishment Environmental Assessment Method) rating.'

(4) Health and safety issues

The key health and safety issues within buildings encompass indoor air quality, thermal comfort, noise and lighting, both natural daylight and artificial lighting. It seems likely that the adoption of a greener approach to the design and management of the internal environment of buildings can result both in reduced risk of health and safety litigation and financial savings through more efficient working. Such savings can then be used to offset any additional initial capital costs that were incurred in raising the design standards of the building above the statutory minima.

A number of studies have concluded that there is a strong correlation between air quality and performance at work. In a series of carefully structured experiments, the performance of groups undertaking similar activities in similar working environments but utilising different cleaning and air-quality control conditions has been compared. The results of these experiments show that there is a relationship between a clean, healthy working environment and better productivity and lower absenteeism (PROBE, 1998).

Although the impact of cleaner, better quality working environments on staff morale is harder to quantify, a sense of physical well-being among building occupiers rather than a high incidence of sore throats, headaches and other respiratory conditions is clearly more likely to promote positive feelings towards work and the working environment (Attenborough, 1996).

The authors of a specially commissioned study of the MOD Abbey Wood project concluded that the higher quality internal environments created by the adoption of a green approach had led to a reduction in the levels of absenteeism among staff within the organisation. An average of 6 days sick leave per annum was recorded for the occupants of the green building as opposed to an average of between 9 and 12 days for staff working in comparable posts but in conventional buildings (MOD/Jones *et al.*, 1998).

Indoor air quality can be significantly improved through a variety of tried and tested techniques including cleaning and filtration of air within the building, adequate supply of clean fresh air and thorough cleaning programmes for furniture, carpets and air-handling ducts and equipment.

At Abbey Wood, the Barclaycard HQ in Northampton and Leeds City Office Park, the buildings have prioritised ease of access to areas such as ducts and spaces above ceiling panels for maintenance and cleaning. The Barclaycard HQ is equipped with localised sensors that can detect poor air quality or uncomfortably high temperatures, triggering the input of cooled, filtered outside-air into the relevant zone.

Lighting levels and lighting quality also have the potential to profoundly affect the way in which occupiers work. A general preference for natural light rather than artificial sources is commonly expressed by building occupiers and many green buildings have incorporated lighting 'baffles' which ensure that as much natural daylight as possible reaches the centre of the building.

Other considerations include ensuring that occupants have a view out of the building and that lighting levels are adequate but not so excessive as to create glare. A high degree of personal control is preferable, one way of achieving this being the use of uplighters for general illumination supported by individual task lighting at workstations.

(5)   *Thermal comfort*

Achieving the right levels of thermal comfort, particularly in commercial buildings, is more often concerned with cooling rather than heating. Heat gain due to the orientation of the building is a common complaint from users particularly when combined with heat gains from equipment, machinery, lighting and the other occupants. The careful use of solar shading and natural ventilation combined with low-energy electrical fittings can do much to improve comfort and reduce cooling costs.

Perceptions of thermal comfort are also very subjective, often varying significantly from one occupant to the next. The principle of user consultation and individual control should therefore be adopted wherever possible and, if successfully implemented, will reduce energy use, improve staff morale and performance and dramatically reduce management and maintenance time spent dealing with complaints, disputes and adjustments to services controls.

Building designers and managers have become increasingly aware of the need to invest in consultation and research at the design stage and that the management of some greener lighting, heating and ventilation systems, often unfamiliar to occupiers, will require a greater input from specialists, at least initially.

In the Barclaycard HQ in Northampton, the Leeds City Office Park and at Abbey Wood, there were concerns regarding the need to 'educate' occupants in the control of their own working environments. A number of problems were, it seems, caused by staff not fully understanding how to control finely tuned environmental systems. Such problems suggest that aspects of current green technologies are still evolving into robust and reliable systems. There is also the important issue of 'ownership', giving staff both greater control and responsibility for their personal environmental comfort. Consequently, the role of the Facilities Manager both in the design and post-occupancy stages of green projects is extremely important.

By contrast, conventional buildings, particularly those with full air conditioning, tend to be a more 'passive' experience for occupants. This could go some way to explaining the lack of enthusiasm on the part of some prospective tenants and the operational difficulties experienced when letting green speculative office space, where natural ventilation systems had been utilised. Such an apparent lack of confidence in the effectiveness of greener comfort systems is perhaps explained in part by a lack of understanding on the part of prospective tenants and also by an unwillingness to actively manage their own environment.

(6) *Marketing and publicity*

Both the property developers BG Properties and Cellnet, the current occupiers of No 1 Leeds City Office Park, considered green projects to represent 'the way ahead' (Shaw/B.G. Properties, 1999) and 'good for the image of the company' (Taylor/Cellnet Ltd, 1999). Letting agents for both the buildings in Leeds and in the previously discussed scheme in Doxford felt that as speculative offices, green buildings were an attractive package and that 'green was good' as a marketing tool.

At present, the decision to 'go green' for organisations is still very much a case of weighing up the various potential financial, health and safety and marketing advantages against the risks associated with innovation and adopting a new approach where learning curves can be steep. However, it is possible that in the future, organisations will have to meet certain green criteria imposed by regulation and the lending institutions, the managers of pension funds and the banks, before building projects will get the necessary funding. Speculative property developers and indeed owner-occupiers may be vetted by the major lenders as borrowers are increasingly expected to subscribe to an environmental agenda.

As lenders become more 'socially responsible' investors, organisations commissioning new buildings could, it seems, be required to show that they are well managed, responsible companies who will protect the value of shareholders' investments. As the Prudential's 1998 Annual Report states:

'We expect companies in which we invest to be able to demonstrate and report on appropriate environmental policies especially where commercial activities have a significant impact. We are unlikely to hold shares in companies where we are not satisfied with the appropriateness of this environmental policy or ability to manage the risks associated with environmental impact.'

As many companies are involved in the procurement and management of their own buildings, they could, in the future, be required to demonstrate implementation of appropriate property-related environmental programmes such as BREEAM or accreditation under ISO 14001, as a condition of loans from lending organisations such as the Prudential. It is also possible that these principles will apply in time to the funding or acquisition of property for investment purposes.

Subsequently, the Prudential has produced an Environmental and Social Report in which they set out a comprehensive set of policy statements dealing with the relationship between property and the environment. The report makes a commitment to 'protect the quality of land, air and water... and the quality and well-being of the communities in which we operate. In this way we will enhance the reputation of our company and develop a sense of pride among our employees' (PruPIM, 2002).

POSSIBLE FUTURE DIRECTIONS

Anticipating future developments in the field of green building design is particularly difficult, as there seems to be a virtually continuous stream of new ideas and initiatives from many diverse sources. It is, therefore, only possible to identify a few key areas in which the more significant changes may occur in the near future.

Because ideas can evolve or change so quickly that it is probable that much of the design guidance produced is out of date even as it is being written, 'the web' and recent specialist journals are essential tools in ensuring that personal knowledge remains current. However, readers are also encouraged to continue to use reliable, established sources of information as they often employ tried-and-tested methods of environmental assessment and are able to draw upon considerable expertise and data built up over time.

As we have seen, the UK government has been a leading player in promoting the green agenda in recent years and it is probable that it will continue to do so for the foreseeable future. It is likely that in time, all construction projects with a link to the government, such as Public-Private Partnership (PPP) projects and those in the public health and education sectors, will be required to meet higher standards of environmental performance, measured by systems such as BREEAM.

Similarly, local government may become more environmentally proactive by requiring that the providers of services such as building maintenance and materials have green credentials such as EMAS or accreditation under ISO 14001. They also may be encouraged by central government to further expand their programmes of upgrading the environmental performance of existing building stock through such measures as improved insulation and the replacement of older heating systems with high-efficiency, low-emission alternatives.

It is also possible that eventually, Local Authorities will insist on proposed building projects reaching a designated environmental standard as a precondition of planning consents; many projects are already subject to sequential testing in terms of preferred locations and this is a logical next step in the 'greening' process.

In the design of new buildings, it is not hard to imagine an even greater emphasis on creating flexible, adaptable homes and offices in the future. As part of this, there may also be a move toward the use of more standardised components which are easier to deconstruct – both for reasons of adaptability and easier maintenance and replacement.

LEARNING MATERIALS

Some questions and issues for discussion

(1) **Define the term 'green building' and give three examples of green design features that you might expect to find as part of a green building project.**

We could say that 'A green building is one which seeks to minimise its environmental impact in an integrated and holistic way'.

Whilst it should be remembered that there is no single view of what constitutes a green building or a green development, most green buildings are characterised by an integrated approach to their design and management; they are projects which seek to reduce environmental impact through careful consideration of *all* aspects of the building's design and post-occupancy management, over the whole life-cycle of the building.

Three design features might include the following:

- Reduced energy consumption through natural ventilation rather than air conditioning, more efficient heating and heat-storage systems, control of solar heat-gain in order to reduce cooling requirements and low-energy lighting, etc.
- Minimal site impact through use of existing site contours and sensitivity to site ecology, flora and fauna.

- The use of 'grey' water recycling for landscape irrigation and the use of low water consumption WCs.
- Careful specification of low-impact building materials including the use of reclaimed materials.
- Minimising the use of harmful chemicals – in the construction process and in the management of the building, for example some timber preservation treatments, cleaning fluids, paints and solvents, landscaping, weed and pest control.
- Minimising waste in the construction phase of the building through more careful ordering of materials thereby reducing the amount of new materials thrown away unused, by separating site waste materials for recycling and in the management of post-occupancy building waste.
- Maximising use of existing transport networks by careful location of proposed buildings close to existing public transport routes and by having greener transport policies within the occupier's organisation, for example car-sharing schemes for building users, facilities for staff using cycles.
- Healthier working and living environments, for example through greater use of natural day-lighting to offices and by ensuring a high standard of air-quality and individual environmental control.

(2) What are the benefits claimed for green buildings and what are the possible downsides in the development, ownership or occupancy of green buildings?

Potential benefits:

- Reduced running costs generally – in particular, dramatically reduced energy costs.
- Comparable or reduced capital costs of construction.
- Buildings easier to let at higher rents because of market distinction and a more appealing product.
- Reduced risk of financial loss arising from health and safety litigation and therefore a safer, more appealing product for investors and lenders.
- Reduced health and safety risks to occupants from Sick Building Syndrome or legionnaire's disease due to improved internal environments through better air quality, etc.
- Lower absenteeism and improved productivity.
- More positive, 'environmentally responsible' and therefore 'socially responsible' image for the organisations involved in projects.

Possible downsides:

- Although many aspects of green buildings utilise tried and tested materials and construction techniques, designs may still involve a level of innovation and therefore risk for the building owner and occupier.
- Still a new field so learning curve can be steep for organisations involved in green projects.

- Some uncertainty regarding the performance of natural ventilation systems in terms of effectiveness and speed of response.
- As a more inclusive process more time is needed for consultation.

(3)   What is the Building Research Establishment Environmental Assessment Method?

BREEAM is a voluntary scheme for the environmental assessment of both new and existing buildings. Credits are awarded for good practice leading to an overall rating for projects on a four-point scale: excellent, very good, good and pass.

Assessments are carried out by accredited assessors for a fee. The scheme was introduced in 1991 and by 2003 some 400 commercial buildings have been assessed under the scheme. Buildings are assessed in terms of:

- Environmental management – policy and procedural issues.
- Health and comfort of occupants.
- Energy use.
- Transport – energy use and location issues.
- Water consumption and leakage issues.
- Materials use – environmental impact issues, for example use of energy in manufacture, responsibly managed sources, recycling (through reference to *The Green Guide to Specification* – percentage of materials achieving 'A' rating).
- Land use.
- Site ecology management and impact.
- Pollution management.

(4)   In what ways can the manufacture of construction materials impact on the environment and how can specifiers select the lowest-impact materials and components?

The ways in which the manufacture of materials, including the winning of the raw materials and transportation, affect the environment include:

- Climate change: global warming or greenhouse gases produced from energy needed in manufacture.
- Fossil fuel depletion: coal, oil or gas consumption.
- Ozone depletion: gases that destroy the ozone layer produced by manufacture and energy use.
- Human toxicity: pollutants that are toxic to humans.
- Waste disposal: material sent to landfill or incineration as by-products of manufacture.
- Water extraction: mains, surface and groundwater consumption.
- Acid deposition: production of gases that cause acid rain, etc.
- Ecotoxicity: pollutants that are toxic to the ecosystem.
- Eutrophication: water pollutants that promote algal blooms, etc.
- Summer smog: air pollutants that cause respiratory problems.
- Mineral extraction: metal ores, minerals and aggregates.

- Recycling issues: recycled material within products, amount capable of being recycled, net saving in embodied energy in using recycled material rather than virgin.

Materials which have the best performance against this range of environmental parameters should then be selected.

Detailed information about the environmental performance of commonly used materials can be found in a range of handbooks including *The Green Guide to Specification* and the *Green Building Handbook* by Tom Wooley.

(5)   What Government-backed initiatives have been introduced in the last five years to promote a more sustainable approach to the location, design and management of buildings?

- In 2000, the Treasury set as an objective that all new government building projects should achieve an *Excellent* BREEAM rating and that refurbishments should be to a *Very Good* BREEAM standard.
- The shift in planning and development policy towards the development of 'brown land' (previously used) rather than 'greenfield' sites, in order to conserve and protect the natural environment and to ensure that towns and cities remain economically viable.
- The 'One Million Sustainable Homes' initiative, sponsored by the World Wide Fund for Nature, is a campaign which has the backing of the UK Government and seeks to construct and refurbish 1 million low environmental impact homes by 2012.
- New legislation such as the Climate Change Levy, also known as CCL – an energy tax on industry – designed to reduce energy consumption in both buildings and manufacturing processes.
- Higher building insulation standards as in the recent amendments to Part L of the Building Regulations.
- The UK government has developed its own set of environmental objectives and targets for the 'greening' of the government estate, including such measures as the use of energy management systems and more environmentally responsible supply chain policies.

Examples of media coverage of the issue of green property

(1)   In the article below by Matt Weaver in *The Guardian* (Thursday 22 November 2001) the idea of introducing financial penalties in order to raise standards of building design and environmental quality was discussed.

- Is there a case for both tougher legislation and the introduction of financial penalty for failure to meet higher environmental standards in the design and management of buildings? In particular, should there be a statutory requirement that new buildings using public money meet certain environmental standards.
- What might be the possible downsides to this approach? Why has the Government been reluctant to use such methods?

'Public money should be withdrawn from housing associations if they do not build new homes of high design quality', the government's architecture tsar has claimed.

Sir Stuart Lipton, chairman of the Commission for Architecture and the Built Environment (CABE) told the Housing Corporation's conference in Manchester there should be a 'sea change' in the quality of new social housing.

He told delegates 'in style terms, there is much room for improvement'. Sir Stuart also urged the Housing Corporation to stop funding poor quality housing. 'We need to make funding conditional on design quality,' he said.

He highlighted good examples of new projects by housing associations including the Joseph Rowntree Foundation Caspar schemes in Birmingham and Leeds, and Peabody Trust's Murray Grove scheme in London and its proposals for the environmentally friendly 'BedZed' scheme in Sutton. But he added: 'Frankly the vast majority of organisations could do better.'

Sir Stuart urged housing associations to appoint 'design champions' to mirror the ministerial design champions now in place in government departments. 'If government can do it, we can all do it,' he said.

He also said housing associations should contact CABE, whose staff would help improve the design of new housing. 'Be better clients,' he said, 'do not treat lowest cost as best value, don't regard design as an optional extra.'

From Weaver (2001). Reproduced with kind permission of the publisher.

(2) **Despite the technology having been available for some considerable time, photovoltaic energy sources have been slow to catch on in the UK. In an article by Paul Brown in *The Observer* on Sunday 31 March 2002, a new government initiative to help remedy this situation is discussed.**

- Why have these technologies not been more widely adopted before now?
- Even with the introduction of this government initiative, what obstacles might continue to stand in the way of more individuals and businesses using such renewable energy sources?

The number of domestic solar power and photovoltaic installations in Britain will increase tenfold by 2005 as a result of a £20 million grant package expected to be announced by Patricia Hewitt, the trade and industry secretary. Hundreds of homes and offices will generate electricity direct from sunlight as part of the government's attempt to kick-start the UK industry, which has so far lagged behind those in the US, Japan and Germany because of lack of government support.

The programme takes up one-fifth of Tony Blair's £100 million support package for the renewables industry announced last November, and involves a series of demonstration projects to show that solar power works in Britain. The panels can be used as cladding on the side of buildings [or] on the roofs of houses and flats. Unlike other renewable power sources, they require no extra space.

Ms Hewitt is visiting one of the projects, the Beddington Zero Energy Development (BedZed) in Sutton, Surrey. BedZed is an 82-home, energy-efficient mix of housing and workshops that aims to be the first 'carbon neutral' community.

The solar part of the project has been funded by the European Union and the Department of Trade and Industry. The Peabody Trust, one of London's largest housing associations, manages the development. A consortium led by the government-sponsored Energy Saving Trust and contractor Halcrow will manage the contracts.

Other parts of the programme include £4 million for the installation of solar systems on public buildings including schools, galleries, church halls and sports centres all over the country, and a similar amount for social and private housing developments. This will provide photovoltaics to power 380 houses, flats and bungalows.

Continued

> Although electricity generated by photovoltaics costs at least three times as much as gas, mass production is expected to make costs competitive by 2020.
>
> From Brown (2002). Reproduced with kind permission of the publisher.

(3)   The idea of large high-tech, lower environmental impact green buildings can, it seems, generate feelings of support and misgivings in equal measure. Projects of the type described below in John Vidal's article in *The Guardian* of Friday 14 December 2001 raise a number of property development, environmental and aesthetic issues. For example, what would be the impact on the existing infrastructures of such large projects? Should inner-city development be more small-scale, community-oriented in nature? Are these projects examples of developers cynically using the green agenda simply to help schemes obtain planning permission?

- Discuss the range of possible objections and concerns as well as potential benefits of such projects.

> Londoners with £350 000 to spend may soon get the chance to live in Britain's tallest housing block if permission is granted for the country's 'greenest' skyscraper.
>
> Plans for the 49-storey, circular 180 m (590 ft) structure, unveiled yesterday suggest that the Vauxhall tower will become as much of a landmark as the NatWest tower or Canary Wharf. Standing on semi-derelict ground on the south bank of the Thames, it would be London's 10th tallest building, 55 m (180 ft) lower than the tallest tower at Canary Wharf five miles to the east. With few tall buildings around it, it will dominate south and west London and may be visible from several counties. St George, the tower's developers, hope that its hi-tech environmental credentials will help persuade the London mayor, Ken Livingstone, and the planners to recommend it. The triple-glazed, mainly glass structure will be topped by a 30 ft tall cylindrical wind generator to provide enough power for the building's communal lights, and will use heat exchangers drawing on the water table below to greatly reduce the need for air conditioning and central heating.
>
> The building, say the architects Broadway Malyan, will use just a third of the energy of a comparable building, reduce carbon emissions by up to 66% and include 'revolutionary' skyscraper features like windows that open and even gardens. None of its environmental initiatives are considered trail blazing but, says the developer: 'It will be the first building of its kind to bring together such a series of initiatives on such a grand scale.'
>
> It was welcomed by Friends of the Earth as an attempt to catch up with green buildings in the US and Europe. 'Architects are waking up to the possibilities of green design which takes pressure off natural resources and which makes people feel good to live in. Tall buildings can have a distinct advantage over sprawling estates because they conserve land,' said Charles Secrett, director of Friends of the Earth. This week Prince Charles condemned skyscrapers as 'overblown phallic structures and depressingly predictable antennae that say more about an architectural ego than any kind of craftsmanship'.
>
> If built the tower will compete in the new London 'green skyscraper' league table with a projected 'bioclimatic skyscraper' expected to be built next year at Elephant and Castle, south London, by Malaysian architect Ken Yeang, and Norman Foster's 41-storey 'erotic gherkin' planned for the City, both of which are billed as ecologically sensitive.
>
> From Vidal (2001). Reproduced with kind permission of the publisher.

(4)   In an Editorial in *Building* in January 2001, 'the voice of the industry' published the article below.

- Why might many in the construction sector empathise with the views expressed here?

- What might be the pro-green response to these issues? What evidence could be used to support a more environment-led approach to design and construction?
- What sources of information, guidance and specialist advice are available for construction professionals seeking to reconcile the issues of development—profit–sustainability?

The green issue now pervades the entire (construction) process, from where to locate offices and homes to how to design and build them – and of course, how construction firms run their own businesses. No environmental debate would be complete without its cynics, and many point out that energy-efficient new building makes up too small a percentage of the housing stock to deliver the hoped for 60% reduction in carbon dioxide emissions. Then there are the arguments about . . . using materials that will last longer but require more energy to make. As experts search for ways to fuse development with sustainability, 'business as usual is the only option we can exclude'. Welcome to the green century.

From Barrick (2001). Reproduced with kind permission of The Builder Group.

REFERENCES

Aho, G. (1987) *William Morris: A Reference Guide*, Gale Group, Boston.

Anderson, J., Shiers, D. & Sinclair, M. (2002) *The Green Guide to Specification*, Blackwell Science, Oxford.

Attenborough, M. (1996) 'Green buildings: benefits and barriers', *Building Services* **18**(5).

Barrick, A. (2001) 'It's got to be green', Editorial, *Building Magazine*, Special Edition, 5 January.

BRE (1998) *BREEAM for Offices '98*, BRE, London.

BRE (2002) Estimate of numbers of BREEAM projects undertaken – discussion with A. Yates of BRE.

Brown, P. (2002) 'Hewitt's £20 m will end solar power eclipse', *The Observer*, 31 March.

CBP (2002) *Rethinking Construction – Accelerating Change*, CBP, London.

Chartered Surveyor Monthly (CSM) (2002) RICS awards edition.

Construction Industry and Research Information Association (CIRIA) (1994) *Environmental Issues in Construction (Energy and Resources Use)*, Vol. 2, Sect. 2, SP94, CIRIA, London.

DEFRA/DETR (1998) Energy Consumption Guides 19, GPG 34 and 35, DEFRA, London.

DETR (2000) *Building a Better Quality of Life: A Strategy for More Sustainable Construction*, DETR, London.

Edwards, B. (1998) *Green Buildings Pay*, Spon, London.

Findlay, J. (PTP Landscape Architects) (1998) unpublished report for MOD, London.

Gauzin-Muller, D. (2002) *Sustainable Architecture and Urbanism*, Birkhauser, Basle.

Goodman, T. (1994) 'Occupiers will pay more for green buildings', survey in *Property Week*, March.

Howard, E. (1898/1965) *Garden Cities of Tomorrow*, Cambridge, MA, MIT Press.

Knutt, E. (2001) 'Wessex man: an interview with Rab Bennetts', *Building Magazine*, Special Edition, 5 January.

Latham, D. & Latham, S. (1991) *An Annotated Critical Bibliography of William Morris*, Macmillan, London.

Macneil, J. (1996) 'MOD Procurement HQ', *Building Magazine*, 9 February, 41–45.

Ministry of Defence (MOD) (1997) Abbey Wood Project Report, unpublished.

PROBE team: Bordass, W. (1998) 'The Elizabeth Fry Building', *Building Services Journal*, April, 37–42.

Prudential (1998) *Annual Report*, London.

Prudential Property Investment Managers (PruPIM) (2002) *Environmental and Social Report*, Prudential, London.

Rocky Mountain Institute (RMI) (1998) *Green Development*, John Wiley & Sons, Chichester.

Shaw, H./BG Properties (1999) Interview.

Stower, W.A. (2002) *The Architecture of Frank Lloyd Wright*, University of Chicago Press, Chicago, IL.

Taylor, D./Cellnet Ltd (1999) Interview.

Vidal, J. (2001) 'Back to the eco-friendly drawing board', *The Guardian*, 14 December.

Water Services Association (1997) *Waterfacts '97*, WSA, London.

Weaver, M. (2001) 'Good housing design is not an optional extra', *The Guardian*, 22 November.

World Wide Fund for Nature (2001) *One Million Sustainable Homes*; statements by stakeholders, WWF website report.

FURTHER RESOURCES AND WEBSITES

ACE & The European Commission (1999) *A Green Vitruvius*, James & James, London.

Bennetts, R. (2001) 'Wessex man', *Building*, 5 January.

Building (2001) *The Green Century*, Special Edition, 5 January.

DETR (1994) *Sustainable Development: the UK Strategy*, HMSO, London.

Egan, J. (1998) *Rethinking Construction*, HMSO, London.

Gilbert, D. & Callaghan, W. (April 1997) photograph and graphics from an original article, RIBA Journal.

Jenks, C. (1975) *Movements in Modern Architecture*, Pelican, London.

Jones Lang & Wootton, McKenna & Company, Gardiner & Theobald (1991) *A New Balance – Buildings and the Environment*, in-house publication.

Jones, O'Sullivan & Bowman (1998) *Guidelines for the Design of Natural and Mixed-Mode Ventilation Systems in Commercial Buildings*, unpublished study, April.

Latham, M. (1994) *Constructing the Team*, HMSO, London.

Leaman, A. (1997) 'Healthier building ventilation systems', *Building Services Journal*, CIBSE, May, 37–41.

Lloyd Jones, D. (2000) *Architecture and the Environment*, Laurence King, London.

MOD (1998) *Office Environment Survey*, unpublished report.

Rao, S., Brownhill, D., Yates, A. & Howard, N. (2000) *EcoHomes: The Environmental Rating for Homes*, BRE, Watford.

Shiers, D. (1999) *Understanding Green Buildings*, College of Estate Management, Reading.

Shiers, D.E. (2000) 'Green developments: environmentally responsible building in the UK commercial property sector', *Property Management*, **18**(5), 352–65, MCB.

Wooley, T. (2000) *Green Building Handbook*, Spon, London.

- The BioRegional Development Group [*info@bioregional.com*] – enquiries can be made regarding information on BedZed – the 'green village' scheme in south London

- Building Regulations and latest on Part L, see www.safety.odpm.gov.uk/bregs/index.htm
  For discussion and background information on range of issues related to sustainable construction, see www.defra.gov.uk, which also contains excellent précis of key facts on Kyoto, ISO 14001 and 18 question/answer sections on Government policy, targets, etc. relating to construction and the environment
- See www.m4i.org.uk for case studies, findings and implications/practical applications of latest sustainability and industry initiatives
- Information and guidance on more efficient waste management, see www.waste-guide. org.uk/
- See www.sustainable-development.gov.uk/news2002/02.htm#0618c for more environment-related press releases
- Design Quality Indicators www.dqi.org.uk
- *Architects Journal* news-based website www.ajplus.co.uk

Procurement: sustainability and the UK construction industry

4

Suggested learning outcomes

After studying this chapter and discussing its contents, you should be able to:

- Define the term 'procurement' and explain the objectives of this stage of the project development process
- Explain how construction practices in the UK could be made more sustainable
- Identify the potential benefits of a 'greener' approach to construction both to the industry and to the wider community
- Appraise the measures taken by the UK Government in order to encourage construction companies to reduce the environmental impacts of their operations
- Discuss the possible barriers to the implementation of greater sustainability in the UK construction industry

---

HEADLINES: BIG ISSUES AND IMPORTANT QUESTIONS

According to most dictionary definitions, the word procurement simply means 'to obtain or to bring about'. In the context of property development projects, whether new-build or works to existing buildings, procurement refers to that part of the process whereby a contractor is appointed and the construction work is undertaken in accordance with a set of design drawings and specifications.

Defining procurement

The term *procurement* refers to that stage of the development process which includes the appointment of a building contractor, agreement on the type of building contract to be used and the construction or refurbishment of the building on site, in accordance with a set of design drawings and specifications.

It is the physical construction of the project which is central to the procurement stage and is the most resource-intensive and fast-moving phase of the

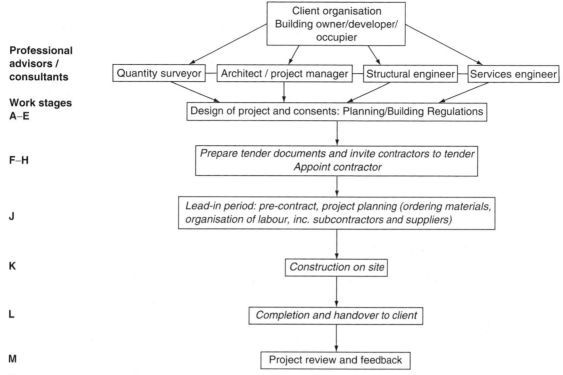

Professional advisors / consultants

Work stages A–E

F–H

J

K

L

M

Figure 4.1   The development process in outline, with procurement in italics.

development process. It is also the clearest demonstration of the construction industry 'in action'. Figure 4.1 shows the project development process in outline, with the procurement stages in italics.

The outline plan of work shown below explains the key stages of a construction project from the outset (inception) to the completion, handover to the client organisation and review of the project. It is set out in the form of a checklist: typical actions to be taken, tasks to have been completed, etc. Normally, the procurement phase includes stages H to L. These work stages are based on the RIBA Plan of Work.

Stage A: inception
Typical tasks to be undertaken are client organisation to consider design requirements, time scales and budget, design team appointed.

Stage B: feasibility
Practical and financial viability of project established in terms of site analysis, design, likelihood of planning consents, costs, legal considerations, etc.

Stage C: outline proposals
Brief established, sketch designs prepared including design and cost options.

Stage D: scheme design
Brief finalised, overall design agreed, planning application submitted.

Stage E: detailed design
Finalise all technical details, submit Building Regulation application.

Stage F: product information
Specification completed, schedules and bills of quantities if required, tender documentation prepared.

Stage H: tender action
Invite contractors to submit a priced bid for the work, tenders reviewed, contractor appointed.

Stage J: project planning
Lead-in period during which materials and labour are organised, insurances checked.

Stage K: operations on site
Management and construction of the project.

Stage L: completion
Handover to client subject to any defects being remedied.

Stage M: feedback
All parties to review project performance.

The construction industry has been identified by the government as being able to make an important contribution to the nation's sustainability aims and objectives as set out in *Sustainable Development: The UK Strategy* (DETR, 1994). As a signatory to the Kyoto Protocol, committing the country to a reduction of energy use and environmental harm, the UK government is looking to all sectors of British industry to adopt more sustainable practices. It is envisaged that the construction industry could reduce its environmental impact through such measures as:

- More careful purchasing of materials to ensure that sources and supply chains are controlled and managed in an environmentally responsible way.
- Minimisation and more careful handling of construction waste.
- Reducing the risk of pollution in the construction process.
- Reducing the levels of energy used in the construction process including fuel used in transportation of materials (i.e. by use of more local suppliers), site lighting and power, etc.
- More efficient, consultative working practices with a greater emphasis on team-working, thus reducing financial and resource wastage.
- Improved client guidance information, for example through simple 'how to' guides provided by the Office of Government Commerce (www.ogc.gov.uk) and access to 'best practice' demonstration project information.
- Encouraging clients to check the environmental credentials of construction companies as a prerequisite to being placed on tender lists.
- Better training and competence programmes.
- The use of targets, Key Performance and Environmental Performance Indicators (KPIs and EPIs) to monitor and measure progress.

However, some important questions which need to be addressed include:

- How can Government targets for lower levels of energy use within the industry, reduced construction waste, etc. best be achieved? Should this be through (1) new legislation, (2) tax breaks and other incentives, or (3) by means of a twin-track 'carrot and stick' approach?
- If legislation were increasingly used to force through change, would this be effective? Would the industry become more sustainable or would it simply become less competitive as companies struggled to finance the costs of compliance?
- Would a greener construction industry be more or less profitable? Recent reports, in particular those chaired by Sir Michael Latham in 1994 and by Sir John Egan in 1998, highlighted a number of shortcomings within the construction industry. Could a green approach to the problems identified offer a way to accelerate positive change or is the green agenda merely a distraction from the main issues, i.e. lack of competitiveness, quality and standards, education and training, etc?
- What community-wide advantages could more sustainable construction practices offer?
- If the industry were to commit wholesale to greener practices, how could such a process of change be best managed?

In 2002, the Strategic Forum for Construction stated that: 'Clients have a key role to play in demanding more sustainable buildings, designed on whole life principles, if the circle of blame is to be broken. Public sector clients can make a real difference by providing leadership in this area. They have committed themselves to doing so in *Achieving Sustainability in Construction Procurement* (see www.property.gov.uk/services/construction/gccp/100700.pdf). They now need to demonstrate publicly that they are delivering the action plan set out in that report. But private clients also need to recognise that investor pressure, regulation and good business practice make sustainability a key business issue in investing for the future' (CBP, 2002).

(Also see www.rethinkingconstruction.org and www.strategicforum.org.uk and www.cbpp.org.uk/acceleratingchange.)

The economic case for greater sustainability is also set out at length in 'Reputation, risk and reward – the business case for sustainability in the UK property sector' (BRE, 2002). As the authors state 'This paper is addressed primarily to chief executives, board members and senior managers in property development and property asset management; as their business partners and key suppliers, it is also of interest to executives in the construction sector. The purpose of the paper is to demonstrate that sustainability is an issue that business leaders can no longer afford to ignore or treat as immaterial. This paper aims to demonstrate that sustainability issues are of critical and strategic importance to business' (see www.projects.bre.co.uk/rrr).

BACKGROUND

The primary aim of the many legal regulations and controls affecting the construction industry is, and always has been, the reduction of risk to the health and safety of building users and the general public, that is, to prevent structural collapse, spread of fire, spread of disease through poor sanitation, etc.

In the legislation following the Great Fire of London in 1666, both the minimum distance and the type of wall construction between buildings were stipulated in the first London Building Act of 1667. The Public Health Act of 1875 determined minimum standards of sanitation within building projects as the fear of epidemics and concern regarding poor housing conditions grew. Over time, common standards of building control have been adopted by Local Authorities throughout the country and many of the controls, which were once voluntary, have become mandatory (see 'A Brief History of the Building Regulations' at www.calderdale.gov.uk and www.safety.odpm.gov.uk/bregs).

Concerns regarding potential hazards continue to drive the process of regulation today. There are now perceived risks associated with the construction and occupancy of buildings which, whilst not perhaps posing such obvious and direct threats as medieval fire traps or Victorian slums, are linked to the *indirect* and long-term effects of buildings. These include energy use from non-renewable sources and the possible link to climate change, the depletion of natural resources, the creation of an enormous waste burden and wasteful and inefficient working practices.

The shift in emphasis of property-related legislation from addressing the more immediate and direct risks to health and safety to controlling longer-term hazards can be seen in the change in Public Health legislation over time. For example, the Factories and Health and Safety at Work Acts of 1936, 1961, 1974 and 1985 deal primarily with the more direct risks of injury to building users. The longer-term risks posed by the handling of deleterious materials such as asbestos, the use of lead in paints and in water pipes and the control of potentially harmful chemicals used in solvents, adhesives and timber treatments have been the subject of more recent legislation such as the Control of Substances Hazardous to Health (COSHH, 1999) (see www.hse.gov.uk/hthdir/noframes/coshh/coshh7).

In addition, health and safety in construction projects is now not only a matter for site managers but must also be considered in the design and subsequent management of buildings as set out in the Construction (Design and Management) Regulations 1994 (CDM Regulations) (see www.hse.gov.uk/condocs/closed/cd161 or www.hse.gov.uk/pubns/cdm).

Since the oil crisis of the early 1970s, changes to the Building Regulations have shown a markedly greater emphasis on energy use in buildings. Recent requirements for insulation and power conservation measures have set significantly higher standards than ever before (see changes to Part L: Fuel and Power Conservation, Building Regulations: www.safety.odpm.gov.uk/bregs/index.htm).

In 1994, a Landfill Tax was introduced which required contractors to pay a tax for every tonne of waste going to a landfill site: currently, this is set at £10/tonne. Since then, the legislation has been modified with additional penalties for unauthorised disposal, etc. and there are further plans to increase the level of the Landfill Tax incrementally over the next five years to £30/tonne (see www.defra.gov.uk/environment/response/landfill/index.htm).

Key stages in the procurement process

The traditional model of the procurement process requires that it is normally the design team that prepares the tender documentation. This means that in most cases, the detail design of the project is undertaken without the input of the contractor who is to build the project. Some regard this as a wasted opportunity to involve the team member who is, arguably, most expert at actually assembling the building – the contractor.

The tender documentation is sent to the prospective contractors so that they may prepare a bid for carrying out the work. They are sent details of the location of the project, required start and finish dates, site access and any working restrictions (e.g. regarding noise, working hours, etc.) and a set of drawings.

The drawings, which will include plans, elevations and technical details, are normally accompanied by a written description of the works in the form of a *specification* or *bill of quantities* (a measured, itemised list of the work to be carried out). This information will have been produced prior to the procurement stage by the design team and the scheme will have received the required Planning and Building Regulation consents. The design team will usually consist of an architect, structural engineer, services engineer and, to provide cost advice, a quantity surveyor. The composition of the team may, however, vary according to the size and nature of the scheme.

In many residential developments, the entire process is executed by a single organisation. Smaller residential development companies will simply pay a consultant architect and an engineer to prepare the necessary designs from which they can build, whilst most large-volume house builders in the UK employ their own architects, engineers and cost estimators 'in-house'. These companies will normally carry out the whole development process from finding and purchasing land through to the design and construction phases before employing an agent to sell individual properties.

In the majority of non-residential projects, that is, commercial, industrial, health-care, retail, leisure, etc., the architect and the other 'consultants' are employed by the client organisation to design, co-ordinate and inspect the work to be carried out by the contractor on site. Work is inspected on site by both the consultants and Local Authority Building Control officers to ensure that the designs are followed correctly and are built to the appropriate standard.

The principles of the system by which contractors are appointed for construction projects and the nature of the contracts entered into by the various parties appear straightforward enough. Contractors are normally selected on the basis of previous experience and capability to bid or *tender* for a project. There would, typically, be a shortlist of between three to six contractors who would receive sets of drawings, specifications and bills of quantities which would describe the work to be undertaken. From this information, the contractor is able to submit a price for the work in competition with the other builders. Normally, the lowest price is accepted and a contract, stating both the agreed cost and the date by which the work is to be completed, is signed by both the builder and the client. There are a number of variations on this basic system, which are discussed later in this chapter.

Prior to commencement of work on site, a pre-construction or 'lead-in' period normally occurs. During this period, typically between two to four weeks, the construction team make all necessary arrangements for the provision of labour, materials and equipment needed for the works. Many in the industry consider this period as, more often than not, far too short and that most projects would benefit from greater project planning further in advance of the project commencing on site.

The great Hollywood film director, Cecil B. de Mille, is said to have meticulously planned every sequence of his epic-scale films of the 1930s and 1940s, long before filming actually commenced. He would use a vast number of sketches and 'storyboards' so that every last detail including camera angles, lighting, sound and stage-set requirements were precisely mapped out well before highly paid actors and technicians were involved. De Mille knew that the detailed planning of large, complex projects on an office desktop is much cheaper and easier than trying to solve problems 'on site' once the project has commenced. This is true of any project involving large numbers of people and resources; reorganising or rescheduling operations, delays whilst decisions are made or unforeseen problems solved can be disruptive and expensive – on a film set it may be actors and camera crews who are kept waiting, on a building site it will be highly-skilled, hourly-paid tradesmen!

Consequently, thorough planning and preparation immediately prior to commencement of construction work on site is critical to the success of any building project. This normally includes:

- Final detail design work and resolution of any outstanding decisions required from the consultants and/or client; the contractor can then programme the work and order materials with confidence, fully aware of client requirements.
- Advance planning of labour requirements, ordering of materials, equipment and machinery and planning of the sequence of the works.
- Agreement of final arrangements for site access and security, storage of materials, waste disposal, working hours and any restrictions on noise and dust, etc.

The contractor will often prepare a 'Gantt' or progress chart showing the proposed sequence of operations of the work on site so that the different trades can be organised in advance and progress and/or delays can be monitored (see Figure 4.2).

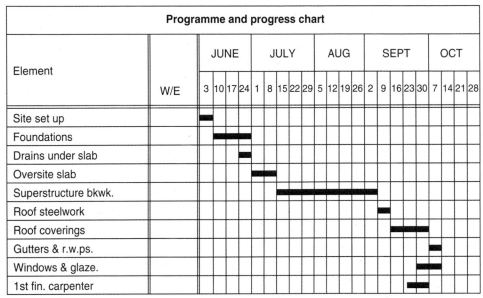

Figure 4.2 Example of a site programme chart or 'Gantt' chart.

Recent industry reports

Whilst much can be done to make the construction industry more environmentally responsible through regulation and control, achieving greater sustainability through changed working practices and through more progressive, inclusive and efficient attitudes is, arguably, a greater challenge.

In the Latham Report of 1994 entitled *Constructing the Team*, the industry was urged to 'improve its public image' and was reminded that 'equal opportunities require urgent attention'. Improvements in productivity and teamwork were also recommended (Latham, 1994, see Executive Summary, pp. viii (20) and Chapter 7, para. 7.25).

In 1998, the Egan Report, *Rethinking Construction*, commissioned by the then Secretary of State for the DETR, John Prescott, was published. In Chapter 1, the report states that

> 'The Construction Task Force has been set up by the Deputy Prime Minister against a background of deep concern in the industry and among its clients that the construction industry is under-achieving, both in terms of meeting its own needs and those of its clients.
>
> Construction in the UK is one of the pillars of the domestic economy. The industry in its widest sense is likely to have an output of some £58 billions in 1998, equivalent to roughly 10% of GDP, and employs around 1.4 million people. It is simply too important to be allowed to stagnate.' (Egan, 1998)

The report concluded that whilst the best organisations could achieve very high standards, the industry generally did not deliver consistent quality and value for money. Too often the performance of the industry was unreliable, projects running neither to time nor budget with too much effort and resources being invested in making-good defects, premature repair and replacement and in litigation (see www.rethinkingconstruction.org/rc/report/2.asp).

Methods of procurement which produce buildings which cannot be sold or let, are unprofitable to own or to manage, are derided and unpopular because of poor visual or construction quality and functional failures or, because of disputes or delays and technical problems in the construction process, result in the insolvency of the developer and/or contractor are clearly *unsustainable*. Moreover, economically unviable projects also represent a loss of space, materials and resources.

Today, the majority of construction projects are still run along very traditional lines, even in the light of the findings of the Latham and Egan reports.

PRACTICAL PROBLEMS AND SOLUTIONS, CURRENT APPROACHES, TECHNIQUES AND MODELS

In May 1999, the UK government published a report, *A Better Quality of Life: A Strategy for Sustainable Development in the United Kingdom*. The principal objective of the strategy set out in the report was to achieve 'a better quality of life for everyone, now and for generations to come' (DETR, 1999) (now DEFRA, see www.sustainable-development.gov.uk).

The government went on to identify the construction industry as having

'a huge contribution to make to improving the quality of life; both directly, by providing safe and secure buildings for people to live and work in, and by ensuring that the industry itself works in a sustainable way, husbanding resources, reducing pollution and waste and valuing its workforce' (DTI, 2001) (see www.dti.gov.uk/sustainability and www.dti.gov.uk/construction/ sustain).

The construction research organisation CIRIA has published a number of guides and reports on improving sustainability in the construction industry. In Report 571, *Sustainable Construction Procurement*, the authors identify a number of opportunities for influencing the sustainability of projects (see Figure 4.3).

As well as employing some 1.4 million people and accounting for 10% of UK GDP, the construction industry in the UK produces 30% of controlled wastes and uses some 29% of all industrial energy to produce building materials (CIRIA/Addis & Talbot, 2001). It is, therefore, not surprising that the UK government has identified the industry as playing an important role in its drive toward more sustainable development.

It should be remembered that the industry is not solely concerned with limiting direct environmental harm or impact through such measures as reducing energy use, waste and minimising pollution. Sustainability, in its widest sense, also encompasses economic viability and growth and promoting efficient working practices: the drive towards greater environmental

Opportunities for influencing environmental/ sustainability issues in a project

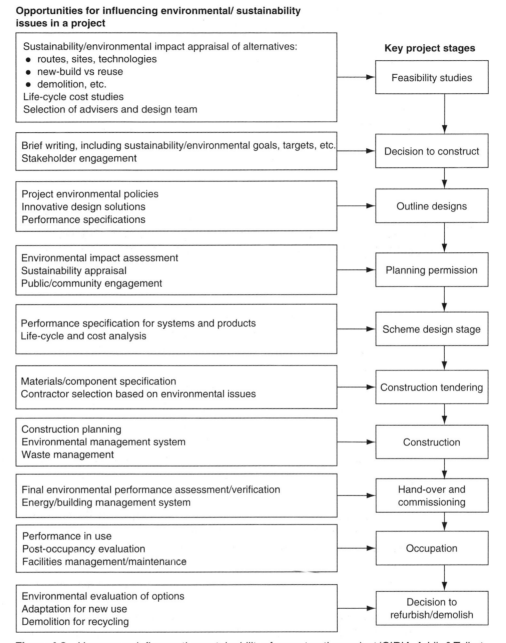

Opportunities	Key project stages
Sustainability/environmental impact appraisal of alternatives: • routes, sites, technologies • new-build vs reuse • demolition, etc. Life-cycle cost studies Selection of advisers and design team	Feasibility studies
Brief writing, including sustainability/environmental goals, targets, etc. Stakeholder engagement	Decision to construct
Project environmental policies Innovative design solutions Performance specifications	Outline designs
Environmental impact assessment Sustainability appraisal Public/community engagement	Planning permission
Performance specification for systems and products Life-cycle and cost analysis	Scheme design stage
Materials/component specification Contractor selection based on environmental issues	Construction tendering
Construction planning Environmental management system Waste management	Construction
Final environmental performance assessment/verification Energy/building management system	Hand-over and commissioning
Performance in use Post-occupancy evaluation Facilities management/maintenance	Occupation
Environmental evaluation of options Adaptation for new use Demolition for recycling	Decision to refurbish/demolish

Figure 4.3   How we can influence the sustainability of a construction project (CIRIA, Addis & Talbot, 2001; Reproduced with permission. This report may be obtained from CIRIA, www.ciria.org.uk).

responsibility forms part of an industry-wide strategy to raise standards of performance generally.

Prompted by the findings of the aforementioned Egan Report in 1998 and, previously, of the Latham Report in 1994, the government has sought to encourage greater efficiency within the construction industry through DTI initiatives such as the Movement for Innovation (M4I) and the Construction Best Practice Programme.

- **The Construction Best Practice Programme** provides support to individuals, companies, organisations and suppliers in the construction industry seeking to improve the way they do business. It is there to offer advice to clients, contractors, consultants, specialists, large or small, public or private. The programme is funded by the Department of Trade and Industry and steered by Government and the construction industry (see www.cbpp.org.uk).
- **The Movement for Innovation** was founded following the work undertaken by the Construction Task Force, chaired by Sir John Egan, in 1997. The Construction Task Force was commissioned to advise the Deputy Prime Minister from the clients' perspective on the opportunities to improve the efficiency and quality of delivery of UK construction, to reinforce the impetus for change and to make the industry more responsive to customer needs. As previously discussed, in July 1998 the Construction Task Force, chaired by Sir John Egan, published their report *Rethinking Construction* (see www.rethinkingconstruction.org/rc/publications/reports.asp). The Construction Task Force highlighted the need for industry to set clear measurable objectives and to create a performance measurement system to aid benchmarking and provide tools for sustained improvement. With these changes, the Construction Task Force believed that the industry could achieve annual improvements of:

  (1)   10% reduction in capital cost and construction time.
  (2)   20% reduction in defects and accidents.
  (3)   10% increase in productivity and profitability.
  (4)   20% increase in predictability of project performance.

- The report also proposed the creation of a 'movement for change' which would be a dynamic, inspirational, non-institutionalised body of people who support the need for radical improvement within the construction industry. *The Movement for Innovation* was subsequently launched in November 1998 to facilitate this cultural change (see www.m4i.org.uk).

Enhanced sustainability forms an important element of many of these programmes to which the industry, including clients, contractors, materials manufacturers and suppliers, is being asked to respond.

As property-owning clients become more aware of their legal, social and environmental responsibilities, contractors may be increasingly asked to provide evidence of their commitment to green building principles through reference to, for example, whole-life costing analysis of key elements of the building. Contractors may also be expected to provide examples of good environmental practice or details of the environmental policy within their company; policies and procedures covering recycling and waste disposal, transport and sources of materials, site pollution, noise and disruption, and health and safety.

For example, in trying to encourage contractors to be more sustainable, the UK Government's Highways Agency now applies a number of checks and indicators to companies bidding to carry out road construction projects. These include asking contractors to provide evidence of:

- Their assessments of the *whole-life* costs of elements of the proposed construction and the materials to be used
- Percentage of products to be provided by suppliers who have adopted *Environmental Management Systems*
- Numbers of accidents on site and complaints from the public and/or other property owners per number of hours worked
- Site fuel and water consumption

(Highways Agency, 2002; also see www.roads.dft.gov.uk/roadnetwork/nextstep/review/5.htm).

Prudential Property Investment Managers are the UK's largest property investment managers with £11 billion under management. They currently ask for evidence of Environmental Management Systems before adding any supplier to their list of building contractors and it is envisaged that '... environmental credentials will become an increasingly important factor over time' (PruPIM, 2002).

Suppliers of building materials are also being encouraged to develop more sustainable practices for reasons of enhanced marketing message ('green is good'), lower energy and transport costs and market differentiation. For example, the Construction Best Practice Programme has provided an Action Sheet for supplier organisations setting out specific actions which can be taken and the benefits which may be obtained as a result (Box 4.1).

The Action Sheet goes on to say:

'Suppliers need to reassure their customers they are not potential environmental liabilities. This is especially important as major construction companies and their clients rationalise their supplier base, allocating a greater percentage of expenditure to fewer suppliers.

It is with suppliers that potential risks to the sustainability of the construction process start, given it is at the raw material extraction stage that some of the greatest sustainability impacts can occur.' (CBPP, 2002; see also www.cbpp.org.uk and for more details)

Freight transport accounts for approximately 10% of total UK energy use, about half of which transports building materials. Contractors are therefore also being encouraged to utilise materials from as many local suppliers as possible. Examples of supplier organisations already taking action using the CBPP guidance sheets include Tarmac Quarry products, Marshalls plc and Timbmet Ltd.

The government has sought to encourage more sustainable practices in construction as part of its 'Framework for Sustainable Development on the Government Estate' (see www.sustainable-development.gov.uk and www.sustainable-development.gov.uk/sdig/improving/index.htm).

The report states that this framework

'is the main vehicle for improving the performance of the Government Estate and will eventually cover all key environmental and social impacts of the running of departments. The Framework also contains guidance to support Departments in achieving targets. All Government Departments have a

Box 4.1   Specific actions and potential benefits of developing more sustainable practices. (CBPP, 2000, reproduced with permission)

Actions	Benefits
Develop sources of environmentally acceptable materials, become involved in sustainable timber organisations such as WWF 1995 'Plus Group'	A positive marketing message. Construction companies are starting to eliminate the use of certain materials, for example the use of wood and wood products that do not come from well-managed forests
Source raw materials locally as much as practicable	Usually results in energy and cost savings, cutting out delays in supply and high transport costs
Talk to customers and encourage them to organise free environmental training – some will do so through the requirements of their corporate environmental commitments	Shows interest and commitment to your customers, increases knowledge of employees, provides differentiation with competitors
Make a commitment to assess and address your impacts, perhaps through formal management systems (ISO14001 and/or EMAS)	This will be an increasingly important feature of supply chain management in keeping existing and gaining new large clients, reassuring those employing you that you are not an environmental liability and demonstrating commitment. Possibly identify financial savings. For example, Shepherd Construction has a policy of prioritising their top 20 suppliers on the basis of environmental considerations and of adopting partnership sourcing principles rather than an adversarial stance
Develop new products and components with lower environmental impact in manufacture, installation and use	An increasing market for these products as clients demand buildings with high environmental performance
If feasible supply reclaimed/recycled materials and use other companies' waste materials as raw materials in your products	Environmentally positive action, growing demand for such materials as customer organizations have their own environmental commitments to meet, possible price differential
Ensure you are knowledgeable of the 'life cycle' (i.e. through extraction, production, transportation, use and disposal) impacts (environmental, social and economic) of the materials in which you deal	It is not necessary to quantify this information, which is a very difficult assessment to achieve. However, if the 'life cycle' is thoroughly thought through it will provide reassurance to customers that you are a competent, aware, outward looking company, wishing to minimise liabilities to all those in the supply chain. This will contribute to winning repeat business from quality customers

significant contribution to make to sustainable development, not just through their policies and services, but through all the support activities that go on every day. Decisions about energy, water and waste management, and the goods and services Departments buy all say a great deal about the Government's commitment to sustainable development.' (DEFRA, 2002)

Under Part F of the report – Procurement – the Government outlines a series of targets and guidance notes under the following headings; all of which can be accessed via the website www.sustainable-development.gov.uk site.

General guidance
- OGC-DEFRA: 'Environmental Issues in Purchasing'
- EC Rules on Green Procurement – Interpretative Communication (4 July 2001)
- Green Guide for Buyers (*Revised*)
- Procurement Guidance Notes
- Green Claims Code
- Suppliers' 'self assessment' checklist

Part G outlines similar guidance for Estates Management:

Guidance
- DTI's Building a Better Quality of Life: A Strategy for More Sustainable Construction
- Guidance on Securing Better Use of Empty Government Homes
- Towards More Sustainable Construction: Green Guide for Managers on the Government Estate
- Towards More Sustainable Construction: How Sustainable Construction can Improve the Performance of Buildings and their Occupants

Tools
- Government Construction Procurement Guidance
- Sustainability Indicator Tool

Related websites: at DEFRA
- DEFRA – Land and Liability Issues

Green taxes

Many of the initiatives discussed, designed to make the construction industry more sustainable, are, of course, voluntary. Such initiatives attempt to persuade the industry to review its current practices in the interests of reduced environmental impact and greater profitability. They are, though, dependent on the goodwill and commitment of individual organisations, often making use of targets to promote changed behaviour.

There are a number of pieces of recent environmental legislation, previously referred to in Chapter 3, which will impact on the construction industry. It is also possible, perhaps even probable, that these will grow in number over time as the Government increasingly adopts a 'stick' rather than 'carrot' approach. Current or imminent legislation relating to property and the environment includes:

- Climate Change Levy; introduced April 2001: energy used by businesses to be taxed at £0.43 per kW for electricity and £0.15 per kW for gas and coal. The objective is to encourage all businesses to become more energy efficient (see www.hmce.gov.uk/business/othertaxes/ccl).
- Aggregates Tax; introduced April 2002: this imposes an additional tax on 'virgin' gravel, crushed rock and sand of £1.60 per tonne. The objective is to encourage the greater use of recycled materials (see www.hmce.gov.uk/business/othertaxes/agg-levy).
- Landfill Tax – incremental increases: this tax is due to be increased from £10 per tonne in annual £1 increments.
- Energy-saving materials VAT cut, from April 2001: VAT to be reduced on some (as yet unspecified) materials from 17.5% to 5%.

Building standards legislation:

- Higher 'U values' in buildings; commenced in 2001: changes to Part L of the Building Regulations to raise the standards of insulation and heating and lighting systems thereby reducing the energy consumption of new buildings.

Other directives and targets which may become law (Building, 2002):

- Government requires that all new government buildings use whole-life cost analysis and post occupancy energy and water consumption review and score an *Excellent* BREEAM rating.
- Renewable energy Government target: by 2010, 10% of all energy comes from renewable sources, i.e. wind and wave power; by 2025, this should increase to 20%.

Key Performance Indicators

As part of *A Better Quality of Life: A Strategy for Sustainable Development in the United Kingdom* (1999), the UK government has developed 15 key headline indicators to monitor and report progress towards sustainable development. They cover what are, for the UK government, the three principal elements of sustainable development, social progress, economic growth and environmental protection, and relate to everyday concerns such as crime, air quality, jobs, wildlife, prosperity and health.

Of the 15 headline indicators for achieving sustainability, three directly relate to the construction industry: H10, air quality; H14, which deals with new homes built on previously developed land; and H15, waste management.

In addition to these headline indicators, there are detailed subsets of 147 National Indicators showing how progress can be measured. These include a series of Environmental Performance Indicators which provide detailed analysis and targets relating to, for example, CO_2 emissions from buildings (e.g. see www.kpizone.com and refer to Environmental Indicators – Carbon Dioxide Emissions: measures in $kgCO_2/m^2/year$ the carbon dioxide produced as a result of the energy from fossil fuels consumed).

Four of these are relevant to the construction industry:

- Primary aggregates used per unit of construction waste.
- Amount of secondary (recycled) aggregates used compared to virgin aggregate.
- CO_2 emissions by end user (energy used).
- Construction and demolition waste going to landfill.

The full document, which includes the available results for these indicators, can be found at www.kpizone.com/homepage.htm or via www.sustainable-development.gov.uk. The full document sets out both current levels and targets and shows how assessments of indicators against target are derived. It is in response to these targets that legislation can be formulated, enacted and reviewed in the light of subsequent progress.

See www.sustainable-development.gov.uk/indicators/headline for a detailed explanation, graphs, targets and examples of full list of KPIs. In Figure 4.4, the amount of waste currently reused in the UK rather than going to landfill or incineration is analysed.

As stated, one of the key recommendations of the Egan Report was the expansion of the construction industry's Best Practice Programme and the formation of the Movement for Innovation Board (M4I), involving individuals and organisations committed to improving the performance of construction by stimulating clients and industry to work together.

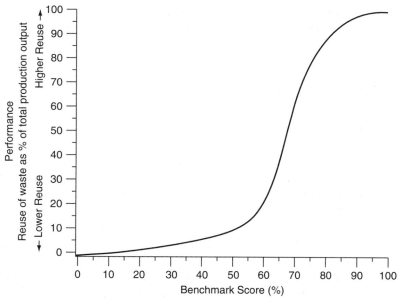

Figure 4.4 Construction products KPI: environment – reuse of waste.

The amount of waste from the manufacturing of construction products recovered, reused or recycled, expressed as a percentage of the total production output. The graph line shows the range of results obtained from the annual national survey.

(Source: Construction Products Ltd.; email: enquiries@constprod.org.uk or see website: www.constprod.org.uk. Also see www.sustainable-development.gov.uk/indicators/headline/h15 for construction waste specific information.)

Therefore, in addition to the indicators described above, and as part of the activities supporting the implementation of 'Rethinking Construction', the Movement for Innovation (M4I) has devised a series of other Key Performance Indicators linked to demonstration projects. Aimed specifically at improving economic and technical performance, these indicators compliment M4I's Environmental Performance Indicators; together, these allow not only individual project monitoring but also the development of benchmarks for the rest of the industry.

Use of demonstration projects or 'case histories' allow construction companies to learn from the experience and successes of others working on similar building projects. Details of some 75 from a total of 300 such project case histories are available at www.m4i.org.uk/m4i/publications/casehistories and include examples which deal with such problems as construction waste reduction, brownfield sites and Sick Building Syndrome.

Such indicators help monitor progress for achieving sustainability and enable the industry to work towards the key overall objectives of:

- More efficient and reduced use of **resources**.
- Prevention of **pollution**.
- Reduction and control of **waste**.
- Good **workforce management**.

Minimising the use of resources

(1) Land

In terms of use of resources, it could be argued that land is the most important resource of all. In a relatively small but densely populated country such as the UK, property development over time can have very major impacts through infrastructure requirements such as road building and can cause the loss of natural habitats, agricultural land and visual and recreational amenities.

As discussed in Chapter 1, the first initiatives to encourage private house builders to utilise 'brown' land (previously developed sites – most commonly found in and around existing towns and cities) date from 2000. Government targets for the development of brown land currently stand at 60%. The House Builders' Federation points out that developers such as Barratt (70%) and Crest (95%) are already exceeding these targets (Boyle, 2001). Prior to the setting of such targets, the location of new residential development was very much a case of developers, whilst working within Development Plans, being given a good deal of latitude in deciding what type of housing they wished to build and where to locate it, in response to market demand.

The 'One Million Sustainable Homes' initiative, sponsored by the World Wide Fund for Nature, the campaign to construct and refurbish one million low environmental impact homes by 2012, will no doubt give very careful consideration to the proposed locations of projects.

(2) *Building materials*

The day-to-day management of the construction process – organising labour, plant, equipment and materials – has traditionally been the responsibility of the contractor with relatively little input from either the design team or the client organisation. Builders have generally used their own preferred sources of building materials, have dealt with the disposal of site waste and have been responsible for site safety. However, as client organisations and designers have been taking on greater environmental responsibility for all aspects of the project, builders too are being asked to look at the way the construction process is managed in terms of minimising environmental impact.

The production and transportation of building materials in the UK accounts for the consumption of a significant proportion of the UK's energy. As previously stated, around 30% of industrial energy and approximately 10% of total UK energy is used in materials production. Building materials also involve the use of considerable quantities of raw materials (over 90% of non-energy producing materials extracted in the UK are used in construction) whilst some production processes contribute to the levels of VOCs, NO_x and SO_2 in the atmosphere (Anderson *et al.*, 2002).

For these reasons, it is important that contractors should seek to minimise the quantities of materials used through adopting such measures as (Baldwin *et al.*, 1998):

- Planning construction processes to suit the standard modules for materials to minimise construction waste.
- Utilising recycled materials, preferably from local suppliers and avoiding excessive transportation.
- Ensuring that suppliers understand the required environmental standards (e.g. timber from sustainably managed sources) through clear product and standards descriptions.

As previously discussed, client organisations are beginning to apply pressure to contractors to obtain materials from environmentally responsible businesses by asking them to state, for example, the percentage of products by value provided by firms with Environmental Management Systems. According to the Construction Best Practice Programme (CBPP, 2000), other types of actions which can be taken by materials suppliers include:

- Use of warning labels on products which contain ozone depleting substances (ODSs) or volatile organic compounds (VOCs).
- Development of sources of environmentally acceptable materials such as for timber from sustainable sources (e.g. WWF 1995 'Plus Group', SFC or Forests Forever).
- Sourcing as many raw materials as locally as possible.
- Encouraging customers to organise/participate in environmental training.
- Assess and address impacts of company through formal management systems such as ISO 14001.

- Developing new products and systems with lower environmental impacts in manufacture, installation and use.
- If possible, supply reclaimed/recycled materials as raw materials in manufacture.
- Research life cycle of products which are supplied (extraction, production, transportation, use and disposal and their social, environment and economic impacts).

(3) Consumption of water

In general, the main issues of concern regarding the use of water are the depletion, disruption or pollution of water sources, including rivers and their ecosystems (Anderson *et al.*, 2002). In practice, this means that contractors should plan their site operations to minimise the consumption of water, to install water-efficient sanitary facilities and ensure that site operatives understand the necessity of such efficiency measures (Baldwin *et al.*, 1998).

Practical procedures and policies designed to minimise water pollution and to protect the ecology of the site and surrounding areas can be derived from the 'best practice' notes provided by organisations such as the Environment Agency (see www.environment-agency.gov.uk/business/techguide). Once such protection measures are formulated, it is essential that they are clearly communicated to the site staff and that they are inspected frequently.

(4) Use of energy

Energy consumption is important in terms of both the use of non-renewable resources, such as oil or coal used to generate electricity, and in terms of climate change, due to the production of greenhouse gases such as CO_2 and other pollution caused by the combustion of such fuels. For these reasons, minimising energy use on site (e.g. by equipment and machinery) is important and client organisations may therefore in future ask contractors for evidence of site fuel used against value of work carried out as an indicator of greener construction policies.

Builders and developers will, of course, have to comply with the new higher standards of Part L of the building regulations designed to reduce energy consumption in buildings. It is also possible that as an additional requirement, developers will have to provide evidence of the amount of CO_2 emissions produced by the end user of the building in order to ensure that the project is low-energy in use over time.

(5) Use of aggregates

The term aggregates is used to describe the sand, gravel and rock normally used in road bases, paths and in the manufacture of concrete. The Aggregates Levy, introduced in April 2002, is designed to tax the environmental costs associated with quarrying: noise, dust, visual intrusion and loss of amenity and damage to biodiversity. The ultimate objective is to reduce aggregate use and encourage the use of alternative materials where possible, such as recycled aggregates.

A levy of £1.60 per tonne is now due on many aggregates purchased by building contractors although there are exemptions such as materials used in the production of lime and cement. It is expected that the tax will raise some £385 million in the first year – all of which will be returned through a cut in employer National Insurance contributions with no net gain for the Exchequer, the construction industry needing to remain as financially competitive as possible (see www.hmce.gov.uk/business/othertaxes/agg-levy and www.energy-efficiency.gov.uk for further details on this and other government initiatives).

Again, as an indicator of green policy implementation, clients' organisations may in future ask prospective contractors to list the actual amounts of primary aggregates used per unit of construction value or amount of secondary/recycled aggregates used compared to virgin aggregates.

Reducing pollution

Although the handling of pollutants and toxic materials on site is controlled under both the Health and Safety at Work Act (1974) and the Control of Substances Hazardous to Health Regulations (1988), contractors may, in the future, need to provide evidence of 'best practice' site pollution management regarding, say, the careful disposal on site of solvents, paints, etc. and ground water pollution control measures. (Guidance can be provided by a number of agencies including the Environment Agency.)

Reducing and managing waste

As discussed in Chapter 3 on green buildings, approximately 29% of all UK controlled waste is generated by the construction industry, each year (Baldwin *et al.*, 1998), amounting to some 70 million tonnes. Although 12 million tonnes of demolition materials are recycled or reused each year, the majority for low-grade uses such as road sub-base construction or land engineering, it is estimated that building contractors could recycle a further 6 million tonnes.

Of all the construction waste generated 30% is disposed of by landfill, incineration or other methods of disposal and 13 million tonnes of new materials ordered for use on site are thrown away unused! (the equivalent of between 10% and 30% of all waste falls into this category) (Baldwin *et al.*, 1998).

There are also significant cost penalties in the wasteful disposal of materials which can still be reused in building. The overall costs of waste can be split into the cost of disposal, whether by landfill or incineration, and the value of the raw materials. Studies have revealed that the value of the raw materials lost in construction waste can be between 10 and 20 times the cost of reuse or more efficient disposal! Case studies have also shown that it is possible to reduce waste disposal costs by between 20% and 60% by effective waste segregation (CIRIA *et al.*, 2001).

In a study by Stuart Coventry of Scott Wilson carried out on behalf of CIRIA (CIRIA, 2001), it was concluded that waste management in construction could be improved through:

- Waste management being taken into account in the design process in terms of standard lengths and quantities in which materials are delivered to site.
- Ordering from suppliers who minimise packaging, supply high quality materials and who can deliver close to time of use in order to avoid storage and therefore possible damage, etc.
- Choosing subcontractors early and involving them in the process and giving them more responsibility.
- Encouraging contractors to be more proactive in waste management.
- Allowing contractors more time to select their team carefully (suppliers, sub-contractors) to allow the contractor to go for a higher standard.
- Design to deconstruct by buying and building simple – fewer 'composites'.
- Less landfill tax = less waste management = good project management.
- Measuring sustainability in companies by indicators such as tonnes of waste going to landfill per £ turnover.

Improving workforce management

The Latham Report made some 30 recommendations for improving the efficiency of construction in the UK and ending 'the culture of conflict and inefficiency that dogs Britain's biggest industry' (Latham, 1994). The report identifies a number of structural problems within the industry including poor training and productivity and legal and contractual arrangements often leading to adversarial disputes and a failure to resolve such disputes in an efficient way.

Before discussing possible ways in which the industry could become more efficient in terms of contract administration, that is the running of construction projects on site, it is necessary to describe the most common approaches currently taken to this aspect of the procurement process.

Common types of contractual arrangement

As previously discussed, in the UK, the traditional model for most commercial, industrial and other non-residential projects has been for the architect to act as the lead consultant within the design team; to act, in effect, as the 'project manager'. This project management role involves establishing the project priorities, co-ordinating the other consultants and acting as the client's main representative during the execution of the project.

Once the designs and specification have been completed, the client and the design team agree the selection of a short-list of prospective contractors, who will then bid or *tender* for the project and, in most cases, the lowest bid wins.

The lowest bidder will then enter into a formal contract with the client organisation to construct the building according to the drawings, specifications and/or bill of quantities (a written description of the values, quantities and standards of materials and components to be used). As part of this contract, the builder will organise site access, security, insurance, labour (including sub-contract labour) and materials in such a way as to deliver the building by an agreed date and at an agreed price. Variations or changes to the design, materials used, completion dates or cost incurred must be agreed between all the parties as the work progresses.

Many builders extensively utilise *sub-contract* labour, particularly on large projects. In the past, many builders employed the vast majority of their own staff on a permanent basis. However, the typical contractor today retains only a core of permanent, experienced tradesmen and site managers and simply buys in additional bricklayers, carpenters and joiners, painters, etc. as required for specific projects on a short-term basis. Employing these sub-contractors may mean employing individuals or, on occasions, a company of, say, plumbers or heating contractors to undertake an entire section of the work. Often, prior to appointing such sub-contractors, the main builder or *main contractor* would ask a number of sub-contractors to bid for the work by submitting their own tenders before choosing the sub-contractor who is cheapest or best value for money.

There are a number of alternative models used in the UK, including Design and Build and Management Contracting. The team may also be augmented by use of a Project Manager, who is not part of the design team, as the lead client representative.

The project manager

The project manager is employed directly by the client organisation to safeguard the latter's interests and whilst he or she may sometimes be an architect, quantity surveying is more common as a professional background. The project manager is there to co-ordinate the project without any direct involvement in the design or specification of the project. The project manager is responsible for the overall co-ordination of the project in terms of flow of information, communication between the different parties and ensuring that the project is completed to the correct standard, on time and within budget.

Design and build

In a design and build contract, a builder takes on the responsibility for both the construction of the project and its design. By employing his or her own architects and engineers, a design and build contractor can offer a 'one-stop' or 'package deal' service in which the client will only have to work with one organisation which undertakes to design and build a building to an agreed specification often for a guaranteed price.

There have been questions raised over the design quality of some design and build projects as they tend to be 'cost driven' rather than being focused on high design standards and detailed client requirements. However, many client organisations now say that they prefer this more straightforward, practical approach to procurement which often also provides 'cost certainty' allowing them to budget accurately for future expenditure.

This cost certainty is an important benefit for clients. Once a design and build contractor undertakes to deliver a project at a fixed cost, the financial risk shifts from the client to the contractor. Whereas under a normal contract, unforeseen extra work is most often paid for by the client, in design and build, unforeseen additional work is part of the risk taken by the contractor, who would, if prudent, have built in a contingency sum to cover this eventuality.

Management contracting

A vital part of the building contractor's job is the programming, co-ordination and management of labour, skilled tradespersons and materials – the management of the building project. These are acknowledged as important and specific sets of skills and in management contracts these skills become a service which is paid for separately.

In management contracts, the main building contractor *manages* the construction of the building – the building work is undertaken by a series of separate, independent sub-contractors. The project is divided into a series of *work packages* which are tendered separately, e.g. foundations, steelwork, external walls, roofing, electrical, decorations, etc. The main contractor's role in this is to act as co-ordinator ensuring that all the various work package sub-contractors start and finish at the right time.

The advantage to the client of this arrangement is that projects can commence on site before all the detailed drawings and designs for the whole building have been completed; this can potentially save many weeks in project programmes and, for this reason, management contracts are sometimes known as 'fast-track'.

The disadvantage of these contracts is that they tend to be more expensive and there is more work for the consultants as they have to organise not just one tendering procedure – drawings, specification and contract documents – but many, often resulting in higher fees.

Accelerating change

It would be reasonable to expect that given the long tradition of construction in the UK, the selection of a builder and the construction of a building project according to a set of drawings and instructions, under the terms of tried-and-tested legal contracts, would be relatively straightforward. However, according to many observers, there continue to be a number of widespread 'structural' problems within the industry acting as barriers to the smooth running of this process. According to the Egan Report:

'The UK construction industry at its best is excellent. Its capability to deliver the most difficult and innovative projects matches that of any other construction industry in the world. Nonetheless, there is deep concern that the industry as a whole is under-achieving. It has low profitability and invests too little in capital, research and development and training. Too many of the industry's clients are dissatisfied with its overall performance.' (Egan, 1998; see also www.dti.gov.uk/construction/rethink/report)

There seems compelling evidence to suggest that far too many projects in the UK cost more than they should, are of poor quality, contain an unacceptable level of defects, are often delayed and result in an excessive level of disputes and litigation. At the root of many of these problems is a culture of mistrust; far from the parties approaching construction projects in a spirit of collaboration with a common interest in delivering a high-quality, successful and profitable building, professional relationships are often adversarial and litigation-conscious.

There are a number of factors which may help explain why the construction process is subject to such difficulties. In many respects, every project is a prototype, each, in its own way, unique. For example, the client, design team and contractor may never have worked together before and may have different working practices. They are also likely to be building at a site or location where neither the designers nor the contractors have built before and the design will almost certainly be a one-off, perhaps involving innovative technologies and materials.

Even if building designs and materials are 'standard' and are familiar to the project team, they may not have been used on that particular site and ground conditions or site access may be problematic. Also, market conditions may change during the procurement stage; availability and quality of labour and materials may be affected or the labour employed may be inexperienced or poorly trained.

A project may also involve many different parties; the designers, quantity surveyors and engineers, contractors and sub-contractors, suppliers of materials and equipment, the Local Authority Development and Building Control officers and the client organisation. Each group may have different priorities and interests and may not function as an integrated team sharing the same objectives.

Finally, the project may be worth many millions of pounds and so the risk of financial loss can be high; delays may result in loss of rents and additional expenditure for clients seeking to let or occupy premises. Because of this, any delays to projects shown to be due to the builder's inefficiency or poor workmanship may mean that the contractor has to pay financial penalties in order to compensate the client organisation. The project may have been priced very competitively and the contractor therefore cannot afford for the work to be made more complex or be delayed by, for example, indecision or poor quality information on the part of the client or the design team. In such cases, the contractor will request an *extension of time*; a delay paid for by the client. Such financial risks can make the parties highly 'defensive' in their working practices, with the attribution of blame for delays or other problems becoming the priority rather than foreseeing and preventing problems or finding solutions.

The latest report produced by the Strategic Forum for Construction, *Rethinking Construction – Accelerating Change* (CBP, 2002), both sets out the progress made since the original Egan report (1998) and recommends action for the future.

Many of the key findings build on previous reports and are an attempt to begin to overcome some of the problems associated with the current adversarial system of procurement. The report recommends:

- Greater use of 'integrated teams' comprising design team consultants, contractors, manufacturers and suppliers. Such teams will resemble the Design and Build teams, but in this case, the wider team will be involved from the outset of the project and will take responsibility for the project as a team. This maximises access to pooled expertise, the latest R&D and newest products, and encourages standardisation; all of which improves quality and reliability.
- Teams having an ongoing 'partnering' relationship with clients, not being appointed on a project-by-project basis but, say, for a five-year period. In this way, working relationships and methods are developed and consolidated over time. Short-termism is replaced by a long-term approach. This apparent lack of competitiveness in the procurement process can be 'sold' even to the public sector on the basis of value for money, whole-life performance rather than lowest price.
- Project insurance to be available to underwrite the whole team. In this way, it is acknowledged that construction projects are high-risk and therefore problems are insured against rather than becoming a source of dispute and litigation between the parties.
- Greater use of 'Quality Mark' and 'Investors in People' type QA schemes as evidence of good practice and to stamp out the 'construction informal economy' within the industry.
- Improved health and safety, education and training and marketing of the industry through such initiatives as recent graduates undertaking ambassadorial work as 'Young Presenters' in schools and colleges.
- Improving environmental performance through whole-life appraisal, reduced energy consumption and reduced waste.

As the report states:

'The Strategic Forum's 2002 report *Rethinking Construction – Accelerating Change* sets a target for 20% of construction projects by value to be undertaken by integrated teams and supply chains by end 2004, this figure to reach 50% by end 2007. It commits the Forum to produce an "Integration Toolkit" by April 2003 to help the industry to achieve this target. The brief for the toolkit is set out in full in paragraphs 5.10 to 5.13 in *Accelerating Change*. A working party of the Forum has now produced a *consultation version of the toolkit* for review by potential users of such a toolkit and other industry stakeholders (see www.cbpp.org.uk/acceleratingchange to access this information).

The toolkit provides guidance on processes and methods, culture and activities, and tools and techniques for integrating whole-life (sustainable) activities of the UK construction industry. The toolkit is aspirational. It represents a summary of the innovations, achievements and best practice of the UK construction industry.

The toolkit is based around the following culture and values: empowerment of people, sharing learning, open communication, trust and integrity, no blame. From a wide-ranging review of successful approaches the Forum has identified the following critical success factors of integration: early involvement, selection by value, the use of common processes and tools, performance measurement, long-term relations based on continuous improvement, and commercial arrangements that facilitate these.

Accelerating Change distinguishes between the integration of supply teams (which include the client, and are formed to provide solutions that meet clients' requirements and then often disbanded) and supply chains (which are long-term relationships often involving design, procurement, inventory management and product installation). The toolkit continues this distinction, but it should be noted that the supply chains' half of the toolkit is not yet as developed. This should not detract from the value of this consultation process.

An important feature of the toolkit is its refusal, in general, to use old labels for people and their roles in the process. All too often, people read in their existing paradigm and they see words which they believe they understand, no matter what effort is made to describe these ideas differently. For this reason some of the language is new, we aim to require people to stop and take stock of the concepts being unveiled, creating and associating a new paradigm.' (CBP, 2002)

TECHNICAL GUIDANCE

When seeking guidance relating to a particular construction problem or area of operations, the first step must always be to ensure that all current statutory regulations and controls are fully understood. Standards within construction are being constantly reviewed and, in some cases, modified on a regular basis; this is particularly true in the case of construction-related environmental issues at present.

Guidance on environmental policy and best practice within the construction industry can be obtained through the CBP, M4I and the sources quoted in this chapter.

POSSIBLE FUTURE DEVELOPMENTS

Possibly the most reliable indicators of likely future developments in the construction industry can be found within the current strategies and objectives of the Construction Best Practice Programme and the Movement for Innovation. In addition to those issues already discussed within the programme for Accelerating Change, a number of possible future developments can be identified:

- Ongoing improvements to health and safety practices which may include assessment of competence of all those working at height, more pre-assembly and prefabrication therefore less site processing.

- Greater efforts to change the image of the construction industry – greater skills levels, more highly qualified operatives with engineering and business backgrounds, fewer unskilled workers as buildings increasingly become the product of off-site, high-tech factory processes.
- Enhanced in-post training – more companies to sign up for such programmes (the take-up is only 15% at present, the target is 50%).
- Better advice available for clients through Constructionline – guidance, toolkits, use of company registers. The target is for 80% of public sector clients to use Constructionline by 2005/6.
- The UK Government is to accelerate the drive to promote greater sustainability through such initiatives as the Property and Construction Directorate, the aim of which is to review the management of property owned or funded by the Government. This involves 'construction and property related procurement, including issues such as hiring consultants, health and safety, energy and environment and procuring new space and disposing of surplus... innovative solutions to workspace issues, the procurement of PPP/PFI schemes and the application of flexible working patterns also have an impact on opportunities to achieve better value for money.' (See www.property. gov.uk/services/construction/gccp or www.ogc.gov.uk)

LEARNING MATERIALS

Some questions and issues for discussion

(1) **If you were the Chief Executive of a large UK construction company, why might you decide to recommend that your organisation adopted greener working practices and what might be the possible obstacles to this?**

Reasons for going green: the company may 'go green' in response to increasing pressure through legislation (CCL, Landfill Tax), client demand (more clients insisting on green credentials held by organisations with whom they do business), government pressure on the industry (government has identified construction as having a key role to play in the light of Kyoto targets), reduced health and safety and legal liability risks, improved public image as a socially and environmentally responsible company.

Barriers: expertise within company may be limited, and a change of culture is required; priorities and approach to management may need to change and may involve use of EMAS; it could require additional investment; it may require a change of business partners, e.g. suppliers who do not comply with raised environmental standards may need to be replaced.

(2) **What legal measures has the UK Government introduced or is considering introducing in order to encourage the construction industry to become more environmentally responsible?**

- *Climate Change Levy; introduced April 2001*: Energy used by businesses to be taxed at £0.43 per kW for electricity and £0.15 per kW for gas and coal. The objective is to encourage all businesses to become more energy efficient.
- *Aggregates Tax, introduced April 2002*: this imposes an additional tax on 'virgin' gravel, crushed rock and sand of £1.60 per tonne. The objective is to encourage more use of recycled materials.
- *Landfill Tax, incremental increases*: this tax is due to be increased from £10.00 per tonne in annual £1.00 increments.
- *Energy-saving materials, VAT cut from April 2001*: VAT to be reduced on some (as yet unspecified) materials from 17.5% to 5%.
- *Higher 'U values' in buildings, commenced in 2001*: changes to Part L of the Building Regulations to raise the standards of insulation and heating and lighting systems thereby reducing the energy consumption of new buildings.

Other directives and targets which may become law:

- All new Government buildings should use whole-life cost analysis and post occupancy energy and water consumption review and score a BREEAM rating of 'excellent'.
- Government has a target for renewable energy which states that, by 2010, 10% of all energy should come from renewable sources, that is wind and wave power; by 2025, this should increase to 20%.

(3) Give three examples of key findings from each of the Latham and Egan Reports into the construction industry

Three examples might include the following:

Latham (1994)
- The industry was urged to 'improve its public image' and reminded that 'equal opportunities require urgent attention.'
- Improvements in productivity and teamwork were also recommended.
- Structures of building contracts tribunals and types of contracts used needed review.

Egan (1998) – the report concluded that whilst the best organisations could achieve very high standards:
- The industry generally did not deliver consistent quality and value for money.
- Too often the performance of the industry was unreliable, projects running neither to time nor to budget.
- Too much effort and resources being invested in making-good defects and premature repair and replacement.
- The industry was dogged by a culture of dispute and litigation.
- (See www.rethinkingconstruction.org/rc/report/2.asp)

(4)   **Describe three areas of operations in which building contractors may be required to show that they are working in an environmentally responsible way**

Three such areas might include the following:

- An assessment of the *whole-life* costs of elements of the proposed construction and the materials to be used.
- Percentage of products to be provided by suppliers who have adopted *environmental management systems*.
- Numbers of accidents on site and complaints from the public and/or other property owners per number of hours worked.
- Site fuel and water consumption.
- How sites are managed to deal with the impacts of noise and pollution on neighbouring properties and occupiers.
- How materials have been supplied from reputable sources and have been manufactured to the correct standard.
- How deleterious materials found in existing buildings during demolition or refurbishment works, such as asbestos and lead-based paints, continue to be handled and disposed of according to the correct health and safety procedures.
- How site operations are monitored to measure the extent to which energy and water use is minimised.

(5)   **What are the key environmental issues which should be taken into account in the specification of building materials and what measures can suppliers take to enhance their green credentials?**

- Planning construction processes to suit the standard modules for materials to minimise construction waste.
- Utilising recycled materials, preferably from local suppliers and avoiding excessive transportation.
- Ensuring that suppliers understand the required environmental standards (e.g. timber from sustainably managed sources) through clear product and standards descriptions.

According to the Construction Best Practice Programme, other types of actions which can be taken by materials suppliers include:

- Use of warning labels on products which contain ozone depleting substances (ODSs) or volatile organic compounds (VOCs).
- Development of sources of environmentally acceptable materials, such as for timber from sustainable sources (e.g. World Wildlife Fund for Nature 1995 'Plus Group', SFC or Forests Forever).
- Sourcing of as many raw materials as possible locally.
- Encouraging customers to organise or participate in environmental training.
- Assessing and addressing impacts of the company through formal management systems such as ISO 14001.

- Development of new products and systems with lower environmental impacts in manufacture, installation and use.
- Where possible, supplying of reclaimed/recycled materials as raw materials in manufacture.
- Researching the life cycle of products which are supplied (extraction, production, transportation, use and disposal) and their social, environmental and economic impacts.

Examples of media coverage of issues relating to the UK construction industry

(1)   **Many large construction companies are also volume house builders and developers. The building of new housing schemes on recycled land has not achieved the land use densities envisaged by the government. In the press release below (28 May 2002), the Planning Minister discusses the current statistics.**

- Why should it be the case that developers are not achieving their targets? Why might developers seem less than enthusiastic about high-density development when profits are likely to be higher than those achievable in lower density projects?

GOVERNMENT ON TARGET FOR HOUSING ON BROWNFIELD LAND

The Government has welcomed figures released today showing 61 per cent of new housing has been built on previously developed land and through conversion of existing buildings in 2001, exceeding the Government target of 60 per cent by 2008.

Planning Minister, Lord Falconer, said many Local Planning Authorities had made a valuable contribution in increasing the re-use of land for housing.

'Reaching the target at such an early stage shows the policy approach set out in Planning Policy Guidance Note 3 – Housing (PPG3) is beginning to work. But clearly there is much more to do to maintain this recycling level over the coming years.

The challenge is to continue to find brownfield sites to accommodate increasing numbers of houses. Each region must play its part in sustaining the rate.'

Lord Falconer said the policies in PPG3 also promoted more efficient use of land through increased densities with good design, although there had been no increase.

'In 2001, dwellings were still built at an average of only 25 dwellings per hectare, compared with the 30 to 50 recommended in PPG3. More than half of the land used for new dwellings is built at density of less than 20 dwellings per hectare. A number of examples of new, well-designed developments built at high density prove that we can do much better.'

The Minister stressed that there needed to be a continued push towards more efficient use of land.

Notes: (1) The 'percentage of new dwellings on previously developed land' is also a headline indicator in the Government's *Indicators for a Strategy for Sustainable Development for the UK* (further information can be found at: www.sustainable-development.gov.uk). (2) The new figures are included in *Land use change in England: residential development to 2001–LUCS-17*, a statistical release by the Department for Transport, Local Government and the Regions. Full results of land use change in England is available on the DTLR website: www.dtlr.gov.uk later in the year.

---

(2) Construction companies are, first and foremost, commercial businesses; the largest of them are quoted on the stock exchange. The article shown below (13 May 2002) describes a new initiative from Morley Fund Management, in which leading FTSE companies are ranked according to their green credentials. This Business Sustainability Matrix is based on a range of social and environmental criteria. As evidence of the growing importance of green issues to business, Morley also included a 'diary' of recent key business initiatives and directives driven by environmental considerations

- Why might an investment fund management company carry out and publish such an appraisal?
- What might be the effect on companies rated at the bottom end of the scale? How would you expect leading construction companies in the UK to perform in such an assessment?
- What does this tell us about likely future priorities within the business community?

MORLEY FUND MANAGEMENT PUBLISHES SUSTAINABILITY MATRIX – RATES FTSE 100 ACCORDING TO SOCIAL AND ENVIRONMENTAL CRITERIA

Morley Fund Management (Morley) today releases its first Sustainability Matrix. This Matrix ranks FTSE 100 companies according to social and environmental criteria and provides a new measure of business sustainability. These gradings:

- Encourage companies to improve their Social and Environmental Performance.
- Protect and increase Shareholder Value by adding another tool for the analysis of companies.
- For the first time provide clear and transparent analysis of companies' social and environmental policies.
- Encourage and stimulate debate and continue raising awareness of Corporate Social Responsibility.

Companies such as Glaxo-Smith-Kline (A2), BG (B2), United Utilities (B2) and Pearson (A3) all gain strong grades on product sustainability.

Management vision and strategy is graded from 1 to 5. Companies awarded a grade 1 have a clear vision of sustainable development and are actively working to achieve it. The poorest grade, 5, denotes management policies and practices incompatible with sustainable development and the concept of corporate responsibility. BP (D2), Shell (D2) and Allied Domecq (D2) gain strong gradings for management, vision and strategy. No FTSE 100 company gains a 1 or 5 grade.

'Many companies now recognise the long term financial risks they face by ignoring environmental and social impacts, but believe the City to be entirely uninterested in sustainable development. Publishing the Matrix will contribute to the debate on the compatibility between economic prosperity and sustainable development. It demonstrates for the first time, that the City has a vested interest in working with companies to develop an economic model where sustained returns are rooted in sustainable development.'

Diary of key environment-related business events since 2000

Date	Event
July 2000	Amendment to 1995 Pensions Act requiring SRI disclosure issued in UK
July 2000	UN Global Compact launched – international business community commits to principles of sustainable development

Continued

January 2001	Regulations requiring SRI disclosure issued in Belgium
March 2001	Myners Report issued in the UK advocating shareholder activism
June 2001	EU begins development of CSR strategy for Europe
July 2001	178 nations commit to Kyoto Global Treaty on Climate
July 2001	UK Company Law Review issued advocating greater accountability for environmental and social impacts
August 2001	Regulations requiring SRI disclosure issued in Germany
October 2001	Association of British Insurers issues SRI disclosure guidelines
February 2002	World Economic Forum – International Business Community subscribe to Statement of Corporate Citizenship
March 2002	French law makes environmental and social reporting mandatory
April 2002	Global Reporting Initiative advocating international environmental and social disclosure becomes permanent institution
September 2002	World Summit on Sustainable Development, Johannesburg

See www.morleyfm.com for more information and a full list of the companies who appeared on the matrix. Reproduced with permission.

(3) Many construction products are manufactured using raw materials obtained through mining and quarrying processes both in the UK and overseas. The mining and quarrying industry has the potential to make a huge contribution in terms of reducing its environmental impacts from wastes, resources depletion, transport and the impacts on wildlife and the natural landscape. Read the article below (1 May 2002) and discuss some practical examples of ways in which this industry might become more sustainable and identify the possible barriers to such changes.

MAPPING OUT A SUSTAINABLE FUTURE FOR THE MINING AND MINERALS INDUSTRY

The findings of a two-year research project on how the mining and minerals industry can maximise its contribution to sustainable development were unveiled today at a press briefing in London.

Recognising that the mining and minerals industry needed to become more engaged in sustainable development, ten of the world's largest mining companies, all members of the WBCSD, established the Global Mining Initiative (GMI) in 1999. Further joined by 20 additional companies and non-industry organisations such as the World Bank, UNEP, IUCN, universities and other institutions, the GMI commissioned the IIED to conduct an analysis on the full mineral cycle, from mine to waste and re-use, in order to identify the opportunities and challenges for the industry to become more sustainable.

See www.wbcsd.org which is the website for The World Business Council for Sustainable Development. Reproduced with permission.

(4) The level of recruitment of skilled personnel, trainees and graduates into the construction industry is still very much an issue of concern. A poor 'image' is often cited as one reason that a career in construction appears less appealing than many other options. The article below by Stephen Hoare from *The Guardian* of 23 October 2001 discusses the problem.

- Do you think that the article has identified the main reasons why recruitment is poor and skills shortages remain a problem? What other factors may help explain this trend?

- How do you think the image of construction in the UK compares with, say, the German or French construction industry?
- What measures could be taken to address recruitment and training problems within the UK industry?

BRICKS 'N' MORTARBOARDS

Forget the muddy boots. Construction workers are building a hi-tech future, says Stephen Hoare.

The ribbon has just been snipped and the gates flung wide at yet another palace of concrete and glass vaunted to be the vanguard of computer technology. Inside, those seated ranks of young people looking fixedly at screens are no doubt destined for a lifetime as keyboard drones.

Actually, no. They are trainee plumbers, sparks, chippies and brickies learning their trades in a new kind of skills centre which opened on Friday as part of National Construction Week. Stourhead College in the Black Country has invested £8.5 m in what it bravely terms an advanced technology centre (ATC) where trainees can learn their crafts using the latest computer-aided design (CAD) and 3D simulations.

Often pilloried as a 'muddy boots' career, construction has been itching to reinvent itself as a hi-tech industry and this seems a move in the right direction. The new ATC facility at Brierley Hills business park expects to attract more than 2,000 full- and part-time students a year to study built environment courses. The centre will become a learning hub for the construction industry and IBM has already chosen it as a showcase for its latest product technology. But does this learning environment reflect the industry young people will be joining?

The construction industry training board has repeated its annual warning about the declining number of trainees. The industry is 15 000 skilled operatives short – even more than at the last count.

So why the worsening skills shortage? Construction training has an in-built problem: the high failure rate – which a new emphasis on IT may even exacerbate. Construction workers need to pass key skills before they can gain a vocational qualification and many never make it. Mark Lunn says: 'Sixty to 70% go into recognised employment after training; the rest find work for cash in hand – the move into the informal economy.'

The 'informal economy' is thriving, as any homeowner who has ever paid cash on small jobs – to avoid VAT – will tell you. It is just that these workers never show up on the CITB's skills shortage calculations. The Construction Confederation, which represents all major contractors, is calling for a crackdown on unskilled, unqualified construction workers. From 2003, all work sites must employ only fully-certificated workers.

Reproduced with permission from Hoare (2001).

REFERENCES

Anderson, J., Shiers, D. & Sinclair, M. (2002) *The Green Guide to Specification*, Blackwell Science, Oxford.

Baldwin, R., Yates, A., Howard, N. & Rao, S. (1998) *BREEAM for Offices '98*, BRE, London.

Boyle, S. (2001) 'The green century', *Building Magazine*, Special Edition, 5 January.

BRE (2002) *Reputation, Risk and Reward – The Business Case for Sustainability in the UK Property Sector*, BRE, London.

CBP (2002) The Strategic Forum for Construction for Construction Best Practice, *Rethinking Construction-Accelerating Charge*. Report by CBP, London.

CIRIA/Addis, B. & Talbot, R. (2001) *Sustainable Construction Procurement, Report C571,* CIRIA, London.

CIRIA/CIEF/Covertry, S. (2001) *Waste Minimisation on Construction Projects,* CIRIA, London.

Construction Best Practice Programme (2000) *Suppliers – Actions for Sustainable Construction,* CBPP, London.

DEFRA (2002) *Framework for Sustainable Development on the Government Estate,* DEFRA, London.

DETR (1999) *A Better Quality of Life – A Strategy for Sustainable Development in the United Kingdom,* HMSO, London.

DTI (2001), *Sustainable Construction,* Report on Progress, HMSO

Egan, J. (1998) *Rethinking Construction,* Report of the Construction Task Force, HMSO, London.

Highways Agency (2002) *Procuring More Sustainable Roads,* proceedings of CIEF meeting Sustainable Construction Procurement, London.

Hoare, S. (2001) 'Bricks and mortar boards', *The Guardian,* 23 October.

Latham, M. (1994) *Constructing the Team,* HMSO, London.

Morley Fund Management (2002) Sustainability matrix, published on their website www.morleyfm.com

Prudential Property Investment Managers (PruPIM) (2002) *Environmental and Social Report,* Prudential, London.

World Business Council for Sustainable Development (2002) 'Report on the Global Mining Initiative', press briefing, www.wbcsd.org

FURTHER RESOURCES AND WEBSITES

DETR (1994) *Sustainable Development: The UK Strategy,* HMSO, London.

DETR (2000) *Building a Better Quality of Life: A Strategy for More Sustainable Construction,* DETR, London.

Greenstreet, R. (1994) *Legal and Contractual Procedures for Architects,* Architectural Press, London.

Sustainable Construction Task Group (2002) *Reputation, Risk & Reward,* HMSO/BRE, London.

- www.cbpp.org.uk/cbpp – search under 'procurement', for example see choice of procurement route: Factsheet Abstract 'There are a number of standard routes or processes, particularly with respect to the construction stage, that need early consideration when procuring construction. Each route places different demands, risk allocation and responsibilities on everyone involved and different cash flow profiles on the client. The chosen route is then supported by standard forms of contract.'
- For discussion, background information on range of issues related to sustainable construction, see www.defra.gov.uk and then follow sustainableconstruction. Also contains excellent précis of key facts on Kyoto, ISO 14001 and 18 question/answer sections on Government policy, targets, etc. relating to construction and the environment
- See www.m4i.org.uk for case studies, findings and implications/practical applications of latest sustainability and industry initiatives
- Building Regulations and latest on Part L, see www.safety.odpm.gov.uk/bregs/index.htm

- KPIs – see www.sustainable-development.gov.uk and then follow indicators and index for results so far on these indicators. Also see www.m4i.org and follow kpis
- All government projects now required to be green including supply of timber and other materials, see www.dti.gov.uk and follow 'greening' the Government estate
- Information and guidance on more efficient waste management, see www.waste-guide. org.uk
- See www.sustainable-development.gov.uk and follow news for more environment-related press releases

Index

CAMBRIDGE UNIVERSITY PRESS
Cambridge, New York, Melbourne, Madrid, Cape Town, Singapore,
São Paulo, Delhi, Dubai, Tokyo, Mexico City

Cambridge University Press
The Edinburgh Building, Cambridge CB2 8RU, UK

www.cambridge.org
Information on this title: www.cambridge.org/9780521547765

First published 2004
6th printing 2010

Printed in the United Kingdom by Short Run Press, Exeter

A catalogue record for this publication is available from the British Library

ISBN 978-0-521-54776-5 Paperback

The authors and publishers are grateful for permission to use the copyright materials
appearing in this book, as indicated in the sources and acknowledgements throughout.
If there are errors or omissions the publishers would be pleased to hear and to make
the appropriate correction in future reprints.

Contents

PART 2 Knowing what's important

PART 3 The tools of research

To the Student

Who is *Study Reading* for?

Study Reading is for students who have to use English textbooks, reference materials and other sources, in print or online, for study purposes.

What does *Study Reading* cover?

Study Reading aims to develop the reading skills you need to find information quickly, to identify what is important in a text, to compare different sources of information and to read critically. To help you with these skills, we study how texts are structured, and how you can best deal with vocabulary problems.

Study Reading includes texts from the Humanities, Social Sciences and Science. Most of these texts are from sources used by college and university students in the English-speaking world. A few have been specially written to highlight particular reading problems. In Part 1, Preparing to study, we examine how textbooks are organised so that you can become familiar with the parts which will help you most. In Part 2, Knowing what's important, we study how to identify the important points in a text. Each Unit within this Part provides a selection of texts on a theme important to the world of study. Part 3, The tools of research, provides help with the skills needed for research reading.

How does *Study Reading* work?

This book by itself cannot make you a better reader but it can help you to think about how you read, compare ideas with your fellow students and experiment with different strategies. In this way, you can develop more efficient reading strategies for yourself.

Each Unit has four Sections. The first section is to help you to think both about a reading skill and about the theme of the unit. The second section provides reading practice and an opportunity to talk about your reading with your fellow students. The third section explores some of the features of texts which can cause problems to the reader. Together, these three sections should help you to develop and refine your reading skills. The fourth section allows you to apply your reading skills, old and new.

One piece of advice before you start this course; when you read, it is important that you have a clear purpose. Purposeful reading saves time for you to spend on other study activities. In this book, the instructions for each task indicate your reading purpose. When you study by yourself, you should set your own purpose. To develop faster reading, set yourself a time to achieve that purpose.

Some activities are designed for pair or group work. If you are studying by yourself, do as many of the tasks as you can playing both parts where this is meaningful. Certainly read all of the texts.

Good luck!

To the Teacher

This new edition of *Study Reading* has been updated to include not only more recent texts in the disciplines represented but also to take account of new media with the growth of online resources. This development affects a number of units, in particular Unit 10 which includes a range of online reference sources. One of the strengths of the first edition was the coverage of academic disciplines. This new edition further expands the range to include texts from the field of Information Technology. Other new features include self-study vocabulary building activities based on key words in Academic English drawn from the New Academic Word List (Coxhead, 1998). The full list, which contains 570 word families frequently encountered in academic texts across a range of disciplines in arts, commerce, law and science, forms the Appendix, p 136. For the first time, too, activities are included for IELTS practice.

Who is *Study Reading* for?

Study Reading is aimed at two groups of readers: firstly, students preparing to enter or in the early stages of study at a college or university where English textbooks or reference materials, in print or online, are used but instruction is in the mother tongue; secondly, students at or preparing to enter English-medium colleges or universities. It also provides useful preparation for the reading section of the IELTS examination. Each of the question types in the Academic Reading Module can be found in this book. However, this book is much more than practice for IELTS; it is preparation for academic reading. The book is intended for students whose English level is Upper-Intermediate or above CEF B2.

What makes *Study Reading* different from other reading textbooks?

1 APPROACH *Study Reading* does not have a particular reading technique to sell. The authors recognise that students already have reading strategies in their own language and in English, however ineffectual these may be. The starting point is to give students insight into their existing strategies. The next step is to refine these strategies by exposure to the ideas of other students. Where students are working alone, this book encourages them to question their approach with the same aim of refining strategies. Only when students have had time to think about reading in this way does the third stage follow, when the authors provide direct advice on improving reading efficiency.

2 METHODOLOGY *Study Reading* recognises that reading lessons can be dull if reading is seen as a passive activity. Consequently, a variety of problem-solving tasks are used to motivate students to

think about reading. The authors have included a range of information and opinion-sharing activities in the belief that these will both motivate and help students to become better thinkers and readers by having to justify their answers to others. Students should compare their answers with a partner or in a group and should be asked to defend their answers wherever this is appropriate.

3 TEXTS The texts are appropriate to the needs of students requiring reading skills for study purposes. As in the first edition, there is a very wide range of text types represented. *Study Reading* uses passages from textbooks, journals, reference works and study guides which have been drawn from current reading lists in a range of college and university disciplines and from a variety of higher education institutions. Use is also made of magazines which present specialist topics in a manner accessible to the lay reader, for example *New Scientist*. Care has been taken to select up-to-date sources or older sources that have become classic texts. US and other international sources have been used as well as British to give students exposure to a wide variety of texts. Some texts have been constructed to highlight particular language points. Where possible, these have been modelled, in terms of discourse structure, on authentic texts. Constructed texts have no source listed.

Theoretical influences

Study Reading has been shaped by classroom experience but has been influenced by theoretical debate. In the absence of any generally accepted theory of reading in a foreign language, we have selected such ideas from competing theories as have passed the classroom filter. In general we accept that readers use a mix of strategies appropriate to their reading purpose and may seek to compensate for weaknesses in one area, for example word recognition, by strengths in another, for example content knowledge. Such a view might be labelled *interactive-compensatory* (see Urquhart and Weir (1998)). We accept the importance of knowledge of the world and familiarity with the way different genres of text are structured in reading, and hence have attempted to activate the students' background knowledge and to draw attention to text structure. We accept too that knowledge of cohesion is important and have therefore provided help with features of discourse. Our approach to word recognition draws in part from the ideas of Nation and Coady (1988) and on acquiring an academic vocabulary from Nation (2001).

How is *Study Reading* organised?

Study Reading is divided into three parts:
1 Preparing to study
2 Knowing what's important
3 The tools of research

PART 1 (Units 1 and 2) introduces basic reading strategies which are returned to again and again throughout the text. The themes are 'Getting to know your textbook' and 'Choosing what to read'.

PART 2 (Units 3 to 9) forms the main body of the text. Each Unit is theme-based round a group of related subjects. For example, Unit 5, 'The natural world', draws texts from the Life Sciences. In this Part we study ways of surveying a text, identifying what is important in a text, evaluating what you read and other important reading strategies.

PART 3 (Unit 10) focuses on the reading strategies required by students who have to consult reference and journal sources to prepare a project or for research.

Each Part consists of a number of Units. Each Unit provides 3 to 4 hours of work and is divided into four Sections.

1 **Before you read:** Tasks to develop insight into the reading process, encourage discussion and provide a reason for reading on.
2 **Reading and interaction:** Information and opinion-sharing activities to encourage intensive reading and develop top-down reading skills.
3 **Text exploration:** Activities to develop bottom-up skills, decoding a text starting from the meaning of words, to make the reader aware of the common discourse features of academic texts and strategies the reader can use to tackle unfamiliar vocabulary and to build an academic vocabulary.
4 **Application:** Tasks designed to encourage the reader to apply the strategies developed in Sections 1 to 3. These tasks are suitable for homework.

Study Reading ends with a 'Key' to the tasks.

How can I use *Study Reading* with my class?

STUDY GROUP The most common work unit is the study group. The size of each will clearly depend on your teaching circumstances. About five or six per study group would be ideal. If your students have adequate oral skills, encourage them to use English within their group. If their spoken English is poor and they have a mother tongue in common, allow discussion in the mother tongue. The

'Key' should be used only when discussion has ended. It provides sample answers. Other answers may also be acceptable.

INFORMATION-GAP AND OPINION-GAP TASKS Throughout *Study Reading* there are tasks which ask students to read different sections of a long text or different texts on related themes. They then exchange information or opinions on the texts. Make sure the instructions are clearly understood. There is a natural tendency to read all of the texts. Encourage your students to do this after they have completed the activity.

PACING It is likely that students using this textbook will vary considerably in their reading proficiency. There is no need to tackle every task in every unit. This is particularly the case with Units 1 and 2 where more proficient students may find some of the tasks quite simple. If so, move on quickly to more challenging material. You may also find that the discussion stage may make some of the later tasks redundant as students learn from each other. Given sufficient time, most students of the target level will be able to cope with all of the tasks. However, in real study situations time is at a premium. This is not a speed-reading course but it is important that students are encouraged to read quickly. Set a target by timing yourself and adding a proportion to match your students' abilities. Try reducing the proportion as you proceed through the book. The fourth section can be set for homework or self-study. Encourage your students to set themselves a target time for completing this work.

Coxhead, A. (1998) *An academic word list* (English Language Institute Occasional Publication No. 18). (Wellington, N.Z.: Victoria University of Wellington)

Nation, P. and Coady, J. (1988) Vocabulary and reading, in *Vocabulary and Language Teaching*, Carter, R. and McCarthy, M. (eds) (London: Longman)

Nation, P. (2001) *Learning vocabulary in another language* (Cambridge: CUP)

Urquhart, S. and Weir, C. (1998) *Reading in a second language: process, product and practice* (London: Longman)

Text Map

Unit	Title	Reading strategies and skills	Word study
1 Text topics	Getting to know your textbook Geography, Marketing, Study skills	Surveying a textbook, Using an index	Words which substitute for other words, Vocabulary cards
2 Text topics	Choosing what to read Study skills	Making predictions about your reading, Surveying a chapter	Dealing with unfamiliar words, Semantic sets
3 Text topics	The spirit of enquiry Biology, Psychology	Surveying a text, Understanding how facts and ideas are connected	Using immediate context, Collocations
4 Text topics	The developing world Development issues	Identifying important points, Understanding text structure	Semantic sets: Cause and effect
5 Text topics	The natural world Life Sciences	Making inferences, Note-taking	More semantic sets, Finding related forms
6 Text topics	The physical world Geology, Physics, Applied Sciences – Engineering	Relating texts and graphics, Reading graphics for main ideas and specific details, Using graphics in note-taking	Using the wider context
7 Text topics	Into the future Information Technology	Comparing sources, Identifying viewpoints	Using word structure, Affixes
8 Text topics	The individual and society Social Sciences	Reading critically 1: Distinguishing between facts and opinions, Analysing an argument	Maximisers and minimisers
9 Text topics	Work Industrial Psychology, Economics, Business Studies	Reading critically 2: Comparing viewpoints, Detecting false forms of argument	Emphasising and distancing, Connotations
10 Text topics	Reading for Research Reference, Education	Choosing the best source, Reading reference sources for specific information, Reading for research	Choosing keywords for database searches
Appendix		*Academic Word List*	

PART 1

Preparing to study

UNIT 1 | Getting to know your textbook

This unit aims to develop the reading strategies and skills required for:

1 surveying a textbook

2 using an index

3 dealing with word problems.

Before you read

During your studies, you will learn from your lecturers, your fellow students and from written information resources, both in print form and online.

TASK 1 Tick the written information resources you expect to use in your course. Then rank your choice (1 to 9, with 1 being the most popular) and compare your ranking with others in your group.

Textbooks		Journals	
Lecture notes		Indexing and abstracting databases	
Encyclopaedias		Websites/e-learning materials	
Dictionaries		Theses and dissertations	
Other – specify			

A textbook can be one of your most valuable sources of information. Knowing the parts of a textbook is the first step to using it properly.

TASK 2 *Parts of a textbook*

Study this list of some of the parts of a textbook. Try to match the parts with the correct descriptions. When you have finished, compare your answers with your neighbour.

Parts of a textbook	Descriptions
a) bibliography	1 the units of the book
b) title page	2 sources used by the author
c) appendix	3 a list of the main topics by chapter
d) preface/introduction	4 a list of books, articles, etc. which provide further reading on the themes covered in the book; usually found at the end

e)	acknowledgements	5	an alphabetical list of topics in detail
f)	contents	6	additional information, often for reference purposes, found at the end of the book
g)	chapters	7	selling points, author information, positive reviews
h)	references	8	thanks to people who have helped with the book
i)	glossary	9	the author's aims and the coverage of the book
j)	index	10	a mini-dictionary of specialist terms used
k)	back cover	11	title, author and publisher
l)	foreword	12	a short introduction to the book written not by the author but by someone familiar with the author's work

TASK 3 Identify the parts of a textbook that are shown below. Then compare your answers with those of your neighbour. What is the book about?

1 Salience.

1) The importance a brand holds for different groups of people. It is a measure or indication of emotional closeness to, or distance from, a brand; it is different from awareness.

2) The extent to which a brand comes readily to mind (e.g. measured by first mentions in answer to a brand awareness question) or the most frequently mentioned brand in connection with a set of associations.

2 First published 1999

Admap Publications

Farm Road

Henley-on-Thames

Oxfordshire RG9 1EJ

United Kingdom

3 I Qualitative Research – New or Old Discipline?   14

II Qualitative Research – Warts & All   52

III A Review of Qualitative Methods   74

4 This book is a very personal effort to explain how I *think* about human beings and their relationships to brands, communications and the delivery of service, and hence what I *do* as a quantitative researcher. My credentials for attempting to do this are 30 years of experience.

5 Lesley Thompson is an excellent quantitative researcher whom I admire. She read each chapter twice, challenged my point of view and willingly contributed additional thoughts and examples.

6 S. Adams, *The Dilbert Principle*, Harper-Collins, 1997.

K. Blanchard, *Mission Possible*, McGraw-Hill, 1997.

J.M. Dru, *Disruption*, John Wiley & Sons, 1996.

7 'This book covers the landscape of qualitative research in a way that inspires the reader new to the subject and stimulates the experienced researcher to think more deeply. Even after 20 years' involvement with research, I found my knowledge both challenged and increased.'

Sally Ford-Hutchinson, Global Planning Director, DMB&B

TASK 4 Why would you read these parts of a textbook?
1 Covers
2 Title page
3 Publishing details – publisher, date, place of publication
4 Foreword, Preface or Introduction
5 Contents
6 Index
7 Bibliography

When you have recorded all your answers, go on to Task 5.

TASK 5 Study this passage to find the reasons given for reading each of the textbook parts listed in Task 4. Discuss with the others in your group any differences between your answers to Task 4 and the reasons given in the passage.

Before accepting information published in a book, you should spend a few minutes examining its structure, for this will assist you in evaluating the book. The dust jacket often contains information on the qualifications of the author and the author's point-of-view. Allowance must, of course, be made for the natural desire of the publisher and author to present the book in its best light. The title page should always be read carefully. It may contain a sub-title explaining the intention or scope of the work, or the qualifications of the author. The imprint (place of publication, publisher and date) is of value. The work is likely to be authoritative if published by a publisher who specializes in the subject of the book. The date will indicate how up-to-date the book is and the reverse of the title page should also be examined, in case this reveals whether the edition is substantially a reprint of an older work. The foreword, preface or introduction will often summarize the purpose of the volume (*see Fig. 53*). The table of contents will not only outline the way the work is arranged and help you to trace a particular piece of information (*see Fig. 28*) if the index is defective, but will also suggest the point-of-view. Every book is based on a combination of objective facts and subjective interpretation of them. The contents will suggest whether the author has set out to prove a theory or to spread a particular belief. The book may be of great value even if it contains propaganda, but greater care must be taken in evaluating the information. The running headlines on the top of the pages may contain useful information on the text. The index can reveal the scope of the book by listing the topics discussed (*see Fig. 54*) and the number of pages devoted to them. It can also reveal the author's sources and will indicate whether they are up-to-date and thorough in their approach.

[Source: Chandler, G. (1982) *How to Find Out: Printed and On-line Sources*, 5th Edition (Oxford: Pergamon Press), pp 1–2]

TASK 6 This form can be used to make a quick survey of a textbook. Look through a textbook which is unfamiliar to you, preferably in your own subject. Try to survey the book in about 10 minutes. Use this textbook if you cannot get one in your own subject.

1 Title

2 Author/s or Editor/s

3 Publisher, Date and Place of Publication

4 Edition

5 Level

6 Aims

7 Main Topics Covered

8 Special Features

9 Library Shelf-mark/Call Number

Scanning

Scanning means reading to find specific information. You have a specific target and you search the text quickly for the information you need. Scanning is one of the reading skills you require to locate information quickly in the index of a textbook. To do this, identify the keywords in your search item. Then let your eye go up and down the index columns until you find references beginning with the keywords. Then focus more finely to search for the specific references you want. With practice, you can become faster at scanning by narrowing the area you scan – moving from coarse to fine focus – as quickly as possible.

Sometimes you may not be able to find the information you want in an index, although the book may contain all the information you need. If you cannot find your topic, first make sure that you are using the correct keyword. (The most likely keywords in the following examples are highlighted.)

Often more than one keyword is possible. For example, 'The eclipse of the Moon' may be listed in an index as:

Eclipse, of the Moon

or

Moon, eclipse of

If you cannot find a very specific reference, try a more general keyword. For example, to find 'The French Revolution of 1789' you may have to try any of the terms highlighted.

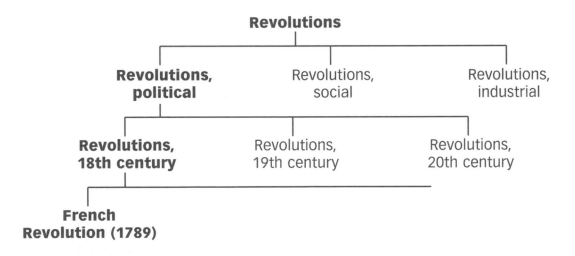

TASK 7 Each of the following topics (1–10) come from a geography textbook; match them with a more general keyword (a–j) from the index.

Topic	Index keyword
1 railways	a) ores
2 cultivation of oranges	b) urbanisation
3 troposphere	c) sea routes
4 cotton growing	d) mining
5 underpopulation	e) transportation
6 Panama Canal	f) climate
7 growth of New York	g) atmosphere
8 uranium	h) population
9 coal production	i) industrial crops
10 rainfall	j) citrus farming

TASK 8 Which page or pages would you refer to first in this extract from the index of *Natural Disasters* to find information on the following? Be prepared to justify your choice. Work as quickly as you can and note the time you take. When you have found your answers, compare them with another student's. Note: a **boldface** entry indicates a figure; an entry in *italics* indicates a table.

1 the reasons for subsidence in Venice
2 the sociology of disasters involving skyscrapers
3 effects of snow in cities
4 aid for developing world countries
5 disasters in Texas
6 frequency of tornadoes in the USA
7 psychological stress
8 relationship between tides and earthquakes
9 assessing the stability of slopes
10 how tornadoes are formed

slope stability	246–51	Small Business Act (USA)	592
Bishop method	249	snow	
factor of safety	246–7	drift	204
Janbu method	250	fall, impact of	201–6
method of moments	247–8	metamorphosis	190–1
stress analysis	249	natural dissipation	202
slopewash erosion	221	sociology of disasters	554–60
slow-onset disaster *see* creeping disaster		and tall buildings	353–5
slump	253	and tornadoes	180

[Source: Alexander, D. (1993) *Natural Disasters* (London: UCL Press Limited), p 630]

Text exploration

Discourse study: Textbook structure

A typical textbook has this structure:

Introduction
Contents
Chapters
1
2
3
etc.
Further Reading
Appendices
Index

The best guide to the organisation of the textbook and the topics it covers is provided by the Introduction and the Contents. Pay particular attention to any section of the introduction labelled 'Advice to the Reader', 'To the Student', 'How to use this book', etc. You can safely ignore the Acknowledgements.

Word study: Words which substitute for other words

Words are one of the first problems that readers face – words which are unfamiliar, words which change, and words which are missing. In this unit we will study ways of dealing with some of these problems.

Writers often use different words in a text to refer to the same thing – the meaning remains the same but the words change. Study the examples that follow.

1 Before accepting information published in *a book*, you should spend a few minutes examining its structure. *The work* is likely to be authoritative if produced by a publisher who specialises in the field. The foreword, preface or introduction will often summarise the purpose of *the volume*.

Work and *volume* do not signal new topics. They are simply different words for *book* in this text. If you meet an unexpected change of topic in your reading, look back in the text for a possible link. The writer may be using a new word for an old topic.

2 *The index* can reveal the scope of the book by listing *the topics* discussed and the number of pages devoted to *them*. *It* can also reveal bias by the number of references under particular topics.

To avoid repeating a noun, writers may change it to a pronoun. In this example *topics* becomes *them*; *index* becomes *It*. If you have difficulty with a pronoun, look back in the text to find the noun referred to.

Sentences which appear to have words missing may also cause problems. Sometimes writers omit words to avoid unnecessary repetition. Study these examples:

Compare versions 3 and 4:

3   It is important that you have a clear purpose when you read. If not, you may waste valuable study time.

4   It is important that you have a clear purpose when you read. If *you do* not *have a clear purpose*, you may waste valuable study time.

Compare versions 5 and 6:

5   Dictionaries and encyclopaedias are important information sources. Both can be found in the reference section of your library.

6   Dictionaries and encyclopaedias are important information sources. Both *dictionaries and encylopaedias* can be found in the reference section of your library.

TASK 9   The following is a preface from a reference book. Study it and answer the numbered questions.

This book has been prepared to provide a guide to sources of information on engineering and its various branches. It [(1) *What does 'It' refer to?*] should prove of interest to all persons engaged in the engineering profession and those [(2) *Add the missing word*] contemplating entering the [(3) *Add the missing word*] profession. It is hoped that Chapters 1 and 8, on careers, and education and training, will assist both advisers and potential students seeking information about these important matters. [(4) *Which important matters?*] This book has been arranged according to the Dewey Decimal classification that is commonly employed in public libraries. Although the work [(5) *Which work?*] is reasonably comprehensive, there are so many textbooks available that it has not been possible to make specific recommendations [(6) *Of what? Add the missing words*]. This matter [(7) *Which matter?*] is better dealt with by tutors and others concerned with teaching. However, in certain chapters selected books have been mentioned in addition to reference books and the like [(8) *The like of what?*] when it has been felt that the details [(9) *Details of what?*] would augment the general information provided [(10) *Information provided where?*]. A number of the books referred to contain neither bibliographies nor guides to further reading.

[Source: Parsons, S.A.J. (1972) *How to find out about engineering* (Oxford: Pergamon Press), p xiii]

Self-study   *Appendix 1* lists some of the key words you will meet when reading academic texts. One way of remembering the important words in Academic English is to keep a vocabulary notebook or a set of word cards. What kind of information do you think it would be useful to note for each keyword? Here are some possible answers:

Translation in your language
Part of speech
Pronunciation
Example sentence
Words with a related meaning
Words which are related grammatically
Words which occur together with the key word (collocations)

Study this example of a word card:

Key word *publication*	**Translation**
Part of speech *noun*	Pronunciation ˈpʌblíkeɪʃən
Example *She is a prolific writer with many publications in her field.*	Related meaning *book, article, paper*
Related grammatically *publish, publisher*	Collocations *official+, research+*

Design your own card to include the information you think is important for your academic reading. Remember that you need not fill in all of the information at the same time.

Application

TASK 10   The extract that follows is from a study skills guide. Study it, then answer the questions: Which part of the publication is it from? Which chapters in the guide will provide help with these problems?

1 planning essays
2 acquiring basic study skills
3 setting out references
4 finding suitable books
5 preparing for examinations
6 looking for a job

How to Read this Book

There are seven chapters in the book, arranged in a sequence which roughly mirrors a student's progress through college. The first chapter deals with 'Starting off in higher education' and is intended mainly for people who are just about to go to university/college or who are in their first year there. If you   5
are an experienced student, you may still find it useful to read this chapter fairly quickly.

Our next three chapters tackle different aspects of normal coursework. Chapter 2 deals with 'Generating information', finding literature, using it effectively, and making notes.   10
Chapter 3 describes 'Analysing concepts and theories', particularly explaining how to place problem concepts within a whole field of ideas. Once you have gathered enough information and you understand the major concepts involved in an area, Chapter 4 moves on to 'Writing essays'. It describes   15
how to de-bug essay topics, plan your response, and write up finished text.

The next two chapters relate to course assessment. You may move on in your final year to 'Writing dissertations', the subject of Chapter 5. Dissertations pose some problems over   20
and above ordinary essay writing, especially in organizing research, writing up a longer piece of text and referencing sources. Chapter 6 deals with the final and most critical stage in most courses, 'Revising for exams' and answering exam questions.   25

Chapter 7 on 'Turning study skills into life skills' is likely to be of immediate relevance if you are beginning the 'milk round' of career interviews and job applications. However, it is worth reading well in advance of this stage, since by then it is generally rather late to do anything about acquiring career-   30
relevant skills. The earlier you think through some ideas about possible career lines, the greater the opportunity you have to undertake relevant activities and develop key personal qualities.

[Source: Dunleavy, P. (1986) *Studying for a Degree in the Humanities and Social Sciences* (London: Macmillan Education Ltd.), pp 1–2]

UNIT 2 Choosing what to read

This unit aims to develop the reading strategies and skills required for:

1. making predictions about your reading
2. surveying a chapter
3. dealing with unfamiliar words.

Before you read

As a student you will find that there is always too much to read. It is important therefore that you can quickly select the most appropriate source for your needs. To do this, you must have a clear purpose for your reading and you must be able to predict which source will help you most to meet that purpose.

TASK 1   Read through the list of seven students. Then study the print-out from an online catalogue search for books on study skills which follows. Choose the best book for each student. Be prepared to defend your choice.

1 A student anxious about a forthcoming examination.
2 A college student wanting advice on how to prepare a report.
3 A student who wants advice on all aspects of study.
4 A student preparing for a BA in Sociology wanting general advice.
5 An MBA (Master of Business Administration) student who does not have enough time to get through long reading lists.
6 A student who has problems taking notes in lectures.
7 A mature student going to college for the first time and worried about studying on her own.

Title (long)	Author	Date
Getting organised	Fry, Ron	1997
Guide to learning independently	Marshall, Lorraine A.	1998
How to manage your study time	Lewis, Roger	1994
How to pass exams without anxiety	Acres, David	1992
Learn how to study: a realistic approach	Rowntree, Derek	1998
Lectures: how best to handle them	Race, Phil	1989
MBA handbook: study skills for managers	Cameron, Sheila	1997
Reading at university: a guide for students	Fairbairn, Gavin	2000

Student's guide to exam success	Tracy, Eileen	2001
Study skills and tomorrow's doctors	Bullimore, David W.	1998
Studying for a degree in the humanities and the social sciences	Dunleavy, Patrick	1986
Successful study for degrees	Barnes, Rob	1995
Writing essays	Williams, Kate	1995
Writing reports	Williams, Kate	1995

TASK 2 Read through the questions below. Then study the Contents pages from *Learn How to Study* that follow. Write down the page numbers of the section to consult for help with each question.

1 How do I learn to read faster?
2 How do I find out about assessment in my course?
3 How do I overcome anxiety about examinations?
4 What is the best way to take notes from a lecture?
5 How can I best timetable my studies?
6 What is the best way to revise for examinations?
7 What do my tutors expect when they set an essay with the title, 'Account for...'?
8 How do I become a successful student?

[Source: Rowntree, D. (1998) *Learn How to Study: a realistic approach*, 4th Edition (London: Warner Books)]

Reading and interaction

Reading with a purpose

When you read, it is important that you have a clear purpose. Having a clear purpose helps you to narrow the choice of book from a reading list then, once you have chosen the book, to select the best chapter and section. Having a clear purpose also helps you to locate the most useful part of a text for your needs and to ignore those parts which will not help you.

Prediction

Prediction means making intelligent guesses about what a textbook, chapter or section contains using only a small sample of the text. In Task 1, we used catalogue entries. In Task 2, Contents pages. It is an important strategy when choosing what to read. The more we know about our subject, the easier it is for us to make predictions because we can relate the samples of new text to our existing knowledge. When our knowledge of the subject is limited, we have to make maximum use of all available clues to predict well. Study this example.

Which of these three chapters from a geography textbook will provide information on how the landscape of coastal regions is formed?

5 The Structure of the Continents
6 The Landscape and the River
7 Wave, Wind, and Ice

Answer: Chapter 5 is unlikely. It seems to be about the formation of continents. Chapter 6 contains the word *landscape* but also *river*. Its topic is the way rivers shape the land, whereas our need is for information on how the coast is shaped. In other words, how the sea shapes the land. Chapter 7 contains the word *wave* – that suggests the sea. It follows a chapter about the formation of landscape by rivers and may therefore continue with other aspects of landscape formation. For these reasons, we can predict that Chapter 7 will include information on how the sea shapes the land and hence how the landscape of coastal regions is formed.

Making accurate predictions from book titles, chapter headings and text samples can help you make the right choice in what to read and can save you valuable study time.

TASK 3 Look at the Table of Contents on page 29. Which chapter would you consult for information on the following? (Then compare answers with your partner.)
1 Changes in population age profiles in Western Europe
2 Oil consumption in Africa
3 Key factors in shaping the recent past
4 The growth of Beijing
5 The role of nations in a unified Europe
6 Euros and dollars – will both prevail?
7 Effects of developed world demand on developing world agriculture
8 Production of Western consumer goods in developing world countries
9 Nomadic peoples in the 21st century
10 Societies before industrialisation

SECTION 1	THE WORLD BEFORE GLOBALIZATION: CHANGING SCALES OF EXPERIENCE	Chapter 10	Alternative geographies of global development and inequality

[Source: Daniels, P., Bradshaw, M., Shaw, D. and Sidaway, J. (2001) *Human Geography: Issues for the 21st Century* (Harlow: Prentice Hall)]

When you have selected a suitable textbook and identified the chapters most appropriate to your needs, it is useful to see what help is given in each chapter to enable you to read it effectively.

TASK 4   The list below shows some common chapter features.
1 Title
2 Introduction
3 Section headings
4 Sub-section headings
5 Highlighted words
6 Diagrams and illustrations (graphics)
7 Summary
8 Suggestions for further reading
9 Problems/Tasks
10 Notes/References

How can these features help you when you are reading a chapter? Discuss your selection in your group. Here is an example of an answer:

(7) Summary This should restate the main points of the chapter. It's a good way of checking that you have understood these points. You can also read it first and then decide which sections of the chapter are important to read in detail.

TASK 5 This task now explores how different parts of a chapter can help you predict its contents. Form yourselves into groups **A**, **B** and **C**.

Group A
Study this chapter introduction from a study guide. Make a list of at least four questions that the chapter will answer and compare it with others in your group. For example:

How can we best prepare for examinations?

All tests and examinations are intended to measure how effectively you have studied a subject, so the best way of preparing for examinations is to develop systematic habits of study. If you follow the advice which has already been given about methods of planning, note-taking, and learning effectively, you should have no difficulty with examinations.

There is no way of passing an examination without doing the requisite work for it. But you can ensure that you are at peak efficiency for an important examination. This means having a thorough knowledge of your subject and having it so well organized and understood that you can write about it from many points of view. It also means being reasonably calm and confident, and not fatigued or over-anxious.

Taking these things for granted, you can improve your performance still more by (1) careful preparation and (2) skill in examination techniques.

[Source: Maddox, H. (1988) *How to Study* (London: Pan Books), p 137]

Group B
Study the following chapter summary from a study guide. Make a list of at least four questions the chapter answered and compare it with others in your group. For example:

How can we best prepare for examinations?

Preparations for examinations should begin at the outset of a course of study, in the sense that you should study the syllabus you are required to cover and the kinds of examinations which you will have to take.

Progressive assessment is now widely used to monitor course performance. Hence final examinations are less of an ordeal. Nevertheless fairly frequent tests and reviews are desirable. Little effort is required to relearn for an important examination what has already been gone over a number of times. To be most effective, review should follow closely on the original learning. For long-term retention intermediate periods of review are also desirable.

The final review preceding important examinations should be carefully planned to a schedule, to avoid any last-minute rush. Examination anxiety can be avoided by regular work, careful planning, and a normal routine which allows for exercise and recreation.

Different kinds of examinations require different kinds of preparation. Suggestions are offered for taking objective tests and for taking essay-type examinations.

[Source: Maddox, H. (1988) *How to Study* (London: Pan Books), p 155]

Group C
Study the following chapter section headings from a study guide. Make a list of at least four questions the chapter will answer and compare it with others in your group. For example:

How can we best prepare for examinations?

Preparing for Examinations
Revision
Methods of Revision
Avoiding Anxiety
Form of Examinations
Objective Tests
Intelligence Quotients
Techniques for Essay-type Examinations
Making Use of Returned Papers
Summary

[Source: Maddox, H. (1988) *How to Study* (London: Pan Books), pp 136–56]

TASK 6 Work in groups of three, one each from Groups **A**, **B** and **C**.
Compare your questions. How similar are they? Read each other's texts and try to answer the questions. Which text provides the most help in predicting the contents of the chapter?

TASK 7 Explain why you agree or disagree with the advice given.

Text exploration

Discourse study: Chapter structure

A typical textbook chapter has this structure:

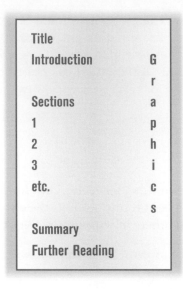

Title
Introduction

Sections
1
2
3
etc.

Summary
Further Reading

G
r
a
p
h
i
c
s

The best guide to the organisation of the chapter and the topics it covers is provided by the Introduction and the Section Headings. Using these samples, you can predict the topics covered. You can check your predictions using the Summary. Summaries can help you in two further ways. They can provide a quick overview of the whole chapter before you read it. They also provide a useful comprehension check after you've read the chapter. If time is short, read the Summary instead of the whole chapter. Refer back to the chapter for help with any points you cannot understand. Graphics sometimes provide easy to read summaries of sections. See Task 13.

Word study: Dealing with unfamiliar words

Students sometimes blame unfamiliar words for their reading difficulties. In this section we will study strategies for dealing with these words.

TASK 8 Study this list of 'difficult words' from a passage. In not more than 3 minutes, try to find the meaning of any of these words which are unfamiliar to you.

intricate resit
hitherto   rush
embarking

TASK 9 Now read the passage in which a student counsellor describes study difficulties. Answer these questions:
1 What is the most common complaint of students?
2 Why do some postgraduates experience this problem?

When I began the work, I expected most of my time to be spent helping students with fairly complex cognitive difficulties with their efforts to grasp higher-order concepts or to reproduce intricate patterns of argument. It surprised me to discover that the most common 'complaint' of students of all ages, levels of study and disciplines, is difficulty in organising and timetabling their work. Many students identify this as a problem fairly soon after embarking on a first year at university, but many do not until after examinations at the end of their first term. Yet others come to discuss methods of organising themselves in something of a rush before resit exams; and I find now that an increasing number of highly successful graduates come with the same concern soon after embarking on a higher degree course that is less structured than anything they have hitherto experienced.

[Source: Main, A.N. (1980) *Encouraging Effective Learning*, (Edinburgh: Scottish Academic Press), p 16]

It has been estimated that you will meet 80,000 to 100,000 different words in your textbooks in a typical course. It is impossible to know the meaning of all of these words. The first decision to make when faced with an unfamiliar word is 'Do I need to know its meaning?' You can only answer this question if you have a clear purpose in your reading. Which of the words listed in Task 8 did you need to know the meaning of to answer questions (1) and (2) above?

TASK 10 In the passage below this grid, some words have been missed out to represent unfamiliar words. The gaps are marked 1 to 6. Which of the missing words do you need in order to briefly answer the following questions?
a) According to Sexton, how are successful and unsuccessful students similar?
b) What differences does Sexton note between successful and unsuccessful students?
c) How do Borrow's ideas differ from those of Sexton?
d) Whose views does Small support, Sexton's or Borrow's?

Question	Missing words needed
a)	
b)	
c)	
d)	

There is a certain amount of ***(1)*** opinion about the characteristics of the successful student. Sexton (1965), reviewing twenty-five years of research into failure, reports that successful and unsuccessful students are likely to ***(2)*** 'bad' study habits with equal frequency. She reports that many investigations find that successful students spend more time in study, and tend to ***(3)*** the amount of study they do to the amount they think is needed for success in different subjects. Borrow (1946) believes that techniques, skills, ***(4)*** and attitudes are more important than the number of hours; his findings are that superior students are characterised by a more ***(5)*** schedule. Small (1966) shows a positive and highly significant relationship between academic success and adherence to a ***(6)*** method of study.

[Source: Main, A.N. (1980) *Encouraging Effective Learning* (Edinburgh: Scottish Academic Press), p 16]

....

TASK 11   Go back to the table in Task 10. If you listed any 'Missing words needed', try to divide the words into two groups:
   1 exact meaning needed
   2 approximate meaning needed

The second decision to make when faced with an unfamiliar word is 'Do I need to know its exact meaning or its approximate meaning?'
   Most of the time when you read, an approximate meaning is sufficient. In this book we will examine strategies for finding approximate meaning. The first step in finding the approximate meaning of an unfamiliar word is to identify what kind of word it is – noun, verb, adjective, etc. This limits the range of possible meanings. You can identify what kind of word it is by noting its position in the sentence and, where these exist, any clues in the form of the word, for example verb endings. Your knowledge of grammar will help you here.

....

TASK 12   In this next text, there are a number of missing words. Try to identify which kind of word (e.g. noun) each blank represents and the most likely word to fill the blank. Some clues to the form of the word are given (for example, an 'ed' ending). Compare with another student and rank your answers (*most likely* to *least likely*).

Strategies for organising yourself and your time

Prioritising
It is likely that you will have several pieces of work to do together, all with similar (1)......s. You may also have non-course commitments or interests to fit in. How will you (2) en... that it all gets done? The following suggestions cover a range of strategies:

- Plan it out on a big piece of paper and tick off items as they are (3)…ed.

- Prioritise using the following system:

  1 urgent and important – do it now
  2 urgent but not important – do it if you can
  3 important but not urgent – start it before it becomes urgent
  4 not important and not urgent – don't do it

- Have three trays and a waste bin. (4)…ate one tray for each of 1, 2 and 3 above and throw category 4 into the bin.

- Make out a list with the most important things first.

- Identify which are your strongest and which are your weakest subjects. Should you allocate equal time to each, or more to the weaker one? Possible dangers are:

  – avoiding giving time to topics you dislike or feel weak at

  – spending so much time on them you neglect areas you are good at

- Is the time you are (5)…ing on something equal to its importance?

- Build in breaks – a coffee, a walk (6)… the block, watching the news.

- Reward yourself with a (7)… when you have achieved a target (or part of a target).

- Allow for (8) un… circumstances (a full bus, a long queue at the library, etc.) and build in (9)….

- Make quick decisions about what action to take. (10)…ly picking up the same piece of paper wastes time.

[Source: Drew, S. and Bingham, R. (1997) *The Student Skills Guide,* 'Strategies for organising yourself and your time' (Aldershot: Gower Publishing Ltd), p 27]

Word study: Building an academic vocabulary

Knowing the headwords in the Academic Word List, Appendix, and the other members of their word families, will help you with your academic reading. Remembering these words is not easy. One way of remembering words with related meanings is to group them in sets.

TASK 13 Add to the following diagram any of the words about academic publications that you have met in Units 1 and 2.

ACADEMIC PUBLICATIONS

TEXTBOOKS	JOURNALS	REFERENCE WORKS
preface	articles	encyclopaedias
contents	abstract	_____
_____	_____	_____
_____	_____	_____
_____	_____	_____
_____	_____	_____
_____	_____	_____

Application

TASK 14 Study this extract from the summary of a chapter called 'Meet Your Memory', from a guide for students on how to improve memory. List at least five main questions this chapter deals with.

There is no such thing as a memory in the sense of some *thing* that can be seen, touched, or weighed. Memory is an abstraction referring to a set of skills rather than to an object. Neither is there a single 5 standard for judging a good or poor memory. There are a number of different ways in which a person may have a 'good' memory.

Memory is generally viewed as 10 consisting of three stages: (1) acquisition refers to learning the material; (2) storage refers to keeping the material in the brain until it is needed; and (3) retrieval refers to getting the material back out when it is 15 needed. These three stages may be viewed as the 3 R's of Remembering: Recoding, Retaining, and Retrieving. Retrieving is where many problems come. We cannot do much about retrieval directly; but since retrieval 20 is a function of recording, we can improve it by improving our methods of recording.

Memory consists of at least two different processes: short-term memory and long-term memory. Short-term 25 memory has a limited capacity and a rapid forgetting rate. Its capacity can be increased by chunking, or grouping separate bits of information into larger chunks. Long-term memory has a virtually unlimited capacity. 30 Short-term memory and long-term memory also differ in several other ways.

One measure of memory is recall, which requires you to produce information by searching the memory for it. In aided 35 recall, you are given cues to help you produce the information. In free-recall learning you recall the material in any order; in serial learning you recall it in the order it was presented; and in paired-associate learning 40 you learn pairs of words so that when the first word is given you can recall the second word. A second measure of memory is recognition, in which you do not have to produce the information from memory, 45 but must be able to identify it when it is presented to you. In a third measure of memory, relearning, the difference between how long it took to learn the material the first time and how long it takes to learn it 50 again indicates how much you remember. Relearning is generally a more sensitive measure of memory than is recognition, in the sense of showing retention where recognition does not; recognition is 55 generally a more sensitive measure than recall.

Some material may be remembered in visual form (pictures), and other material may be remembered in verbal form 60 (words). Some research evidence indicates that there are two different memory processes for these two kinds of material. Pictures may be processed differently from words, and concrete words high in imagery may be 65 processed differently from abstract words low in imagery. Visual images are easier to remember than words alone, leading some researchers to suggest that we should try to use visual images as much as possible in 70 memory.

There are several explanations of why we forget. Passive-decay theory says that learning causes a physical 'trace' in the brain that decays with time. Repression 75 theory says that we purposely push unpleasant or unacceptable memories into our unconscious mind. Systematic-distortion theory says that our memories may be distorted by our values and interests, to be 80 consistent with how we want the memories to be or how we think they should be. Interference theory says that forgetting is due to problems in retrieving the information, and that we can remember almost anything if given the right cues.

85

[Source: Higbee, K.L. (1977) *Your Memory, How It Works and How to Improve It* (Englewood Cliffs, N.J.: Prentice-Hall, Inc.), pp 18, 34–6]

TASK 15 Study the following illustration from the same chapter. Write three questions answered by this illustration.

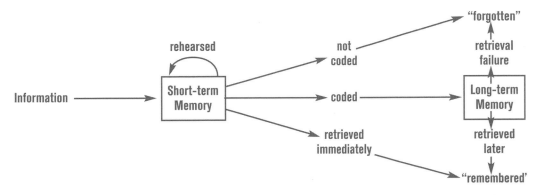

TASK 16 Compare your questions from Task 14 with the section headings for the same chapter (below). How similar are they to your questions?

MEET YOUR MEMORY
WHAT ARE THE STAGES OF MEMORY?
WHAT ARE SHORT-TERM AND LONG-TERM MEMORY?
  Short-Term Memory
  Long-Term Memory
HOW CAN WE MEASURE MEMORY?
  Recall
  Recognition
  Relearning
HOW DO WE REMEMBER PICTURES VERSUS WORDS?
WHY DO WE FORGET?
  Passive decay
  Repression
  Systematic distortion
  Interference

PART 2

Knowing what's important

UNIT 3 The spirit of enquiry

This unit aims to develop the reading strategies and skills required for:

1. surveying a text
2. understanding how facts and ideas are connected
3. understanding unfamiliar words from their immediate context
4. understanding collocations.

Before you read

Having a spirit of enquiry is an important part of being a student. One aim of study is to increase your personal understanding of the world. The purpose of research is to add to the sum of human knowledge. In this unit you will read about methods of enquiry to increase both your own understanding and advance the frontiers of knowledge. The topics covered in this unit are: designing experiments, problem-solving, carrying out surveys and making questionnaires.

You will not only read about methods of enquiry, you will also take part in an experiment to find out how to read more effectively.

TASK 1 Look at this statement.

Male birds sing to attract female birds.

Working with a partner, try to devise an experiment to investigate this claim. Note briefly the method you would use.

TASK 2 Study this introduction to a report of an experiment to investigate why male birds sing. The text contains some specialist vocabulary. Use the strategies you studied in Unit 2 to decide if you need to know the meaning of any of these words.

Male passerine birds are noted for their singing. Considerable study has been made of the frequency, duration and even regional variation in their song (Swales, *et al*, 1994). Most ornithologists have taken it for granted that they sing to attract females. But no one has produced any evidence to support this assumption. Our study focused on the pied flycatcher (*Ficedula hypoleuca*) and the collared flycatcher (*Ficedula albicollis*). It involved setting up nesting-box traps in a known nesting site near Uppsala, Sweden.

Does this text give you any new ideas about how to conduct your experiment? Think again about your method. Note any changes.

TASK 3   We will study another text which may help you with the design of your experiment. The title is *Conducting Biological Experiments*. Before you read it, try to predict some of the words and ideas that may come up in the text. Note them down; then share your ideas with the others in your group.

TASK 4   The following diagram shows some of the words which appear in the text. Are any of them on the list you made in Task 3? Try to explain what the connection is between the title and each of the words surrounding it. In what order would you expect to find these words? Share your ideas with the others in your class.

hypothesis	confirmed	conclude
significant	CONDUCTING BIOLOGICAL EXPERIMENTS	results
investigation	suggest	predict

TASK 5   As you read the text 'Conducting biological experiments', you will find a choice of endings to some of the sentences. Try to predict how a sentence will continue at each numbered point. Test your prediction by selecting what you consider the most logical of the alternatives given. You will probably find when you read on, that you have not always chosen correctly. If this happens, go back and read the section again. Check whether you have failed to make the correct guess because the text is not clear or because you have missed some clues which could have helped you. Mask the text with a piece of paper as you read so that you cannot read ahead.

When you have completed this task, compare your answers with your neighbour.

CONDUCTING
BIOLOGICAL EXPERIMENTS

A hypothesis stands or falls on the experiments that are carried out to test it. It is therefore essential to

1 **a** make a sensible hypothesis.   **b** do the right experiment in the right way.

The predictions made from the hypothesis should tell the investigator exactly what experiments need to be done. This might seem obvious, but it is surprising how often a student, having formulated a very sensible hypothesis, goes on to

2 a devise experiments which do not test it at all. **b** make highly inaccurate predictions.

Often a single crucial experiment is enough to settle the matter. Here is an example. On the basis that all cells have one, we conclude that the nucleus is

3 a essential for life. **b** the central part of cells.

From this we predict that a cell without a nucleus will die. The experimental test is obvious: assuming that it is technically feasible, we must

4 a examine as many cells as possible. **b** remove the nucleus from a cell and see what happens.

Enucleation of cells is possible, at any rate with a large cell like Amoeba. The nucleus is carefully sucked out with a very fine pipette. It is found, as predicted, that

5 a the cell dies. **b** the cell survives.

But can we be certain that it is the absence of the nucleus which causes death, and not

6 a factors in the environment? **b** the damage inflicted on the cell during the operation?

To find the answer to this we must set up a control: a second Amoeba has its nucleus removed in exactly the same way, and then immediately

7 a destroyed. **b** put back again.

The same amount of damage is done to the cell but it is not permanently deprived of its nucleus. Apart from this the two Amoebae must be

8 a treated quite differently. **b** kept in exactly the same conditions.

The control Amoebae do in fact survive, suggesting (proving?) that it is

9 a the absence of the nucleus **b** the damage done in removing the nucleus

which causes death. Setting up appropriate controls is an essential part of any investigation. It provides a standard with which the experimental situation can be compared.

One further point before we leave this topic. It is not sufficient to do the experiment on only one pair of Amoebae, even though

10 a they may give the expected results. **b** this is very time-consuming.

The experiment must be repeated many times, and consistent results obtained, before this prediction can be regarded as confirmed. The quickest way of doing this in the case described above is to set up a group of enucleated Amoebae, perhaps fifty in all (the experimental group). At the same time we prepare a control group of non-enucleated specimens. If we are lucky it may turn out that all the individuals in the experimental group die, whereas

11 a all those in the control group survive. **b** all those in the control group die.

But in biological experiments it often turns out that only a proportion of the tests

12 a prove anything. **b** give the expected results.

In such cases it may be necessary to repeat the experiment over and over again, and subject the results to statistical analysis, to establish whether the results are significant or merely the result of chance.

[Source: Roberts, M.B.V. (1976) *Biology: A Functional Approach* (London: Nelson), pp 5–6]

TASK 6 Does Task 5 give you ideas for further improving the design of your bird song experiment? Discuss your ideas with your partner.

  When you have completed your discussion, read the brief report in the Key on page 144. Note any differences between your experiment and the one described.

Reading and interaction

Surveying a text

Surveying a text means reading to obtain a general idea of its contents. Reading for a general idea depends on good sampling – knowing where to look, knowing which parts of the text can help us most. We read a little – take a sample – and predict what will come next. The sample provides clues as to how the text will continue. Then we take another sample and adjust our prediction. Each time, the sample provides clues as to how the text will continue. Because we don't read everything when we read to get a general idea, this kind of reading also depends on good prediction skills.

  As you become a more experienced reader, you will sample more effectively. Consequently your predictions will become more accurate. In the tasks that follow we will try to find out what parts of a text can provide the best samples.

TASK 7 You will be studying three samples taken from 'Functional fixity: A barrier to creative problem solving'. You will use the information gained to answer the six questions below. When you can answer all of the questions, you will have gained a general idea of the text you are sampling. Look at the first sample to find out how much it helps you to answer the questions. Give as full an answer to each question as you can *before* you read the next sample. Then repeat this process for the other samples.

  1 What is functional fixity?
  2 What task were the groups asked to do?
  3 What was the single difference between the groups?
  4 What were the results?
  5 What conclusion can we make from these results?
  6 What was the effect of the extra objects?

Our aim is to find out which samples help us most to get a general idea of the text. Which questions does Sample 1 help us to answer? Think about this before you read on.

Sample 1 (Title and illustrations)

FUNCTIONAL FIXITY: A BARRIER TO CREATIVE PROBLEM SOLVING

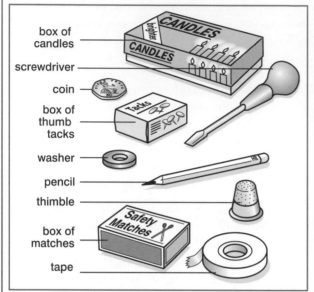

Figure A

Figure B

Now study Sample 2. Does it help you to answer more of the questions or give better answers to some of the questions?

Sample 2 (First sentence of each paragraph added)

FUNCTIONAL FIXITY: A BARRIER TO CREATIVE PROBLEM SOLVING

The German psychologist Karl Duncker first proposed the concept of functional fixity about 1930, and he illustrated it with a few simple experiments.

The task: Mount three candles vertically on a soft wooden screen, using any object on the table.

For one group (twenty-nine college students), the candles, matches, and tacks were placed *in* the three boxes before they were presented to the subjects (Figure A).

Of the first group, only twelve of the subjects (or 41 percent) were able to solve the problem: apparently the remaining subjects in this group could not perceive the boxes with the meaning of platform or shelf.

These results give striking evidence that functional fixity may be an important barrier in creative problem solving.

Give as full an answer to each question as you can *before* you read on.

Now study Sample 3. Does it help you to answer more of the questions? Does it help you to give better answers to some of the questions? Try to draw the solution to the problem the subjects were set.

Sample 3 (First and last paragraphs added)

FUNCTIONAL FIXITY: A BARRIER TO CREATIVE PROBLEM SOLVING

The German psychologist Karl Duncker first proposed the concept of functional fixity about 1930, and he illustrated it with a few simple experiments. Because these experiments were done with so few subjects, several American psychologists repeated them, and they obtained results similar to Duncker's. R.E. Adamson at Stanford University did one such experiment.

The task: Mount three candles vertically on a soft wooden screen, using any object on the table.

For one group (twenty-nine college students), the candles, matches, and tacks were placed *in* the three boxes before they were presented to the subjects (Figure A).

Of the first group, only twelve of the subjects (or 41 percent) were able to solve the problem: apparently the remaining subjects in this group could not perceive the boxes with the meaning of platform or shelf.

These results give striking evidence that functional fixity may be an important barrier in creative problem solving. Note also the mental dazzle operating here, as a result of the useless, hence distracting, extra objects.

[Source: Krech, D., Crutchfield, R.S. and Livson, N. (1982) *Elements of Psychology*, 4th Edn, (New York: Knopf), p 158]

TASK 8 Compare your answers and your drawings with the others in your study group. Discuss any differences. Then check the accuracy of your answers and your drawings with the complete text in the Key, page 144.

Which samples of the text gave you the most help with the questions? Which questions could not be answered fully? Do you think that sampling in this way could be useful for all texts?

Text exploration

Discourse study: Linking words

While sampling will help us to obtain a general idea of a text, we need to know how the facts and ideas which compose the text are linked to understand the meaning of the text in detail. We will study here how writers link facts and ideas.

TASK 9 Complete these sentences about questionnaires and interviews. Compare your completed sentences with your partner.

1 Questionnaires are cheaper than interviews because ...
2 Interviews are expensive whereas ...
3 People often fill in questionnaires without much thought. As a result ...
4 Postal questionnaires have a poor response rate; i.e. ...

TASK 10 Here is another example for you to try. This time try to predict how the text will continue at each numbered point.

When making a questionnaire, avoid imprecise terms like 'occasionally' and 'sometimes' since
1 a) people understand such words in different ways.
    b) you should use shorter words.

Consequently, if your questionnaire includes such terms,
2 a) it will be very lengthy.
    b) it will not be reliable.

In other words,
3 a) it will not provide consistent results.
    b) it will be very expensive to produce.

For example, a teenager may answer that he plays computer games 'occasionally' but his parents may respond that he plays
4 a) 'very often'.
    b) about three hours a week.

Authors sometimes use linking words and phrases to mark the connections between the ideas in their writing. Knowing these words will help you both to understand how the ideas in a text are connected and also to make more accurate predictions as you read.

Self-study Study these examples and try to add further linking words and phrases to the table.

Idea	Marked by
Reason	because, since
Contrast	whereas, but
Conclusion	consequently, as a result
Rephrasing	in other words, i.e.
Example	for example, for instance
Addition	furthermore, in addition

TASK 11 Select the correct linking word or phrase from the two alternatives given.

RELIABILITY AND VALIDITY

Reliability and validity are key concepts in any form of enquiry. Reliability is a measure of consistency. *Furthermore/For example*, if a clock is sometimes fast and sometimes slow, it is unreliable. If a questionnaire produces different results for the same group of people each time it is used, then the questionnaire is unreliable.

Validity is a measure of truth. It is possible for a questionnaire to be highly reliable yet invalid, like a clock which is always ten minutes slow. *In contrast/In other words*, a clock which is always right provides a valid and reliable measure of time. Similarly, a questionnaire which really measures what it claims to measure is a valid questionnaire. We can assess how valid our questionnaire is by comparing its results with an independent measure. *In addition/For instance*, if we ask people how often they visit their local theatre and then check the results against ticket sales, we will know how valid our questionnaire is. *However/Because* often independent measures are themselves unreliable and of low validity. *Furthermore/Consequently*, in many cases there are no independent measures. *In other words/However*, a 'true' answer does not exist.

Word study: Using immediate context

....

TASK 12 The extract below contains some words in **bold** type that may be unfamiliar to you. Identify the part of speech each word belongs to (e.g. noun). Then try to guess the meaning of each word as it is used in the text. Complete the following grid with your answers. Do not use a dictionary at this stage.

Word	Part of speech	Meaning
drawbacks		
spontaneous		
ambiguity		

Questionnaires have certain obvious advantages, but they also have **drawbacks.** **Spontaneous** answers cannot be distinguished from thought-out answers. Questions can be misunderstood because it is difficult to avoid **ambiguity** except in the most simple questions. Different answers cannot be treated as independent since the subject can see all the questions before answering any one of them.

In Unit 2 we studied the first steps in finding out the approximate meaning of unfamiliar words – identifying the kind of word, and the part of speech, as a means of limiting the range of meaning. The second step in working out the meaning of an unfamiliar word is to examine the immediate context of the word – the sentence in which it appears. Often the sentence contains enough clues to help you to get an approximate meaning of the word. Linking words can help. Here are some examples.

1 Questionnaires have certain obvious advantages,
   but (= expect a contrast)
   they also have drawbacks.

The contrast is between 'advantages' and 'drawbacks'. Hence we can work out that 'drawbacks' means 'disadvantages'.

Sometimes words which are opposites are contrasted in a sentence. If you know the meaning of one of these words, you can find out the meaning of the other. For example,

2 Spontaneous answers cannot be
   distinguished from (= expect an opposite)
   thought-out answers.

Hence we can work out that a spontaneous answer is one which is not thought-out. In other words, 'spontaneous' means 'without thinking'.

3 Questions can be misunderstood
   because (= expect a reason)
   it is difficult to avoid ambiguity.

In this case the linking word tells us that 'ambiguity' is the reason why something may be misunderstood/something which causes misunderstanding.

Check in your dictionary for more accurate definitions of these three words.

TASK 13 Read the sentences 1–8 and try to guess the meaning of each of the words in *italics*. Underline the clues in the sentence which help you. When you have finished, compare ideas with your partner. Then check the accuracy of your guesses using a dictionary.

1 The interview is a *flexible* tool which can be altered to suit its role in the study.
2 Replies can be more *candid* since respondents do not have to commit themselves in writing.
3 The interviewer can distinguish between a genuine and an *insincere* response.
4 Interviewers can control the sequence of items; hence the respondent cannot look ahead and *anticipate* the trend of the inquiries.

5 The problem of taking full notes of a conversation during an interview is usually solved by *restricting* writing to marks or numbers.

6 Interviewers may give an *inkling* of their own opinion or expectations by their tone of voice, the way in which they read the questions, or simply by their appearance, dress and accent.

7 Questionnaires can be *anonymous* – but not if identification is required for follow-up study.

8 Respondents fill in their own answers and so cannot be *misheard*.

Word study: Collocations

Part of knowing what a word means and how to use it is knowing which words occur with it. For example, we *devise, conduct* or *carry out* an **experiment**. *Devise, conduct* and *carry out* are common collocations of **experiment** whereas *make* is not. Study these key words from *Conducting Biological Experiments* and some of the words which collocate with them:

test	+	**hypothesis**
significant	+	**results**
statistical	+	**analysis**
	confirm +	prediction

TASK 14 The table on the next page lists a number of common academic headwords with spaces for their collocates alongside. Match each of the headwords with one of their collocates from the list below.

agreement	law
changes	legitimate
circumstances	limits
class	market
come to	medical
education	progress
evolution	response
experimental	scientific
findings	situation
gravity	transfer

collocates	headword	collocates
	appropriate	
	assess	
	authority	
	conclude	
	conclusion	
	design (N)	
	display (V)	
	economy	
	enforce	
	evaluate	
	exceed	
	method	
	normal	
	occur	
	positive	
	primary	
	research (N)	
	specific	
	structure	
	theory	

TASK 15 Decide in which context the collocates in Task 14 may occur, e.g. *positive transfer* is likely to occur in the context of psychology. Add any other collocates from your own discipline.

Application

In this section we will practise sampling and prediction skills. Each of the texts are short reports of experiments and investigations.

TASK 16 Study this list of titles. Try to predict what each text will be about. You may use a dictionary.
1 Predators key to forest survival.
(*New Scientist* Online News 30/12/01)
2 Knock-out pig clones advance transplant hopes
(*New Scientist* Online News 3/1/02)
3 Electron beams could be used to irradiate post
(*New Scientist* Online News 24/10/01)
4 Thermal camera captures guilty faces
(*New Scientist* Online News 2/1/02)

TASK 17 The following two illustrations each belong to a text listed in Task 16. Match the illustrations to the texts. Refine the predictions you made earlier about these two texts.

Photo: PPL Therapeutics

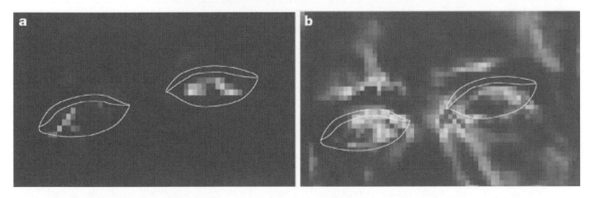

Periorbital, high-resolution thermal images of the face of a 'guilty' subject. Images were obtained before (a) and after (b) lying in reply to the question 'Did you steal the $20?'

TASK 18 The texts listed in Task 16 are given in full in the Key on page 145 to 148. Study the texts there and sample the parts which you think will help you most with predicting the main points. Do not spend more than one minute on any one text.

TASK 19 Write down your predictions of the main points of each text that you read in Task 18 – without looking back at the text. Then read the text at your own speed to check your predictions.

UNIT 4 The developing world

This unit aims to develop the reading strategies and skills required for:

1 identifying important points

2 understanding text structure

3 grouping words in semantic sets.

Before you read

Wherever we live, the issues which confront the three-quarters of the world's population who inhabit the developing world are important to all of us. The texts in this unit deal with some of these issues.

TASK 1 Make a list of five countries of the developing world. Why do you think they should be classified in this way? What issues are of particular importance to such countries? Discuss your answers with your study group and make a joint list of the important issues.

TASK 2 Study this Contents page. Which headings will cover the issues you listed in Task 1? Match your list with the Contents headings.

INTERNATIONAL DEVELOPMENT ABSTRACTS

Agriculture and Rural Development
Environment and Development
Economic Conditions
Comparative Development Strategies
Adjustment Policies, Economic Reform
Financial Sector, Debt
Private Investment Flows, Multinationals
Industry, Industrial Policy
Small Business Promotion and the
    Informal Sector
Parallel and Illegal Economy
Tourism
Labour and Management, Economic
    Policy
Water

Forestry
Hydrocarbons and Mining
Energy
Demography and Population
Migration, Refugees, Resettlement,
    Labour Migration
Urbanisation and Urban Planning
Regional and Spatial Development and
    Planning
Hazards and Disaster Planning
Health, Health Systems and Services
Food, Food Supply
Nutrition
Education and Training
Housing

Social Policy, other Social Services
Poverty, Welfare and Income
    Distribution
Ethnicity and Fourth World Issues
Women and Gender Issues
Nongovernmental Organisations and
    People's Participation
Aid Flows and Policies
Project Design and Appraisal
International Relations, Conflict and
    Cooperation
Trade and Trade Policy

Transport and Communications
Technology and Science Policy
Development Theory and Concepts
Culture and Development
Institutional Framework and
    Administration
Politics

[Source: Amos, M. (Ed.) (1996) *International Development Abstracts*, (Amsterdam: Elsevier), pp iii, iv]

TASK 3 Study the following brief texts and graphics on developing world issues (numbered 1–8). Sample the text; then match each extract to one of the Contents headings given in Task 2.

1

Households with dishwashers, washing machines and sprinklers: 1,000 litres a day

Households using a public hydrant in the street: 20–70 litres a day

Households with a piped supply and taps: 100–350 litres a day

Households using a stream or distant water: 2–5 litres a day

2

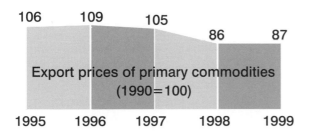

106   109   105   86   87

Export prices of primary commodities (1990=100)

1995   1996   1997   1998   1999

3

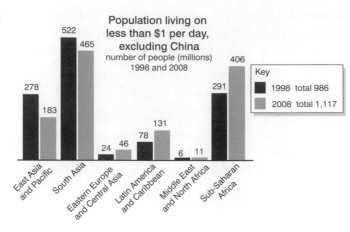

Population living on less than $1 per day, excluding China
number of people (millions)
1998 and 2008

Key
■ 1998 total 986
■ 2008 total 1,117

East Asia and Pacific: 278, 183
South Asia: 522, 465
Eastern Europe and Central Asia: 24, 46
Latin America and Caribbean: 78, 131
Middle East and North Africa: 6, 11
Sub-Saharan Africa: 291, 406

4 The price of a jar of instant coffee

Growers 10%
Exporters 10%
Shippers and Roasters 55%
Retailers 25%

5

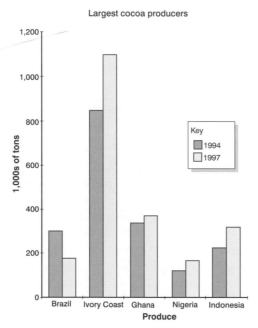

Largest cocoa producers

Key
■ 1994
□ 1997

1,000s of tons

Brazil, Ivory Coast, Ghana, Nigeria, Indonesia

Produce

6 The 'tyranny of distance' has so far kept most of the islands out of the reach of tourism – but the world's largest and ultimate consumer 'industry' will not be denied for long:

- Only Nadi in Fiji among the Pacific Member Countries of the World Bank can cope with a fully-laden Boeing 747 jet.
- Tourist arrivals in the East Asia Pacific region increased by 8.7% between 1988 and 1993 but in the South Pacific by just 6.8% – from 330,000 to 450,000. This suggests that tourism in the South Pacific is set to expand considerably.
- Around a third of the hotel rooms are in 7% of the total number of establishments: the large 'resort' hotels. These hotels are owned and operated by overseas investors and managers – only a small proportion of the income remains locally.

7 Many forests on the west coast of the US, in the Philippines, Indonesia and Malaysia have been logged out. So Sarawak and Papua New Guinea have become the substitute source of supply for the plywood and veneer mills of Japan and Korea. The small South Pacific islands are now following suit.

   In 1993 natural forest still covered 45% of Fiji, 78% of the Solomon Islands, 75% of Vanuatu and 77% of Western Samoa.

   In 1995 the 'sustainable' annual cut for the Solomon Islands was estimated at 286,000 m^3 – in 1994 the actual cut was 700,000 m^3 and seemed likely to increase to 1,300,000 m^3. At this rate, the islands will be logged out in less than five years.

   Similar rates of deforestation apply in Vanuatu and Western Samoa. Major logging contracts are planned for Fiji.

   Profits described as 'excessive' by the World Bank itself are made by the logging companies and average 30 per cent of the value.

8 **Girls' primary enrolment as % boys (UNESCO 1998)**

| Yemen 40% | Pakistan 45% | Chad 49% | Afghanistan 50% | Somalia 53% |
| Guinea 54% | Liberia 55% | Benin 57% | Guinea Bissau 58% | Ethiopia 62% |

[Sources: 1 New Internationalist Publications, Oxford: NI322, April 2000, Factfile on Water; 2 and 3 NI334 May 2001, WTO the facts, Export prices of primary commodities. Population living on less than $1 per day, excluding China; 4 NI271 Coffee – the facts; 6 and 7 NI291, June 1997, South Pacific; 8 NI315, August 1999, Gender canyon.]

TASK 4 Underline what you think are the most important points in the text *Too many mouths*. Compare your choice with a partner. Discuss how you made your selection of points.

   This text draws on ideas from *Worlds Apart, the economic gulf between nations*, Peter Donaldson, BBC, London, 1971.

Too many mouths

One of the most important problems facing developing countries today is the rapid increase in population. In the last twenty-five years, the population of the world has doubled. As the developing world has a population growth rate which is twice that of the developed world, most of that population increase has taken place in the poorer countries of the world. The main point 10 to be made here is that more and more people are concentrated in those countries which are least able to provide a living for them.

   What is responsible for this 15 population rise is not an increase in fertility, but a sharp decline in the death rate in developing countries. In the absence of birth control, the maximum birth rate is around 4%. For a 20 population to remain static in these circumstances, the death rate would have to be the same. Improving food supplies can reduce the death rate to 3%. Better public health and medical care can $\qquad$ 25 cut the death rate by a further 2%. The resultant population growth of 3% will double the population every twenty-five years.

The main reason for the reduction in $\qquad$ 30 the death rate in the developing world has been improved public health measures. For example, in Sri Lanka the death rate was halved over ten years by spraying the mosquitoes which carry $\qquad$ 35 malaria. Why is it so easy to cut the death rate in this way and yet so hard to reduce the birth rate? One answer is that public health measures can be very cheap. Anti-malarial spraying is $\qquad$ 40 inexpensive. But this is not the important point. For birth control programmes to be successful, a change in attitude is required whereas death control can be achieved autonomously. In other $\qquad$ 45 words, the death rate can be cut without anything else changing.

Reading and interaction

Reading for important points

In Unit 3 we studied how to survey a text to obtain a general idea of its contents. We found that good sampling (knowing where to look) and good prediction skills (making intelligent guesses based on these samples) were important when reading for a general idea.

Identifying what is important in a text depends on good sampling but it also depends on knowing what to look for – the clues that help us to identify the important points and to separate them from the less important details.

Look again at the text from Task 4 (see below). Some of the words have been highlighted for you.

The main reason for the reduction in the death rate in the developing world has been improved public health measures. **For example**, in Sri Lanka the death rate was halved over ten years by spraying the mosquitoes which carry malaria. **Why** is it so easy to cut the death rate in this way and yet so hard to reduce the birth rate? **One answer** is that public health measures can be very cheap. Anti-malarial spraying is inexpensive. **But this is not the important point.** For birth control programmes to be successful, a change in attitude is required whereas death control can be achieved autonomously. **In other words**, the death rate can be cut without anything else changing.

The highlighted words are signposts. They can help you to find the important parts of a text. They can also warn you that some things in the text are not so important. Let's examine some of the signposts writers use.

1 These phrases indicate an important point.
The main/important point/conclusion/reason ...
The point to note here ...
Above all ...

2 Sometimes we are told how many important points to expect. For example:
There are three major reasons ...

3 Important points may be highlighted using *italics*, **bold** type or CAPITALS.
*An important requirement for development is **freedom from debt**.*
In this example the word order also emphasises the phrase in bold type. Compare it to:
***Freedom from debt** is an important requirement for development.*

4 *But* and *however* often indicate an important contrast, qualification or correction. For example:
The rising birth rate is not due to increased fertility, but to a sharp decline in the death rate.

5 Asking a question in a text is a way of highlighting the answer that follows. For example:
Why is a piped water supply so important? Disease due to contaminated water is a common cause of death in childhood.

6 A writer may repeat an important point to make sure it is understood. For example:
Death control can be achieved autonomously. In other words, the death rate can be cut without anything else changing.

7 Conclusions are usually important. Look out for signposts such as:
therefore   the result
in conclusion   we can conclude
one of the primary conclusions

8 Examples are usually less important, although a key example can help you to remember a main point. Examples are signposted by phrases such as:
for example/instance like
such as   these include
to illustrate   among these are
They may also be shown simply by punctuation. For example,
The developing countries are dependent on cash crops – sugar, coffee, cacao, cotton.
Precipitating factors are those which reduce the food supply (droughts, floods, wars, epidemics) ...

Now read the text again (below). This time the meaning of each signpost has been added in brackets [ ].

The main reason for [*this is important*] the reduction in the death rate in the developing world has been improved public health measures. **For example,** [*this is only to illustrate*] in Sri Lanka the death rate was halved over ten years by spraying the mosquitoes which carry malaria. **Why** [*the answer to this question is important*] is it so easy to cut the death rate in this way and yet so hard to reduce the birth rate? **One answer** [*this is only one answer – not the important one*] is that public health measures can be very cheap. Anti-malarial spraying is inexpensive. **But this is not the important point.** [*now I'm going to tell you what the important point is*] For birth control programmes to be successful, a change in attitude is required whereas death control can be achieved autonomously. **In other words,** [*this is so important, I'll repeat it in simpler words*] the death rate can be cut without anything else changing.

TASK 5 The signposts in this text have been highlighted. Put a tick [✓] after those which indicate an important point and a cross [✗] after those which indicate information which is less important.

Why is it so difficult to solve the unemployment problems of the developing world? [ ] There are **three main reasons**. [ ] **Firstly** [ ] there is the constant pressure of a rapidly rising population. This problem is made worse in cities by the drift of people from country areas to escape the poverty of rural life. **Then** [ ] there are problems of bad manpower planning. **For example**, [ ] a feature of unemployment in the developing world is the educated unemployed – the lawyers or arts graduates who have been trained at great expense for jobs which do not exist. **The point here** [ ] is that the manpower plan has not been matched to the production plan. **However, the major reason** [ ] for many countries failing to solve the unemployment problem has been their governments' preference for large-scale capital-intensive projects which use up scarce resources and have little impact on unemployment. **In fact**, [ ] by destroying local craft-based industry, such projects may even create further unemployment.

TASK 6 In Task 7 you are going to read a text with the following title and opening sentence.

The Famine Process
It is useful to identify three categories of cause of famines.

First, make a list of all the reasons you can think of why famines sometimes occur in the developing world.

TASK 7 Work in groups of three. Each choose a different text, **A**, **B** or **C**, which are from **The Famine Process**. Identify the main points and note them in your section of the table on page 60. Use the strategies described in Unit 2 to deal with unfamiliar vocabulary. Do not compare answers at this stage; wait until Task 8.

Text A

First there are *long-term* causes of household income loss or income instability which increases the vulnerability of poor people. High among these in Africa is environmental degradation, affecting pastoralists but also cultivators in arid and semi-arid areas. The Sahel, the Horn and western southern Africa are the areas where long-term factors have been increasing famine risk most. Social changes, particularly increased assetlessness among rural people, also increase famine risk. Among these are occupation of the best land by the rich and consequent loss of access by the poor and the breakdown of traditional social obligations to the poor.

Text B

Second there are *precipitating factors*, the events which dislodge the last food security of the poor, setting off the secondary events which worsen the situation – spiralling food prices, collapsing prices of rural assets (particularly livestock, because of lack of feed and the need to sell), calling in debts, laying-off of employees, ultimately abandoning the aged, the sick and the very young, and migration to towns. Precipitating factors include all those which actually reduce the food supply (drought, flood, war, epidemics) as well as those which it is feared will do so, and any which reduce the purchasing power of the poor.

Text C

Third there is *relief failure*. For famine to be precipitated, governmental famine-prevention administration must be inadequate, incompetent, or unable to operate. In Bengal, 'administrative chaos' in the famine relief operation worsened the famine. In Bangladesh, improvement in famine relief administration during the 1970s greatly reduced famine in the early 1980s (see Ch.5). Effective relief has prevented famine in Botswana and Gujerat state in India (see Ch.5). Delays in relief have been a major factor in recent famines in Sudan and Ethiopia (see Ch.3). The politics of famine relief (international and national) have played their part in worsening the Ethiopian and Mozambique famines through the delivery of food aid (Tickner 1985:91) while civil wars have severely hampered food distribution.

[Source: Curtis, D., Hubbard, M. and Shepherd, A. (1988) *Preventing Famine, Policies and Prospects for Africa* (London and New York: Routledge), pp 5–6 abridged]

Causes of famine

Text A

First category

_____

Causes

1 _____

2 _____

Example of social changes

1 _____

_____

Text B

Second category

_____

Types of precipitating factors

1 _____

2 _____

Example of secondary events

1 _____

_____

Text C

Third category

_____

Example of relief failure

1 _____

Example of relief success

1 _____

Find out from the others in your group the important points in their texts. Note them in the table. Make sure each section is complete.

When you have finished, read the remaining texts yourself. Do you agree with the choice of main points made by your group? Discuss any differences.

Text exploration
Discourse study: Signpost expressions
In the 'Reading and interaction' section, we studied how signpost expressions may help you to identify the important parts of a text. Writers may also use signpost expressions to indicate how the text is organised and to show when new topics are introduced.

Study the following four extracts from a text on *Desertification*. Note the expressions which have been highlighted.

1 Deserts cover much of the world's surface. Each year over 100,000 km² of new desert is formed. This process is called desertification. **There are three major causes** of desertification: over-cultivation, over-grazing and deforestation. Over-cultivation and over-grazing are related causes and **I will discuss them first**.

2 **Let us consider now** deforestation which affects many parts of the developing world from the Himalayas to the Amazon basin.

3 **Can the process of desertification be halted?** A number of solutions have been attempted. One of the commonest is to plant belts of drought-resistant trees.

4 Given that the factors which lead to the misuse of land are unlikely to change in the next decade, **we may conclude that** the process of desertification will be slowed but not halted.

Study these signpost expressions for text organisation.

1 Signposts which show the order in which topics will be covered.
   There are three major causes: … I will discuss them first.

2 Signposts which indicate a change of topic:
   Let us consider now …
   Having dealt with …
   Next …
   Lastly …
   Asking a question in a text can both indicate a change of topic and highlight the answer.
   Can the process of desertification be halted?

3 Signposts which indicate the end of a topic or the end of a text – a time to read carefully as the main points are often made here.
   We may conclude that
   In conclusion

Word study: Building an academic vocabulary

One way to remember your growing vocabulary is to group the new words into sets according to their meanings. All of these verbs share the idea of causing something to happen. Group them into the following sets:

Cause + START   Cause + MORE   Cause + LESS
Cause + HARM

aggravate	dislodge	increase	reduce
create	double	lower	restrict
cut	halve	precipitate	set off
damage	hamper	raise ✓	worsen

Here are some of the ways these words are used in this book:
1 Deforestation and desertification *aggravate* floods and droughts.
2 The environment makes it difficult to *create* the agricultural surplus required for development.
3 Many animals, especially predators, need a wide territory. If this is *reduced*, in the short term drought, disease or war may *cut* their numbers.
4 Overfishing will *damage* fish stocks.
5 There are precipitating factors, the events which *dislodge* the last food security of the poor, *setting off* the secondary events which *worsen* the situation
6 In the last 25 years, the population of the world has *doubled*.
7 In Sri Lanka the death rate was *halved* over ten years by spraying the mosquitoes which carry malaria.
8 Civil wars have severely *hampered* food distribution.
9 Fertilizer and irrigation can *increase* the productivity of the developing world.
10 Small-scale, labour-intensive technologies and basic health care involving the community can *lower* the cost of investment.
11 For famine to be *precipitated*, governmental famine-prevention administration must be inadequate, incompetent, or unable to operate.
12 The sea water is warmed but not *raised* to boiling point.
13 Water shortage *restricts* the areas where three crops a year are possible.

Application

TASK 10 Five extracts from *Inside the Third World* are given below. Underline the main points in each paragraph. Then select the best summary from the alternatives (a–c), which appear after each paragraph.

Disasters, of course, are not entirely due to the injustice of nature: the injustice of man also plays its part. Poverty contributes both to the causation and impact of disaster. It is a major cause of deforestation and desertification which aggravate floods and droughts. Poverty and the pressure of population drive the poor to live in increasingly dangerous places, like slums perched on steep slopes, or the flood- and cyclone-ridden islands of the Ganges delta in Bangladesh. Poor people can afford only flimsy houses of wood, mud and straw, liable to collapse in a heavy storm. Serious disasters appear to be increasing in frequency. A study by the University of Bradford found that the average number per year rose from five between 1919 and 1971, to eleven between 1951 and 1971, and over seventeen between 1968 and 1971. It seems unlikely that nature's inclemency is growing at this rate. The increase is probably due to the increasing disaster-proneness of the poor. But disasters of themselves accentuate poverty and make their victims more disaster-prone for the future.

1 a) Poverty makes the poor more disaster-prone, which results in more disasters and hence more poverty.
  b) The homes of poor people are easily destroyed in disasters.
  c) Poverty results in deforestation and desertification which contribute to other disasters.

All in all, the physical environment has not favoured the developing countries. The low productivity of the soil and of man has hampered growth and, along with the setbacks of variable rains and disasters, helped to prevent the emergence of a large and stable agricultural surplus. Such a surplus is the first requirement of development.

2 a The soil in many developing countries is not very productive.
  b Development requires a stable agricultural surplus.
  c The environment makes it difficult to create the agricultural surplus required for development.

There are some potential advantages in being closer to the sun. Given enough fertilizer and water, year-round sunshine can create an extraordinary agricultural potential, allowing as much as three crops a year. But water shortage restricts the areas where this is possible. As the oil runs out and solar power becomes more economical, the Third World will have greater supplies of endlessly renewable energy than the developed temperate zone countries.

3 a Fertilizer and irrigation can increase the productivity of the developing world.
  b Two potential advantages of ample sunshine are increased agricultural output and solar energy.
  c The developed world has less solar energy potential than the developing world.

But these prospects are as yet only hypothetical. Up to the present day, the hostile environment has been one of the key restraints in holding back economic development. It has raised 85 the threshold of investment that the developing countries need to leap before they can industrialize. They need to invest more than western countries did at similar stages, in 90 irrigation, flood control and erosion control for agriculture, and in human resources, to combat the effect of disease and heat on labour productivity. 95

4 a) Development has been held back because of the higher investment needed to overcome the effects of the environment.
   b) Irrigation and erosion control 100 are very expensive for developing countries.
   c) Heat and disease reduce labour productivity.

This investment hurdle was leapt in 105 water control by the ancient empires of the Middle East, Asia and South America. It can be leapt again. Small-scale, labour-intensive technologies and basic health care involving the 110 community can lower the cost of investment, while foreign aid and loans can help provide the necessary funds.

5 a) The ancient empires of the Middle East, Asia and South America 115 solved the problem of irrigation.
   b) The investment problem can be overcome by focusing on less-expensive technologies and community health care and by 120 using loans and aid money.
   c) Foreign aid and loans can help development.

[Source: Harrison, P. (1993) *Inside the Third World*, 3rd Edition (London: Penguin Books Ltd)]

UNIT 5 The natural world

This unit aims to develop the reading strategies and skills required for:

1. making inferences
2. taking notes
3. grouping words in semantic sets
4. finding related word forms.

Before you read

In this unit you will study the importance of making inferences when you read. You will also study ways to understand text structure and to make it easier to remember the main points in a text by note-taking. The texts in this unit are concerned with the life sciences.

TASK 1 Answer, in a sentence, the questions that follow each of these statements.

1 Parents who do not have their children vaccinated put not only their own children at risk but the whole community. *Why is this so?*
2 Bats eat moths. One species of moth has developed exceptional hearing which gives it a considerable advantage over other moths. *Why is this an advantage?*
3 Some types of fishing net are killing large numbers of immature fish. Increasing the size of the mesh would solve the problem. *How would this help?*
4 Before Ross's research into malaria, it was considered dangerous to spend the night in damp areas. *What did Ross disprove?*

TASK 2 Find the answers to questions 1–3 in the text that follows.

1 Why did a species of antelope become extinct in the Sahel?
2 Why is only one of the wild dog populations in Africa viable?
3 Why is captive breeding essential for some large animals?

Most people would agree that the best way to conserve rare animals is to preserve their habitat. Many habitats are vulnerable. The poor, the hungry and those involved in war have no time for conservation. In the Sahel, a species of antelope became extinct in the 1980s. 5

Many animals, especially predators, need a wide territory. If this is reduced, in the short term drought, disease or war may cut their numbers. In the long term, inbreeding will 10 cause extinction. Only one of the remaining wild dog populations in Africa is viable. For many animals, breeding in zoos is desirable. For larger animals, captive breeding is essential.

Reading and interaction

Making inferences

Sometimes it can be difficult to understand a text because it contains few linking words and few signpost expressions. In such situations we have to make use of two kinds of information to make sense of what we read.

1 Information from the text, i.e. clues from the words, sentences and ideas which make up the text.
2 Information we provide ourselves, i.e. clues from outside the text, from our own knowledge of the world.

To answer Task 1, we needed to link information in the text with information from our knowledge of the world. Here is an example.

Question: Why is it an advantage that one species of moth has developed exceptional hearing?

From the text
Bats eat moths.
+
One kind of moth has exceptional hearing.

Knowledge of the world
Bats produce high-frequency sound inaudible to many species.

Answer: This moth can hear the sound of hunting bats and evade them.

To answer Task 2, we needed to link different pieces of information in the text as well as draw on our knowledge of the world. Here is an example.

Question: Why is captive breeding essential for some large animals?

From the text
Many animals need a wide territory.
+
Reduced territory means inbreeding and therefore extinction may occur.

Knowledge of the world
To remain viable an animal species needs a wide genetic pool.
+
Zoos can provide animals from different areas so the available genetic pool is large.

Answer: Captive breeding is essential for some large animals because their territory is so reduced that extinction may occur through inbreeding, whereas in zoos a sufficiently wide genetic pool exists to allow healthy animals to be bred.

Combining information in this way is called making inferences. It is one of the most important reading skills to develop.

TASK 3 Note down the information you required from the text and from your own knowledge of the world for the remaining questions in Tasks 1 and 2.

Note-taking: Linear notes

Most of you will already have your own system for note-taking. If you are content with your system, omit this section.

Taking notes is an important way of learning from a text and making it easy to revise our knowledge in the future. When we take notes on a text, we have to do three things:

1 recognise what's important
2 reduce the important points to note form
3 show how the important points are linked.

In Unit 4 we studied how to recognise what's important. We will deal here with points (2) and (3).

We can reduce the important points by omitting all but the key words and by using abbreviations, either standard or personal. Some students like to use text messaging abbreviations. We can use symbols to show the relationship between the points.

TASK 4 Study this list of symbols and abbreviations. Work out what they mean. Compare your answers with others in your study group and give other examples of your own.

Symbols		Standard abbreviations		Other abbreviations	
1	=	9	re.	17	govt.
2	>	10	etc.	18	hypoth.
3	<	11	viz.	19	prob.
4	+++	12	c.f.	20	impt.
5	→	13	a.k.a	21	temp.
6	←	14	n.b.	22	std.
7	?	15	ca.	23	v.
8	??	16	e.g.	24	discussn.

The following symbols and abbreviations are commonly used in note-taking to show how important points are linked. Add other examples of your own.

Idea	Linking words	Symbols & abbreviations
Reason	because, since	∴, b.
Contrast	but, in contrast, whereas	BUT
Result	as a result, consequently, so, therefore	∴, t.
Rephrasing	in other words	i.e.
Example	for example, for instance, such as	e.g.
Addition	furthermore, in addition, moreover	&

State	Example	Symbols
Increase	accelerate, increase, rise,	↗
Decrease	fall, reduce, slow down	↘
No change	equal, static	=
Pace of change	sharp/ly, steep/ly	⇑, ⇓
Change by a set amount	double, treble, halve	2×, 3×, ½×
Possibility	could, may, might	?, ??
Cause and effect	cause, lead to, result in	→
Effect and cause	caused by, due to, result from	←

TASK 5 Underline the most important points in *Forest pyre* as preparation for note-taking. Then compare your choice with others in your study group. Discuss how you know which points are the most important.

FOREST PYRE

In 1996, there was an estimated 3.3bn hectares of forest worldwide. But this figure is rapidly decreasing. A 1982 survey showed that up to 11.3m hectares of rainforest are [5] felled annually. In Africa alone, 85% of tropical forest has been felled or degraded. The forests are destroyed by plantations and cash crops, log-ging, urbanisation and construction [10] projects such as dams, roads and mines.

Rainforests play a vital role in regulating the Earth's climate, pre-venting soil erosion and storing and purifying water. Furthermore they [15] are home to over half the world's species. In just 0.4 hectares of rain-forest there are some 1500 plant species and 750 tree species. The rainforest has also provided us with [20] many products such as chocolate, vanilla, chicle, bananas and various medicinal cures. The deforestation of the world's rainforests has mas-sive environmental implications, [25] threatens the homes of many in-digenous peoples and endangers the habitat of many creatures.

[Source: *Guardian Education*, 23/4/02, 'Forest pyre', adapted]

TASK 6 Use your own system of note-taking to reduce the main points to note form. Compare your notes with others in your group. Discuss any differences in the points noted. Justify your choice.

Text exploration

Discourse study: Identifying text structure

Texts may be divided into sections, each marked by section headings. Texts are usually further divided into paragraphs. When we come to a text, we have expectations about its structure. For example, we may expect the first paragraph to give an introduction and the last to provide a conclusion. A new paragraph may indicate a minor shift of topic and a new section a major shift.

However, these can only be expectations. A new paragraph does not always mean a new topic. A single topic may be developed over several paragraphs. A paragraph may include more than one topic. Identifying text structure is useful because it helps us understand how the topics in a text relate to each other. It also helps us to give a structure to our notes and summaries.

TASK 7 Study the following title and first paragraph of a text about the attempts to save Australia's famous koalas from extinction. How do you expect it will be structured?

More than one cure for extinction

A The fight to save Australia's koalas is being waged on three fronts: in the laboratory, the forest and the political arena.

TASK 8 The text has 9 paragraphs, A to I. Put the paragraphs in the right sections in this table.

Sections	Paragraphs
Introduction	A
The laboratory	
The forest	
The political arena	

B Microbiologists are striving to identify all strains of chlamydia that affect koalas. Their goal is to develop a vaccine that can be used to protect koalas in zoos and game parks from the disease. Scientists are also attempting to find an effective treatment for infected animals.

C So far, the most promising drug is trospectomycin, an antibiotic developed in the US to treat human chlamydia. Other drugs often kill the koala along with the bacteria.

D Biologists and ecologists are collecting field data to improve government strategies for managing the wild koalas in Australia's forests. They are evaluating the risks and benefits of moving animals from overpopulated to underpopulated areas of the country, a tactic used in the state of Victoria since the 1920s.

E Other studies are proposed to find out how much land koalas need. The amount of land needed to sustain those animals living in fragmented or sparsely wooded areas is clearly greater than in 'quality' habitat, well-endowed with eucalyptus. But as yet there is no reliable method to enable ecologists to assess 'quality' in this sense.

F Other biologists are investigating the koala's highly specialised digestive system to understand better the animal's nutritional requirements. This information could lead to improved diets for captive koalas. At present, they are fed eucalyptus leaves almost exclusively.

G As supplies of the leaves are not always reliable, a variety of dietary supplements would help to keep the koalas fed and fit. Experts at the University of Sydney and the Taronga Zoo in Sydney have created a 'koala biscuit' that begins to fill the nutritional gap.

H Wildlife officers are encouraging land owners to safeguard koala colonies on their property, while city planners seek to 'build' koalas into rapidly expanding communities. The planners are trying to introduce innovative designs that maintain good koala habitat within new residential developments; road systems that bypass koala territory or force people to drive slowly; and civic bylaws that regulate human activities and control dogs in koala country.

I Most importantly, conservationists and scientists are urging city, state and federal governments to protect koala habitat. Their message is clear: the trees cut down to make way for housing, logging and tourism, are home and kitchen to Australia's most famous marsupial.

[Source: Deyton, L., *More than one cure for extinction, can koalas bear the twentieth century?*, *New Scientist*, 26 September 1990, p 44]

TASK 9 Note down the key words and phrases that helped you with Task 8. For example, paragraph B belongs in the *laboratory* section. Words which help us are *microbiologists, vaccine, scientists.*

TASK 10 Complete the gaps (a–k) in the notes below to show the main points of the text. Use the notes to give a brief oral report in your group on one way to conserve koalas.

Ways to conserve koalas

Sources of possible solutions
  Lab
  Forest
  Political arena
1 Lab: Tackle prob. disease through
    ident. (a)............
    devpt. (b)............
    and (c)............

2 Forest: Improve mgt. wild koala pop. through evaluatn. risks and benefits of moving animals from
    (d)............
    investigatn. amount (e)..........
3 Lab: Improve diet captive animals through:
    research into (f)..........
    devpt (g)...........

4 Political Arena: Protectn. colonies through:
    encourage land owners to (h)..........
    innovative town planning to (i)..........
    bylaws to control (j)..........
    pressure to legislate on (k)..........

Word study: Building an academic vocabulary, academic words and related forms

TASK 11 Here are three of the Unit titles from this textbook followed by a list of words in random order. Sort the words into sets under the appropriate titles. Then compare with your partner.

The developing world

The natural world

The spirit of enquiry

a) hypothesis
b) territory
c) urbanisation
d) control group
e) erosion
f) unemployment
g) habitat
h) questionnaire

i) labour migration
j) interview
k) education
l) wildlife
m) validity
n) conservation
o) health

TASK 12 Each of the academic headwords in the Appendix has a number of related forms, for example:

verb	noun	adjective
analyse	analysis	analytical

When you learn a new headword, try to learn the other members of the word family at the same time. This will help you to read with more understanding.

Try to find the related forms of each of these headwords. More than one answer is possible in some cases. Check your answers in a dictionary.

verb	noun	adjective
benefit		
compensate		
consume		
contradict		
cooperate		
create		
define		
		distinct

verb	noun	adjective
distort		
		diverse
	emphasis	
	environment	
finance		
	generation	
	hypothesis	
	ignorance	
illustrate		
induce		
innovate		
invest		
	licence	
	logic	

Application

TASK 13 This text has eight paragraphs. Match each paragraph to one of the headings (a–h).

a) Chimps are genetically like humans
b) Importance of identifying genetic differences
c) Resistant to HIV
d) Resistant to cancer
e) Chimpanzee survival important for humans
f) Important differences
g) Consequences of identifying differences
h) Reason for HIV resistance

1 Chimpanzees will soon be extinct. If the present rate of hunting and habitat destruction continues, then within 20 years, there will be no chimpanzees living in the wild. But this is more than an environmental or moral tragedy. Chimpanzee extinction may also have profound implications for survival of their distant relative – human beings.

2 In 1975 the biologists Marie-Claire King and Allan Wilson discovered that the human and chimpanzee genomes

match by over 98%. Compare this to the mouse, used as a model for human disease in lab tests, which shares only 60% of its DNA with us. In fact, chimpanzees are far more similar to humans than they are to any other species of monkey. As well as resembling us genetically, chimpanzees are highly intelligent and able to use tools. These facts alone should be enough to make protection of chimps an urgent priority. But there is another, more selfish reason to preserve the chimp.

3 The chimpanzees' trump card comes in the field of medical research. Chimpanzees are so similar to humans that veterinarians often refer to human medical textbooks when treating them. Yet chimpanzees do show differences in several key areas. In particular, chimps are much more resistant to a number of major diseases. It is this ability that is so interesting.

4 For example, chimps seem to show a much higher resistance than humans to HIV, the virus that causes Aids. Indeed, their use as experimental animals in Aids research has declined because they are so resistant.

5 The reason for this resilience is that while HIV is new to humans, chimps have had their own variety – simian immunodeficiency virus (SIV) – for many thousands of years. Over a long period of time, chimpanzees have been able to evolve resistance to SIV. This resistance is encoded in their DNA.

6 Another area of interest is cancer. While it is one of the biggest killers in the western world, chimps suffer very little from the most common human cancers. This may be simply due to a healthier lifestyle and diet, but many scientists suspect that genes play a significant role.

7 By sequencing the chimp genome and pinpointing the place where the chimpanzee DNA sequence differs from that of humans, scientists hope to be able to discover which parts of the genetic code gives chimps their increased resistance to some diseases. This, they hope, will allow them to develop new and more effective treatments for the human forms of these diseases. Such treatments could include the production of new drugs or even the alteration of the human genetic sequence. The recently completed human genome sequencing project has shown that such an endeavour is now well within our reach.

8 In addition to disease treatment, the sequencing project could open up new possibilities that verge on science fiction. The argument that if there is less than 2% difference between chimp and human genes, then that must account for everything that makes us human, from our increased intelligence to our ability to use language. Comparing sequences will allow us to isolate the genes responsible for our 'humanness'. Once we know what the genes are, we may be able to alter them to give future generations desirable characteristics such as improved intelligence.

[Source: Heddle, J., *The Guardian Science*, 29/11/01, p 9 extract]

TASK 14 Underline the main points in the text in Task 13 and make notes to show the relationship between the main points.

TASK 15 Study the following map of the text structure. How does it compare with the main points you have noted? Use your notes to complete the gaps.

Topic *Importance of chimpanzees for human survival*

Chimpanzees ⇓ b. (1)...... but impt. +++ for humans   **Para 1**

Chimpanzees ≈ humans   **Para 2**
1 genomes 98%   c.f. (2) 60%
2 IQ
3 (3) ......
Differences impt. for (4)......: because resistance to diseases   **Para 3–6**
e.g. HIV b. evolved resistance to (5)...... cancer ?b. diet & (6)......
but ? genetic
Sequencing chimp genome cd.:   **Para 7–8**
1 identify (7).........
2 → new drugs or alteratn. (8)......
3 identify 2% genes responsible for (9)......
4 → (10)...... e.g. IQ

UNIT 6 The physical world

This unit aims to develop the reading strategies and skills required for:

1. relating texts and graphics
2. reading graphics for main ideas and specific details
3. using graphics in note-taking
4. understanding unfamiliar words using the wider context.

Academic writers use graphics for many reasons. What reasons can you think of? Graphics are used in all subjects but are particularly common in the sciences. The texts and graphics in this unit are largely drawn from sciences and applied sciences relating to the physical world.

Before you read

TASK 1 Discuss what the following diagram shows and explain how this device works. When you have finished, check the Key on page 151.

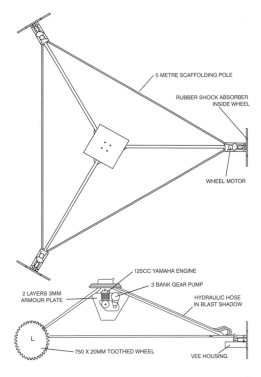

5 METRE SCAFFOLDING POLE

RUBBER SHOCK ABSORBER INSIDE WHEEL

WHEEL MOTOR

125CC YAMAHA ENGINE

3 BANK GEAR PUMP

2 LAYERS 3MM ARMOUR PLATE

HYDRAULIC HOSE IN BLAST SHADOW

L

750 X 20MM TOOTHED WHEEL

VEE HOUSING

[Source: Professor S.H. Salter, University of Edinburgh]

Graphics are sometimes stand-alone but often they have to be read with text to be understood. Both text and graphic contribute to the meaning. If we read only the graphic or only the text, we have to make much greater use of inference skills to find the meaning. We therefore increase the risk of error.

Some of the most common types of graphics are:

1	table	5	horizontal bar chart
2	graph	6	pie chart
3	flowchart	7	tree diagram
4	vertical bar chart	8	schematic diagram.

TASK 2 There are seven different types of graphic shown below. Identify each type of graphic and explain what it shows. For each graphic consider why the information has been presented in this way. Would any other form of graphic be possible for this kind of information?

1

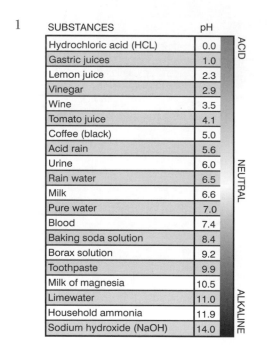

SUBSTANCES	pH	
Hydrochloric acid (HCL)	0.0	ACID
Gastric juices	1.0	
Lemon juice	2.3	
Vinegar	2.9	
Wine	3.5	
Tomato juice	4.1	
Coffee (black)	5.0	
Acid rain	5.6	
Urine	6.0	NEUTRAL
Rain water	6.5	
Milk	6.6	
Pure water	7.0	
Blood	7.4	
Baking soda solution	8.4	
Borax solution	9.2	
Toothpaste	9.9	
Milk of magnesia	10.5	
Limewater	11.0	ALKALINE
Household ammonia	11.9	
Sodium hydroxide (NaOH)	14.0	

2

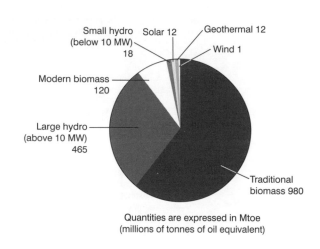

Quantities are expressed in Mtoe
(millions of tonnes of oil equivalent)

3

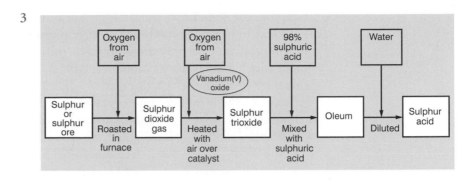

4

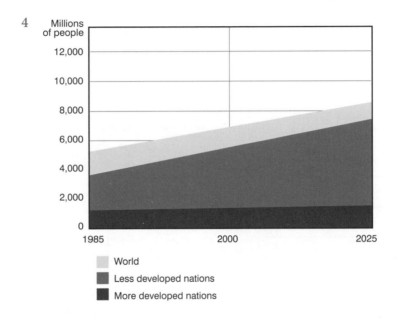

World

Less developed nations

More developed nations

5

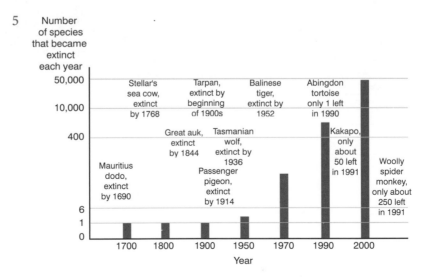

6

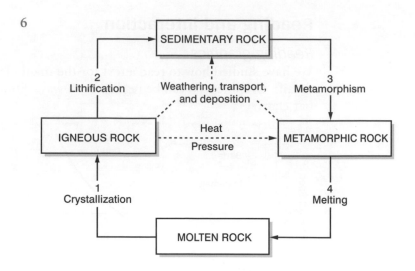

7

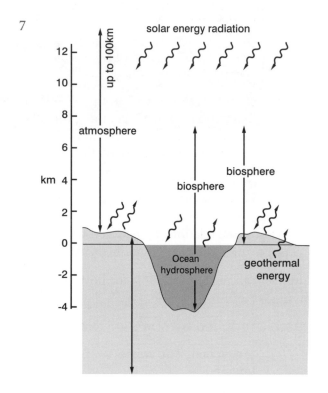

[Sources: (1) to (6) *Encarta Encyclopaedia*, Microsoft, (7) Bartelmus, P. (1986) *Environment and Development*, (Boston: Allen & Unwin), p 2]

Reading and interaction

Reading graphics

We have studied how to read a text for the main idea and for specific details. Graphics too can be read in both ways. Study the following bar chart.

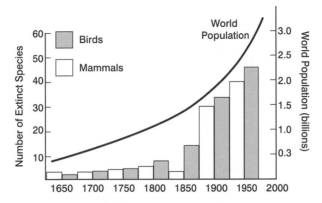

[Source: Keller, E.A. (1982) *Environmental Geology*, 3rd Edition (New York: Macmillan), p 18, Fig 2.5 Increase in human population paralleled by increase in the extinction of birds and animals]

Using the graphic (above) we can find specific details such as:

1 How many species of birds became extinct between 1800 and 1850?
2 What was the population of the world in 1900?
3 To what extent did world population increase between 1700 and 1800?

But at a more general level the diagram provides the answer to the question:

4 What is the relationship between the increase in the human population and changes in the bird and animal population?

Thus we can read this graphic for both specific details and for the main idea. Study this table.

Domestic waste produced by some of the richest nations

Country	Annual domestic waste (tonnes)	Equivalent per person (kilogrammes)
United States	177,500,000	721
Japan	50,441,000	411
Germany	28,401,000	360
United Kingdom	20,000,000	348
France	18,510,000	328

Main idea: The richest nations produce large amounts of
              domestic waste.
Specific   The United States produces twice as much waste
detail: per person as Germany.

TASK 3 Look again at the graphics shown in Task 2. Note down a specific
detail and the main idea for each graphic where possible. Compare
answers in your study group.

TASK 4 Work in pairs, **A** and **B**.
A Read questions 1–4 and try to answer them with the help of the
graphic that follows.

How is a 'crag and tail' formation caused? Account for the:
1 origin of the rock forming the crag
2 shape of the crag
3 shape of the tail
4 composition of the tail.

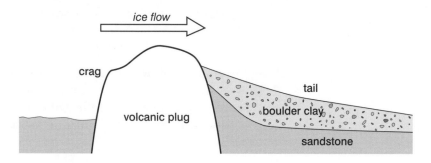

B Read the questions 1–4 and try to answer them with the help of
the text that follows.

How is a 'crag and tail' formation caused? Account for the:
1 origin of the rock forming the crag
2 shape of the crag
3 shape of the tail
4 composition of the tail.

Erosion and deposition may occur in close proximity, not only at the margin of an area of erosion, but elsewhere on local topographic irregularities. A small hill, formed by an igneous intrusion, may be eroded by ice until a steep craggy face is left facing the ice flow; but, protected by it, a streamlined tail of softer rock or thick till is preserved on the lee side. The resultant land form is called a crag and tail.

[Source: McLean, A.C. and Gribble, C.D., (1979) *Geology for Civil Engineers* (London: Allen & Unwin), p 73, Figure 3.9]

TASK 5 Compare your answers. Then read each other's source. Agree on the correct answers.

TASK 6 For this task there are three graphics but just one set of questions (1–6). Work in groups of three, **A**, **B** and **C**. Use the information in your graphic to answer as many of the questions as you can.

1 What is the difference between transpiration and evaporation?
2 What is 'run off'?
3 How does precipitation become part of groundwater flow?
4 What is the most direct route for precipitation to return to the atmosphere?
5 What is magmatic water?
6 What is the water table?

Graphic A   Graphic B

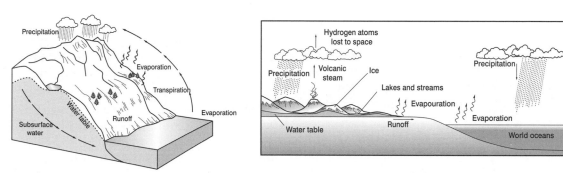

Graphic C

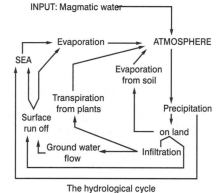

The hydrological cycle

[Source A: Keller, E.A. op cit, p 52, Figure 3.19. Source B: Waddington, C.H., (1978) *The Man Made Future* (London: Croom Helm), p 54, Figure 2.4
Source C: Blyth, F.G.H. and de Freitas, M.H., (1978) *A Geology for Engineers*, 7th Edn., (London: Edward Arnold), p 213, Fig. 13.1]

TASK 7 Compare your answers to Task 6; then compare graphics. Which graphic provided the most complete answers?

TASK 8 Now check your answers to Tasks 6 and 7 by using the following
text.

Water

The second most important constituent
of the biosphere is liquid water. This can
only exist in a very narrow range of
temperatures, since water freezes at 0°C
degrees and boils at 100°C. This is only a 5
tiny slice between the low temperatures of
some of the other planets and the hot
interior of the earth, let alone the
temperature of the sun. Life as we know it
would only be possible on the surface 10
of a planet which had temperatures
somewhere within this narrow range. If
there is anything that can be called living
on parts of the solar or other systems of
the universe at a different temperature, it 15
would have to be of an entirely different
character.

The earth's supply of water probably
remains fairly constant in quantity. A
certain number of hydrogen atoms, which 20
are one of the main constituents of water,
are lost by escaping from the atmosphere
to outer space, but they are probably just
about replaced by new water brought up
from the depths of the earth during 25
volcanic action. The total quantity of
water is not known very accurately, but it
is about enough to cover the surface of
the globe (510 million sq. km) to a depth
of about two and three-quarter km. Most 30

of it is in the form of the salt water of the
oceans − about 97 per cent. The rest is
fresh, but three-quarters of this is in
the form of ice at the Poles and on
mountains, and cannot be used by living 35
systems until melted. Of the remaining
fraction, which is somewhat less than one
per cent of the whole, there is 10–20 times
as much stored underground water as is
actually on the surface. There is also a 40
minute, but extremely important fraction
of the water supply which is present as
water vapour in the atmosphere.

This tiny fraction of the water supply,
existing as water vapour in the 45
atmosphere, is the channel through which
the whole water circulation of the
biosphere has to pass. Water evaporated
from the surface of the oceans, from lakes
and rivers and from moist earth is added 50
to it; so is the small amount from
volcanoes. From it the water comes out
again as rain or snow, falling on either the
sea or the land. There is, as might be
expected, a more intensive evaporation 55
per unit area over the sea and oceans
than over the land, but there is more
precipitation over the land than over the
ocean, and the balance is restored by the
runoff from the land in the form of rivers. 60

[Source: Waddington, C.H., op cit, pp 52, 53]

Text exploration

Discourse study: Marking text structure

Simple graphics can be used to show how a text is structured. This
can be useful in two ways:
1 in marking parts of the text for later revision and reference
2 in note-taking.

The text below has this structure.

Topic: **Using sea-water in agriculture**	
Introduction: problems	Para 1
Methods for removing salt: problems	Para 2
Evaporation methods:	
Solar methods: problems	Para 3
Arizona scheme:	
Basics	Para 4
Potential	Para 5

We can also show this structure by using margin brackets and labels. **Warning:** do this only if the book belongs to you!

1   Control of evaporation, and particularly transpiration of water through plants, is obviously of crucial importance in all regions of the world where water is scarce. It is being investigated most thoroughly 5 in connection with the use of sea water for agriculture. Sea water can actually be used as such for watering certain plants, on certain soils. But it seems unlikely that it can be at all widely used for growing 10 plants useful for food, and it is not at all certain how long it can be carried on before the accumulation of salt in the lower parts of the soil makes it unusable.

2   Most attempts to use sea water for 15 agriculture depend on first removing the excess salt. There are two basic methods of desalination. One depends on using a membrane which will allow the water to pass, but will hold back the salts (reverse 20 osmosis). The other is distillation, that is to say water vapour or steam is produced and this, which does not contain salts, forms fresh water when it is condensed. The production of steam can be done by 25 actually boiling the sea water or, more gently, by encouraging evaporation from the surface of sea water which is warmed but not raised to boiling point. Both the membrane-filtering techniques and the 30 boiling technique require large amounts of concentrated energy. They are essentially industrial processes of a very energy-consuming kind. The evaporation methods are much less demanding, and I 35 will discuss them first.

3 The cheapest way of evaporating sea water is to use the heat of the sun. The sea water is run into shallow tanks of concrete or plastic, preferably with a ₄₀ black bottom which absorbs the sun's heat. The tanks, which are usually built long and narrow, are covered with a transparent roof with curved or sloping sides. The water in the tanks is warmed, ₄₅ evaporates, and the water vapour condenses again on the cooler glass roof and runs down the sides to be collected in a trough at the bottom. Installations of this kind are already in use in many arid re- ₅₀ gions near the sea, from the coasts of Chile to the Aegean islands. It is a very satisfactory process provided one does not want too much water. It has mostly been used to provide drinking water. The ₅₅ quantities required for agricultural irrigation would require enormous areas of tanks.

4 A much more sophisticated low temperature evaporation scheme is being ₆₀ developed in Arizona. The scheme involves using cold water which is pumped into the installation to aid the condensation of the water vapour which has been produced by hot sea water. ₆₅ Originally solar energy was used to heat the sea water, but since any place that wanted to run such a scheme would certainly be generating its own electricity, probably with a diesel engine, use ₇₀ was later made of the 'waste heat' in the cooling water of the engine.

5 They also introduced another improvement which is of very general application. The fresh water was used on ₇₅ plants grown in plastic greenhouses. A large sheet of plastic is attached to a low brick or stone wall, and a small pump keeps the air pressure inside the plastic a little above the air pressure ₈₀ outside, so the plastic is inflated in the form of a long low sausage. The plastic is transparent to the sunlight which the plants need, while the water, led to the plant roots and transpired through their ₈₅ leaves, is trapped inside and not allowed to escape back into the general atmosphere; it can be used again and again. There are quite a large number of areas in the world in which arid ₉₀ deserts come near enough to the sea coast for developments of this kind to make important contributions to the world's food supply.

[Source: Waddington, C.H. (1978), *The Man-Made Future* (London: Croom Helm), pp 98–100, abridged]

Discourse study: Spider notes

Spider notes (also known as spider diagrams) are a useful alternative to linear notes as they give a better visual display of the text structure. It is also simple to add supporting detail and to show links between any parts of your notes.

Study these spider notes for the text on page 83. With the help of the notes, make an oral summary of the text.

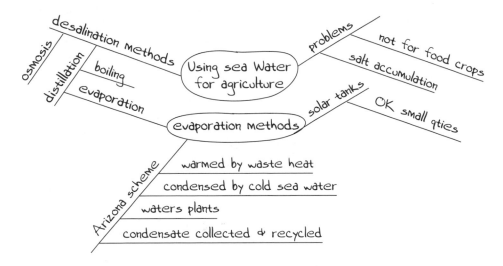

Some kinds of texts can be represented easily by rough diagrams. The kind of diagram you produce will depend on the type of text you have to deal with. For example, a text which describes a process can be represented by a flowchart. A text which classifies can be shown by a tree diagram. If quantities or percentages are given for each class, a pie chart may be more suitable. A text which explains how two variables relate to each other can be represented by a graph.

Often you may have to use a mixture of graphics and more conventional notes.

TASK 9 Draw a rough diagram to illustrate the solar method described in paragraph 3, p. 84. Compare your drawing with others in your group.

Word study: Using the wider context, academic words and related forms

In Units 2 and 3 you studied how to work out the meaning of a word by identifying the kind of word and using its immediate context, the sentence in which the word occurs. Try to work out the meaning of the following highlighted words using these methods.

1 Many phenomena produce sound in an **incidental** but unavoidable fashion.
2 These usually have two primary components: a mechanism for producing a vibration and a **resonant structure**.

In these cases, the immediate context may not give you enough help. It is necessary then to look at the wider context for more clues. Underline the parts of the text *Sound Sources* that help you with the meaning of 'incidental'.

Sound Sources

Many phenomena produce sound in an incidental but unavoidable fashion. For example, the combustion of fuel in an engine always produces some sound as a by-product. This sound is both annoying and wasteful of energy.

However, there are many man-made and natural sources for which sound is the desired output. These usually have two primary components: a mechanism for producing a vibration and a resonant structure.

The second sentence tells us that sound made by burning fuel in an engine is an example of sound produced in an **incidental** fashion – as a by-product. By joining this information from the wider context of the text with our own knowledge – that fuel is burned in an engine to produce power not sound – we find that incidental means here 'unplanned'.

For **resonant structure** we have to look at a wider context – the next paragraph of the text. Which parts of the following paragraph help you know the meaning of this term? (Ignore the use of **bold** type for now.)

Musical instruments present a variety of arrangements for the production of sound. In a violin the strings vibrate, and their vibrations are efficiently transmitted to the air by the resonant hollow body of the instrument. In woodwinds and **brasses** the vibrations are produced by causing the air in the mouthpiece to puff, swirl, and **eddy**. This causes the reeds in woodwinds to vibrate. In **brasses** the lips themselves vibrate as air is blown in the mouthpiece. In both cases the oscillatory flow of air results in standing waves in the extended hollow body of the instrument, and the energy is then efficiently transmitted to the air outside. Similarly the oral and nasal **cavities** in humans serve as resonant structures for vibrations produced by the vocal cords.

[Source: Kane, J.W. and Sternheim, M.M. (1984), *Physics*, 2nd edn., (Hoboken, NJ: Wiley), p. 452]

TASK 10 Find approximate meanings for the words in **bold** type as used in the text, *Sound Sources*, above. Use any of the methods we have covered. The words are:

1 brasses
2 eddy
3 cavities.

Compare meanings with your group. Discuss how you decided on these meanings.

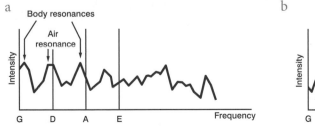

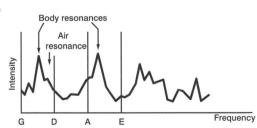

TASK 11 Graphics are part of the wider context you can use when searching for the meaning of unfamiliar words. Underline the terms in 'The Violin' which are explained by the graphics that accompany it (below).

Pegs
Nut
Finger board
Strings
Top plate
F-holes
Bridge
Sound post
Tail piece
Back plate
Tail piece
Brass bar
Bridge
Strings
Sound post
Back plate

(a)   (b)   (c)

Figure 22.8 (a) Front and (b) side view of a violin. (c) An enlarged view of the bridge and part of the body.

The Violin

The body of a violin is a more complex resonant structure than the tube. When the strings of a violin are plucked or bowed, their vibrations are transferred to the body through the bridge (Fig 22.8). Although the strings may vibrate with many different frequency components, the body resonates at and amplifies only certain frequencies.

The violin body vibrates so that its volume varies, and the air is forced in and out through the f-holes. This is called the air resonance. The front and back plates of the body can also vibrate at characteristic frequencies called body resonances. Just as a string can vibrate at more than one frequency, so also can the violin plates, and several body resonances exist (Fig 22.9). The frequencies of the air and body resonances should be at or near the fundamental string frequencies. If this is not achieved, some notes will be muted or distorted.

a Body resonances
Air resonance
Intensity
G D A E   Frequency

b Body resonances
Air resonance
Intensity
G D A E   Frequency

Figure 22.9 (a) The intensity-versus-frequency graph for a good violin. The vertical lines represent the characteristic frequencies of the four violin strings. Note that the resonances occur at nearly the same frequencies as those characteristic of the strings. (b) The spectrum of a poor violin.

[Source: Kane, J.W. and Sternheim, M.M. op cit, pp 453–4]

TASK 12 Try to find the related forms of each of these academic headwords. More than one answer is possible in some cases. Check your answers in a dictionary.

verb	noun	adjective
manipulate		
	margin	
	mechanism	
		minimal
modify		
	norm	
▓▓▓▓		nuclear
participate		
perceive		
	philosophy	
▓▓▓▓		precise
publish		▓▓▓▓
pursue		
	▓▓▓▓	random
react		

verb	noun	adjective
recover		
regulate		
reinforce		
respond		
		significant
		specific
		stable
stress		
submit		
	symbol	
▓▓▓▓		technical
	theory	
unify		
		valid
vary		
	vision	

TASK 13 Which of the words in Task 12 do you think are likely to occur in texts on the physical world? Use each word in a sentence.

Application

TASK 14 Study the following graphic. Note the main idea in one sentence and three specific details.

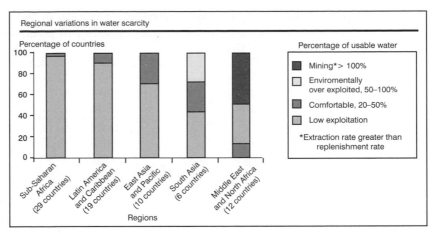

Regional variations in water scarcity

[Source: World Bank (2003), *World Development Report*, Ch 5, Fig 5.2 Regional variations in water scarcity, p 88]

TASK 15 Find the specific information needed to answer the following questions by using the graphic in Task 14.

1 Which areas have the most serious water problems?
2 What techniques are these areas using to find more water?
3 Which area is exploiting its water resources least?
4 What is the situation in South Asia?
5 Does the East Asia and Pacific region have a serious water problem at this time?

TASK 16 Read the text below; then the instructions that follow.

Water – the issue of this century

The world is running short of fresh water. Populations are growing bigger and thirstier, with the result that fresh water is becoming increasingly scarce. Half the world's wetlands have disappeared during 5 the last century, while estimates suggest that water use will rise by 50% in the next 30 years.

The World Bank report estimates that as much as half of the world's population, 10 concentrated in Africa, the Middle East and south Asia, will face 'severe water shortages' by 2025. 'Local water conflicts and the loss of freshwater ecosystems loom in some regions.' 15

A similar picture emerges from the globe's salt water regions. Three-quarters of the world's people may live within 100km of the sea in 2025, putting even more pressure on stretched coastal 20 ecosystems. Two-thirds of fisheries are exploited at or beyond their sustainable limits, and half the world's coral reefs may perish in 100 years. Almost 60% of coral reefs and 34% of fish species are at 25 risk from human activities, the Bank says.

The report concludes that there is ample evidence to justify immediate and coordinated action to safeguard supplies and use water more efficiently. 30

'Fresh water consumption is rising quickly, and the availability of water in some regions is likely to become one of the most pressing issues of the 21st century.'

A third of the world's population – around two billion people – live in countries that are experiencing moderate to high water shortages. 'That proportion could [at current population forecasts] rise to half or more in the next 30 years unless institutions change to ensure better conservation and allocation of water.'

China is one country where the portents are gloomy. The most water-stressed country in East Asia, China is exploiting 44% of its usable water, a figure projected to rise to 60% by 2020.

'Primary withdrawal of water of more than 60% is widely considered by water experts to exceed the environmental carrying capacity of a river basin system. Although China's aggregate use appears still to be reasonable, it has several basins that are severely stressed environmentally.'

Withdrawals exceed environmental limits in Afghanistan and Pakistan, and will exceed them in India by 2020. In the Middle East and North Africa, only Morocco has unexploited water resources. The rest have exceeded environmental limits and many are mining aquifers – bodies of water-bearing rock – the report says.

[Source: Elliott, L., *Guardian*, 22 August 2002, p 26.]

Do these statements agree with the information given in the text? Write:

True　　　　if the statement is true according to the text.
False　　　　if the statement is false according to the text.
Does not say　if the information is not given in the text.

1　Half the world's wetlands were lost in the twentieth century.
2　It is estimated that water use will rise by 50% in the next 30 years.
3　Some Mediterranean countries will face 'severe water shortages' by 2025.
4　Most of the world's population may live within 100km of the sea in 2025.
5　Almost 60% of coral reefs may perish in 100 years.
6　Some species of fish in the Atlantic are at dangerously low levels.
7　In the next 30 years, around three billion people could experience moderate to high water shortages.
8　India exceeds environmental limits for water use.

TASK 17　This summary of the text has had words removed. Select the missing word for each gap from the box that follows. (Use each word only once.)

According to a World Bank …1…, as the world's population grows, the demand for fresh water is …2… rapidly but supplies are falling and wetlands are disappearing. Up to half the world's population will have …3… water problems by 2025. This may lead to …4… . Coastal regions will …5… similar problems. Overfishing will damage fish stocks and coral reefs may be …6… . Immediate action is needed to …7… water supplies and encourage more efficient use. If this is not done, the numbers suffering …8… will rise by 50% in the next 30 years. China has the most serious problem in East Asia with freshwater withdrawal set to …9… environmental limits by 2020. Other countries with severe problems include most of the Middle East, North Africa, and the Indian sub-continent.

exceed	disappearing
gloomy	increasing
picture	serious
destroyed	projected
report	safeguard
availability	face
experience	reasonable
shortages	limit
consumption	conflict

UNIT 7 Into the future

This unit aims to develop the reading strategies and skills required for:
1 comparing sources
2 identifying viewpoints
3 understanding word structure.

For essays, assignments and dissertations you have to demonstrate that you have consulted a range of sources and taken different viewpoints into account. It may also help your understanding of a particular topic to refer to texts with different viewpoints. The texts in this unit mainly concern technology.

Before you read

TASK 1 Predict developments within the next 25 years for each of the areas listed below.

For example: (1) Most of the world's population will live in cities.
1 urbanisation
2 information technology
3 communications
4 globalisation
5 transport
6 food production
7 transplant surgery
8 robotics
9 control of disease
10 genetic engineering

TASK 2 What are your feelings about the future? Write down a list of words and phrases that you associate with the word FUTURE. Put them under two headings – POSITIVE and NEGATIVE.

Compare them with the rest of your group; then the rest of your class. On balance, are the feelings of your class mainly positive or mainly negative?

TASK 3 Study the following article titles and introductions. Can you identify the authors' viewpoints? For each, select whether it is optimistic, pessimistic, neutral, for or against.

1 **Fuelling the future**
How can we continue to consume vast amounts of energy without filling the atmosphere with smog, heating up the planet and depleting valuable natural resources such as oil and natural gas? A 160-year-old technology called the fuel cell is finally coming of age and may well be the answer.'Inside Science' 141, Author: David Hart, 16/6/2001

2 **Small is great**
Imagine what could be done with machines as small as those inside a living cell, whose components consist of individual molecules and are measured in nanometres. We could yet have a computer that fits inside a shirt button or health monitors that circulate in our bloodstream. 'Inside Science' 147, Author: Steve Adams, 14/7/2001

3 **Mass extinctions**
Five times in the past, the global ecosystem collapsed and most of the life forms of the planet suddenly went extinct. Today the world may well be in the middle of the sixth mass extinction triggered not by any external influence but by mankind's own destructive ways.'Inside Science' 126, Author: Gail Vines, 11/12/1999

4 **Life, but not as we know it**
Imagine a world where biotechnology controls every aspect of human behaviour and narrows the range of 'acceptable' emotions. The future is already with us in the shape of drugs such as Prozac, warns Francis Fukuyama. 'Opinion', Author: Nick Saunders, 20/4/2002

5 **Not now, Dr Miracle**
Cloned babies are a bad idea when the science is still in its infancy. 'Comment', 17/3/2001

6 **Time to come clean**
With or without a climate deal, the game's up for the carbon economy. 'Comment', 21/12/2000

7 **Chic geek**
Clothing of the future will be smart, so smart it will organise your day. It'll take you jogging, massage your ego and even fix your love life, says Scott Lafee. 'Features', Author: Scott Lafee, 24/2/2001

8 **Designed for life**
They caused a sensation when they first appeared in the 1990s but now robots COG and Kismet are not enough for the man who helped create them. Rodney Brooks, Professor of Robotics at MIT's Artificial Intelligence Lab, wants more. In his new book *Robot: The future of flesh and machines*, he argues that there's something lacking in our maths. We need 'new stuff' that will zero in on the vital difference between living and non-living systems and help us transform robots from the lumbering arms of the car factory or the single-use cute little home machines. 'Opinion', 1/6/2002

9 **Much ado about nothing**
So far the prophets of doom have drawn a blank. But where are the spectacular benefits of genetic modification we were promised? *New Scientist* watches the dust settle on the GM crop controversy. 'Opinion', 18/5/2002

10 **The search for perfection**
As a new age of genetics looms, how free should we be to design our children? Should we eliminate defects and tweak embryos to enhance intelligence? Or should society do what it failed to do with cosmetic surgery – clamp down hard from the start? 'Opinion', Author: John Harris, Tom Shakespeare, Kathy Phillips, Donald Bruce. 11/5/02

[Source: *New Scientist Archive*]

Reading and interaction

Comparing sources

When we consult several sources we should have a clear purpose. This may include:

1 clarifying something we are not sure about
2 checking the accuracy of our information
3 getting additional information on a topic
4 comparing viewpoints on a topic.

It helps to have specific questions in mind before comparing sources. These help to guide us to the information we need.

TASK 4 When we think about the future, we usually think about the role of science and technology. Conduct a survey to find the views of your class on the importance of science and technology to the future of your country and the world. Use the following questionnaire and record the responses in the grid that follows.

1 Do you believe that many of the world's problems can be solved by scientific research?
2 Do you believe that the benefits of science are greater than any harmful effects?
3 Do you believe that your country's national prosperity depends on science and technology?
4 Do you think that it is important for your country to be a leading nation in science?
5 Do you believe that politicians know enough to judge the importance of science and technology?

Question	Agree strongly	Agree	Neither agree nor disagree	Disagree	Disagree strongly	Don't know
1						
2						
3						
4						
5						

TASK 5 The two tables below report some of the findings of two surveys conducted in the United Kingdom. Your purpose is to:

1 compare the questions asked
2 compare the results
3 make conclusions from this comparison.

Table 1: 'Overall do science and technology do more good than harm, more harm than good, or about the same of each?'

	Totals %
More good than harm	44
More harm than good	9
About equal	37
Don't know	10

[Source: Gallup Poll conducted on behalf of *New Scientist* June/July 1989 and reported in *New Scientist*, 16 September 1989]

Table 2: 'The benefits of science are greater than any harmful effects.'

	Totals %
Agree strongly	11.8
Agree	33
Neither agree nor disagree	17.4
Disagree	21.6
Disagree strongly	10.2
Don't know	6

[Source: Oxford University Department for External Studies, published in *Nature*, Vol 340, p 11]

TASK 6 Now read this next text which compares the two studies. Does it identify the same similarities and differences that you noted?

The Oxford study also provides a number of checks with our own survey. For example, in a long list of questions, the survey team asked people to respond to the statement: 'The benefits of science are greater than the harmful effects.' While the question isn't quite the same as that we asked (Table 1), and the results are presented differently, the sentiment is similar. On a scale of 5 (agree strongly) to 1 (disagree strongly), 44.8 per cent agreed (11.8 per cent strongly), 17.4 per cent were in the middle and 31.8 per cent disagreed (10.2 per cent strongly) the rest (6.0 per cent) 'don't know'. In our survey, 44 per cent thought that science does more good than harm, while a larger number (37 per cent) were in the middle (about equal).

[Source: Science stays up the poll, *New Scientist*, 16 September 1989, p 57]

TASK 7 Compare your own poll with the results from the two studies.

Text exploration

Identifying viewpoints

Identifying differences in the factual content of texts is fairly straightforward. Identifying different viewpoints is more difficult. Understanding the writer's purpose and the structure of the text can help. These are the first steps in critical reading.

TASK 8 Survey 'The Robot Man' to identify the writer's main purpose. Choose one from this list. Is it to:

a) support the view that robots will take over the world?
b) describe the life of Hans Moravec?
c) explain the differences between Moravec's robot generations?
d) describe the views of Hans Moravec?
e) criticise the views of Hans Moravec?
f) make fun of the views of Hans Moravec?

The Robot Man

1 According to Hans Moravec, universal robots will take over all the physical activities that we engage in, leaving us with little to do.

2 Moravec sees four generations on the road to true universal robots. The first generation will be here by 2010 and will consist of free-ranging robots that can navigate by building an internal mental map of their surroundings. In new situations they'll be able to adapt, unlike today's mobile industrial robots. These robots will have the computing power to cope with simple speech and text recognition, and will be used for tasks such as domestic cleaning.

3 The second generation will arrive around 2020 and will be distinguished by the ability to learn. Second generation robots, are programmed with suites of primitive tasks and with feedback that provide 'pleasure' and 'pain' stimuli. For example, a collision provokes a negative response, a completed task would be positive. The robots could be trained in the same way as a dog, by words of praise or rebuke.

4 Move forward another ten years to 2030 and you get to generation three. This robot can build internal simulations of the world around it. Before beginning a task, it can imagine what will happen in order to predict problems. If it has a free moment, it can replay past experiences and try variations in order to find a better way of doing things next time. It could even observe a person or another robot performing a task and learn by imitation. For the first time, we have here a robot that can think.

5 By the time we get to generation four in 2040, Moravec predicts that robots will be able to: match human reasoning and behaviour; generalise abstract ideas from specific experience; and, conversely, compile detailed plans of action from general commands such as 'earn a living' or 'make more robots'.

6 The Moravec manifesto runs something like this. As robots start to become useful in generation one, they'll begin to take on many tasks in industry. Driven by the availability of this cheap and tireless labour force, the economy will boom and the demand for robots will grow so rapidly that they will soon become low-cost commodity items. So much so that they'll move into the home, where the domestic robot will relieve us of many chores.

7 With increasing automation in generations two and three, the length of the average working day will plummet, eventually to near zero. Most people will be unemployed

as robots take over not just primary industry, but the service economy too. Companies will have the potential to become very wealthy, but not unless people have an income with which to buy their goods and services. So there will need to be a major redistribution of wealth, with companies being taxed in order to support a social security system that will pay us all to do nothing. Relieved of the stresses and demands of both work and poverty we will be happier and healthier.

8 Moravec sees the fourth generation as an opportunity to transcend our puny human limitations. Unhampered by the constraints of our genetic and cultural heritage, fourth generation robots will evolve rapidly. Being able to rationalise and optimise their actions so much more effectively than we can, they will inevitably supersede us.

9 In Universal Robots Moravec writes, 'I consider these future machines our progeny, "mind children", built in our image and likeness, ourselves in more potent form. Like biological children of previous generations, they will embody humanity's best hope for a long-term future. It behoves us to give them every advantage and to bow out when we can no longer contribute.'

[Source: adapted from: Weber, J. (1998) The Robot Man, *PC Pro*, October 1998, pp 221–6]

TASK 9 Work in groups of three: A, B and C. Using 'The Robot Man' text from Task 8, read the appropriate paragraphs (as listed below) to answer the questions that follow.

Student A   Read paragraphs 1, 2, 3, 6, 9
Student B   Read paragraphs 1, 2, 4, 6, 9
Student C   Read paragraphs 1, 2, 5, 6, 8, 9.

1 What differences are there between the four robot generations?
2 What is the author's viewpoint?
3 What is Moravec's viewpoint?
4 How does Moravec's viewpoint compare with yours?

TASK 10 Note which paragraphs belong to each part of this text.

Part	Paragraphs
a) Introduction	....
b) Evolution of robots	....
c) Consequences	....

TASK 11 Part (c), 'Consequences', summarises Moravec's views. It consists of a series of cause and effect statements. For example:

Cause	Effect
robots start to become useful	they begin to take on many tasks in industry
cheap and tireless labour force available	the economy will boom

Match each of the following causes with one of their effects from the list a)–i).

1 demand for robots will grow so rapidly
2 robots will move into the home
3 automation will increase
4 robots will take over not just primary industry, but the service economy too
5 companies will become wealthy only if people have an income to buy their products
6 companies will be taxed
7 without the stresses and demands of both work and poverty
8 without the constraints of human genetic and cultural heritage
9 Being able to rationalise and optimise their actions so much more effectively than we can

a) the domestic robot will relieve us of many chores
b) most people will be unemployed
c) robots will inevitably supersede us
d) we will be happier and healthier
e) to support a social security system that will pay us all to do nothing
f) fourth generation robots will evolve rapidly
g) robots will soon become low-cost commodity items
h) the length of the average working day will fall to near zero
i) there will need to be a major redistribution of wealth

TASK 12 Which of the cause and effect links in Task 11 do you accept? Give reasons.

Word study: Word structure

One way of working out the meaning of an unfamiliar word is to look for clues in the structure of the word. For example, we can break down the word 'uncertainty' into its components like this:

		Word class	Meaning
Root	certain	adj.	sure
+ *suffix*	certain + ty	noun	sureness
+ *prefix*	un + certainty	noun	not being sure

Working out the meaning of a word from its structure can only be done with a minority of English words. Use this method once you have tried all the other ways of identifying an unfamiliar word. Be careful – some apparent prefixes are in fact part of the root. Compare, for example, *restart* and *respect*.

One way to remember English affixes (prefixes and suffixes) is to make your own checklist. Here is an example.

Affix	Meaning	Effect	Examples
en –	make/cause	adj → verb	ensure
– en			soften

TASK 13 Work out the word class and meaning of each word in the list below. They are taken from texts in this book. Check your answers in a dictionary.

1 inactive   7 transformed
2 disproportionate   8 employment
3 reintroduced   9 futility
4 improbable   10 rationalise
5 irrelevance   11 shortening
6 unquestionably   12 standardise

Self-study Study these examples. The words are from this book. You can find a full list of affixes in many learners' dictionaries.

Affix	Meaning	Effect	Example
a-	without	adj → adj	amoral
-able/ible	having qualities of	noun → adj	sustainable, variable responsible
anti-	against	adj → adj	anti-malarial
-ator	object or person doing	verb → noun	cultivator, predator
auto-	of oneself, independent		autonomously automatic
de-	opposite of		deforestation
dis-	negative, opposite of	verb → verb	disappear, disagree
-ic		noun → adj	specific
-ify	cause to be	noun → verb adj → verb	modify, unify clarify
inter-	between		international
-ity		adj → noun	instability, security
mis-	bad, wrong		misuse
over-	above, to excess		overfishing

We can summarise our approach to unfamiliar words as follows:

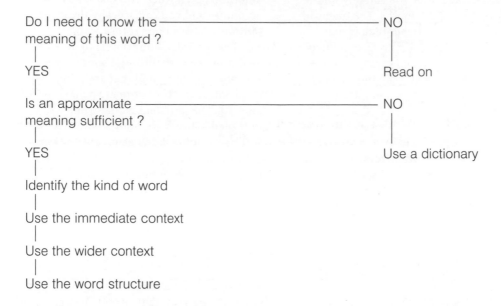

Do I need to know the ——————————— NO
meaning of this word ?
| |
YES   Read on
|
Is an approximate ——————————— NO
meaning sufficient ?
| |
YES   Use a dictionary
|
Identify the kind of word
|
Use the immediate context
|
Use the wider context
|
Use the word structure

Application

TASK 14 Survey the text 'How smart is that?' to identify the writer's main purpose and viewpoint.

How smart is that?

WE'VE all seen the movie. Super-intelligent machines are about to inherit the Earth. And we're going to end up as members of an underclass.

Unfortunately, the current advocates of 5 this idea are not movie makers but certain robotics researchers. Worse they are being taken seriously everywhere, even by the Royal Institution, where roboticist Kevin Warwick is giving this year's Christmas 10 Lectures. Worse still – and every researcher should have this imprinted on their forehead – silly idea equals loss of cash from serious funding agency.

So what are these roboticists saying? 15 Well, Hans Moravec reckons the robots-rule scenario is a good thing because we will hand on civilisation to our cyber-children.

Warwick envisions robots snatching the world before we want to hand it over. In 20 Belgium, Hugo de Garis fears a war between robots and humans. Meanwhile, Ray Kurzweil sees nanocomputers in our brains letting us join the super-intelligence party. 25

For my money, all this is closer to conjuring tricks than science. As with all the best conjuring tricks, the effect is achieved by distracting us with 'astonishing facts' while two enormous assumptions 30 are sneaked by. The astonishing facts are to do with Moore's law, which predicts that computers double in power every 18 months. That doubling is why everyone buys it. That and the fact that Moore 35 used it to come up with a very useful benchmark: the power you can buy for $1000 doubles in 18 months. The magic of this kind of exponential growth is that it doesn't matter if we have underestimated the power of the human brain by a factor of 100 – we'd only have to wait another 10.5 years for computers to be a hundred times more powerful.

The first assumption, then, is that this increase in computer processing power automatically means an increase in the intelligence of whatever is using these computers for brains. This increase in 'intelligence' has happened in some areas of robotics and Artificial Intelligence research, but for machine intelligence to keep step with machine power, it must always happen, not often happen. So far, we've done badly with giving machines humanlike common sense or ability to learn – prerequisites for AI. Add to this Hofstadter's law of software development – the problem is much more difficult than you think, even when you take this into account – and you can see why the optimists have a poor record.

The second assumption is to do with evolution. Now evolution disposes us to stay alive by supposing that anything displaying aspects of animate behaviour is animate. Our problem is that while we know teddy bears are not real, we are willing to endow intelligent contraptions with the full orchestra of creaturehood on hearing a few flute-like notes. None of which would matter were it not for the little matter of government funding. Funding agencies have a nasty habit of making funds harder to get in an area which has been guilty of making very exaggerated claims. So let's be careful. We don't want the world's most interesting science to be confused with marketing hyperbole.

[Source: Malcolm, C., *New Scientist* vol 168 issue 2270, 23 December 2000, p 73]

TASK 15 Which of the statements 1–10 accurately reflect the author's views? Answer using: *Yes*, *No*, or *Not given*
1 The idea that robots will take over the earth is silly.
2 It is unfortunate that some authorities are taking seriously such claims by robotics reseachers.
3 Humans will become an underclass in the future.
4 Tiny computers will be inserted in our brains to allow us to link directly to computers.
5 The predictions of some robotics researchers are based on false assumptions.
6 Regarding computing power, Moore's Law has proved to be correct.
7 An increase in processing power does not mean an equal increase in robotic intelligence.
8 Not everything which displays aspects of animate behaviour is animate.
9 Making exaggerated claims for robotics is dangerous because this may put government funding for robotics at risk.
10 Robotics is like marketing.

....

TASK 16 Complete the following summary of the text by choosing the correct words from the box and writing them in the spaces provided.

The idea that robots will take over the earth is …1… and it is …2… that some authorities are taking seriously such claims by some robotics reseachers.

Their predictions are based on two false …3… . We accept them because we are …4… by 'astonishing facts' linked to Moore's Law on the doubling of computing power every 18 months. The first is that an increase in …5… power equals an increase in robotic intelligence. This is false because we haven't done well in giving machines …6… sense and the ability to learn. In addition a problem is always more difficult than we …7… even when we take this unanticipated difficulty into account (Hofstadter's Law). The second assumption is that anything which displays aspects of …8… behaviour is animate. Because robots show some minor aspects of animate behaviour, we assume they are animate. Making …9… claims for robotics is dangerous because government …10… for robotics may be put at risk.

common	anticipate
researchers	intelligent
animate	benchmark
assumptions	automatically
tricks	computers
funding	distracted
doubling	marketing
silly	processing
underestimated	unfortunate
increase	exaggerated

....

TASK 17 Does the writer provide a convincing argument against the views of Moravec described in the text on page 96? Discuss in your groups. What other arguments could you use against Moravec?

UNIT 8

The individual and society

This unit aims to develop the reading strategies and skills required for:

1 reading critically
2 distinguishing between facts and opinions
3 analysing an argument
4 understanding words which maximise and minimise.

This unit and Unit 9 focus on critical reading. Critical reading means testing the strength of an argument, proposal or explanation in a text. It also means measuring the ideas in a text against your own ideas and against those of other writers. Critical reading is an important skill for any student but is of particular importance to the social scientist because sociology is a subject in which conflicting viewpoints are common. For this reason, Social Science has been described as an argumentative subject. The texts in this unit are drawn from Social Science sources.

Before you read

TASK 1 Study these statements about education. Divide them into facts and opinions. Compare your answers with your study group. Discuss how you can recognise a fact and how you can recognise an opinion.

1 In the United States the per capita costs of schooling have risen almost as fast as the cost of medical treatment.

2 Equal obligatory schooling must be recognised as at least economically unfeasible.

3 Paradoxically, the belief that universal schooling is absolutely necessary is most firmly held in those countries where the fewest people have been – and will be – served by schools.

4 We have all learned most of what we know outside school.

5 A good educational system should provide all who want to learn with access to available resources at any time in their lives.

6 I believe that a desirable future depends on our deliberately choosing a life of action over a life of consumption.

7 The university graduate has been schooled for selective service among the rich of the world.

[Source: Illich, Ivan D. (1971) *Deschooling Society* (London: Calder and Boyars)]

8 Half the people in our world never set foot in school.

9 School groups people according to age.

10 Schools create jobs for schoolmasters, no matter what their pupils learn from them.

TASK 2 Note down points to use in an argument either to support or to oppose the statement:

> Even with schools of equal quality, a poor child can seldom catch up with a rich one.

Work with another student who has prepared the same argument, i.e. both for or both opposed. Read each other's points. Try to agree on the best argument.

Now pair with another student who has prepared an argument opposed to yours. Try to find faults in their argument.

TASK 3 Discuss in your group what makes a persuasive argument.

TASK 4 Now study the following argument. Does it persuade you to agree with the writer? If so, why? If not, why not?

It should be obvious that even with schools of equal quality a poor child can seldom catch up with a rich one. Even if they attend equal schools and begin at the same age, poor children lack most of the educational opportunities which are casually available to the middle-class child. These advantages range from conversation and books in the home to vacation travel and a different sense of oneself, and apply, for the child who enjoys them, both in and out of school. So the poorer student will generally fall behind so long as he depends on school for advancement or learning.

[Source: Illich, Ivan D. (1971) *Deschooling Society* (London: Calder and Boyars), p 6]

TASK 5

I.D. Illich is a famous writer on education. How far should this alter your evaluation of the views and arguments he puts forward?

Reading and interaction

Critical reading

A first step in critical reading is to break down the argument into points. You can do this in your head or by making notes using the techniques you studied in Units 5 and 6. Study the following notes on the text in Task 4.

1 Even with equal schools, poor child cannot catch up with rich.
2 ∵ Lack m/c educational opportunities.
3 e.g. conversation & books at home
   vacation travel
   diff. sense self
4 Apply in/out school.
5 ∴ Poor child falls behind if depends school.

Then ask yourself these questions:
a) Are all the points supported (or are some just assertions)?
b) Are unsupported points either known facts or generally accepted opinions?
c) If a point is supported by examples, are they well-chosen?
d) Does the conclusion follow logically from the points?

TASK 6 Half the group read Text A and the other half Text B. The notes which follow each text summarise the points of the argument. Show how the points are linked by completing the blanks in the following notes with the appropriate symbol or word from the list given in Unit 5 (and shown below).

∵ b.   because   ALTHO'   although
∴ t.   therefore   BUT
&   and   ALSO   in addition
e.g.   for example

Text A

A second major illusion on which the school system rests is that most learning is the result of teaching. Teaching, it is true, may contribute to certain kinds of learning under certain conditions. But most people acquire most of   5 their knowledge outside school, and in school only insofar as school, in a few rich countries, has become their place of confinement during an increasing part of their lives.

Most learning happens casually, and even   10 most intentional learning is not the result of programmed instruction. Normal children learn their first language casually, although faster if their parents pay attention to them. Most people who learn a second language   15 well do so as a result of odd circumstances and not of sequential teaching. They go to live with their grandparents, they travel, or they fall in love with a foreigner. Fluency in reading is also more often than not a result of such   20 extracurricular activities. Most people who read widely, and with pleasure, merely believe that they learned to do so in school; when challenged, they easily discard this illusion.

[Source: Illich, Ivan D. (1971) *Deschooling Society* (London: Calder and Boyars), p 12]

---

1 Most learning NOT because teaching.
2 _____ teaching may help in s. conditions.
3 _____ most knowledge out/s school.
4 _____ in/s school only insofar as confined there.
5 Most learning casual (not intentional).
6 _____ 1st lang. learnt casually.
7 Even most intentional learning NOT because teaching.
8 _____ if 2nd lang. learnt well, learnt because odd circumstances like travel.
9 _____ fluent reading because out/s school activities.
10 Good readers merely believe learned at school.
11 _____ when challenged, discard this illusion.

Text B

Equal obligatory schooling must be recognised as at least economically unfeasible. In Latin America the amount of public money spent on each graduate student is between 350 and 1,500 times the amount spent on the median citizen (that is the citizen who holds the middle ground between the poorest and the richest). In the United States the discrepancy is smaller, but the discrimination is keener. The richest parents, some 10 per cent, can afford private education for their children and help them to benefit from foundation grants. But in addition they obtain ten times per capita amount of public funds if this is compared with the per capita expenditure made on the children of the 10 per cent who are poorest. The principal reasons for this are that the rich children stay longer in school, that a year in a university is disproportionately more expensive than a year in a high school, and that most private universities depend – at least indirectly – on tax-derived finances.

[Source: Illich, Ivan D. (1971) *Deschooling Society* (London: Calder and Boyars), p 9]

1 Equal obligatory schooling is economically unfeasible.
2 _____ in Latin America 350/1,500 × more public money spent on graduate student than median citizen.
3 _____ in US discrimination worse.
4 _____ richest educate children privately.
5 _____ richest obtain 10 × more per capita public money than poorest.
6 _____ rich children longer at school.
7 _____ university year more expensive than school year.
8 _____ most private universities depend on tax-derived finances.

TASK 7 Work in pairs, **A** and **B**.

A Check your notes with another student who has read the same text. Then with the help of the completed notes, explain the argument to your partner, B. Together, discuss how persuasive you find the argument.

B Check your notes with another student who has read the same text. Then with the help of the completed notes, explain the argument to your partner, A. Together, discuss how persuasive you find the argument.

Text exploration

Discourse study: Forms of argument 1

You are going to study two texts on marriage. They reflect the views of the sociologist, J. Bernard. The form of argument in each text differs.

TASK 8 Read Text 1. Underline the main idea. Then look at the grid below and show what stage in the argument each 'summary' refers to by putting the following words in the spaces:

supporting reasons, conclusion, opinion, counter-argument dismissed

Text 1

Marriage has a beneficial effect on men. Compared to single men of the same age group, married men enjoy better physical and mental health. Their lives are likely to be longer and happier. In addition, they enjoy more successful careers, fill higher status occupations and consequently earn more money. Critics may argue that it is simply that more successful men tend to get married, but the evidence shows that it is marriage which brings about these beneficial effects. Hence the best guarantee of a long, happy, healthy and successful life for a man is to have a wife devoted to homemaking and the care of her husband.

Argument	Summary
1	Marriage is beneficial to men.
2	Better health. Longer, happier lives. Better careers.
3	Not the case that more successful men marry but that marriage makes men successful.
4	Marriage is the best guarantee of health, happiness, success for a man.

TASK 9 Now read Text 2. Underline the main idea. Label each section of the summary to show the steps in the argument. Use your own labels.

Text 2

Surveys show that more wives than husbands express dissatisfaction with their marriage and consider their marriages unhappy. More wives start divorce proceedings. In addition, wives are much more likely to suffer from stress, anxiety and depression than their partners. Compared to their single peers, wives have poorer physical and mental health. It is clear that for many women, marriage cannot be considered a beneficial experience.

Argument	Summary
1	More wives are unhappy. More wives start divorce. Wives suffer more stress. Single women are healthier.
2	For many women, marriage is not beneficial.

Text 1 has this structure:
Opinion
Supporting reasons
Counter-argument dismissed
Conclusion (opinion restated in stronger terms)

Text 2 has a simpler structure:
Evidence
Conclusion

Both these forms of argument are common in texts. Careful reading of the first and last sentence will often disclose the writer's main point. If you do not accept their point, check the rest of the text for the supporting points.

Paragraphs are often steps in an argument rather than complete arguments. What conclusion could follow from Texts 1 and 2 if they were read as steps in an argument? Compare your answer with the key on page 155.

Word study: Maximisers and minimisers

TASK 10 Read the following text with and without the highlighted words. What effect do these words have?

The traditional approach to parenthood is **completely** unsatisfactory. Women have to spend many hours in child-rearing. Those with professional skills may sacrifice their career **in all respects** for the benefit of only one child. Because women spend time caring for their children, the services of many expensively trained teachers, nurses, doctors and other professionals are **altogether** lost to society. Even if child-rearing is shared by the father, it **simply** means that two people waste time on an unproductive task for which they may be **entirely** ill-equipped. Society would be **much** better served if parenthood was made the responsibility of well-trained professional parents who would look after groups of children as a paid occupation. This would end amateur child-rearing and allow the biological parents to **fully** develop their careers for the benefit of society. Critics may argue that children reared in this way would feel rejected, **at least to some extent**, by their natural parents. This is **quite** untrue. Evidence from societies where collective childrearing is practised shows that children **merely** experience minor upsets and are **hardly** affected by the separation.

TASK 11 Divide the highlighted words into two sets. Label the sets. Discuss your selection with your partner.

Writers try to persuade not only by well-structured argument, but also by well-chosen words. They may try to maximise the points in favour and to minimise the points against their opinion using words such as those highlighted.

Application

⋮ ⋮

TASK 12 Study these statistics on marriage and divorce in England and Wales. What conclusions can you make? What explanations can you give for these conclusions? Compare your findings with your study group.

Marriage and divorce rates, 1989–99 England and Wales						
Year	Persons marrying per 1,000 population	First marriages: number marrying per 1,000 single population aged 16 and over		Remarriage: number remarrying per 1,000 widowed and divorced population		Divorces: persons divorcing per 1,000 married population
		Men	Women	Men	Women	
1989	13.7	42.6	53.5	53.1	21.4	12.7
1990	13.1	40.4	51.0	48.9	20.2	13.0
1991	12.0	37.0	46.6	43.5	18.5	13.4
1992	12.2	36.8	46.3	43.7	19.1	13.7
1993	11.6	34.7	43.8	41.3	18.5	14.2
1994	11.3	33.1	41.6	39.7	18.4	13.7
1995	10.9	31.2	39.3	38.4	18.1	13.6
1996	10.7	29.8	37.3	37.7	18.4	13.8
1997	10.4	28.4	35.6	36.2	17.8	13.0
1998	10.2	27.5	34.6	34.0	16.8	12.9
1999	10.0	26.6	33.5	32.5	16.4	13.0

TASK 13 Read the following three texts, each of which gives an explanation for marital breakdown. Make brief notes to show the structure of each explanation. Which explanation do you find the most convincing? Justify your answer.

Text 1
The value of marriage

Functionalists such as Talcott Parsons and Ronald Fletcher argue that the rise in marital breakdown stems largely from the fact that marriage is increasingly valued. People expect and demand more from marriage and [5] consequently are more likely to end a relationship which may have been acceptable in the past. Thus Ronald Fletcher argues that 'a relatively high divorce rate may be indicative not of lower but of higher [10] standards of marriage in society' (Fletcher, 1966).

The high rate of remarriage apparently lends support to Parsons' and Fletcher's arguments. Thus, paradoxically, the higher [15] value placed on marriage may result in increased marital breakdown.

Text 2
Conflict between spouses

Hart (1976) argues that the second set of factors that must be considered in an explanation of marital breakdown are those which affect the degree of conflict between the spouses. From a functionalist perspective 5 it can be argued that the adaptation of the family to the requirements of the economic system has placed a strain on the marital relationship. It has led to the relative isolation of the nuclear family from the wider kinship 10 network. William J. Goode argues that, as a result, the family 'carries a heavier emotional burden when it exists independently than when it is a small unit within a larger kin fabric. As a consequence, this unit is relatively 15 fragile' (Goode, 1971). Edmund Leach (1967) makes a similar point. He suggests that the nuclear family suffers from an emotional overload which increases the level of conflict between its members. 20

In industrial society, the family specializes in fewer functions. It can be argued that, as a result, there are fewer bonds to unite its members. The economic bond, for example, is considerably weakened when the family 25 ceases to be a unit of production. N. Dennis (1975) suggests that the specialization of function which characterizes the modern family will lead to increased marital breakdown. Dennis argues that this can 30 place a strain on the strength of the bond between husband and wife. Put simply, when love goes, there is nothing much left to hold the couple together.

Text 3
The ease of divorce

The third set of factors that Hart considers essential to an explanation of marital breakdown are those which affect the opportunities for individuals to escape from marriage. If, as the functionalists argue, 5 behaviour is directed by norms and values, a change in the norms and values associated with divorce would be expected. It is generally agreed that the stigma attached to divorce has been considerably reduced. 10 This, in itself, will make divorce easier.

Goode (1971) argues that the change in attitudes to divorce is part of the more general process of secularization in Western societies. During the nineteenth century, the 15 church strongly denounced divorce. During the twentieth century the church had to accommodate the rising divorce rate by taking a less rigid view.

However, the official church position is 20 probably less important than the declining influence of religious beliefs and values in general in industrial society. Many sociologists argue that secular (that is non-religious) beliefs and views increasingly 25 direct behaviour. In terms of divorce, Goode argues that this means that 'Instead of asking, "Is this moral?" the individual is more likely to ask, "Is this a more useful or better procedure for my needs?"' 30

[Adapted from: Haralambos, M. (2000) *Sociology, Themes and Perspectives*, 5th Edn., (London: Collins), pp 568–9]

TASK 14 Read all the texts from Task 13 again, then complete the gaps in the summary using words from the list that follows.

Any explanation of marital …¹… from a functional viewpoint would consider three factors:

1 the value of marriage
2 …²… between spouses
3 the ease of divorce

Parsons and Fletcher argue that the higher value placed on marriage leads to higher …³… . When these are not realised, breakdown follows. Functionalists argue that the economic …⁴… today means that the family unit is no longer part of a larger family network. Therefore it is more vulnerable to …⁵… pressures which lead to conflict within the family. In addition, because families no longer …⁶… the same work, the ties which hold husband and wife together are weaker. Finally it is now easier for individuals to …⁷… from marriage because …⁸… to divorce have changed. Society in the West has become more …⁹… and self-interest rather than religious belief influences behaviour regarding divorce.

secular	expectations
breakdown	rigid
relationship	attitudes
reduce	emotional
conflict	couple
suffer	bonds
strain	share
value	production
escape	system

TASK 15 Prepare notes for a short debate on this topic: half the group prepare the case for and half the case against. Pair with someone who has prepared the opposite case and debate the issue.

UNIT 9 Work

This unit aims to develop the reading strategies and skills required for:

1 comparing viewpoints
2 detecting false forms of argument
3 understanding how writers emphasise and distance themselves from viewpoints
4 understanding connotations.

The end point of studies for most students is work. Attitudes to work create friction or harmony in the workplace. The wealth of a nation depends on work. With the introduction of new technology, the future of work is changing. In this unit we will read about work in texts from Industrial Psychology, Labour Relations, Economics and Business Studies.

Before you read

TASK 1 Thinking about the topic of a text and related vocabulary can help you prepare for reading. Write down as many words associated with WORK as you can think of in 1 minute. Compare your list with your neighbour. Then try to group your words into categories, for example: *Rewards of work, Reasons for work, Attitudes to work.*

TASK 2 You are going to read a text about work. Before you read, note your own views on the following aspects of work.

Your views
1 NATURE OF WORK   What is work?
2 EFFECT OF WORKING CONDITIONS   How do working conditions affect workers' attitudes?
3 MOTIVATION FOR WORK   Why do people work?

TASK 3 Work in pairs, **A** and **B**.

Pair A Read Text A. Note briefly the 'orthodox' view on the three aspects of work listed in Task 2.

Pair B Read Text B. Note briefly the author's views on the three aspects of work listed in Task 2.

Text A 'Orthodox' view

The orthodox view of work which has been accepted by most managers and industrial psychologists is a simple one, and fifty years of industrial psychology and more than a century of managerial practice have been founded upon it. Regarding the *nature* of work, the orthodox view accepts the Old Testament belief that physical labour is a curse imposed on man as a punishment for his sins and that the sensible man labours solely in order to keep himself and his family alive, or, if he is fortunate, in order to make a sufficient surplus to enable him to do the things he really likes. Regarding the *conditions* of work, it is assumed that improving the conditions of the job will cause the worker's dislike of it to be somewhat mitigated, and, in addition, will keep him physically healthy and therefore more efficient in the mechanistic sense. Finally, regarding the *motivation* of work, the carrot and stick hypothesis asserts that the main positive incentive is money, the main negative one fear of unemployment.

[Source: Brown, J.A.C. (1954) *The Social Psychology of Industry* (London: Penguin), p 186]

Text B Author's view

1 Work is an essential part of a man's life since it is that aspect of his life which gives him status and binds him to society. Ordinarily men and women like their work, and at most periods of history always have done so. When they do not like it, the fault lies in the psychological and *social* conditions of the job rather than in the worker. Furthermore, work is a social activity.
2 The morale of the worker (i.e. whether or not he works willingly) has no *direct* relationship whatsoever to the material conditions of the job. Investigations into temperature, lighting, time and motion study, noise, and humidity have not the slightest bearing on morale, although they may have a bearing on physical health and comfort.
3 There are many incentives of which, under normal conditions, money is one of the least important. Unemployment is a powerful negative incentive, precisely because (1) is true. That is to say, unemployment is feared because it cuts man off from his society.

[Source: Brown, J.A.C., op cit, p 187]

TASK 4   Find out from your partner the views expressed in their text. Note them in a table with one column for the 'orthodox' view and one for the 'author's' view.

Now read each other's text to check if anything has been missed out.

TASK 5   Work in groups. Discuss your own views and those expressed in the texts. Do you agree with either text? Have your views changed through reading the texts?

Reading and interaction

Critical reading: Comparing viewpoints

In Unit 8 we studied how to break down an argument into points. When comparing different viewpoints, we can proceed in the same way; then compare the arguments point by point. Before doing this, it is useful to be clear about your own opinions on the topic so that you do not simply absorb what you read but react to the writer's views. You can then argue with the text, deciding whether to accept or reject each idea or to wait for further evidence before deciding.

A useful discipline, encouraged by some modern university learning materials, is to record your changing ideas and opinions as you read about your subject.

A useful tool in comparing viewpoints is to make a summary of each text.

TASK 6   Note some possible solutions to unemployment. Discuss your proposals with others in your study group. Try to decide on the best solution.

For the next three tasks, work in groups, **A** and **B**.
Group A Do Tasks 7, 8 and 9
Group B Do Tasks 10, 11 and 12

TASK 7   **Group A**
Read Text A and complete the gaps in the summary that follows. You need several words for each gap. When you have finished, compare your summary with other students from your group.

Text A

One argument used to support the idea that employment will continue to be the dominant form of work, and that employment will eventually become available for all who want it, is that working time will continue to fall. 5 People in jobs will work fewer hours in the day, fewer days in the week, fewer weeks in the year, and fewer years in a lifetime, than they

---

do now. This will mean that more jobs will be available for more people. This, it is said, is the way we should set about restoring full employment.

There is no doubt that something of this kind will happen. The shorter working week, longer holidays, earlier retirement, more sabbaticals, job-sharing – these and other ways of reducing the amount of time people spend on their jobs – are certainly likely to spread. A mix of part-time paid work and part-time unpaid work is likely to become a much more common work pattern than today, and a flexilife pattern of work – involving paid employment at certain stages of life, but not at others – will become widespread. But it is surely unrealistic to assume that this will make it possible to restore full employment as the dominant form of work.

In the first place, so long as employment remains the overwhelmingly important form of work and source of income for most people that it is today, it is very difficult to see how reductions in employees' working time can take place on a scale sufficiently large and at a pace sufficiently fast to make it possible to share out the available paid employment to everyone who wants it. Such negotiations as there have recently been, for example in Britain and Germany, about the possibility of introducing a 35-hour working week, have highlighted some of the difficulties. But, secondly, if changes of this kind were to take place at a pace and on a scale sufficient to make it possible to share employment among all who wanted it, the resulting situation – in which most people would not be working in their jobs for more than two or three short days a week – could hardly continue to be one in which employment was still regarded as the only truly valid form of work. There would be so many people spending so much of their time on other activities, including other forms of useful work, that the primacy of employment would be bound to be called into question, at least to some extent.

[Source: Robertson, J. (1985) *Future Work: Jobs, self-employment and leisure after the Industrial Age* (London: Gower/Maurice Temple Smith), pp 23–4]

	lines
If working time falls, then _____. The	5–9
result will be _____. Working time will	9–10
fall because of _____, longer holidays,	14
earlier retirement, more sabbaticals and _____	16
This means a mix of part-time paid and part-time	
unpaid work will become more common but _____	25–28
_____. The first reason is that	
the reduction of working time cannot take place on	
a scale and at a pace sufficient to _____.	35–37
The second reason is that if _____	42–45
_____ , it would create a situation where	
full employment would no longer be the main form	
of work.	

TASK 8 Group A

Here are the steps which make up the argument in the text. Try to complete them. When you have finished, compare your answers with another student from your group.

			lines
1	IF working time falls	THEN _____	5–9
2	THEREFORE	_____	9–10
3	Working time will fall	BECAUSE OF _____	14–16
4		longer holidays,	
5		_____,	
6		more sabbaticals,	
7	AND	_____.	16
8	THEREFORE	_____	19–25
9	BUT	_____	25–28
10	BECAUSE	the scale and pace are insufficient	34–35
11	and BECAUSE IF	_____	42–45
	THEN	full employment would no longer be the only form of work.	

TASK 9 Group A

Consider each step (1 to 11) in the argument in Task 8. Then decide whether you accept, reject or require further evidence for each step.

TASK 10 Group B

Read Text B and complete the summary that follows. You will need several words for each gap. When you have finished, compare your summary with other students from your group.

Text B

There is an apparently simple solution to mass unemployment: the shortening of working hours by 10, 15 or 20%. For several reasons such simplicity is more apparent than real. Given the comparatively low level of British wages and salaries, organised labour would not and could not accept wage cuts by the same proportion. Any attempt to create employment for all by such cuts might create social upheaval on a scale larger than that of riots. To pay the same wages for significantly reduced hours to a larger workforce, however, would lower British competitiveness on the world market even further. But even if the world market could absorb more expensive goods – an unlikely assumption anyhow – the attempt could not succeed because of the geographical distribution of unemployment and the mismatch between the skills of the unemployed and the skills required by modern enterprises.

And yet, in the long run the shortening of working hours per day, per year or per life-time is the most constructive measure if new technologies actually reduce the amount of work required to give the population a respectable standard of living. The psychological benefits of employment are not tied to an eight-hour day or a forty-hour week. They would accrue even in the improbable case for this century that working hours could be halved without lowering the standard of living. In this country as elsewhere a gradual reduction of working hours is actually taking place and there are efforts afoot to cut overtime, one of the few positive aspects of an otherwise dark picture. The immediate impact of such developments will be mostly an improvement in the quality of working life for the employed; it is inevitably a slow way of reducing the number of the unemployed.

[Source: Jahoda, M. (1982) *Employment and Unemployment* (Cambridge: CUP), pp 98–9]

	lines
It may seem that if working hours are cut by 10 to 20%, then _____. But labour will not accept wage cuts on such a scale. If wage cuts are imposed,	1–3
_____. If hours are cut but wages maintained, Britain will be unable to compete in world markets because her goods will be so expensive. Even if	10–12
Britain's goods could be sold, unemployment would not fall because of _____ and the mismatch between the skills the unemployed can offer and the skills required for modern employment.	20–21
Shortening working hours has value because _____ from employment even when we work less.	31–34
Cutting hours will improve the quality of working life for the employed but _____	46–48

TASK 11 **Group B**

Here are the steps which make up the argument in the text. Try to complete them. When you have finished, compare your answers with other students from your group.

			lines
1	IF working hours are cut	THEN _____	1–3
2	BUT labour will not accept wage cuts on such a scale		7–9
3	IF _____	THEN there will be serious social upheaval	10–12
4	IF _____	THEN Britain will be unable to compete in world markets	12–14
5	BECAUSE	her goods will be so expensive	14–16
6	IF Britain's goods could be sold	THEN _____	19–20
7	BECAUSE OF its geographical distribution		20–21
8	AND _____		22–24
9	_____	BECAUSE we get the psychological benefits of work even when we work less	25–31
10	THEREFORE	cutting working hours will improve the quality of life for the employed	43–46
11	BUT _____		46–48

TASK 12 **Group B**
Consider each step (1 to 11) in the argument. Then decide whether you accept, reject or require further evidence for each step.

TASK 13 Work with a student from the other group. Explain the argument in your text and give your reaction to that argument. Listen to their explanation and note the points of agreement and disagreement between the texts using the techniques studied in Units 5 and 6. Which argument do you find the most convincing? Justify your answer.

Text exploration

Discourse study: Forms of argument 2

In Unit 8 we studied two forms of argument. Here, to sharpen your critical reading abilities, we will study some false forms of argument you may meet.

TASK 14 Read the following texts carefully. Think about the argument presented in each text. Does the argument convince you that the writer's conclusion is justified? If so, why? If not, why not?

Text 1

Women are more likely to strike than men because they take a more emotional attitude to problems at work. The majority of workers in the clothing industry are female. Hence labour disputes are a common feature in factories which produce garments.

Text 2

The 1920s in Western Europe were a period of high unemployment. In the late 20s and early 30s extreme right-wing political parties developed in Germany, Spain, Portugal and Italy. It seems obvious, therefore, that unemployment leads to the rise of fascism.

Text 3

Much of the success of Japanese industry is due to the way in which management and workers are treated as equal partners. There is no gap between white collar and blue collar workers. Both share the same canteens and there is only one entrance for all employees. If these measures were adopted in our country there would be much less industrial friction.

Text 4

Japan and Switzerland are both countries with few natural resources. Like Japan, Switzerland imports much of its fuel and almost all of its raw materials. Both countries base their economies on the production of high-quality, high-value goods like watches and machine tools. Like Japan therefore, Switzerland should have few labour problems.

Text 5

As Marx states, labour creates wealth and this wealth is divided between capitalist and worker. If wages rise, profits fall and if wages fall, profits will rise. Hence capitalists everywhere seek to keep wages at as low a level as possible so that they can maximise their share of the wealth.

Text 6

During the strike of power workers in the UK in 1975, factories were only able to operate for three days per week instead of the usual five. Nevertheless, productivity showed little change. This evidence shows that manufacturers have nothing to fear from reducing the working week by 40%.

Text 7

Workers who do boring, repetitive tasks, like assembly line workers, are more likely to strike than those who have varied and interesting work like craftspeople. Requiring workers to do the same thing, day in, day out, is likely, therefore, to lead to strikes.

Word study: 1 Emphasising and distancing

Study the following extracts from texts used in this unit. Why has the writer included the highlighted words? Try reading the texts without the highlighted words; then with the highlighted words.

1 The morale of the worker has no direct relationship **whatsoever** to the material conditions of the job. Investigations into temperature, lighting, time and motion study, noise and humidity have not **the slightest** bearing on morale.

2 This, **it is said**, is the way we should set about restoring full employment.

3 **There is no doubt that** something of this kind will happen.

4 But it is **surely** unrealistic to assume that this will make it possible to restore full employment as the dominant form of work.

5 There would be so many people spending so much of their time on other activities, including other forms of useful work, that the primacy of unemployment would **be bound to** be called into question, at least to some extent.

6 There is an **apparently** simple solution to mass unemployment: the shortening of working hours by 10, 15 or 20%.

Writers may try to convince their readers by adding words to emphasise their message. In Unit 8 we studied how maximisers could be used in this way. Writers may also try to distance themselves from statements which they do not agree with or are not completely confident about. Which of the phrases above were included to emphasise and which to distance?

Read the following message then study the ways in which writers may emphasise the message differently.

Employers should ensure that the views of the workforce are represented in the boardroom.

1 Choice of modal verb:
Employers **must** ensure that the views of the workforce are represented in the boardroom.

2 Using a maximiser – often an adverbial:
Clearly employers should ensure that the views of the workforce are represented in the boardroom.

3 Changing the structure:
What employers should ensure is that the views of the workforce are represented in the boardroom.

4 Repetition by rephrasing:
Employers should ensure that the views of the workforce are represented in the boardroom. **In other words** they should appoint worker directors.

Word study: 2 Connotations

Some words have associated meanings, not just for individuals but for societies. For individuals, *work* may have connotations as diverse as *rewarding, exciting, tiresome, depressing. Organic* as in *organic food,* for many people has connotations such as *healthy, promoting long-life.*

It is important to be aware of connotations as writers may choose words with particular connotations to reinforce their arguments. Study these examples from the *How smart is that?* text on p 100. Look at the text again to understand the context.

1 For my money, all this is closer to conjuring tricks than science. As with all the best conjuring tricks, the effect is achieved by distracting us with 'astonishing facts' while two enormous assumptions are *sneaked* by.

2 Our problem is that while we know teddy bears are not real, we are willing to endow intelligent *contraptions* with the full orchestra of creaturehood on hearing a few flute-like notes.

Sneak means *to go or take something quietly or secretly.* The connotations are *acting like a thief, acting dishonestly.*
   Contraption means *a strange piece of apparatus or machinery.* The connotations are *unreliable, likely to break down, a product of mad scientists.*

TASK 16 What connotations have these words for you? Compare answers in your group.

1 society	6 master (noun)
2 globalisation	7 confinement
3 drone	8 sacrifice (verb)
4 Old Testament	9 GM (genetically modified)
5 amateur	10 clone (verb)

Application

What are your views on the future of work in your society? Think of these points:
   1 Will there be full employment?
   2 Who will work?
   3 Where will people work?
   4 What will work consist of?

Note your views before reading further.

TASK 18 As you read the following text, answer each of the in-text questions before going on to the next section of text. Mask the text with a piece of paper as you read so that you cannot read ahead.

LEISURE IN PLACE OF WORK – A REALISTIC GOAL?

1 What will the text be about?
2 What do you think is the writer's attitude to his topic?

The idea that in a post-employment society employment could be largely replaced by leisure activities and that increasing numbers of people could live lives of leisure, is open to serious question from two points of view.

3 What arguments do you think the writer will use?

First, many people without employment would resist the idea that they were expected to make no useful contribution, either towards meeting their own needs or towards meeting those of other people, and were merely expected to keep themselves amused and out of trouble. They would resent the sense of uselessness and futility which this would imply, and feel that their lives were condemned to be empty of value and meaning. It is not as if most of us today are heirs to an aristocratic tradition of cultured leisure. We have inherited the protestant work ethic, and the need to feel useful which goes with it.

4 Break the argument in the paragraph above into steps and note them. Which steps do you accept?
5 Do the same for the argument in the paragraph below.

Second, many of the people still in employment would resent the idea that they were expected to support large numbers of idle drones. The situation would be one in which the employed were perceived as doing all the useful work and the unemployed were seen, on a larger scale and a more permanent basis than today, as making no useful contribution to society. The question of how to finance the leisure of the unemployed in a leisure society would thus be a difficult one.

6 Explain why this would be difficult.

They would need a money income. Thus some extension of today's unemployment and social security benefits systems would be needed, perhaps going as far as the introduction of a Guaranteed Basic Income (GBI).

7 What do you think a GBI would be ?

But this would be much more difficult to introduce in the context of a society clearly split between workers and non-workers, than in the context of a society in which it was understood that the purpose of the basic income was to give all citizens the freedom to choose their own mix of paid and unpaid work.

8 Is it possible to say what kind of society the writer would like?
9 Explain why the writer has used the highlighted words in the following paragraph.

Finally, if anything resembling the leisure society **did come** about, **one thing is sure**. Many of those at leisure would **in fact** use their time for useful activities of many kinds. **In other words**, they would find ways of working on their own account, to provide useful goods and services for themselves and for one another. A leisure society would automatically transform itself, **at least to some extent**, into an ownwork society.

10 What will the writer's conclusion be?

In short, the prospect of moving towards a leisure society cannot be accepted as providing a realistic solution to the present crisis of unemployment and work.

11 Do you share his conclusion? [Source: Robertson, J., op cit, pp 24–5]

PART 3

The tools of research

Reading for research

This unit aims to develop the reading strategies and skills required for:

1 choosing the best source
2 reading reference sources for specific information
3 reading for research
4 choosing keywords for database searches.

Before you read

Often you can't find all the information you need in your textbooks. You need to look for other sources. Sometimes you will need specific information, too detailed for a textbook. For research you need the most up-to-date information available. In this unit you will consider the kinds of help that different reference and research sources can provide and how to read these sources effectively.

1 Choosing the best source

TASK 1 What's the best way to read more about your subject?
1 Ask your tutor for a reading list.
2 Use your textbook. You may find a recommended reading list after each chapter or at the end of the book.
3 Look up the topic in an encyclopaedia online or in the library. The entry may give a bibliography for further reading.
4 Look for a specialist bibliography online or in your library.
5 If your library catalogue is online, conduct a subject search.
6 Check the library shelves for titles with the same shelf-mark/call number as a textbook you know in this area.
7 Use a search engine to conduct a search for web resources.
8 Find a journal article on the topic and check the References for relevant sources.

TASK 2 Bibliographies are available for many subjects. Look at the following subjects and select the most appropriate bibliography for each from the list that follows.
a) Women in children's literature.
b) Women and environmental issues.
c) Women in business.
d) Noted women physicists.
e) Women writers of the 20th century.

1 Annotated Bibliography of Feminist Aesthetics in the Literary, Performing and Visual Arts, 1970–1990, by Linda Krumholz and Estella Lauter (1992)
2 Brave, Active Resourceful Females in Picture Books, by Claudia Morrow (1992)
3 Contemporary Women Novelists: A Selected Annotated List, by Helene Androski (1996)
4 Ecofeminism: An Introductory Bibliography, by Julie Knutson (1995)
5 Feminist Perspective on the Ethic of Care, by Virginia Dudley (1994)
6 Gender and Creative Writing: A Bibliography, by Susan Hubbard and Gail Stygall (1997)
7 The Glass Ceiling: A Selective Bibliography, by Melba Jesudason, assisted by Janet Rother-Harris (1995)
8 The History of Women and Science, Health, and Technology: A Bibliographic Guide to the Professions and the Disciplines, by Phyllis Holman Wesibard and Rima D. Apple (1993)
9 Information Technology and Women's Lives, by Linda Shult (1996)
10 Selected Recent Books and Articles on the State of Welfare and the Single Mother: An Annotated Bibliography, by Elizabeth F. Dill (1998)
11 Women and World Literature: Bibliography of Anthologies of Women's Literature in Translation, by Carolyn J. Kruse (1992)
12 Issues Related to Women in Management, by Marge Karsten (1993)
13 Women Mystery Writers, by Helen Androski (1995)

[Source: Wisconsin bibliographies in women's studies, University of Wisconsin System Women's Studies Librarian]

TASK 3 What sort of information would you expect to find in these reference sources?
1 Dictionaries of acronyms and abbreviations.
2 Dictionary of national biography.
3 Directory of organisations.
4 Dictionary of quotations.
5 Encyclopaedias.
6 Gazeteers.
7 Database of patents.

TASK 4 Where would you look for help with these problems? Be prepared to defend your choice.
a) The title of Bruce Lee's last film.
b) The location of Mpwapwa.
c) The most recent figures for the amount of rice produced by major rice exporters.
d) The difference between the behaviourist and the cognitive view of language learning.
e) The main political parties in India.
f) Who was W.K. Kellogg?
g) Which spelling is correct – enrolment or enrollment?
h) The difference between RAM and ROM in computing.

i) The number of single-parent families in the UK at present.
j) The number of Internet users in Nepal.
k) The number of Spanish speakers in Florida in the 2000 census.
l) US energy consumption last year.

TASK 5 Which of these reference sources, 1–14, could help you with the problems in Task 4?

1 Whatis.com: Definitions for thousands of the most current IT-related words.
2 Document Service Center (Columbia University): US government reference resources online.
3 World Factbook: Information online compiled by the CIA including area, demography, disputes, economy, political system and a map of each country listed.
4 OED Online: Oxford English Dictionary online.
5 Encyclopaedia Britannica online.
6 UKOP Online: Catalogue of United Kingdom Official Publications.
7 FOLDOC: Free On-line Dictionary Of Computing.
8 The Internet Movie Database: www.imdb.com.
9 The Statesman's Year Book.
10 The Cambridge Encyclopaedia of Language.
11 UN Monthly Bulletin of Statistics.
12 Encyclopedia Americana.
13 The Times Index-Gazeteer of the World.
14 Webster's Biographical Dictionary.

2 Locating specific information

Locating specific information quickly is an important skill when using reference sources. Remember that no reference source can contain all the information on a particular topic. Knowing when it is time to give up and try another source is important.

TASK 6 Try to find the answers to these questions in this online encyclopaedia entry as quickly as you can. Warning! You will not be able to find one of the answers. How would you find the missing answer?

1 When was breakfast cereal first developed?
2 Who started the first breakfast cereal businesses?
3 What types of breakfast cereal exist?
4 At what stage in the process are vitamins added?
5 Why did the sale of breakfast cereals increase dramatically from the 1950s?
6 Which manufacturer has the biggest share of the breakfast cereal market?
7 Most breakfast cereals are directed towards what section of the market?

breakfast cereal ...

... grain food, usually pre-cooked or ready-to-eat, that is customarily eaten with milk or cream for breakfast in the United States and elsewhere, often sweetened with sugar, syrup, or fruit. The modern commercial concept of cereal food originated in the vegetarian beliefs of the American Seventh-day Adventists, who in the 1860s formed the Western Health Reform Institute, later renamed the Battle Creek Sanitarium, in Battle Creek, Mich. The entrepreneurial possibilities of the ground, thin-baked cereal dough served to the Sanitarium's patients inspired two men, C.W. Post and W.K. Kellogg, each to found his own business. In the late 20th century the ready-to-eat breakfast cereal industry sold the equivalent of several billion bowls of cereal to Americans yearly, having far surpassed the market for the traditional 'hot' cereals made from rolled oatmeal or enriched wheat farina.

Ready-to-eat breakfast cereals are of four basic types: **flaked**, made from corn, wheat, or rice that has been broken down into grits, cooked with flavours and syrups, and then pressed into flakes between cooled rollers; **puffed**, made by exploding cooked wheat or rice from a pressure chamber, thus expanding the grain to several times its original size; **shredded**, made from pressure-cooked wheat that is squeezed into strands by heavy rollers, then cut into biscuits and dried; and **granular**, made by a process in which a stiff dough made from wheat and malted barley flour, salt, yeast, and water is fermented, baked thoroughly, and then, after being crumbled and rebaked, is ground into rough grains. As a final step in each process, the cereal is treated to restore vitamins lost through cooking and often coated with sweet flavouring.

Until the mid- to late 1950s, the market for ready-to-eat breakfast cereal was relatively small, making its subsequent rapid growth one of the most dramatic success stories in modern advertising. By skilful product diversification and promotion, ready-to-eat products took over the breakfast food market. Children found a prize in every package or associated a cereal with their favourite cartoon characters, while their parents, ever reminded of the convenience and the nutritional value of fortified cereals, could enter manufacturer-sponsored contests for prizes of their own. Late in the century, the majority of breakfast cereals continued to be directed toward the children's market, with entertainment-oriented packaging and a wide variety of 'treat' flavours. Alongside these, the so-called health food movement fostered, or revived, cereals composed of 'natural' whole grain and fruit in the old-fashioned granola style.

[Source: Encyclopaedia Britannica Online, 2002]

TASK 7 Write six questions on either of the following encyclopaedia entries to test your partner's speed at locating specific information.

If you are working alone, refer to the *Key*. It contains questions for you to try.

Text A
dendrochronology
also called tree-ring dating the scientific discipline concerned with dating and
interpreting past events, particularly paleoclimates and climatic trends, based on the
analysis of tree rings. Samples are obtained by means of an **increment borer**, a simple
metal tube of small diameter that can be driven into a tree to get a core extending
from bark to centre. This core is split in the laboratory, the rings are counted and   5
measured, and the sequence of rings is correlated with sequences from other cores.

Dendrochronology is based on the fact that many species of trees produce growth
rings during annual growing seasons. The width of the ring (i.e. the amount of growth)
for each year is determined by various internal and external factors, but it tends to
vary mainly in proportion to either the amount of available precipitation or the   10
prevailing temperatures. The ring measurements taken from trees with overlapping
ages can extend knowledge of climates back thousands of years. The **bristlecone pines**
of California have proven to be particularly suitable for such chronologies, since some
individual trees are more than 4,000 years old.

[Source: © 2002 Encyclopaedia Britannica Inc.]

Text B
radiocarbon dating
Scientists in the fields of geology, climatology, anthropology, and archaeology can
answer many questions about the past through a technique called radiocarbon, or
carbon-14, dating. One key to understanding how and why something happened
is to pinpoint when it happened. (See also Anthropology, 'Dating'.)

Radiocarbon dating was developed in the late 1940s by physicist Willard F. Libby   5
at the University of Chicago. An atom of ordinary carbon, called carbon-12, has six
protons and six neutrons in its nucleus. Carbon-14, or C-14, is a radioactive, unstable
form of carbon that has two extra neutrons (see Carbon). It returns to a more stable
form of carbon through a process called decay, which involves the loss of the extra
neutrons and energy from the nucleus.   10

In Libby's radiocarbon dating technique, the faint radioactive emissions from this
decay process are counted by instruments such as a radiation detector and counter or a
particle detector and counter. The decay rate is used to determine the proportion of
C-14 atoms in the sample being dated.

Carbon-14 is produced in the Earth's atmosphere when nitrogen-14, or N-14,   15
interacts with cosmic rays. Scientists believe that cosmic rays have been bombarding
the atmosphere ever since the Earth was formed, while the amount of nitrogen in the
atmosphere has remained constant. Consequently, C-14 formation is thought to occur
at a constant rate. Although the current ratio of C-14 to other carbon atoms in the
atmosphere is known, scientists are not certain that this ratio has been constant.   20

Most of them agree, however, that these processes and ratios are useful for dating items back to at least 50,000 years.

Since all life on Earth is made of organic molecules that contain carbon atoms derived from the atmosphere, all living things have about the same ratio of C-14 atoms to other carbon atoms in their tissues. Once an organism dies it stops taking in carbon in any form, and the C-14 already present begins to decay. Over time the amount of C-14 in the material decreases, and the ratio of C-14 to other carbon atoms declines. In terms of radiocarbon dating, the fewer C-14 atoms in a sample, the older that sample is. 25

The rate of decay seems to be steady. The half-life of C-14 is about 5,730 years. This means that half of the C-14 has decayed after 5,730 years. Then half of the remaining C-14, or one fourth of the original amount, decays in the next 5,730 years. After 50,000 years the amount of C-14 still present is essentially unmeasurable. Errors in radiocarbon dating can be caused by inaccurate radiation or particle counts, contamination of a sample with more modern carbon, and stray radiation striking the counter. (See also Archaeology, 'Chronological Analysis'.) 30 35

[Source: Britannica Student Encyclopaedia online]

Reading and interaction

Reading for research

For most research, you will need to use recent information from journal articles. The best way of searching journals is to use a database of abstracts and indexes. To find the information you want quickly, you need to develop an effective search strategy. This involves:

1 posing the search question
2 identifying the main topics
3 deciding how to search for the main topics
4 formulating the search query.

For example:

1 The search question:
  What information is available on the language problems of international students at universities?
2 The main topics:
  international students, language problems, universities
3 Searching for the main topics:
  Databases search for information by keywords. If your topics do not match these keywords, use synonyms or variants. Some databases help you to focus your search by suggesting alternatives or more specific keywords. Here is an example.

international students   foreign students
language problems   English (second language)
universities   postgraduates, undergraduates

4 The search query:

Most databases allow you to combine your keywords using AND so the search query becomes:

foreign students AND English (second language) AND postgraduates

TASK 9   Underline the main topics in these search questions and suggest possible keywords.

1 What are the main kinds of disease amongst fish kept in freshwater ponds?
2 How are working practices affected by the introduction of computers?
3 What information is available on the links between exposure to asbestos and lung disease?
4 How has the economy of Japan changed in the last 20 years?
5 What were the causes of the civil war in the USA?
6 Which countries will suffer water shortages in the next 50 years and to what extent?
7 What factors cause corrosion in aluminium?
8 Why do girls perform better than boys in school examinations in the UK?
9 What are the advantages and disadvantages of GM cereal crops?
10 What differences are there between male and female management styles?

TASK 10   Formulate search queries for each of your search questions from Task 9.

Compare queries with your partner. Try your questions using an online database.

TASK 11   Research one of these questions or a question of your own.

Take brief notes on the information you find and report your findings to the rest of your class. Cite the references you use.

TASK 12   Which of these citations from a database search would you refer to for further information on topics a) to e) below? Compare answers with your partner.

a) The language problems of Asian international students.
b) The writing problems of international students.
c) The best way to teach international students.
d) The importance of previous learning for international students.
e) Factors in addition to language problems which may affect international students.

1 Hall, Helena. When background matters: Three Writing Center Employee's Views on ESL Students. 19p March 2001.

2 McClure, Joanne. Developing Language Skills and Learner Autonomy in International Postgraduates. *ELT Journal.* v55 n2 p142–8 Apr 2001.

3 Walfish, Daniel. Intimate Program Tries to Break Barriers between Chinese and American Students. *Chronicle of Higher Education.* v47 n20 pA52–A54 Jan 26, 2001.

4 Jin, Wenjun. A Quantitative Study of Cohesion in Chinese Graduate Students' Writing: Variations across Genres and Proficiency Levels. 34p. January 17, 2001.

5 Cadman, Kate. 'Voices in the Air': Evaluation of the Learning Experience of International Postgraduates and their Supervisors. *Teaching in Higher Education.* v5 n4 p 475–91, 2000.

6 Book of Readings. Delta Pi Epsilon National Conference [Proceedings] (1999). 189p. 1999.

7 Wan, Guofang. The Learning Experience of Chinese Students in American Universities: A Cross-Cultural Perspective. 25p. 1999.

8 Collingridge, Dave S. Suggestions on Teaching International Students: Advice for Psychology Instructors. *Teaching of Psychology.* v26 n2 p 126–8.

9 Brickman, Bette. Nuzzo, Richard. International versus Immigrant ESL Students: Designing Curriculum and Programs to Meet the Needs of Both. 15p. 1999

10 Shaw, Philip. Liu, Eric Ting-Kun. What develops in the Development of Second-Language Writing? *Applied Linguistics.* v19 n2 p 225–54 Jun 1998.

11 Mills, Colleen. Interaction in Classes at a New Zealand University: Some International Students' Experiences. *New Zealand Journal of Adult Learning.* v25 n1 p 54–70 May 1997.

12 Lee, Debra S. What Teachers Can Do To Relieve Problems Identified by International Students. *New Directions for Teaching and Learning.* n70 p 93–100 Sum 1997.

13 Cargill, Margaret. An Integrated Bridging Program for International Postgraduate Students. *Higher Education Research & Development.* v15 n2 p 177–88 1996.

14 Huxur, Gulbahar. Mansfield, Earl. Nnazor, Reginald. Scheutze, Hans. Segawa, Megumi. Learning Needs and Adaptation Problems of Foreign Graduate Students. 18p. *Csshe Professional File.* n15 Fall 1996.

15 Bailin, Song. What Does Reading Mean for East Asian Students? *College Esl.* v5 n2 p 35–48 Dec 1995.

[Source: ERIC database, Ovid Technologies, Inc.]

TASK 13   Abstracts provide a useful summary of a paper. Match the abstracts
a) to f) with six of the papers cited in Task 12.

a)

Data from 5 Indonesian, 5 Thai, 21
Singaporean, and 85 Malaysian students in
a New Zealand college were obtained
through interviews, surveys, and
observations. Differences in level and style
of teacher–student interaction, difficulties
learning English, perceptions of local
students, lack of a common experience,
and acculturation were the issues
identified. (SK)

b)

A University of Adelaide (Australia)
program to assist international students in
adjustment to Australian academic and
discipline-related norms is described. The
program focuses on language and
academic skill development, and has been
found to be effective. Factors in the
program's success and their potential for
wider application are discussed. (MSE)

c)

Describes a Johns Hopkins University
program based in Nanjing, China, which
gives Chinese and American students a
close look at each other and the ideas that
shape or divide their two worlds. The
program, which is challenged by deep
divisions between the countries, brings
about 100 Chinese and foreign (mostly
American) college graduates to live and
study together each year. (SM)

d)

Evaluated the Integrated Bridging
Programme (IBP) of the University of
Adelaide, South Australia, which offers
international postgraduates the
opportunity to develop languages and
skills for successful acculturation.
Responses of all IBP participants for
2 years and of supervising staff show the
importance of recognising that it is not
only the newly recruited students who
need to evaluate their own academic goals
and practices. (SLD)

e)

Discusses reasons for behavior of East
Asian college students in their approach to
reading, including their respect for the
teacher as a spiritual guide, belief that
asking a question is a sign of slow
learning, and conviction that the goal of
reading is to decode words and recite
whole text fluently rather than to analyze
a reading passage. (14 references) (CK)

f)

International students have identified
problems in the college classroom that
hinder their learning, including listening
difficulties, lack of understanding of
differences in cultural background, poor
oral communication skills, insufficient
vocabulary, and poor writing skills. The
students suggest both general and specific
ways in which professors can help them
overcome these problems. (Author/MSE)

[Source: ERIC database]

Text exploration

TASK 14 Research papers often have the following structure. What would you expect to find in each component?

Title
Authors and their affiliation
Abstract
Introduction
Methods
Results
Discussion
Acknowledgements
References

TASK 15 Study these extracts from a paper on psychological stress and heart disease. From which part of the paper did each extract come?

1 Psychosocial factors – for example, psychological stress, are widely believed to be important determinants of heart disease.
2 In our study, heightened stress showed typical associations with unhealthy behaviour.
3 Table 3 shows a higher rate of hospital admission with higher stress.
4 Our investigation is based on a cohort of men recruited from 27 workplaces in Scotland between 1970 and 1973.

[Source: McLeod, J., Smith, G.D., Heslop, P., Metcalfe, C., Carroll, D. and Hart, C. (2002) Psychological stress and cardiovascular disease, *BMJ*, 324:1247–50]

Often we have to make a quick decision on how valuable a paper will be for our research. Here is how one researcher reads:

Sample	Reason
Title	To know what the topic is
Authors and affiliation	Are they or their institution known and respected in this field?
Abstract	To find out what's special about their research, what question they asked, what answers they found.
Discussion	To see if I agree with their analysis and conclusions.

TASK 16 Which parts of a paper would you read first and in what order? In which sequence would you read the rest of the paper? Discuss your answers with others in your group.

Word study: Choosing keywords

When searching a database, you may find the first keyword you use does not produce helpful results. You may have to use a broader, narrower or related keyword to get the results you want. For example:

keyword:	computer crime
broader:	information technology
narrower:	viruses
related:	computer security

TASK 17 For each topic, classify the keywords given below it into broader, narrower and related terms.

1 **Sports**
   exercises, physical activity, bowling, games, archery

2 **Reading**
   decoding, literacy, critical reading, language skills, reading aloud, language processing

3 **Engineering**
   manufacturing, technology, civil engineering

4 **Sanitation**
   waste disposal, health, hygiene, public health, cleaning

5 **Fish studies = icthyology**
   fisheries, zoology, cod stocks

Application

TASK 18 Study these three abstracts from a range of papers. In each case identify:
   a) the discipline
   b) what's special about the research
   c) what questions the researchers asked
   d) what answers they found.

1

The attitudes of faculty members toward international students were studied through comparative case studies of four academic departments at three professional schools of a Midwestern university. The focus was on graduate students because most international students at a 4-year institution study at the graduate level. In all 54 faculty members in the public health, architecture, mechanical engineering, and materials science and engineering departments were interviewed. Faculty members displayed a range of awareness of any problems international graduate students might have. Some observed few differences between domestic and international students, but most indicated an awareness of academic and personal issues such students face. Most recognized difficulties with English as a major hurdle for these students, and more

---

faculty members were aware of language problems than any other issue. Many acknowledged the difficulties in cultural adjustment. Faculty members tended to identify the same areas students in other studies had indicated as obstacles in their studies in the United States. Some differences among departments are noted.

2

A flat plate solar collector can easily supply hot water at temperatures up to 90–95°C. At these temperatures, rice, potatoes and vegetables can be cooked without much difficulty. However, to design an efficient solar system for cooking, one must know the exact energy and time required for cooking at these temperatures. Our experiments show that the actual energy consumed in cooking rice, potatoes or green vegetables is only 216 to 360 kJ/kg at cooking temperatures of 82–88°C and the cooking time at these temperatures is 30–45 mins.

3

Factors that relate to the stability of the West Antarctic ice sheet are of global importance because of its potential impact on sea level. The Ross Sea sector of the ice shelf is currently growing, but suggestions that the Holocene retreat of the ice sheet has ended may be premature. New data from remote sensing and on-site measurements show that the crucial drainage system of the Ross Sea ice is changing — for instance, an ice stream that flowed north less than 300 years ago is now flowing south. The rapidly changing drainage patterns cause short-term changes in ice balance that may mask or accentuate long-term trends.

[Sources:
1 Trice, A.G. Faculty Perceptions of Graduate International Students: The Benefits and Challenges.
2 Popali, S.C., Yardi, N.R. and Jain, B.C. (1980) Cooking at low temperatures: energy and time requirements, in Redy, A.K.N. (Ed.), *Rural Technology*, (Indian Academy of Sciences, Bangalore: Indian Institute of Sciences)
3 Conway, H., Catania, G., Raymond, C.F., Gades, A.M., Scambos, T.A. and Engelhardt, T. (2002) Switch of flow direction in an Antarctic ice stream, *Nature* 419, 465–7]

Appendix

Headwords of the *Academic Word List*

This appendix contains the headwords of the families in the *Academic Word List*. The number beside each word indicates the sublist in which it appears. For example, *abandon* and its family members are in Sublist 8 of the *Academic Word List*. Sublist 1 contains the most frequent words, and Sublist 10 the least frequent. The list comes from Coxhead (1998).

abandon	8	analyse	1	benefit	1
abstract	6	annual	4	bias	8
academy	5	anticipate	9	bond	6
access	4	apparent	4	brief	6
accommodate	9	append	8	bulk	9
accompany	8	appreciate	8	capable	6
accumulate	8	approach	1	capacity	5
accurate	6	appropriate	2	category	2
achieve	2	approximate	4	cease	9
acknowledge	6	arbitrary	8	challenge	5
acquire	2	area	1	channel	7
adapt	7	aspect	2	chapter	2
adequate	4	assemble	10	chart	8
adjacent	10	assess	1	chemical	7
adjust	5	assign	6	circumstance	3
administrate	2	assist	2	cite	6
adult	7	assume	1	civil	4
advocate	7	assure	9	clarify	8
affect	2	attach	6	classic	7
aggregate	6	attain	9	clause	5
aid	7	attitude	4	code	4
albeit	10	attribute	4	coherent	9
allocate	6	author	6	coincide	9
alter	5	authority	1	collapse	10
alternative	3	automate	8	colleague	10
ambiguous	8	available	1	commence	9
amend	5	aware	5	comment	3
analogy	9	behalf	9	commission	2

commit	4	contract	1	deviate	8
commodity	8	contradict	8	device	9
communicate	4	contrary	7	devote	9
community	2	contrast	4	differentiate	7
compatible	9	contribute	3	dimension	4
compensate	3	controversy	9	diminish	9
compile	10	convene	3	discrete	5
complement	8	converse	9	discriminate	6
complex	2	convert	7	displace	8
component	3	convince	10	display	6
compound	5	cooperate	6	dispose	7
comprehensive	7	coordinate	3	distinct	2
comprise	7	core	3	distort	9
compute	2	corporate	3	distribute	1
conceive	10	correspond	3	diverse	6
concentrate	4	couple	7	document	3
concept	1	create	1	domain	6
conclude	2	credit	2	domestic	4
concurrent	9	criteria	3	dominate	3
conduct	2	crucial	8	draft	s
confer	4	culture	2	drama	8
confine	9	currency	8	duration	9
confirm	7	cycle	4	dynamic	7
conflict	5	data	1	economy	1
conform	8	debate	4	edit	6
consent	3	decade	7	element	2
consequent	2	decline	5	eliminate	7
considerable	3	deduce	3	emerge	4
consist	1	define	1	emphasis	3
constant	3	definite	7	empirical	7
constitute	1	demonstrate	3	enable	5
constrain	3	denote	8	encounter	10
construct	2	deny	7	energy	5
consult	5	depress	10	enforce	5
consume	2	derive	1	enhance	6
contact	5	design	2	enormous	10
contemporary	8	despite	4	ensure	3
context	1	detect	8	entity	5

environment	1	format	9	incline	10
equate	2	formula	1	income	1
equip	7	forthcoming	10	incorporate	6
equivalent	5	found	9	index	6
erode	9	foundation	7	indicate	1
error	4	framework	3	individual	1
establish	1	function	1	induce	8
estate	6	fund	3	inevitable	8
estimate	1	fundamental	5	infer	7
ethic	9	furthermore	6	infrastructure	8
ethnic	4	gender	6	inherent	9
evaluate	2	generate	5	inhibit	6
eventual	8	generation	5	initial	3
evident	1	globe	7	initiate	6
evolve	5	goal	4	injure	2
exceed	6	grade	7	innovate	7
exclude	3	grant	4	input	6
exhibit	8	guarantee	7	insert	7
expand	5	guideline	8	insight	9
expert	6	hence	4	inspect	8
explicit	6	hierarchy	7	instance	3
exploit	8	highlight	8	institute	2
export	1	hypothesis	4	instruct	6
expose	5	identical	7	integral	9
external	5	identify	1	integrate	4
extract	7	ideology	7	integrity	10
facilitate	5	ignorance	6	intelligence	6
factor	1	illustrate	3	intense	8
feature	2	image	5	interact	3
federal	6	immigrate	3	intermediate	9
fee	6	impact	2	internal	4
file	7	implement	4	interpret	1
final	2	implicate	4	interval	6
finance	1	implicit	8	intervene	7
finite	7	imply	3	intrinsic	10
flexible	6	impose	4	invest	2
fluctuate	8	incentive	6	investigate	4
focus	2	incidence	6	invoke	10

involve	1	minimum	6	participate	2
isolate	7	ministry	6	partner	3
issue	1	minor	3	passive	9
item	2	mode	7	perceive	2
job	4	modify	5	percent	1
journal	2	monitor	5	period	1
justify	3	motive	6	persist	10
label	4	mutual	9	perspective	5
labour	1	negate	3	phase	4
layer	3	network	5	phenomenon	7
lecture	6	neutral	6	philosophy	3
legal	1	nevertheless	6	physical	3
legislate	1	nonetheless	10	plus	8
levy	10	norm	9	policy	1
liberal	5	normal	2	portion	9
licence	5	notion	5	pose	10
likewise	10	notwithstanding	10	positive	2
link	3	nuclear	8	potential	2
locate	3	objective	5	practitioner	8
logic	5	obtain	2	precede	6
maintain	2	obvious	4	precise	5
major	1	occupy	4	predict	4
manipulate	8	occur	1	predominant	8
manual	9	odd	10	preliminary	9
margin	5	offset	8	presume	6
mature	9	ongoing	10	previous	2
maximise	3	option	4	primary	2
mechanism	4	orient	5	prime	5
media	7	outcome	3	principal	4
mediate	9	output	4	principle	1
medical	5	overall	4	prior	4
medium	9	overlap	9	priority	7
mental	5	overseas	6	proceed	1
method	1	panel	10	process	1
migrate	6	paradigm	7	professional	4
military	9	paragraph	8	prohibit	7
minimal	9	parallel	4	project	4
minimise	8	parameter	4	promote	4

proportion	3	restrict	2	strategy	2
prospect	8	retain	4	stress	4
protocol	9	reveal	6	structure	1
psychology	5	revenue	5	style	5
publication	7	reverse	7	submit	7
publish	3	revise	8	subordinate	9
purchase	2	revolution	9	subsequent	4
pursue	5	rigid	9	subsidy	6
qualitative	9	role	1	substitute	5
quote	7	route	9	successor	7
radical	8	scenario	9	sufficient	3
random	8	schedule	8	sum	4
range	2	scheme	3	summary	4
ratio	5	scope	6	supplement	9
rational	6	section	1	survey	2
react	3	sector	1	survive	7
recover	6	secure	2	suspend	9
refine	9	seek	2	sustain	5
regime	4	select	2	symbol	5
region	2	sequence	3	tape	6
register	3	series	4	target	5
regulate	2	sex	3	task	3
reinforce	8	shift	3	team	9
reject	5	significant	1	technical	3
relax	9	similar	1	technique	3
release	7	simulate	7	technology	3
relevant	2	site	2	temporary	9
reluctance	10	so-called	10	tense	8
rely	3	sole	7	terminate	8
remove	3	somewhat	7	text	2
require	1	source	1	theme	8
research	1	specific	1	theory	1
reside	2	specify	3	thereby	8
resolve	4	sphere	9	thesis	7
resource	2	stable	5	topic	7
respond	1	statistic	4	trace	6
restore	8	status	4	tradition	2
restrain	9	straightforward	10	transfer	2

transform	6	uniform	8	virtual	8
transit	5	unify	9	visible	7
transmit	7	unique	7	vision	9
transport	6	utilise	6	visual	8
trend	5	valid	3	volume	3
trigger	9	vary	1	voluntary	7
ultimate	7	vehicle	8	welfare	5
undergo	10	version	5	whereas	5
underlie	6	via	8	whereby	10
undertake	4	violate	9	widespread	8

Originally from Coxhead, A. (1998) An Academic Word List, Occasional Publication Number 18, LALS, Victoria University of Wellington, New Zealand.

Key

Unit 1
Task 2
a)	4	g)	1
b)	11	h)	2
c)	6	i)	10
d)	9	j)	5
e)	8	k)	7
f)	3	l)	12

Task 3
1 glossary
2 publishing details
3 contents
4 introduction
5 acknowledgements
6 bibliography
7 back cover

Task 7
1	e	6	c
2	j	7	b
3	g	8	a
4	i	9	d
5	h	10	f

Task 8
1 the reasons for subsidence in Venice   281–82
2 the sociology of disasters involving skyscrapers   353–5
3 effects of snow in cities   201–06
4 aid for developing world countries   511–4
5 disasters in Texas   161, 285
6 frequency of tornadoes in the USA   174–80
7 psychological stress   564, 569
8 relationship between tides and earthquakes   65
9 assessing the stability of slopes   246–51
10 how tornadoes are formed   171–4

Task 9
1 this book
2 those people/students
3 engineering
4 careers, education and training
5 this book

6 of textbooks
7 making specific recommendations of textbooks
8 the like of reference books
9 details of selected books
10 general information provided in certain chapters

Task 10
1 Ch 4
2 Ch 1
3 Ch 5
4 Ch 2
5 Ch 6
6 Ch 7

Unit 2
Task 1
1 *How to pass exams without anxiety*, Acres, David
  Student's guide to exam success, Tracy, Eileen
2 *Writing reports*, Williams, Kate
3 *Learn how to study: a realistic approach*, Rowntree, Derek
  Guide to learning independently, Marshall, Lorraine A.
  How to manage your study time, Lewis, Roger
  Getting organised, Fry, Ron
4 *Studying for a degree in the humanities and the social sciences*, Dunleavy, Patrick
5 *MBA handbook: study skills for managers*, Cameron, Sheila
  Reading at university: a guide for students, Fairbairn, Gavin
6 *Lectures: how best to handle them*, Race, Phil
7 *Guide to learning independently*, Marshall, Lorraine A.

Task 2
1	117	5	67
2	44	6	215
3	212	7	183
4	160, possibly 121	8	9

Task 3

1 Population age profiles/changes in Western Europe Ch 7
2 Fossil fuel use/oil consumption in Africa Ch 14
3 Key factors in shaping the recent past Ch 3
4 The growth of Beijing Ch 4
5 The role of nations in a unified Europe Ch 16
6 Euros and dollars – will both prevail? Ch 13
7 Effects of developed world demand on developing world agriculture Ch 9
8 Production of Western consumer goods in developing world countries Ch 12
9 Nomadic peoples in the 21st century Ch 5
10 Societies before industrialisation Ch 1

Task 5 (examples)

Group A

1 How can we best prepare for examinations?
2 How can we avoid being over-anxious about examinations?
3 What examination techniques are there?
4 How can we best organise subject knowledge in preparation for an examination?
5 How can we become skilled in examination techniques?

Group B

1 How can we best prepare for examinations?
2 How should we review for examinations?
3 How can we schedule revision?
4 How can we avoid anxiety?
5 What examination techniques are there?

Group C

1 How can we best prepare for examinations?
2 What is the best way to revise?
3 How can we avoid anxiety?
4 What kinds of examinations are there?
5 What is the best way to answer essay questions?

Task 9

1 Difficulty in organising and timetabling work.
2 Their course may be less structured than previously experienced.

Task 10

a) They both show bad study habits.
b) Successful students spend more time on study and adjust the time spent to that needed for success.
c) Sexton stresses the time successful students spend on study. Borrow stresses technique, not time.
d) Borrow's.

Task 12

1 deadlines
2 ensure
3 completed
4 Allocate
5 spending
6 around/round
7 treat
8 unforeseen
9 leeway
10 Repeatedly

Task 13

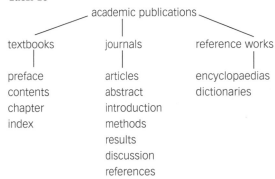

Task 14

1 What is memory?
2 What do we mean by 'a good memory'?
3 What are the stages of memory?
4 What is the difference between short-term and long-term memory?
5 How do we measure memory?
6 In what form do we best remember material?
7 Why do we forget?

Task 15

1 What is the difference between short-term and long-term memory?
2 Why do we forget things?
3 How can we retain information in short-term memory?

Unit 3
Task 2

Words to ignore are *passerine*, *pied flycatcher* and Latin names for birds. *Ornithologist* can be worked out from context. *Nesting-box traps* should help refine ideas for a suitable experiment.

Task 4

In addition to the order in the text, one possible order would be: *hypothesis, predict, investigation, results, significant, confirmed, suggest, conclude.*

Task 5

1	b	7	b
2	a	8	b
3	a	9	a
4	b	10	a
5	a	11	a
6	b	12	b

Task 6
Why male birds sing

Most ornithologists take it for granted that male passerine (perching) birds sing to attract females. But, until now, no one has produced any direct evidence to support the idea. Although the males of many species certainly sing much less once they have acquired their mates, and some female birds respond to male song with courtship display, this evidence is circumstantial. Now Dag Eriksson and Lars Wallin, two zoologists from the University of Uppsala in Sweden, have proved the point – for two species at least (*Behavioural Ecology and Sociobiology*, vol 19, p297).

Eriksson and Wallin studied the pied flycatcher (Ficedula hypoleuca) and the collared flycatcher (F. albicollis). In May, they set up nest-box traps occupied by dummy male birds. Some of the nest boxes broadcast recordings of flycatcher song, while others remained silent. Normally, male flycatchers arrive at the nest site earlier than females, establish and defend a small territory, and sing frequently from a perch near the nest hole. When the researchers checked their nest boxes, they found that nine of the ten trapped flycatchers were in nest boxes with the 'singing' dummy males, which seems to indicate what amateur ornithologists have thought all along.

[Source: *New Scientist*, No.1544, 22 January 1987, p 28]

Task 7 and 8

1 Seeing things only in terms of their function. The boxes are seen as containers, not as potential support.
2 To mount three candles vertically on a soft wooden screen using any object on the table.
3 For one group the candles, matches and tacks were presented in their boxes. For the other, these boxes were presented alongside their contents, but not as containers.
4 41% of the first group solved the problem. 86% of the second group solved the problem.
5 Functional fixity can hinder problem solving by preventing us thinking of uses for objects other than their normal function.
6 The extra objects distracted the subjects.

The only information which cannot be derived directly from these samples is the result for the second group, but this can be inferred.

Figure C

FUNCTIONAL FIXITY: A BARRIER TO CREATIVE PROBLEM SOLVING

The German psychologist Karl Duncker first proposed the concept of functional fixity about 1930, and he illustrated it with a few simple experiments. Because these experiments were done with so few subjects, several American psychologists repeated them, and they obtained results similar to Duncker's. R.E. Adamson at Stanford University did one such experiment.

The task: Mount three candles vertically on a soft wooden screen, using any object on the table. Among the objects are three cardboard boxes and a number of matches and thumbtacks. *The solution*: Mount one candle on each box by melting wax on the box and sticking the candle to it; then tack the boxes to the screen (see Figure C).

For one group (twenty-nine college students), the candles, matches, and tacks were placed in the three boxes before they were presented to the subjects (Figure A). *The boxes were thus seen functioning as containers*; whereas in the solution of the problem the boxes would have been seen as supports or shelves. For the second group (twenty-eight subjects), the boxes were empty and placed among the other objects (Figure B). There the boxes were not seen functioning as containers. Twenty minutes were allowed for the solution.

Of the first group, only twelve of the subjects (or 41 percent) were able to solve the problem: apparently the remaining subjects in this group could not perceive the boxes with the meaning of platform or shelf. Of the second group, twenty-four (or 86 percent) were able to solve the problem.

These results give striking evidence that functional fixity may be an important barrier in creative problem solving. Note also the mental dazzle operating here, as a result of the useless, hence distracting, extra objects.

Task 9

1 they do not require expensive interviewers.
2 questionnaires are cheap.
3 they may not be reliable.
4 many people do not return them.

Task 10

1 a   3 a
2 b   4 a

Task 11

For example   However
In contrast   Furthermore
For instance   In other words

Task 12

drawbacks (noun) *disadvantages, limitations*
spontaneous (adj) *unplanned, immediate, without thinking*
ambiguity (noun) *when the meaning is unclear because something can be understood in more than one way*

Task 13

1 flexible *adaptable* 'can be altered'
2 candid *frank* 'since…not have to commit themselves'
3 insincere *not genuine* 'distinguish between a genuine…'
4 anticipate *predict* 'look ahead'
5 restricting *limiting* 'problem…full notes…solved…marks or numbers'
6 inkling *hint* 'tone…way…appearance, dress and accent' (all very indirect)
7 anonymous *without identification* 'but not if identification is required'
8 misheard *misunderstood* 'fill in their own …and so cannot be…'

Task 14

collocates	headword	collocates
	appropriate	response
	assess	situation
legitimate	authority	
	conclude	agreement
come to	conclusion	
experimental	design	
	display	findings
market	economy	
	enforce	law
	evaluate	progress
	exceed	limits
scientific	method	
	normal	circumstances
changes	occur	
	positive	transfer
	primary	education
medical	research	
	specific	gravity
class	structure	
	theory	evolution

Task 17

Fig 1 Thermal camera captures guilty faces
Fig 2 Knock-out pig clones advance transplant hopes

Task 18

Text 1
Predators key to forest survival
18:35 30 November 01
A forest without predators may not be a forest for

long – that is the ominous conclusion of a unique new study by an international team of scientists. The team has found that when predators vanish, herbivore populations can explode, leading to the mass destruction of plant life. The team, led by John Terborgh of Duke University, conducted a census of the herbivores and trees on several islands in Lago Guri, a 4300 square kilometre lake in Venezuela that was created in 1986 when a river was dammed for hydroelectric power. When the water rose, the smallest of the islands lost nearly all of the predatory animals that inhabit the mainland, such as jaguars, snakes and raptors. The situation provided a unique natural experiment to test two competing theories of how ecosystems are structured. The so-called bottom-up theory, says, in effect, that the plants are in control. Proponents of this idea argue that the availability of edible plants determines how many herbivores an ecosystem can support, which in turn determines how many predators it can support. The top-down theory, on the other hand, argues that the predators are in charge. They keep the herbivores in check, thereby determining the abundance of plants.

Population explosion

'Some theoretical ecologists have argued that these top-down effects aren't very important or very common,' says Michael Pace of the Institute of Ecosystem Studies in Millbrook, New York. 'But these kinds of observations are very hard to make in terrestrial ecosystems, which is why it's been so hard to tell.' Until now. The bottom-up theory predicts nothing much should have changed in the Lago Guri after the predators disappeared. But Terborgh's findings show that the absence of predators has had a profound effect on the islands' ecosystems. His team found that herbivores such as howler monkeys, iguanas and leaf-cutter ants were 10 to 100 times more prevalent on the lake's six smallest islands than they were on the mainland. The density of young trees on these islands was less than half that on six larger islands in the lakes, which had retained some of their predators.

Back lash

Pace says the study illustrates nicely that top-down processes can shape ecosystems, at least in some situations. However, he adds that the pendulum could swing back to bottom-up forces if the herbivores gobble up all the edible plants on the islands. If that happens, the remaining plants could begin limiting animal populations. The study's authors argue that predators play a key role in maintaining biodiversity. An overabundance of herbivores 'threatens to reduce species-rich forests to an odd collection of herbivore-resistant plants,' they write. 'Along the way, much plant and animal diversity will probably be lost.' This process is already happening in North America, they say, where deer populations have ballooned, and in Malaysia, where wild pigs run rampant through some forests.
Journal reference: *Science* (vol 294, p 1923)
Greg Miller

Text 2
Knock-out pig clones advance transplant hopes
11:05 03 January 02

Five cloned piglets, genetically modified so that their organs are much less likely to be rejected by a human donor recipient, have been born in the US. More than 62,000 people in the US alone are waiting to receive donated hearts, lungs, livers, kidneys and pancreases. The number of human donors falls far short of demand. Pig organs are of a similar size to human organs, and some scientists hope they might be used to help meet the shortfall. But previous attempts to transplant unaltered pig tissue into humans have failed, due to immune rejection of the tissue. The five piglets, born on Christmas Day, lack a gene for an enzyme that adds a sugar to the surface of pig cells. The sugar would trigger a patient's immune system into launching an immediate attack.

'This advance provides a near-time solution for overcoming the shortage of human organs for transplants, as well as insulin-producing cells to cure diabetes,' says David Ayares, vice president of research at PPL Therapeutics' US division, where the pigs were created. 'This is the key gene for overcoming the early stage of rejection,' he told

New Scientist. Several other teams are working on knocking out the same gene. One, led by researchers at the University of Missouri, is using a strain of pig that they believe will be more suitable for transplantation than the strain used by PPL. This team is expected to publish results of their cloning programme imminently.

Double knock out

However, scientists warn that much more work is necessary before organs from copies of the pigs could be transplanted into humans. Human genes will need to be added, to prevent rejection of the organ in the long-term. There are also concerns that pig viruses could infect organ recipients. Cloning techniques were vital to the production of the pigs. Genes can only be knocked out in a single cell. Cloning of these single cells then allowed the creation of a whole animal in which the gene was knocked out in every cell. But the PPL researchers have succeeded in knocking out only one copy of the gene for the enzyme, called alpha 1,3 galactosyl transferase. The team will now attempt to knock out both copies of the gene.

Human genes

'There will also be other genes we will incorporate into our program,' Ayares says. 'We don't think that one gene is going to produce an organ that's going to be the end-all for transplantation. We're going to have to add two to three human genes as well.' The team will also conduct tests to investigate whether so-called porcine endogenous retroviruses (PERVS) from the pigs could infect human cells in culture. But Ayares hopes that organs created from PPL pigs could be transplanted into patients within five years. Other approaches to combating the human donor shortage have been successfully tried. Mechanical hearts are functioning in several patients. But creating artificial lungs and livers is much more difficult.

Stem cells, which can in theory be coaxed into forming any kind of cell in the body, have been transplanted into patients suffering the loss of a particular type of cell, for example. 'But although a lot of the stem cell work is very exciting, we're still very far off being able to grow an organ in a culture dish,' says Julia Greenstein of Immerge BioTherapeutics in Charlestown, US, who is working on creating similar knock-out pigs with researchers at the University of Missouri.
Emma Young

Text 3
Electron beams could be used to irradiate post
12:20 24 October 01

The US Postal Service is installing irradiation equipment in an attempt to destroy biological weapons, such as anthrax, concealed in envelopes and parcels. Jack Potter, the US Postmaster General, announced on Monday that the first piece of equipment has already been bought. But he will not reveal which irradiation technology will be used, or when or where postal irradiation will start. The USPS processes 200 billion pieces of small mail each year, so it seems unlikely that it could offer comprehensive coverage. On Tuesday the White House announced that small quantities of anthrax had been found at a military sorting office that serves the White House. Two US postal workers have already died after contracting anthrax from contaminated mail. Another worker in New Jersey is suspected of having pulmonary anthrax and more than a dozen others are showing symptoms of infection. There are a number of ways to kill anthrax spores, says Wil Williams of Titan, a San Diego-based company which produces irradiation equipment. But most are too slow to be practical for use on mail, he says.

Electron beams

Gamma rays are used to irradiate food and sterilise medical equipment. They are known to damage DNA in anthrax spores, says Williams. But he thinks electron beam technology would work faster. 'Anything that's done with gamma rays you can do with electron beam, but in a fraction of the time,' he says. Titan's irradiation equipment, called SureBeam, uses high energy electron beams to break down molecules within DNA, either killing a micro-organism or rendering it unable to reproduce. SureBeam bombards its target with energy levels of around five million electron volts. At these energy levels, says Williams, 18,000 kilograms of ground beef could be sterilised in a few seconds.

Dead in seconds

Anthrax spores are particularly difficult to kill, says Anne-Brit Kolstø a microbiologist at the University of Oslo, in Norway. 'A very thick wall is created surrounding the DNA, protecting it against dryness, chemicals and ultraviolet light,' she says. But Williams told *New Scientist* that SureBeam has been successfully tested on anthrax and anthrax spores. It can kill spores in seconds, he says. The technique could be used on boxes of mail prior to or after sorting. Kolstø believes that all machinery within the postal system needs to be scrutinised. If rollers apply pressure to an envelope containing anthrax it could force spores out and increase the spread, she says.
Duncan Graham-Rowe

Text 4

Thermal camera captures guilty faces

19:00 02 January 02

A camera that detects liars by monitoring the temperature of their face could lead to more effective screening procedures at airports and other high-security locations, according to US researchers. Norman Eberhardt and James Levine of the Mayo Clinic and Ioannis Pavlidis of Honeywell Laboratories, both in Minnesota, have developed the high-resolution thermal imaging camera. This can identify an instant rush of blood to the area around the eyes, a phenomenon that has been linked with lying.

The changes around the eyes after telling the truth (upper image) and telling a lie (lower image) are detected (Photo: Pavlidis *et al*). The temperature of the eye region can rise by several degrees. However, the thermal camera needs to be many times more sensitive to detect this change accurately at a distance. In tests the system picked out liars with comparable accuracy to conventional polygraph equipment, which is more complicated and time consuming to use. The team say that the new camera could potentially be used at busy security checkpoints. 'If the technology proves this accurate in the airport, it could revolutionise airport screening' says Levine. 'The ultimate concept that you would ask someone if they were carrying a weapon and get an immediate response from the camera.' The researchers did not test how factors such as heating levels and recent exertion could impact the reliability of the camera. 'Further testing and development are needed,' concedes Levine.

Guilty faces

The thermal imaging camera can detect temperature changes of just 0.025°C and is calibrated between 29°C and 38°C. In 20 tests performed at the US Department of Defence Polygraph Institute the device correctly identified 75 per cent of those who had lied and 90 per cent of those who were telling the truth. Traditional polygraph equipment used on the same subjects was only 70 per cent accurate, although Levine says that the two techniques are probably equally reliable. Levine speculates that increased blood flow to the eyes could be linked to identifying a means of escape. The same reaction has in the past been recorded when subjects hear a startling noise. But not all experts are convinced that the system would work in practice.

Aldert Vrij of the Department of Psychology at Portsmouth University, UK, believes the system is unlikely to work perfectly and could lead to complacency at high-security checkpoints. 'There is the risk that people start to rely on it too much,' he says. Vrij says that the camera's results could vary significantly between individuals and believes that some people may even be able to fool the camera by altering their emotional state, as is the case with polygraph tests.
Journal reference: *Nature* (vol 415, p 35)
Will Knight

Unit 4

Task 3

1 Water
2 Trade and Trade Policy
3 Economic Conditions/Poverty
4 Trade/Agriculture
5 Trade
6 Tourism

7 Forestry

8 Women and Gender Issues

Task 4

The main points are all signposted:

1 *One of the most important* problems facing developing countries today is the rapid increase in population.

2 *The main point to be made here* is that more and more people are concentrated in those countries which are least able to provide a living for them.

3 *What is responsible for this population is not…but* a sharp decline in the death rate in developing countries.

4 *The main reason* for the reduction in the death rate in the developing world has been improved public health measures.

5 *In other words*, the death rate can be cut without anything else changing.

Task 5

Only *For example* (line 5) marks an unimportant point. All the other signposts indicate important points, although of the three reasons given, the third is clearly marked as the most important.

Task 8

Text A

First category: *Long-term causes of household income loss or income instability which increases the vulnerability of poor people.*

Causes:

1 *environmental degredation*

2 *social changes*

Example of social changes: *breakdown of traditional social obligations to the poor.*

Text B

Second category: *Precipitating factors setting off the secondary events which worsen the situation.*

Types of precipitating factors:

1 *those which reduce the food supply*

2 *those which it is feared will do so*

3 *those which reduce the purchasing power of the poor*

Example of secondary events: *spiralling food prices*

Text C

Third category: *Relief failure, i.e. governmental famine-prevention administration which is inadequate, incompetent or unable to operate*

Example of relief failure: *Sudan and Ethiopia (delays in relief)*

Example of relief success: *Bangladesh in the early 1980s*

Task 9

cause + START	*cause + MORE*
create	increase
set off	raise
dislodge	double
precipitate	
cause + LESS	*cause + HARM*
reduce	aggravate
halve	worsen
restrict	damage
cut	hamper
lower	

Task 10

1 a	4 a
2 c	5 b
3 b	

Unit 5

Task 1

1 They may infect other children and unimmunised adults.

2 They can detect approaching bats.

3 The young fish can escape through the larger spaces.

4 That malaria was caused by breathing bad night air from wet areas.

Task 2

The amount of information provided by the reader will depend on their knowledge of the world. Possible answers:

1 The antelope were killed off because people were poor, hungry and involved in war.

2 Only one wild dog population has a territory wide enough to avoid inbreeding. The genetic pool in a small territory is not large enough to ensure a vigorous population.

3 The territories of large animals are so reduced that inbreeding is a danger. Zoos

have animals from a number of territories and can avoid this problem.

Task 4

1 equals, is equal to
2 more than, greater than
3 less than
4 very, greatly
5 leads to, causes, results in, is the cause of
6 caused by, results from, is the effect of
7 possibly
8 unlikely
9 regarding, with reference to
10 etcetera, and so on, and other things
11 that is to say, they are, namely
12 compare
13 also known as
14 note well
15 circa, about
16 for example, for instance
17 government   first syllable, last letter
18 hypothetical important syllables
19 probably   first syllable only
20 important   first syllable, last letter
21 temporary   first syllable only
22 standard   key consonants
23 very   first letter
24 discussion   *ion* ending reduced to *n*

Task 6 (Example)

Destructn.forests
1996 ca. 3.3bn hectares but ⇓ ++ 11.3bn/yr.
e.g. Africa 85%
b.farming,
logging,
construction.

Rainforests impt. b.
regulate climate,
prevent erosion,
store/clean water,
home 50% world's species,
produce e.g. chocolate, drugs.
Destructn. → environmntl problems & habitat loss.

Task 8

Sections	Paragraphs
Introduction	A
The laboratory	B,C,F,G
The forest	D,E
The political arena	H,I

Task 10

a) all chlamydia strains
b) vaccine
c) treatment
d) overpop. to underpop. areas
e) land needed
f) koala's specialist digestive system
g) dietary supplements
h) safeguard koala colonies
i) 'build' koalas into communities
j) dog/human activities in koala country
k) protecting koala habitat

Task 11

The developing world: c, f, i, k, o
The natural world: b, e, g, l, n
The spirit of enquiry: a, d, h, j, m

Task 12

verb	noun	adjective
benefit	benefit	beneficial
compensate	compensation	compensatory
consume	consumption	consuming
contradict	contradiction	contradictory
cooperate	cooperation/ cooperative	cooperative
create	creation/creator	creative
define	definition	defining
distinguish	distinction	distinct
distort	distortion	distorting
diversify	diversification	diverse
emphasise	emphasis	emphatic
	environment	environmental
finance	finance	financial
generate	generation	
hypothesise	hypothesis	hypothetical
ignore	ignorance	ignorant
illustrate	illustration	illustrated
induce	inductance/induction	induced
innovate	innovation	innovatory
invest	investment/investor	investing
license	licence	licensing
	logic	logical

Task 13

Para 1 (e) Chimpanzee survival important for humans

Para 2 (a) Chimps are genetically like humans

Para 3 (f) Important differences

Para 4 (c) Resistant to HIV

Para 5 (h) Reason for HIV resistance

Para 6 (d) Resistant to cancer

Para 7 (b) Importance of identifying genetic differences

Para 8 (g) Consequences of identifying differences

Task 15

Topic **Importance of chimpanzees for human survival**

Chimpanzees ⇓ b.(1)hunting & habitat destruction *Para 1*

but impt.++ for humans

Chimpanzees ≈ humans *Para 2*

1genomes 98% c.f.(2) mice 60%

2IQ

3(3) tool use

Differences impt. for (4) medical research: *Para 3–6*

because resistance to diseases

e.g. HIV b.evolved resistance to (5) SIV

cancer ?b. diet & (6) lifestyle

but ?genetic

Sequencing chimp genome cd.: *Para 7–8*

1 identify (7) genes for disease resistance

2 → new drugs or alteratn. (8) human genes

3 identify 2% genes responsible for (9)"humanness"

4 → (10) ways to improve human genes, e.g. IQ

Unit 6

Task 1

The diagram shows a device for exploding landmines developed by Professor Salter of the University of Edinburgh. It can be constructed from materials easily available in the developing world. It sweeps an area in a series of overlapping circles.

Task 2

1 table, the pH of common substances, could be given by a bar chart

2 pie chart, annual energy consumption excluding fossil fuels

3 flowchart, how sulphuric acid is made

4 graph, the growth in world population, could be shown by a vertical bar chart

5 vertical bar chart, the extinction of species

6 flowchart, the rock cycle

7 schematic diagram, the physical world

Task 3 (*examples* of specific ideas)

1 Specific Sodium hydroxide is highly alkaline.

 Main Substances range from very acidic with a pH of 0 to highly alkaline with a pH of 14.

2 Specific Solar energy provides the equivalent of 12 million tonnes of oil.

 Main Alternative energy sources produce the equivalent of more than 1,600 million tonnes of oil.

3 Specific Water is added in the final stage to dilute the acid.

 Main Sulphuric acid is produced from sulphur by a process involving heat and a catalyst.

4 Specific World population will exceed 8,000 million by 2025.

 Main The population of the less developed world is increasing much more quickly than that of the developed world.

5 Specific The passenger pigeon was extinct by 1914.

 Main The pace of extinction of species has accelerated rapidly since 1900.

6 Specific Metamorphic rocks may be formed by heat or pressure.

 Main The formation of the different types of rocks is a cyclical process.

7 Specific The lithosphere is about 60km in depth.

 Main The physical world consists of the lithosphere, hydrosphere, biosphere and atmosphere.

Tasks 4–5

1 igneous intrusion, volcanic plug
2 eroded by ice
3 streamlined by the ice flow
4 softer sandstone protected by the crag and boulder clay deposited in the ice

Tasks 6–8

1 transpiration is from plants, evaporation is from soil and water
2 water which is not absorbed but runs off the land to the sea in the form of rivers
3 by infiltration
4 evaporation
5 water from volcanic steam
6 the level below which the ground is saturated

Task 9

Cheapest method of evaporation

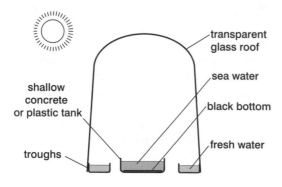

transparent glass roof

sea water

shallow concrete or plastic tank

black bottom

fresh water

troughs

Task 10

Check these approximate meanings worked out from the text with a good dictionary.

1 **brasses** musical instruments played by blowing air into the mouthpiece and vibrating the lips; they have long hollow bodies.
2 **eddy** a movement of air.
3 **cavities** hollow places like the mouth and nose.

Task 11

violin, strings, bridge, f-holes, front (top) plate, back plate, body resonances, string frequencies, distorted

Task 12

verb	noun	adjective
manipulate	manipulation	manipulatory
marginalise	margin	marginal
mechanise	mechanism	mechanical
minimise	minimum	minimal
modify	modification	modifying
normalise	norm	normal
	nucleus	nuclear
participate	participation/participant	participating
perceive	perception	perceptive
philosophise	philosophy	philosophical
	precision	precise
publish	publication/publishing	
pursue	pursuit	pursuing
randomise		random
react	reaction	reactive
recover	recovery	recovering
regulate	regulation	regulatory
reinforce	reinforcement	reinforcing
respond	response	responsive
signify	significance	significant
specify	specification	specific
stabilise	stability	stable
stress	stress	stressed/stressful
submit	submission	submissive
symbolise	symbol	symbolic
	technique/technology	technical
theorise	theory	theoretical
unify	unification	unifying
validate	validation	valid
vary	variation	varying
visualise	vision	visual

Task 14

Main   There are considerable differences in regions affected by water scarcity with the Middle East and North Africa having the greatest problems.

Specifics More than half the water resources in the Middle East and North African region are overexploited.
About 25% of water resources in South Asia are overexploited.
The Latin America and Caribbean region does not have serious water problems at present.

Task 15

1 Middle East and North Africa
2 Mining
3 Sub-Saharan Africa
4 About 30% of water resources are over-exploited
5 No

Task 16

1 Half the world's wetlands were lost in the twentieth century. T
2 It is estimated that water use will rise by 50% in the next 30 years. T
3 Some Mediterranean countries will face 'severe water shortages' by 2025. DNS
4 Most of the world's population may live within 100km of the sea in 2025. T
5 Almost 60% of coral reefs may perish in 100 years. F
6 Some species of fish in the Atlantic are at dangerously low levels. DNS
7 In the next 30 years, around three billion people could experience moderate to high water shortages. T
8 India exceeds environmental limits for water use. F

Task 17

According to a World Bank (1) *report*, as the world's population grows, the demand for fresh water is (2) *increasing* rapidly but supplies are falling and wetlands are disappearing. Up to half the world's population will have (3) *serious* water problems by 2025. This may lead to (4) *conflict*. Coastal regions will (5) *face* similar problems. Overfishing will damage fish stocks and coral reefs may be (6) *destroyed*. Immediate action is needed to (7) *safeguard* water supplies and encourage more efficient use. If this is not done, the numbers suffering (8) *shortages* will rise by 50% in the next 30 years. China has the most serious problem in East Asia with freshwater withdrawal set to (9) *exceed* environmental limits by 2020. Other countries with severe problems include most of the Middle East, North Africa, and the Indian sub-continent.

Unit 7
Task 3

1 optimistic about the future
2 optimistic about the future
3 pessimistic about the future
4 pessimistic about the future
5 against human cloning
6 against carbon economy
7 optimistic about these developments
8 neutral – reporting only
9 unconvinced about benefits of GM
10 probably against 'designer babies'

Task 6

Similarities: In both surveys approximately 44% feel that the benefits of science outweigh the negative aspects.
Differences: The phrasing of the questions; the presentation of the results – the scales used.

Task 8

d.

Task 9

1 1st   can navigate, recognise speech and text
  2nd   can learn from experience
  3rd   can think, problem-solve, learn by imitation
  4th   match human reasoning; then supersede humans
2 Neutral – simply reporting
3 It is inevitable and even to be welcomed that robots will supersede mankind.

Task 10

a) Introduction 1
b) Evolution 2, 3, 4, 5
c) Consequences 6, 7, 8, 9

Task 11

1 g
2 a
3 b OR h
4 b OR h
5 i
6 e
7 d
8 c OR f
9 c OR f

Task 13

1 adj., not active
2 adj., not in proportion
3 p.p. (past participle), introduced again
4 adj., not probable
5 noun, something not relevant
6 adv., without question
7 p.p. (past participle), changed into another form
8 noun, being employed
9 noun, being futile
10 verb, make rational
11 pres.p. (present participle), making something shorter
12 verb, make something standard

Task 14

To refute the claims of certain robotics researchers and to warn that their exaggerated claims may put research funding at risk.

Task 15

1 The idea that robots will take over the earth is silly. /Yes/
2 It is unfortunate that some authorities are taking seriously such claims by robotics researchers. /Yes/
3 Humans will become an underclass in the future. /No/
4 Tiny computers will be inserted in our brains to allow us to link directly to computers. /Not given/
5 The predictions of some robotics researchers are based on false assumptions. /Yes/
6 Regarding computing power, Moore's Law has proved to be correct. /Not given/
7 An increase in processing power does not mean an equal increase in robotic intelligence. /Yes/
8 Not everything which displays aspects of animate behaviour is animate. /Yes/
9 Making exaggerated claims for robotics is dangerous because this may put government (research) funding for robotics at risk. /Yes/
10 Robotics is like marketing. /No/

Task 16

The idea that robots will take over the earth is (1) *silly* and it is (2) *unfortunate* that some authorities are taking seriously such claims by some robotics researchers. Their predictions are based on two false (3) *assumptions*. We accept them because we are (4) *distracted* by 'astonishing facts' linked to Moore's Law on the doubling of computing power every 18 months. The first is that an increase in (5) *processing* power equals an increase in robotic intelligence. This is false because we haven't done well in giving machines (6) *common* sense and the ability to learn. In addition a problem is always more difficult than we (7) *anticipate* even when we take this unanticipated difficulty into account (Hofstadter's Law). The second assumption is that anything which displays aspects of (8) *animate* behaviour is animate. Because robots show some minor aspects of animate behaviour, we assume they are animate. Making (9) *exaggerated* claims for robotics is dangerous because government (10) *funding* for robotics may be put at risk.

Unit 8
Task 1

Facts can be verified by experiment or by reference to other facts. They are true statements supported by evidence. This does not mean that every statement presented as a fact is true. Facts can also change when new evidence becomes available. Opinions are personal beliefs. They are subjective.

This task is to promote discussion. There is room for disagreement in this division.
Facts: 1, 3, 8, 9
Opinions: 2, 4, 5, 6, 7, 10

Task 6
Text A

1 Most learning NOT because teaching.
2 ALTHO' teaching may help in s. conditions.
3 BUT most knowledge out/s school.
4 & In/s school only insofar as confined there.
5 Most learning casual (not intentional).
6 e.g. 1st lang. learnt casually.
7 Even most intentional learning NOT because teaching.

8 e.g. If 2nd lang. learnt well, learnt because odd circumstances like travel.

9 ALSO fluent reading because out/s school activities.

10 Good readers merely believe learned at school.

11 BUT when challenged, discard this illusion.

Text B

1 Equal obligatory schooling is economically unfeasible.

2 b. in Latin America 350/1500 × more public money spent on graduate student than median citizen.

3 & in US discrimination worse.

4 b. richest educate children privately.

5 & richest obtain 10 × more per capita public money than poorest.

6 b. rich children longer at school.

7 & university year more expensive than school year.

8 & most private universities depend on tax-derived finances.

Task 9

Conclusion to Texts 1 and 2 on marriage:

If there are winners and losers in marriage, it is hard to avoid the conclusion that men are more often the winners and women the losers.

Task 11

Maximisers	*Minimisers*
completely	only
in all respects	simply
altogether	at least to some extent
entirely	merely
much	hardly
fully	
quite	

Task 14

Any explanation of marital (1) *breakdown* from a functional viewpoint would consider three factors:

1 the value of marriage

2 (2) *conflict* between spouses

3 the ease of divorce

Parsons and Fletcher argue that the higher value placed on marriage leads to higher (3) *expectations*. When these are not realised,

breakdown follows. Functionalists argue that the economic (4) *system* today means that the family unit is no longer part of a larger family network. Therefore it is more vulnerable to (5) *emotional* pressures which lead to conflict within the family. In addition, because families no longer (6) *share* the same work, the ties which hold husband and wife together are weaker. Finally it is now easier for individuals to (7) *escape* from marriage because (8) *attitudes* to divorce have changed. Society in the West has become more (9) *secular* and self-interest rather than religious belief influences behaviour regarding divorce.

Unit 9
Tasks 3 and 4

	Text 1	Text 2
Nature of work	A curse	Essential, a social activity
Effect of working conditions	Reduce dislike, Improve mechanical efficiency	No direct effect on morale but can affect health and comfort
Motivation for work	Money and fear of unemployment	Money unimportant, Fear of unemployment because it cuts one off from society

Task 7

If working time falls, then *people will work less*. The result will be *more employment*. Working time will fall because of *the shorter working week*, longer holidays, earlier retirement, more sabbaticals and *job-sharing*. This means a mix of part-time paid and part-time unpaid work will become more common but *it will not restore full employment*. The first reason is that the reduction of working time cannot take place on a scale and at a pace sufficient to *create work for all who want it*. The second reason is that if *it could be done on such a scale and at such a pace*, it would create a situation where full employment would no longer be the main form of work.

Task 8

1 IF working time falls THEN *people will work less.*
2 THEREFORE *there will be more employment.*
3 Working time will fall
   BECAUSE OF *the shorter working week,*
4 *longer holidays,*
5 *earlier retirement,*
6 *more sabbaticals,*
7 AND *job-sharing.*
8 THEREFORE *a mix of part-time paid and unpaid work will become more common.*
9 BUT *it will not restore full employment*
10 BECAUSE the scale and pace are insufficient
11 and BECAUSE IF *it could be done on such a scale and at such a pace* THEN full employment would no longer be the only form of work.

Task 10

It may seem that if working hours are cut by 10 to 20%, then *mass unemployment will fall.* But labour will not accept wage cuts on such a scale. If wage cuts are imposed, *there will be serious social upheaval.* If hours are cut but wages maintained, Britain will be unable to compete in world markets because her goods will be so expensive. Even if Britain's goods could be sold, unemployment would not fall because of *its geographical distribution* and the mismatch between the skills the unemployed can offer and the skills required for modern employment.

Shortening working hours has value because *we still get psychological benefits* from employment even when we work less. Cutting hours will improve the quality of working life for the employed but *it is a slow way to reduce unemployment.*

Task 11

1 IF working hours are cut THEN *mass unemployment will fall*
2 BUT labour will not accept wage cuts on such a scale
3 IF *wage cuts are imposed* THEN there will be serious social upheaval
4 IF *hours are cut but wages maintained* THEN Britain will be unable to compete in world markets

5 BECAUSE her goods will be so expensive
6 IF Britain's goods could be sold THEN *unemployment would not fall*
7 BECAUSE OF its geographical distribution
8 AND *the mismatch between skills offered and required*
9 *Shortening working hours has value* BECAUSE we get the psychological benefits of work even when we work less
10 THEREFORE cutting working hours will improve the quality of life for the employed
11 BUT *it is a slow way to reduce unemployment.*

Task 14

Each argument contains a flaw.

1 The argument appears to be well-constructed but would you accept that women strike more than men because they are more emotional? The statement on which the argument is based is false.
2 B happens after A. Therefore A causes B. Because two actions happen in sequence does not mean that the first causes the second. After taking medicine you may recover from an illness but was it the medicine that cured you or would you have recovered in any case?
3 A is true in one situation. Therefore A is true in all situations. Such arguments are often used to justify importing foreign solutions to solve local problems.
4 A is like B in some ways. Therefore A is like B in all ways. This argument is often used to make false parallels with situations which are similar in some aspects but very different in others.
5 A is true because an authority says so. Appeals to philosophical, religious and political 'truths' are often used to justify unacceptable conclusions.
6 A is true once. Therefore A is always true. No scientist would accept a conclusion based on only one observation. In this argument there is simply not enough evidence to support such a major claim.
7 This is a circular argument. Saying the same thing twice does not make it true. The writer does not present an argument. The opening statement is merely repeated in different words.

Task 15

1 emphasis
2 distancing
3 emphasis
4 emphasis
5 emphasis
6 distancing

Task 18

1 and 2 The question mark in the title indicates the writer's doubts about this goal.

4 Unemployed people would feel resentful because they would feel their lives had no value. This is because most people have no tradition of leisure, but on the contrary feel the need to work and be useful.

5 The employed would be resentful because they would feel they had to support the idle.

7 A secure minimum wage for the unemployed and low paid.

8 A society in which citizens could choose their own mix of paid and unpaid work.

9 *did come* instead of *came* emphasises the writer's belief that it will not happen.
one thing is sure emphasises his next point
in fact gives further emphasis
in other words restates his point, giving further emphasis and clarity
at least to some extent hedges his conclusion

Unit 10

Task 2

a) Women in children's literature. 2
b) Women and environmental issues. 4
c) Women in business. 12, possibly 7
d) Noted women physicists. 8
e) Women writers of the 20th century. 3, possibly 6

Task 3

1 The meaning of acronyms such as NATO and abbreviations such as *temp*
2 Lives of a country's famous people
3 Information on organisations such as the FAO
4 Origin of famous sayings
5 Comprehensive information on all important topics
6 Help on locating places and natural features throughout the world

7 Information on inventions, processes, etc. – who devised them, when and details on what makes them unique

Task 4

All could be checked using a search engine.

a) a database of films or a film guide
b) a gazeteer or atlas (It's in Tanzania)
c) any source of up-to-date statistics, e.g. UN statistics online
d) a specialist encyclopaedia in either psychology or language
e) a reference book such as *The Statesman's Year Book*
f) an encyclopaedia or dictionary of biography
g) a dictionary – print or online
h) a technical dictionary, a dictionary of acronyms and abbreviations
i) UK government statistics online
j) UN statistics online
k) US statistics online
l) US statistics online

Task 5

1 Problem h)
2 Problems k) and l)
3 Problems e) and j)
4 Problem g)
5 Problem f)
6 Problem i)
7 Problem h)
8 Problem a)
9 Problem e)
10 Problem d)
11 Problem c)
12 Problems possibly k) and l)
13 Problem b)
14 Problems a) and f)

Task 6

1 1860s
2 American Seventh-day Adventists
3 flaked, puffed, shredded, granular
4 the final stage
5 advertising – diversification and promotion
6 *not stated*
7 children

Task 7
Text A
1 What is another name for dendrochronology?
2 What is an increment tree borer used for?
3 What is done once the tree rings have been counted and measured?
4 What is a tree ring?
5 What determines the width of a ring?
6 How can this technique provide information on climate over thousands of years?

Answers
1 tree-ring dating
2 to bore into the centre of a tree to obtain a complete record of the tree rings
3 the sample is correlated with sequences of rings from other trees
4 the amount of growth a tree makes in a year
5 the amount of rain and the temperature
6 overlapping samples are used and very old trees such as the bristlecone pine

Text B
1 Which sciences use radiocarbon dating?
2 Who developed the technique?
3 What does decay mean in this context?
4 Up to what age can this form of dating be used?
5 When does C-14 decay begin?
6 How much C-14 remains after 5,730 years?

Answers
1 geology, climatology, anthropology and archaeology
2 William Libby
3 the return of unstable C-14 to stable C-12
4 50,000 years
5 when an organism dies
6 half

Task 9 (successful keywords will depend on the database used)
1 disease, fish, freshwater
2 work, information technology
3 asbestos, respiratory diseases
4 Japan, economy
5 civil war, USA
6 water shortages
7 aluminium, aluminum, corrosion

8 UK secondary education, achievement tests, women's education
9 GM crops
10 management, female

Task 12 Other answers may be possible
a) 7 Wan
b) 4 Jin, 1 Hall
c) 12 Lee
d) 1 Hall
e) 14 Huxur

Task 13
a) 11 Mills
b) 13 Cargill
c) 3 Walfish
d) 5 Cadman
e) 15 Song
f) 12 Lee

Task 15
1 Introduction
2 Discussion
3 Results
4 Methods

Task 17
1 Sports
broader: physical activity
narrower: archery, bowling
related: exercises, games
2 Reading
broader: literacy, language skills
narrower: critical reading, reading aloud
related: decoding, language processing
3 Engineering
broader: technology
narrower: civil engineering
related: manufacturing
4 Sanitation
broader: public health
narrower: waste disposal, cleaning
related: health, hygiene
5 Fish studies = icthyology
broader: zoology
narrower: cod stocks
related: fisheries

Task 18

Text 1

a) Education
b) Surveyed a large sample of faculty members on problems international students face.
c) What problems do international graduate students have? Are these different from the problems domestic students face?
d) The problems identified by faculty members were similar to those that students identified as problems.

Text 2

a) Rural technology
b) Investigated the exact energy and time required for cooking rice, potatoes and vegetables at the temperatures generated by a solar cooker.
c) What are the amounts of energy required for cooking these foods? How long must they be cooked?
d) The exact amounts of energy and temperatures.

Text 3

a) Climatology
b) It investigated the Ross Sea ice.
c) Is the ice growing or retreating? Have the ice streams changed?
d) The Ross Sea ice drainage system is changing.